How to Design and Report
Experiments

How to Design and Report Experiments

Andy Field
Graham Hole

Los Angeles | London | New Delhi
Singapore | Washington DC

SAGE Publications Ltd
1 Oliver's Yard
55 City Road
London EC1Y 1SP

SAGE Publications Inc.
2455 Teller Road
Thousand Oaks, California 91320

SAGE Publications India Pvt Ltd
B 1/I 1, Mohan Cooperative Industrial Area
Mathura Road
New Delhi 110 044

SAGE Publications Asia-Pacific Pte Ltd
33 Pekin Street #02-01
Far East Square
Singapore 048763

British Library Cataloguing in Publication data

A catalogue record for this book is available from the British Library

ISBN 978 0 7619 7382 9
ISBN (pbk) 978 0 7619 7383 6

Library of Congress Control Number: 2002108293

Typeset by Keyword Typesetting Services
Printed in Great Britain by the MPG Books Group

Mixed Sources
Product group from well-managed forests and other controlled sources
www.fsc.org Cert no. SA-COC-1565
© 1996 Forest Stewardship Council

Contents

Part 2:   Analysing and Interpreting Data   107

Part 3:   Writing Up Your Research   285

Preface

A long time ago in a galaxy far, far away there lived a race of aliens who had no difficulty with the finer points of experimental design. For centuries the forces of the 'dark side' imposed a rigid regime of learning and practising experimental design. The strain of writing lab-report after lab-report day in, day out, proved too much for some. A small rebel alliance escaped from the planet in an old x-axis star-fighter. They found their way to an attractive small blue-green planet called Earth where they inter-married with a set of hairy apes that were scratching their heads about how to work out whether their leader had significantly more bananas than them. We are their descendants. The rest is what we now call history, but this aversion to designing and reporting experiments has stayed in our racial memory. So, if you want to know whether your leader has significantly more bananas than you, this is the book for you!

There are many worthy books on experimental design on the market, so why have we written another one? Well, few books take you logically through the process of doing an experiment (from the stage of having the initial idea right through to delivering the finished lab-report). Those that do probably don't have as many jokes in them as this one (and they certainly don't have dogs and cats). Over the years that we've both lectured on experimental design and statistics, we've noticed that a bit of humour (well, we think it's humour at least) goes a long way in helping to relieve the potential stress of the topic—for the students and for us. So, this book isn't as big as it looks and certainly not as scary!

Acknowledgements

Joint: We are grateful to many people who've read bits of this book and provided invaluable comments (in alphabetical order): Tricia Maxwell, Julie Morgan, Brenda Smith, Liz Valentine, Leonora Wilkinson. Thanks also to Jayne Grimes, for letting us mutilate her paper into the example write-up that's presented in Chapter 16. Two anonymous reviewers made extremely valuable comments that helped us with the final version. We are also grateful to Michael Carmichael for being not only a wonderful editor, but also a very nice bloke!

Andy: Listening to music while I write keeps me sane (arguably). I listened to the following while writing this book: Fugazi, Arvo Pärt, System of a Down, Slipknot, Korn, Radiohead, Tom McRae, more Fugazi, George Harrison, The White Stripes, Frank Black and the Catholics, Slayer, some more Fugazi, Weezer, Air, Favez, and the Foo Fighters.

I am very grateful to all of my friends who persist in being my friends even though I never phone them because I'm too busy writing books! Most of my thanks go to Graham Hole for being such a great teacher, an immensely clever guy, and one of the funniest people I know. He made writing this book a truly entertaining process and so most of all I'm grateful that he was too well-mannered to say 'piss off' when I went to his office one day and said 'hey, Graham, fancy writing a text book ...'.

Graham: Listening to music also keeps me sane (or so my wardens say), but I'm not sure that would be true if I listened to Andy's choice of music – with the exception of George Harrison. My thanks go to C.P.E. Bach (a deeply under-rated composer who even Mozart thought was great) and his dad (who everyone thinks is great these days, so no problems there). I can't top what Andy has written about me, except to say that it is actually all true of him – he is a really great person to write a book with, and he has made it all a genuinely enjoyable experience (partly by writing all the tricky bits and doing all the tedious stuff like headings, corrections, formatting, etc.). He is a very generous person, in every sense of the word (as you can tell from his acknowledgements above). Bloody hell, this is turning into a TV awards ceremony! Oi, reader! You've spent your entire student grant on this book to find out about experimental design, so why are you wasting your time reading this page? Just get on with reading the rest of the book, will you? And if you haven't paid for the book, I hope the bookstore security guard gives you a good kicking as you try to smuggle it out of the shop.

Dedications

I'd like to dedicate this to the memory of my father, John Ernest Hole, who taught me to read, amongst many other things.

G. H.

For Mum and Dad because, although they are not nearly as cute as my cat, they have done (and still do) so much in return for so little.

A. F.

PART 1   DESIGNING AN EXPERIMENT

1 Before You Begin

Scientists spend most of their lives trying to answer questions: why do some people get nervous when they speak to others? does smoking cause cancer? does reading a book on experimental design help you to design experiments? The traditional view is that the fundamental premise of science is that there are absolute truths – facts about the world that are independent of our opinions of them – to be discovered. There are fundamentally two ways in which these sorts of research questions can be answered (and the absolute truths discovered): we can observe what naturally happens in the real world without interfering with it (e.g. *correlational* or *observational* methods), or we can manipulate some aspect of the environment and observe its effect (the *experimental* method). These two approaches have many similarities:

- *Empirical*: both methods attempt to gather evidence through observation and measurement that can be replicated by others. This process is known as empiricism.
- *Measurement*: both methods attempt to measure whatever it is being studied (see Box 1.1).
- *Replicability*: both methods seek to ensure that results can be replicated by other researchers (Box 1.1 illustrates how measurement can affect the replicability of results).
- *Objectivity*: both methods seek to answer the research question in an objective way. Although objectivity is a scientific ideal, arguably researchers' interpretations of their results are influenced by their expectations of what they hope to discover.

Nevertheless, correlational and experimental methods have one fundamental difference: the manipulation of variables. Observational research centres on unobtrusive observation of naturally occurring phenomena (for example, observing children in the playground to see what factors facilitate aggression). In contrast, experimentation

---

■ Box 1.1: Why do scientists measure things?

Imagine you were a chemist (heaven forbid!) and you wanted to demonstrate that eating a newly discovered chemical called 'unovar' made your brain explode. You force-fed 20 people with unovar and indeed their brains did explode. These results were written up and published for other chemists to read and you were awarded the Nobel science prize (which you enjoyed in the comfort of the prison cell assigned to you for murdering 20 innocent people). A few years pass and another scientist Dr. Smug-git comes along and shows that when he fed unovar to his participants their brains did not explode. Why could this be? There are two measurement-related issues here:

1. Dr. Smug-git might have fed his participants less unovar than you did (it may be that brain explosion is dependent on a certain critical mass of the chemical being consumed)
2. Dr. Smug-git might have measured his outcome differently – did you and Smug-git assess brain explosion in the same way?

For the former point, this explains why chemists and physicists have devoted many hours to developing standard units of measurement. If you had reported that you'd fed your participants 100 grams of unovar, then Dr. Smug-git could have ensured that he had used the same amount – and because grams are a standard unit of measurement we would know that you and Smug-git used exactly the same amount of the chemical. Importantly, direct measurements such as the gram provide an objective standard: an object that weighs 10 g is known to be twice as heavy as an object weighing only 5 g.

It is easy enough to develop scales of measurement for properties that can be directly observed (such as height, mass and volume). However, we rarely have this luxury in psychology and other social sciences because we are interested in measuring constructs that cannot be directly measured; instead we rely on indirect measures. For example, if I were to measure undergraduates' anxiety at having to do a statistics course on a scale ranging from 0 (not anxious) to 10 (very anxious), could I claim that a student who scores 10 is, in reality, twice as anxious as a student who scores 5? Although I couldn't claim that a student who scored 10 was twice as anxious as a student who scored 5, I probably could claim that the student scoring 10 was more anxious (to whatever degree) than the student scoring 5. This relationship between what is being measured and the numbers obtained on a scale is known as the *level of measurement*. In a sense, the level of measurement is the degree to which a scale informs you about the construct being measured – it relates to the accuracy of measurement.

The second proposed explanation for the difference between your experiment and that of Dr. Smug-git illustrates this point rather nicely. In both cases the observed outcome was an exploding brain, but how was this measured? Clearly a brain can either explode or not, so it should be easy to observe the brain and then classify its response to the chemical as exploding or not exploding. Easy eh? Well, perhaps not, what constitutes an explosion? Does the brain have to literally pop – propelling small fragments of blood and tissue onto the nearby walls – or will it suffice to have a large internal haemorrhage? Perhaps Dr. Smug-git required a more dramatic response before he would classify a brain as exploding – hence his differing conclusion. This example illustrates what psychologists face all of the time: an inability to directly measure what they want to measure. When we can't measure something directly there will always be a discrepancy between the numbers we use to represent the thing we're measuring and the actual value of the thing we're measuring (i.e. the value we'd get if we could measure it directly). This discrepancy is known as *measurement error*.

deliberately manipulates the environment to ascertain what effect one variable has on another (for example, giving someone 15 tequilas to see how it affects their walking).

1.1   Variables and Measurement

Scientists are interested in how variables change and what causes these changes. If you look at any research question, such as the one above – 'why do some people get nervous when they speak to others?' – inherent within it is something that changes in some way (it is not constant). In this case it is nervousness: the question implies that some people will be more nervous than others; therefore, nervousness is not constant – it changes (because it will differ both in different people and across different situations). In much the same way 'does watching horror films make children more anxious?' implies that anxiety will change or be different in different children. Anything that changes in this way is known as a *variable* – something that varies. As you'll see later in this section variables can take many forms (see page 6), and can be both manipulated and observed (see page 10).

To draw meaningful conclusions about the relationships between variables, scientists have to measure them in some way (see Box 1.1). Psychologists cannot measure psychological constructs directly and so instead we use techniques such as self-report (e.g. asking people how they feel) and questionnaires. Any device we use to measure something will provide a different quality of data. There are basically four levels at which variables can be measured:

1. Nominal (a.k.a. categorical)   **Non-parametric**
2. Ordinal
3. Interval   **Parametric**
4. Ratio

We'll discuss each of these levels in turn, but for those wanting a gentler introduction Sandy MacRae (1994) covers the material excellently.

Nominal Data

The word *nominal* derives from the Latin word for *name* and the nominal scale is literally a scale on which two things that are equivalent in some sense are given the same name (or number). With this scale, there is no relationship between the size of the number and what is being measured; all that you can tell is that two things with the same number are equivalent whereas two things with different numbers are not equivalent. The classic example is numbers in a football team. A player with number 7 on his back should play in mid-field, whereas a player with number 1 on his back plays in goal. However a number 7 player is not necessarily better than a number 1 (most managers would not want their midfielder playing in goal!). The numbers on the back of shirts could equally well be letters or names (in fact, until recently many rugby clubs denoted team positions with letters on the back of shirts).

Data from a nominal scale should not be used for arithmetic because doing so would be meaningless. For example, imagine if the England coach found that his number 7 (David Beckham) was injured. Would he consider replacing him with seven David Seaman (who plays number 1) or – heaven forbid – combine Phil and Gary Neville (at numbers 2 and 5)? Even more ludicrous, I used to play wing in rugby (number 11 – the fast good-looking ones who score all the tries, ahem, well maybe not!). Imagine if one day the coach replaced a number 11 with a number 8 (burly bloke at the back of the scrum) piggy-backing a number 3 (huge bullock-like blokes at the front of the scrum)! They certainly wouldn't be as fast (or good looking!) as a number 11. The only way that nominal data can be used is to consider frequencies. For example, we could look at how frequently number 11s score tries compared to number 3s. Having said this, as Lord (1953) points out in a very amusing and readable article, numbers don't know where they came from and will behave in the same way, obeying the same arithmetic rules regardless.

Ordinal Data

Ordinal data give us more information than nominal data. If we use an ordinal scale to measure something, we can tell not only that things have occurred, but also the order in which they occurred. However, these data tell us nothing about the differences between values. Figure 1.1 illustrates ordinal data: imagine you went to a frog race in which there were three frogs (Silus, Hoppy and Flibbidy – or Flibbs to his mates). The names of frogs don't give us any information about where they came in the race, however if we label them according to their performance – first, second and third – then these labels do tell us something about how the frog performed; these categories are *ordered*. In using ordered categories we now know that the frog that came second was better than the frog that came third.

The limitation of ordinal data is that it tells us little about the differences between ordered categories; we don't know how much better the winner was than the frogs that came second and third. In Figure 1.1 the two races show Flibbs winning, Hoppy coming second and Silus losing. So, the ordered categories attached to each frog are the same in the two races: Flibbs is 1, Hoppy is 2, and Silus is 3. However, in the first race Flibbs and Hoppy tightly contested first place but Silus was way behind (so first and second place were actually very similar to each other in terms of performance), but in the second race Flibbs is a long way ahead whereas Hoppy and Silus are very similar (so first and second place are very different in terms of performance). This example shows how ordinal data can tell us something about position but nothing about the relative differences between

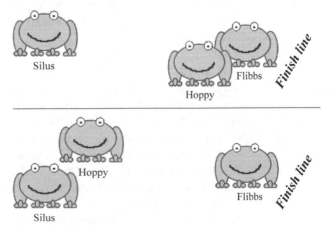

Figure 1.1 Two frog races

positions (first place is always better than second place, but the difference between first and second place can vary). Nominal and ordinal scales don't tell us anything about the differences between points on the scale and need to be analysed with *non-parametric* tests (see Chapter 7).

A lot of psychological data, especially questionnaire and self-report data, are ordinal. Imagine we asked several socially anxious individuals to think of embarrassing times in their lives, and then to rate how embarrassing each situation was on a 10-point scale. We might be confident that a memory they rate as 10 was more embarrassing than one they rate as 5, but can we be certain that the first memory was twice as embarrassing as the second? How much more unreliable does this become if we compare different people's ratings of their memories – would you expect a rating of 10 from one person to represent the same level of embarrassment as another person's or will their ratings depend on their subjective beliefs about what is embarrassing? Most self-report responses are likely to be ordinal and so in any situation in which we ask people to rate things (e.g. rate their confidence about an answer they have given, rate how scared they are about something, rate how disgusting they find some activity) we should regard these data as ordinal although many psychologists do not.

Interval Data

Interval data are considerably more useful than ordinal data and most of the statistical tests we use in psychology rely on having data that are measured on an interval scale. To say that data are interval, we must be certain that equal intervals on the scale represent equal differences in the property being measured. So, for example, if a psychologist took several spider phobic individuals, showed them a spider and asked them to rate their anxiety on a 10-point scale, for this scale to be interval it must be the case that the difference between anxiety ratings of 5 and 6 is the same as the difference between say 1 and 2, or 9 and 10. Similarly, the difference in anxiety between ratings of 1 and 4 should be identical to the difference between ratings of 6 and 9. If we had 4 phobic individuals (with their anxiety ratings in brackets): Nicola (10), Robin (9), Dave (2) and Esther (3), an interval scale would mean that the extra anxiety that Esther subjectively experiences compared to Dave is equal to the extra anxiety that Nicola experiences compared to Robin. When data have this property they can be analysed with *parametric* tests (see Chapter 6).

Ratio Data

Ratio data are really a step further from interval data. In interval data, all that is important is that the intervals between different points on the scale represent the same difference at all points along the scale. For data to be ratio they must have the properties of interval data, but in addition the ratios of values along the scale should be meaningful. We use ratio measurement scales all the time in every day life; for example, when we measure something with a ruler we have a ratio scale because not only is it true that, say, the difference between 25 and 30 cms (a difference of 5 cms) is the same as the difference between 80 and 85 cms or 57 and 62 cms, it is also true that distances along the scale are divisible (e.g. we know that something that is 20 cms is twice as long as something that is 10 cms and twice as short as an object that is 40 cms).

It is possible for a scale to be interval but not ratio (although by definition if a scale is ratio then it must be interval). One good example is temperature (when measured in Celsius). On the Celsius scale it is the case that the difference between, say, 20° and 27° is the same as the difference between 85° and 92° (for both the difference is 7° and in both cases this 7° difference is equivalent), however, it is not the case that 40° is twice as hot as 20°. The reason is because the Celsius scale has no absolute zero value (you can have minus temperatures). One example of a ratio measure used in psychology is reaction time; if, in our spider phobia example above, we measured the speed at which each phobic reacted to the spider (how long it took them between seeing the spider and running away from it) this would give us ratio data. We can use other measures though, such as the percentage score on a test or the number of errors someone makes on a task.

Can a measure be interval but not ratio?

Discrete versus Continuous Variables

Earlier on we mentioned that variables could take many forms, and two important forms are whether variables are continuous or discrete. A *discrete* variable is one for which no underlying continuum exists; in other words, the measure classifies items into non-overlapping categories. One example would be being pregnant: a woman can be either pregnant or not, there isn't such a thing as being 'a bit pregnant'. Other variables are measured in a *continuous* way: for example aggression probably runs along some kind of continuum (beginning at calm and ending at extremely violent). The distinction between discrete and continuous variables can be very fuzzy indeed. For example, at first glance gender seems like a discrete variable (you can be either male or female but not both), however there probably is some kind of under-lying continuum because some genetic females can be quite masculine and some genetic males can be very feminine (either in looks or beha-viour); there are also chromosomal disorders that can confuse the genetic gender of a person. To confuse matters further, some contin-uous variables can be measured in discrete terms; for example, although reaction times are continuous, they may, in practice, be measured in discrete terms (i.e. we tend to measure to the nearest millisecond even though in theory it could be measured in infinitely small steps!).

1.2   Experimental versus Correlational Research

So far we've learnt that scientists do experiments to answer questions, and that questions can usually be answered either by observing what naturally happens, or by manipulating some aspect of the environ-ment and observing the effect it has on some variable of interest. In addition any question that you want to answer will involve some variables that need to be measured in some way. The main distinction between what might be termed correlational research (that is, where we observe what naturally goes on in the world without directly inter-fering with it) and experimental research is the fact that experimenta-tion involves the direct manipulation of variables. In correlational research we either observe natural events (such as facial interactions between a mother and child) or we take a snapshot of many variables (such as administering several questionnaires, each measuring a dif-ferent aspect of personality, at the same point in time, to see whether certain personality characteristics occur in the same people at that moment in time). The good thing about this kind of research is that it provides us with a very natural view of the question we're research-ing: we are not influencing what happens and so we get measures of the variables that should not be biased by the researcher being there (this is an important aspect of *ecological validity*). If research ques-tions can be answered using the correlational method then why bother doing experiments? To answer this question we need to look at the philosophy underlying science.

Claws (... groan!) and Effect

We began the chapter by discussing some research questions and mentioned that these questions implied some outcome had changed as a result of some other variable. As such, research questions often

imply some kind of causal link between variables. Sometimes this could be in a direct statement such as 'does smoking cause cancer?' or sometimes the implication might be subtler. Taking one of the other examples ('does reading a book on experimental design help you to design experiments?'), the implication is that reading a book on experimental design will have an effect (one way or another) on your ability to design experiments. Many research question can basically be broken down into a proposed cause (in this case reading a book) and a proposed outcome (your ability to design an experiment). Both the cause and the outcome are variables: for the cause some people will have read this book whereas others won't (so it is something that varies), and for the outcome, well, people will have different abilities to design experiments (again, this is something that varies). The key to answering the research question is to uncover how the proposed cause and the proposed outcome relate to each other; is it the case that the people good at designing experiments are the same people that read this book (hopefully so, but probably not!)?

Hume

How do we discover a causal relationship between variables? Well, this question has been long-debated by people much cleverer than I am (I don't speak for Graham) and philosophers and methodologists have spent (literally) centuries arguing about it (did they have nothing better to do?). Much of what we accept as conventional wisdom on cause and effect stems from David Hume's (1739–40, 1748) ideas about causality. Hume stressed the importance of observed temporal regularities between variables. In essence Hume proposed three criteria that need to be met to infer cause and effect: (1) cause and effect occur close together in time (contiguity); (2) the cause must occur before an effect does; and (3) the effect should never occur without the presence of the cause. In essence, these conditions imply that causality can be inferred through corroborating evidence, and cause is equated to high degrees of correlation between contiguous events. However, Hume also pointed out that the inference to causality was a psychological leap of faith and not one that was logically justified. What is the problem with these ideas? Think about it while we have a look at an illustration of the principles.

Figure 1.2 illustrates some of Hume's principles; in this example we are trying to confirm the causal statement 'Andy talking about causality causes boredom'. According to what we've learnt about Hume, proving this statement requires three things: (1) boredom and me talking about causality must occur contiguously (close in time); (2) me talking about causality must occur before boredom does; and (3) boredom should not occur without me talking about causality (so the correspondence between boredom and me talking about causality should be strong). Looking at Figure 1.2 it's clear that me talking about causality and boredom occur close in time. Also in all situations in the diagram talking about causality precedes boredom; hence conditions 1 and 2 are satisfied. You should also note that in 5 out of 6 of the situations shown in the diagram talking about causality results in boredom, so the correspondence between cause and effect is very strong, and at no point do we see a bored face preceded by anything other than me talking about causality (which satisfies condition 3).

Earlier on I asked you to think about possible problems with these criteria, and one already emerges: there is an instance in Figure 1.2 in which talking about causality leads to happiness (not boredom). This instance doesn't contradict any of Hume's criteria yet surely poses a doubt about the causal connection between talking about causality and boredom (because in one situation the proposed cause does not have the desired effect). There are also mathematical reasons why a correlation between variables does not imply causality (see Field, 2000, Chapter 3 for some general discussion of this issue). There are two main reasons why correlation does not imply causality:

1. *The tertium quid*: This always makes me think of seafood for some reason ('I'll have the grilled quid, please'), but it actually

Figure 1.2   A demonstration of Hume's criteria for causality

means a third person or thing of indeterminate character. In this context it is another variable that has an effect on both the proposed cause and the outcome. For example, we might observe a strong correlation between having dreadlocks and supporting environmental issues. However, it is unlikely that having dreadlocks causes an interest in the environment – presumably, there is an external factor (or factors) that causes both. These extraneous factors are sometimes called *confounding variables* or *confounds* for short. So, in the example of me talking about causality and people being bored it could be that some other factor is causing the boredom (perhaps the person I'm talking to is tired and hungover and that is what's making them bored – I live in hope!).

2. *Direction of causality:* Although Hume's condition of temporal precedence (cause must precede effect) allows logical inference about the direction of causality, mathematics cannot prove the direction of cause. So, although it might look as though me talking about causality causes boredom, there is no reason why it cannot be that boredom causes me to talk about causality (it certainly causes me to write about it!).

Run of the (John Stuart) Mill?

How do we isolate causal variables?

John Stuart Mill was one of the main proponents of Inductivism, which is a view that science should be based on inductive reasoning. Inductive reasoning is just reasoning based on probable outcomes. For example, 'Andy likes statistics, Andy writes statistics books, therefore Andy is a dullard' is an example of inductive reasoning: based on the two premises the conclusion is probably accurate. It could be false – I might be interesting – but it is more likely to be true that I'm as dull as dishwater. In science, inductive reasoning really relates to extrapolating from a set of observations to some more general conclusions.

Mill (1865) 'borrowed' many of Hume's ideas to formulate his thinking about causality and ultimately expanded upon Hume's original ideas considerably. He described three conditions necessary to infer cause:

1. Cause has to precede effect.
2. Cause and effect should correlate.
3. All other explanations of the cause-effect relationship must be ruled out.

The first two conditions mirror those of Hume: temporal precedence of the cause and a strong correlation between cause and effect. Mill's main contribution was to add the third condition, which suggests that the effects of a tertium quid should be ruled-out. To verify that the third criterion is true, Mill proposed several methods:

1. *The method of agreement*: an effect should be present when the cause is present.
2. *The method of difference*: when the cause is absent the effect will be absent also.
3. *The method of concomitant variation*: when the two previous relationships are observed, causal inference will be made stronger because most other interpretations of the cause-effect relationship will have been ruled out.

Figure 1.3 illustrates some of these points. Here we have a situation in which we have two events (me talking about causality or my cat talking about being fed – in cat language of course) that precede two outcomes (boredom or happiness). According to Mill's criteria, to infer that talking about causality causes boredom: (1) talking about causality must precede boredom (in all situations in the diagram this is true); (2) the correlation between boredom and my talking about causality must be strong (in the diagram 4 out of 4 occasions when I talk about causality boredom is observed so the correlation is perfect in this case); (3) whenever boredom occurs I have previously (and recently) been talking about causality (again in the diagram every instance of boredom is preceded by my talking about causality); (4)

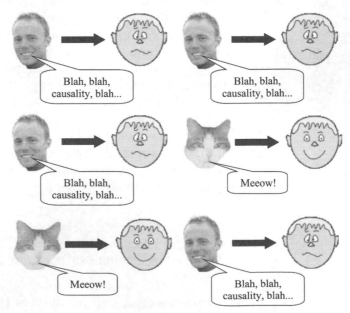

Figure 1.3   Me talking about causality appears to correlate with boredom!

when cause is absent effect is also absent (when I don't talk about causality in the diagram – and instead my cat talks about food – no boredom is observed so boredom is not elicited by anything other than me); and (5) the manipulation of cause leads to an associated change in effect (so if we manipulate whether I'm talking about causality or my cat is mewing, the effect elicited changes according to the manipulation – again, in the diagram the change in the cause is always associated with a change in the effect). This final manipulation serves to rule out external variables that might affect the cause-effect relationship.

It would be fair to sum up Mill's ideas by saying that the only way to infer causality is through comparison of two controlled situations: one in which the cause is present and one in which the cause is absent. These situations should be identical in all senses except the presence of cause (for an applied example of these ideas read Field & Davey, 1998).

The Evolution of Theories

In psychology, we typically generate theories from which we develop hypotheses that we test (either with experiments or correlational methods). If we want to be certain about the causal relationships between variables then we typically design experiments. If the results confirm our hypotheses then they are published in academic journals (provided we haven't tested a theory of little importance, or tested a theory of great importance in a ridiculously flawed way, or tested a theory that disproves the long espoused beliefs of the editor of the journal!). Once published, the theory is (hopefully) accepted as a valid contribution to our understanding of psychology. This approach is inductive in that we collect evidence to corroborate theories (you can see now just what an impact Mill's ideas had).

How do theories change over time?

Nevertheless, I'm sure you'll be pleased to learn that the inductive approach that dictates all of scientific knowledge has a logical flaw! The flaw is really an extension of Hume's critique of induction, which can be summarized as 'just because we observe that night always followed day in the past does not prove that night will follow day again in the future'. Although if we were really bored you could argue about whether night follows day, or day follows night, this simple example also illustrates why correlation is no indication of causality, although night and day are perfectly correlated, neither causes the other (both are caused by an external factor – the spinning of the Earth in relation to its sun).

Duhem and the conventionalists

Karl Popper also believed in the inherent ambiguity of confirmation. In his books, *The logic of scientific discovery* (1959) and *The poverty of historicism* (1957) Popper developed Hume's critique to devise a system of scientific discovery. Popper was hugely influenced by the conventionalist philosophers such as Pierre Duhem, Francis Bacon and possibly more importantly, Henri Poincaré. We've seen that the prediction of some outcome involves sets of laws and hypotheses about predictive events, or causes. It logically follows that if these causes are present but the outcome is not then one of the causes must be false (i.e. it is not actually a cause). The main contribution of the conventionalists was to contradict this logic; they argued that all that would be disconfirmed in this situation is the conjunction (combination) of the causal events. In fact Duhem in particular went on to suggest that when the observed evidence contradicts the causal relationships that a scientist has proposed then that scientist is free to alter one or more of their hypotheses in such a way as to explain the observed data. An example might be that I predict that when he is hungry, and when I am in the house my cat, Fuzzy, will meow. The outcome is my cat meowing and the predictive events are hunger and my presence at home. If one day I get home and my cat doesn't meow, then this observation contradicts my hypothesis. There are three obvious explanations: (1) Fuzzy isn't hungry; (2) I am not at home (despite the fact I think I am!); or (3) one of these variables is not really a cause. However, Duhem would've argued that Fuzzy did not meow because the combination of Fuzzy being hungry and me being home is wrong. Furthermore, as a scientist I would be entitled to explain away the disconfirming evidence by suggesting other explanations: perhaps some other causal variable is necessary; perhaps Fuzzy wasn't hungry; perhaps I only thought I was at home when actually I was somewhere else (being a philosopher Duhem would love to question my belief in my own perception); maybe Fuzzy did meow but I'd suddenly gone deaf; or maybe Fuzzy had been replaced by a non-meowing doppelganger cat by the evil Dr. Catthief who spends his life deliberately stuffing up everyone else's experiments. Duhem believed that the scientist should be left to exercise his (or her) expert and objective judgment (yeah, right!) in deciding which part, or parts, of the original hypothesis to change. Although it might sound as if Duhem was endorsing doggedly sticking to preconceived scientific ideas even in the face of contradictory evidence, he was actually astute in recognizing the role of outside influences on data and experiments (the tertium quid on page 12). He also, along with Francis Bacon, was one of the first to acknowledge the idea of a critical experiment that might distinguish between two competing hypotheses. This idea was key in Popper's later thinking regarding how theories should develop.

Popper's logic of scientific discovery

Popper distinguished between scientific and non-scientific statements. Scientific statements are ones that can be verified with reference to empirical evidence, whereas non-scientific statements are ones that cannot be empirically tested. So, statements such as 'Korn are a great band', 'cats are better than dogs', 'Gonzo is the funniest Muppet' and 'beating children is morally wrong' are all non-scientific; they cannot be proved or disproved and although we might all agree that beating children is morally wrong, the morality of the issue cannot be tested empirically (it is a subjective value). Scientific statements can be confirmed or disconfirmed empirically. 'Eating blue Smarties makes you hyperactive', 'drinking wine and beer gives you a worse hangover than drinking beer alone' and 'depression increases the risk of suicide' are all things that can be tested empirically (provided you can quantify and measure the variables concerned). Non-scientific statements can sometimes be altered to become scientific statements, so, 'cats are better than dogs' is non-scientific but by changing the statement to 'cats are better than dogs at climbing trees' it becomes testable (we can collect data about the success of cats and dogs when climbing trees and prove or disprove the statement). Popper believed that non-scientific statements were nonsense, and had no place in science (Box 1.2).

However, although a statement of hypothesis might be testable (unless you're Freud!), Popper was aware that verification through corroborative evidence was insufficient evidence of the truth of a statement. He went as far as to say that such statements could be assigned only the status of 'yet to be disconfirmed'. So, even when there was a wealth of corroborative evidence in favour of a theory, Popper would argue that this theory was merely waiting to be disproved (falsification). Popper believed that it is more powerful to disprove a theory than to corroborate it, therefore, scientists should seek disconfirming evidence. To take an example always close to the hearts of young females, suppose we had a theory that all men are unreliable (that wasn't the word I was going to use, but I need to get this past the editor) based on an observation that all of the men we had previous experience of were indeed unreliable. The more unreliable men we experience, the more this theory is corroborated. However, we have to encounter only one man who is reliable to disconfirm this theory. Hence, one instance that disconfirms a hypothesis is more powerful than many instances that confirm the hypothesis.

■ Box 1.2: Scientific statements?

Popper believed that non-scientific statements had no place in science. Have a look at the following theories and ideas and think about whether these statements, or theories, are scientific (in Popper's view):

	Scientific	Non-Scientific
1. We sometimes behave in a way opposite to how we feel (Freud's 'Reaction Formation', 1901), but sometimes we don't.	☐	☐
2. There are five key dimensions to personality (Costa & MacRae, 1995)	☐	☐
3. Humans and apes are descended from a common ancestor. (Darwin, 1859, 1871)	☐	☐
4. Dogs can learn that a certain sound predicts being fed (Pavlov, 1927).	☐	☐
5. Social phobic people dwell on the bad aspects of social events more than non-anxious individuals do (Clark & Wells, 1995)	☐	☐

Answers to Box 1.2: (1) Freud's theory of reaction formation has come under fire for being non-scientific because it doesn't predict when someone will behave oppositely to their true feelings and when they will not (as such it cannot be tested); (2) dimensions of personality can (arguably) be measured and counted and so this statement can be scientifically tested; (3) Darwin's ideas rely on speculation about past events, in the absence of a time machine it is impossible to test his speculations and so in a sense it is a non-scientific statement (however, we can collect corroborative evidence through fossils and so on); (4) it is possible to see whether a dog learns that a noise predicts food by measuring salivation to both stimuli before and after learning (see Davey & Field, in press) and so this statement is scientific; and (5) it is also possible to measure thoughts after social events in anxious and non-anxious individuals and compare them, so this statement is scientific also.

It's interesting that in Popper's terms two key theories (evolution, and Freud's theory of personality) centre on largely unscientific statements and yet have still been hugely influential!

The idea of falsification can be further demonstrated by reference to a familiar psychological task: Wason's (1966) 4 card task. In this task, participants are presented with four cards known to have a letter on one side and a number on the other side (see Figure 1.4) and are told the rule that if a card has a vowel on one side then it must have an

Figure 1.4   One example of Wason's card task

even number on the other side. The task is to decide which card or cards should be turned over to determine whether this rule is true.

Wason found that most people (about 79%) responded by turning over the card labelled E, and sometimes the card labelled 4 also. In a sense, this is a sensible thing to do because it could confirm the theory: if the E (a vowel) has an even number on the back of it then the rule is supported, and if the 4 has a vowel on the back then the rule is also supported. However, these actions alone do not disconfirm the rule provided the E does indeed have an even number on the back. Turning over the 4 is irrelevant because the rule does not say that even numbers cannot occur on the back of consonants. To fully test the rule, the 7 must be turned over (as well as the E) because if this card has a vowel on the back then the rule is disconfirmed. Therefore, the card labelled 7 has power to determine the truth of the rule whereas the card labelled 4 does not. So, people have a natural bias to try to confirm hypotheses and yet science is based on the opposite – we try to disconfirm hypotheses.

The kind of falsification just described was Popper's fundamental basis for his theory of scientific discovery. He took this idea and set up principles on which to base scientific investigation in which he proposed that when generating hypotheses, scientists should attempt to disconfirm past hypotheses. As such, any new scientific study should do two things:

1. Disconfirm an old hypothesis
2. Confirm (or corroborate) a new hypothesis.

He went on to say that

> ... if we test two such systems which differ in one hypothesis only, and if we can design experiments which refute the first system while leaving the second very well corroborated, then we may be on reasonably safe ground if we attribute the failure of the first system to that hypothesis in which it differs from the other (Popper, 1957: p. 132).

This idea is similar to Mill's thinking on causality. Mill believed that by comparing two situations that differ only in the presence of the causal variable, causality could be isolated. In a similar vein, Popper was suggesting that the truth of a scientific statement or theory could be tested only by comparing two hypotheses that differ in a single respect. Both Mill and Popper saw the fundamental importance of controlling all factors other than the one that is of interest to the scientist.

Combining Popper's beliefs about scientific statements and falsification we might sum up his work by suggesting that all theories should be open to test, or falsification, and that any such test must involve direct comparison with a competing theory that is similar in all but one respect. Over time, the theory will therefore evolve by gradual falsification of incorrect elements of the initial proposal. Ultimately all theories are awaiting falsification and can only be assigned the status of a truth when all attempts to falsify the theory have failed (i.e. all alternative models have been tested), and, of course, this situation will never be reached.

Putting Theories to the Test

How do we test theories?

We have already learnt two important research principles: (1) to isolate causal variables we must rule out all other explanations of the effect we observe (we must compare two situations that are identical in every respect except the supposed causal variable); and (2) we must attempt to falsify theories by designing experiments that compare one theory with another. The next obvious thing to learn is how we actually put these principles into practice. There are two issues here, the first is how we rule out other explanations of the supposed cause, and the second is how we gain confidence that one theory is correct and another is not.

Isolating cause: control conditions

Mill proposed that causal factors could be isolated only by comparing two conditions: one in which supposed cause is present and one in which supposed cause is absent. For example, if we wanted to see whether using mobile phones causes brain tumours, we are proposing a cause (mobile phones) and an effect (tumours). To verify that mobile phones do cause tumours we would need to have one condition in which mobile phones are present and one in which mobile phones are absent. The condition in which cause is absent is known as a *control condition* and it acts as a baseline against which to compare behaviour when a proposed cause is present.

Earlier on, I explained that the difference between experiments and correlational research was that in experiments we manipulate one variable to observe its effect on another. The variable that we typically manipulate is the one we have proposed as a cause and in the simplest situation we manipulate it by changing whether the cause is present or absent. These manipulations are known as *levels* of the variable. The most basic experiment manipulates the causal variable so that it has two levels (supposed cause present versus supposed cause absent) but we can go on to have more levels. For example, we could manipulate not only whether mobile phones are used or not, but also how much they are used. So, we could look at when a mobile phone is not used, when it is used for up to 7 hours a week, up to 14 hours a week and up to 21 hours a week. The mobile phone variable now has 4 levels (0, up to 7, up to 14 and up to 21). The variable that is manipulated is called the *independent variable* (because its value is independent of the other variables in the experiment, it instead depends on the experimenter) whereas the outcome variable, the one that is not manipulated by the experimenter, is called the *dependent variable* (because its value depends on the other variables in the experiment). Students often confuse these terms, but really if you think of it in terms of cause and effect, the outcome variable should depend on the causal variable so anything that is an outcome of your experiment is a dependent variable, and anything that you, as an experimenter, propose as a cause of the outcome you're measuring is an independent variable.

What happens when control conditions are not used?

Box 1.3 shows a real-life research example of the principles of control conditions and the dramatic effects they can have. The example is from my own research on the learning of likes and dislikes. It illustrates that when control conditions are not used, the conclusions that researchers reach can sometimes overlook other factors that they might never have conceived would explain their findings. We'll talk about some different types of control conditions in Chapter 3.

Killing the tertium quid I: controlling other factors

The second stage in ruling out other explanations of causal relations is to minimize the risk of random factors influencing your experiment. Mill showed that he was aware of these factors when he suggested comparing conditions that were *identical* in all respects except the proposed cause. What he meant by this is that all random factors should be held constant. To do this we have to ensure that all aspects

■ Box 1.3: When is a control condition not a control condition?

There are many years of research indicating that if you present a stimulus that evokes a neutral response alongside one that evokes an affective response (positive or negative) then after many of these pairings the neutral stimulus will come to evoke the same emotional response as the stimulus with which it was paired. This process is rather like what happens in advertising: a relatively neutral product (e.g. a car) is presented alongside a favourable stimulus (e.g. a semi-naked celebrity) in the hope that the product will become associated with the positive emotion evoked by the celebrity. This kind of learning is called evaluative learning. The reason why the neutral stimulus comes to evoke an affective response is thought to be that it becomes associated with the other stimulus (i.e. the thought of one evokes some connection in memory to the other).

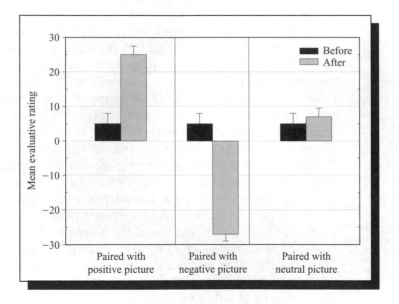

In a typical experiment, several neutral stimuli are rated according to how much a person likes or dislikes the stimulus. Then, some of these neutral stimuli are presented alongside liked stimuli, some presented with disliked stimuli and some with other neutral stimuli. The neutral stimuli are then re-rated to see how much participants now like or dislike them. Typically, neutral stimuli presented alongside positive images are subsequently rated more positively, those paired with negative imagery are rated more negatively, and those paired with other neutral stimuli do not change rating (see the example graph). So, the responses evoked by the neutral stimuli change because of them being presented with stimuli that are liked (or disliked) – see De Houwer, Thomas and Baeyens (2001) for a review.

Researchers in this area had agreed that this paradigm was a suitable way of showing that presenting a neutral stimulus with an affect-evoking stimulus causes the change in response to the neutral stimulus. The proposed cause is the 'pairing' process (i.e. repeated presentation of a neutral stimulus with one that evokes a response). They argue that because ratings to neutral stimuli presented alongside other neutral stimuli do not change whereas those presented with liked or disliked stimuli do change, the only explanation is that subjects associate the neutral pictures with those that evoke an affective response (e.g. Baeyens, De Houwer, Vansteenwegen, & Eelen, 1998; Baeyens, Eelen & Crombez, 1995). Is this conclusion correct?

An alternative explanation
Graham Davey and I argued (Field & Davey, 1998) that the paradigm just described does not demonstrate that the pairing process is the causal factor because there is no condition in which neutral stimuli are not paired with anything. So, even though there is a control in the sense that some neutral pictures are paired with other neutral pictures, this control does not eradicate the predicted cause. How does this fit in with Mill's ideas about isolating cause and effect? What is needed is some condition in which participants are exposed to the same pictures, the same number of times, but the neutral pictures are never presented alongside positive or negative pictures. I even devised such a control condition (Field, 1996, 1997) that allowed researchers to compare one situation in which neutral pictures are presented alongside affect-evoking pictures with one in which the neutral pictures are presented completely separately to positive and negative ones. Interestingly, I used this control condition (Field & Davey, 1997, 1999) and found identical results to those of the experimental condition. This showed that the effects that had previously been attributed to the presentation process (the pairing of neutral pictures with liked or disliked pictures) could not possibly have been caused by this factor because even when neutral pictures were not presented alongside affect-evoking pictures the results were the same. It turned out that participants were doing something completely different in the experiment that created the illusion of them learning (there was a tertium quid at work). Without the kinds of controls derived from Mill's thinking, these confounding variables cannot be ruled out.

Some things to think about
How does this real-life example fit in with Popper's notion of falsification? Well, there was a lot of corroborating evidence for Baeyens et al.'s interpretation of this paradigm. However, Field and Davey's use of a new paradigm threw up evidence that contradicted Baeyens' hypothesis. This illustrates Popper's idea of falsification in that we took an established hypothesis and compared it with a competing one and then used the data to falsify one and corroborate the other.

of our experimental conditions are the same and you can take this idea to varying degrees of extreme. In our mobile phone example it would, for instance, be sensible to ensure that everyone used the same phone (to ensure everyone was exposed to the same level of microwaves), and had similar degrees of brain health to begin with. In other experiments, you would hope to test everyone in the same room and use identical instructions to ensure that no variable has a systematic influence on the outcome.

Killing the tertium quid II: randomization

In the previous section, I mentioned in passing that in the mobile phone experiment we might want to make sure that all participants had an equivalent level of brain health. This comment actually hid an important point about how we allocate participants to our various groups. We can rule out many random influences on our experiment simply by randomizing parts of the study. The first important thing to do is to make sure participants are randomly allocated to your experimental and control groups. Imagine we worked in a head-injury unit at a hospital and we decided to use these people as participants in our experimental group and we then found a group of strangers for our control. The experimental group contains people that we know have head injuries so they might already have tumours or abnormalities from their injury. The other group (who have been allocated to the control) has no such history. If you gave your head-injury friends phones to use for a week and then concluded that phones caused brain abnormalities, would this conclusion be accurate? Well, of course it wouldn't because the group that used phones already had problems. Although this example is extreme, it illustrates the point I'm trying to make: we should not allow any systematic bias into our experiment. We could use our head-injury friends only if we randomly (and preferably evenly) allocated them to both groups (that way we know that any existing head injuries are present in both groups and so should cancel out). If you think of how complex the average human is (how much humans differ in intelligence, motivation, emotional expression, physical characteristics) you should realize how important it is to randomly allocate people to experimental groups: it ensures a roughly equivalent spread of attributes across all groups.

Comparing theories: statistics

Section 2 of this book talks in more detail about statistics. Suffice to say at this stage that once we have our experimental conditions that have controlled for confounding variables and have isolated causal

Did someone say 'milk'?

factors, we need some objective way of comparing one condition with another. In fact, we use mathematics to help us out with this task. The basic idea behind most modern statistics can be illustrated with an example from the man who you should blame next time you're bored witless in a statistics lecture: Ronald Fisher. Fisher's (1925) contribution to statistics and methodology was so groundbreaking that it was republished some 66 years later. In Fisher's (1925) book, he describes an experiment designed to test a claim by a lady that she could determine, by tasting a cup of tea, whether the milk or the tea was added first to the cup. Anyway, Fisher's line of thinking was that he should give the lady some cups of tea, some of which had the milk added first and some of which had the milk added last and see whether she could correctly identify them (a bit like the Pepsi challenge[1] for those of you old enough to have seen the adverts). In all cases discussed, the lady knows that there are an equal number of cups in which milk was added first or last. If we take the simplest situation in which there are only two cups (so, literally like the Pepsi challenge) then the lady has 50% chance of guessing correctly. If she did guess correctly would we, therefore, be confident in concluding that she can tell the difference between cups in which the milk was added first from those in which it was added last? Probably not: most of us could perform fairly well on this task just by guessing. Imagine we complicate things by having 4 cups (two with milk added first and two with milk added last). There are 6 orders in which these cups can be arranged, so if the lady gets the order correct then she would only do this by chance 1 in 6 times; our confidence in her genuine ability to detect when the milk was added has increased because the task is more difficult. If we now use 6 cups, there are 20 orders in which these can be arranged and the lady would only guess the correct order 1 time in 20 (or 5% of the time). Again, if she got the correct order we would now be very confident that she could genuinely tell the difference. Finally, if, as Fisher did, we use 8 cups there are 70 orders and the lady has only a 1 in 70 chance of getting the order correct by guessing (she will correctly guess only 1.4% of the time). The task has become incredibly difficult and so we'd certainly be very confident that she could genuinely tell the difference if she got the answer correct.[2]

This example illustrates an important point about science: we draw inferences based on confidence about a given set of results. As the probability of the result occurring by chance decreases, our confidence in the result being genuine increases. So, when we compare groups in which supposed cause is present (experimental group) with one in which supposed cause is absent (control group) the difference between these groups has to be sufficiently large that we have confidence that the difference is not a chance result. Just like with Fisher's tea experiment, the more unlikely a chance result is, the greater our confidence in our results being genuine. Fisher actually suggested that an appropriate level of confidence is 95%, so that if the probability of our results being due to chance is less than 5% (or 1 in 20 – just as in the 6 cups example) then we should conclude that a result is genuine. This example lays the foundations of the statistical ideas presented in Chapter 2.

Fisher also noted a couple of other important points. The first was that he realized how important randomization is to experimentation. He correctly noted that his tea experiment depends upon the cups being ordered randomly, so the lady could have no way of predicting the order other than by taste. So, he recognized that randomization is an important tool in isolating causal factors. Second, he noted that although his single tea experiment was impressive in itself (if the lady correctly identified the order of the cups), it would be much more convincing if she could replicate the feat. Again, this is an important concept: our confidence in a given scientific statement will increase if a given set of results can be replicated many times (and by different researchers).

So, What is the Difference Between Experimental and Correlational Research?

We've covered many concepts including the isolation of cause and effect, and the basic framework for the experimental method. To answer our initial question now becomes easy. Experiments seek to isolate cause and effect by manipulating the proposed causal variable or variables. All that we have so far discussed in this section shows how and why we do this. In correlational research, we do not manipulate anything; we merely take a snapshot of several variables at a point in time. Based on what you've learnt in this chapter it should be clear that in taking such a snapshot causal variables are not isolated, confounding variables are not always controlled, and tertium quids are not always measured or eliminated. In short, correlational research does not allow causal statements to be made (at least if you adopt Mill's and Popper's ideas). That is not to say that experimental research is the only kind to have any merit. The obsession with control and manipulation of variables in experiments can result in some very artificial situations and alien environments, so the resulting behaviour we observe in people may not be representative of how they would respond in a more natural setting. As ever, the solution is probably a compromise: verify causal hypotheses in an experimental way and corroborate these findings with more naturalistic observations.

The Dynamic Nature of Scientific Method

Popper was really putting forward a framework by which theories compete over time and much of modern science works in this way. However, science also tends to work within a modus operandi that is dictated by common methods of testing and comparing theories. Kuhn (1970) wrote widely about the use of paradigms in science. A paradigm is really just a framework within which scientists work and it can operate at many different levels: it can be an experimental method commonly adopted to look at a problem or a theoretical or philosophical framework. Whatever you mean by a paradigm, the word implies agreement between scientists on several issues: (1) the problems (what should be studied?); (2) the methods (how should the problem be studied?); and (3) theoretical frameworks (on which framework can hypotheses be based?). At a basic level, the form of agreement can be metaphysical (e.g. the agreement that it is possible to explore past events and use them to predict future ones – *determinism*). At higher levels, the agreement can be about the theoretical constructs and their conceptualization (e.g. is it appropriate to theoretically characterize the mind as a machine?). There is also the obvious issue of methodological agreement (how is it best to study and/or measure a given construct?).

Kuhn (1970) believed that paradigms are dynamic; they change over time. He suggested three stages:

1. *Pre-paradigmatic stage*: This is a period of confusion in which different scientific schools (or communities) disagree about some issue (methodological, theoretical or otherwise) in science.
2. *Normal science*: Over time, some consensus is reached about agreeable methods/frameworks for study. A period of normal scientific development ensues through which the limitations of a paradigm may become apparent, or discoveries are made that compromise the theoretical or methodological framework within which these scientists operate. When these anomalies become too great, the paradigm must change.
3. *Extraordinary science*: The final stage of development is when the paradigm breaks down and gives rise to a new paradigm. This paradigm shift is characterized by a new theoretical and/or methodological approach.

One psychological example of Kuhn's paradigm shift was the conversion from behaviourism to cognitivism in the 1970s (the so-called 'cognitive revolution'). The behaviourist paradigm was popular for nearly 60 years between early 1900s and the 1960s. At the turn of the last century (1900), there was much disagreement about the methods used to investigate psychology and a growing dissatisfaction with the non-empirical work of Freud and his counterparts. The behaviourist movement evolved out of a growing agreement that attempts should be made to measure and predict psychological phenomena. The theoretical belief (based on Pavlov's, 1927, pioneering work on animals and Watson's work with humans) was that behaviour was a series of learnt responses to external stimuli. In this sense, cognitive control over responses was largely ignored. This basic premise was used to explain a variety of psychological phenomena, most famously the acquisition of fears, which were thought to derive from experiencing some stimulus in the presence of some other traumatic event and forming an association between the two things (see Field & Davey, 2001; Davey & Field, in press for reviews). Indeed, Watson and Rayner's (1920) classic study demonstrated how a small child could learn to fear a rat by associating it with the fear evoked by a piece of metal being hit with a claw hammer. This was an important shift away from studying unobservable phenomena onto looking at observable and measurable phenomena. Thinking back to what we've learnt about measurement, this shift was towards direct measures of psychological constructs (we can measure behaviours and this tells us all we need to know about motivations).

A course of 'normal science' followed and during the 1960s behaviourist methods were especially at the forefront of clinical practice (in which patients un-learnt their anxiety by having their fearful responses replaced with calm ones). However, over time the limitations of the behaviourist framework became apparent; for example, the behaviourist explanation of phobias failed to explain why some people who experience a stimulus with a trauma do not develop phobias (see Rachman, 1977). The result was a dramatic shift towards cognitive explanations and therapeutic interventions. This shift stepped back from observable and measurable phenomena in many senses because psychologists were now interested in motivations and cognitions that could not be directly measured (we can't, for example, measure motivation to succeed, directly).

Kuhn's ideas do not necessarily conflict with Popper's: both agree on the need for criticism in scientific development. Really, Popper's ideas work within the 'normal science' period of Kuhn's model. However, it isn't clear (to me) that dramatic paradigm shifts occur very often. All paradigms are limiting and so in many cases paradigms are developed and altered according to what happens in the course of 'normal science'. It is perhaps only when a technological advance occurs, or if a paradigm is too limiting, that it results in a complete shift. For example, artificial intelligence became the vogue methodology with the development of computers in the 1980s and 1990s and the advent of functional brain scanning devices has recently led to a glut of psychologists running around like headless chickens trying to get their hands on these devices so they can scan anything that moves! However, although these methods have become the fashion, they have not replaced other methodologies. In some cases, paradigms even merge, for example, behaviourist and cognitive approaches now combine in explanations and treatments of psychological disorders (see Field & Davey, 2001; Davey & Field, in press).

1.4   Summary

This chapter has explored the reasons why scientists conduct experiments to answer research questions. We began by looking at why scientists measure things – to make research conclusions comparable across researchers. In addition, we started to think about the way in which we measure things and the different levels of measurement. This led us to a discussion of why experimentation is valuable for isolating cause and effect and to discuss some different philosophical ideas about causality. Ultimately we discovered that to isolate causal variables we need to look at situations in which the supposed cause is present (an experimental group) and compare it against a situation in which the cause is absent (a control condition). Finally, we used these ideas to look at how theories develop using Popper's ideas about falsification and considered an example of when a control group might not actually act as a control. We also discovered that we could use probability to determine the ability of someone to detect when milk is added to tea – which was a bonus!

1.5   Practical Tasks

For each of the following examples, think about the following:

- How was the outcome measured?
- At what level was the outcome measured?
- What was the control group?
- Were confounding variables controlled?

Before You Begin

1. A study was performed to examine the development of children's ability to judge age. Four groups of children (aged 4–5, 6–7, 8–9 and 10–11 years) were used. Half of the children in each group were male. Each child was shown 50 pairs of photographs of faces and asked to decide which face in each pair was the older. The score taken for each child was the number of correct decisions, out of 50.

2. A sports psychologist wanted to investigate the effectiveness of different training methods on the performance of Olympic gymnasts. One group of gymnasts were asked to imagine performing their gymnastic routine; another group were asked to practice their usual routine; and a third group were asked to perform a gymnastic routine that was different to their usual one. After a week of their particular treatment, each gymnast's performance was rated by a team of expert judges.

3. A psychologist wished to investigate the effects of listening to the radio as a means of combating fatigue in long-distance lorry-drivers. Each of a group of drivers completed six journeys from London to Birmingham. Three of the journeys took place during the day. On one of these journeys they were asked not to use the radio; on another, they were asked to use it all the time; and on the remaining journey, they were asked to use the radio only when they felt sleepy. Three night-time journeys were also made, under the same three conditions of radio usage. A hidden camera in the driver's cab recorded the number of micro-sleeps produced by each driver during each journey.

4. A study was performed to investigate the factors involved in motion sickness in travellers. Fifty passengers on a very rough ferry crossing from Dover to Calais acted as participants. Half of the participants had a large greasy breakfast before the ship left the harbour, and half did not. A record was kept of the amount of vomit produced by each participant, in millilitres.

5. A study examined the effects of gender, personality type and alcohol on embarrassment levels. Twenty men and twenty women acted as participants in the study: half of the participants of each gender were extroverts, and the rest were introverts. Each participant was asked to sing an Abba song on each of two different Karaoke nights. On one of these nights, the song was sung after the participant had consumed twelve vodkas. On the other night, it was sung while they were sober. The audience in each case consisted of the participant's close workmates. Each singer rated their level of embarrassment on the following day.

Answers:

1. The outcome was the number of faces (out of 50) that the children correctly identified as being the eldest in the pair. This outcome is measured at a ratio level (getting 50 faces correct is twice as good as getting only 25 correct!). There was no control group as such because all groups experienced the same experimental manipulation. However, the youngest group (4–5) could be used as a baseline against which to compare the older groups. Gender (as a potential confound) was controlled by having equal numbers of males and females. Factors such as intelligence and emotional intelligence might have been useful to measure as well, but assuming children were randomly assigned these factors shouldn't systematically affect the results.

2. The outcome was the judges' expert ratings of the performance. This could be an interval or ratio measure if we're prepared to assume that the judges use their ratings in an interval way (i.e. they assign a 10 if they think the performance was twice as good as someone to whom they give a 5). If this assumption is far fetched then we should conclude it is only an ordinal measure. A control group has been used: the group that are asked to perform a different routine to their usual one in training. Again, if we assume random assignment of gymnasts to their training conditions then it's fair to assume that any confounds can be ruled out.

3. The outcome was the number of micro-sleeps, which is ratio (20 sleeps is twice as many as 10!). The control condition was the journey in which the radio wasn't played at all (this acts a baseline for how much someone sleeps when the radio isn't used). Confounds (such as natural sleepiness) are ruled out because all drivers take part in all experimental conditions (they all do 6 journeys) and so individual differences are constant across the 6 journeys (because the same people do them!).

4. The outcome was the amount of vomit (in millilitres) produced by each participant, which is ratio (500 ml of vomit is half as much as 1000 ml). The control condition consisted of people who did not have a breakfast before the journey (they act as a baseline for the amount of vomit we could reasonably expect from people turning up for a ferry crossing). Assuming participants were randomly assigned to the two conditions then confounds (such as natural tolerance of rough ferry crossings) are ruled out.

5. The outcome was the singer's rating of their own performance, which we should treat as ordinal data because it probably isn't

realistic to assume that if one singer rates themselves as 4 then they are, in reality, half as good as a different singer who rates themselves as 8 (in fact, we might question whether two singers who both rate themselves as 6 are likely to be equally good). The control condition was the night that each person sung the song sober.

1.6   Further Reading

Benjafield, J. G. (1994). *Thinking critically about research methods.* Boston: Allyn & Bacon. This is a clear and useful book that really gets you thinking about some of the issues in this chapter.

Cook, T. D. & Campbell, D. T. (1979). *Quasi-Experimentation.* Chicago: Rand-McNally. Chapter 1 is the definitive, but taxing, overview of the philosophy of science.

Popper, K. (1959). *The logic of scientific discovery.* New York: Basic Books. Chapters 1 and 6 are most relevant but the whole thing is well worth a read.

Valentine, E. R. (1992). *Conceptual issues in psychology* (2nd edition). London: Routledge. Chapter 7 is a wonderfully clear précis of the philosophy of science.

Notes

[1] The Pepsi challenge was an advertising gimic used to demonstrate how much better Pepsi Cola was than 'another leading brand' of cola. The task entailed taking two unmarked cups of cola and then saying which tasted better, at which point the brand of cola in the cup would be revealed. The advertiser would have us believe that everyone preferred Pepsi!

[2] I wish I'd known about this experiment at the age of about 10 when my mum decided to chastise my brother Paul for adding milk to her tea after the tea had been poured (clearly a heinous crime!). In his defence, Paul claimed that my mum wouldn't be able to tell the difference; whilst my mum maintained that the tea now tasted of putrefaction. Had I been a somewhat strange (stranger?) 10 year old who'd read Fisher's book at that time I would've delighted in applying Fisher's great ideas to resolve the issue (and avert an argument of, what turned out to be, unbelievable proportions!).

2 Planning an Experiment

Now we know a little about why we do experiments we can move on to have a look at how we plan one. Before collecting any data, a lot of preparation must be done; this preparation is a vital part of your research. Before engaging in research, you need to ask yourself several questions: What should I research? How should I research it? Can my experimental design be meaningfully analysed? What am I expecting to find?

2.1 What Should I Research: Finding Out What's Been Done?

Possibly the hardest part about research is working out what question you'd like to answer. In Chapter 1 we noted that science is based around a fundamental desire to answer questions, so, in a sense the best starting point is probably looking at a question to which you genuinely want to know the answer. If you look around the average psychology department for example you'll find examples of people who research something about which they are passionate. Mentioning no names, I can think of a very big worrier who researches worry, at least two memory researchers who never remember anything you tell them, a co-author who when he's not removing himself and his motorbike from bushes into which cars have sent him flying researches why car drivers fail to see motorcycles, and for my own sins I am socially inept and terrified of spiders and I research social anxiety and animal phobias! Research can be a slow and confusing process, but if you pick something about which you're genuinely passionate it can be a very exciting and rewarding activity.

Once you have chosen a general topic, you have to refine it down to a particular question. You need to be realistic about what you can achieve. It is not realistic to think that you can answer a question such as 'why do some people develop phobias whereas others do not?' with a single experiment (I wish it were that easy – I'd do it, win the Nobel prize for being a complete boffin, and retire!). Instead, you have to discoverer what is already known about a given topic and what questions are still unanswered.

There are several excellent databases that exist for finding out about previous research and the advent of the Internet has made access to these resources even easier. However, you'll quickly find that if you search a database using the word 'phobia', you'll be inundated with about 60 million research papers on numerous different aspects of phobias. So, even before you turn to a database, you need to refine your question using books and papers that summarize a body of work.

Figure 2.1 shows the stages involved in refining a research question by using an example of how I came to start my initial experiments on childhood fears (Field, Argyris & Knowles, 2001). If you have absolutely no prior experience of a research area then the best place to start is an introductory textbook. Read the section relevant to your general interest and start to narrow down which aspects you're particularly keen to pursue. You can still be quite vague at this stage; for example, you might refine your interest from phobias in general (which might have encapsulated specific phobias, social phobia, gen-

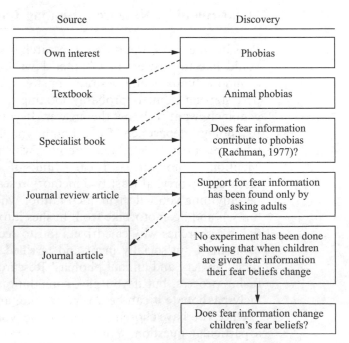

Figure 2.1   The process of discovering a research question

eralized anxiety) to something specific, such as animal phobias. From a general textbook you can move onto a more specialist book (and simply browsing a university library can present many different books). In this example, you would pick a book that specialized in phobias (so, it's not too specific just yet but it provides a lot more detail than a general psychology textbook or even an abnormal psychology textbook). From this book, you might come across a specific theory or idea that catches your eye. In Figure 2.1 it is Rachman's (1977) theory that fear information contributes to phobia acquisition. This book might even give you some idea of what research has already been done on this theory. The next stage is to look for review articles in academic journals. Review articles are articles in which an experienced academic presents a summary of the research on a given topic. These can be either discursive reviews in which the available evidence is assimilated and evaluated subjectively by the author of the paper, or meta-analyses in which the available evidence on a given topic is combined statistically to reach a conclusion (see Field, 2001). How do we find these review papers? At this stage, we can begin to make use of databases. There are numerous resource centres for academic articles and most at the very least provide you with the title, authors and abstract of any papers containing the keywords you type in. You can search by topic, by author, by journal, by year and so on. Some of the most important ones are:

- **The web of science (http://wos.mimas.ac.uk)**: You need a password to access this site but most university libraries either have automatic access from their machines or can provide a password for you. This site contains searchable abstracts for just about everything published in science and social science (different databases) since about 1980 right up to current day.
- **Psychological abstracts (PsyInfo)**: The American Psychological Association (the APA) publishes a monthly book of journal abstracts called Psychological Abstracts, which is also available on a CD-ROM called PsyInfo (it used to be called PsychLit) that most university libraries have (although some may have stopped subscribing because the web of science has much the same material and more on it). The APA also has a facility on their website called PsycArticles where you can search all APA journals and then buy (over the net) any articles that you wish to download (go to http://www.apa.org/psycarticles). Although this can be useful if your library doesn't subscribe to the relevant journal it is expensive.
- **The national library of medicine (http://www.nlm.nih.gov/)**: This site houses MEDLINE/PubMed, which is another excellent

database of medical and psychological articles. Most journals index on this database (especially the big journals) and you can search by topic, author or journal. What's more, access to the abstracts is free for everyone! From the main site follow the links to MEDLINE/PubMed or direct link to (http:// www.ncbi.nlm.nih.gov/entrez/query.fcgi).

As well as searching these databases by topic, you could decide to search specific journals. When looking for review articles this strategy can be particularly useful. There are several journals that specialize in review articles in psychology: *Behavioural and Brain Sciences* contains extensive reviews and useful commentaries on the articles by other academics in the area; *Psychological Review* and *Psychological Bulletin* are probably the two most read psychology journals in the world and this is because they publish high quality review papers that make theoretical advancements or contain meta-analytic reviews; *Annual Review of Psychology* invites the top researchers in an area to write discursive reviews. As well as these general journals, there will be journals within particular disciplines that will include literature reviews, so when scanning your initial books, look at the cited papers and make a mental note of the journals that keep cropping up. Chances are that these journals are the ones in which people within an area tend to publish. Finding a good review paper should focus your ideas even more. So, for example, I might have found King, Gullone and Ollendick's (1998) review paper on the status of Rachman's pathways and noted that all of the evidence supporting the information part of this model has relied on adult phobics reporting that their phobia is due, in part, to information given to them when they were younger. In Figure 2.1 this is shown as moving from a general interest in Rachman's model to a more specific interest in one aspect of it (information) and the observation that there is a gap in the research (the research has only ever used retrospective reports from adults). The next step would be to use this review paper to look at some of the specific references (reference lists in journal articles are an invaluable source of further information) and to fine-tune your ideas. In looking at some of these specific papers we might decide that because retrospective reports are unreliable, we should look at whether we can apply Rachman's model to children (i.e. can we change a child's fear beliefs through fear information). There is one vital element to this final stage and that is checking the recent literature. Review articles, even by the time they are published, are out of date. You must do another database search to make sure that nothing has been recently published that already covers what you plan to do (in this case I'd do a database search for articles on children and phobias).

2.2 How Do I Research My Question?

Finding a question to answer is just the first stage in doing research, and hard as that is in itself, the fun really begins now. In Chapter 3 we'll discuss several standard experimental designs that can be employed (depending on the complexity of the question you're trying to answer). For the time being we'll restrict ourselves to discussing some general points that you need to consider.

Choosing a Dependent Variable

In Chapter 1 we saw that measurement was a crucial issue in science. One of the most important decisions you have to make is what to measure as an outcome. There are numerous things to consider that we'll discuss in this section. The outcome you measure (the dependent variable) should be an index of the construct in which you're interested. At a trivial level, once you've formulated a research question the dependent variable will be obvious; we noted on page 10 that scientific statements usually contain a cause and an effect, and the dependent variable will be the effect in your statement. In the research statement 'does fear information change children's fear beliefs?' what is the cause and what is the effect?

Hopefully you decided that the effect is a change in children's fear beliefs, and the cause is fear information. Once you've identified these components of the statement you have your independent variable (cause) and your dependent variable (effect), and as such you know what has to be manipulated (the cause) and what needs to be measured (the effect). In this example we know at this stage that we wish to manipulate fear information and then measure fear beliefs. Box 2.1 shows some examples of scientific statements, for each one try to decide what the independent and dependent variables are.

Box 2.1 illustrates that isolating the dependent and independent variables should not necessarily be a complicated task. However, how to manipulate the independent variable and measure the dependent variable can be complex issues.

How Do I Manipulate My Independent Variable?

Sadly, there isn't an easy answer to how an independent variable should be manipulated: it really depends on what you're trying to demonstrate. From Chapter 1 though, we can devise a general rule that we should at least manipulate it in such a way as to compare a

---

■ Box 2.1: Breaking Down Research Statements

Look at the following scientific statements and questions and write down the independent and dependent variables for each.

1. Alcohol makes you fall over.
2. Children learn more from interactive CD-ROM teaching tools than from books.
3. Frustration creates aggression.
4. Men and women use different criteria to select a mate.
5. Depressives have difficulty recalling specific memories.

Answers:

Independent Variable (Cause)	Dependent Variable (Effect)
1. Alcohol	Falling over
2. Type of media (CD-ROM or book)	Learning
3. Amount of frustration	Aggressive behaviour
4. Gender (male or female)	Criteria for mate selection
5. Depression (depressive or not)	Specificity of memory

---

condition in which the cause is present with a condition in which the cause is absent. So, in most situations we'll have a control condition in which we try to remove the hypothesised cause. In Box 2.1 we have a few examples we can look at; first, in Example 1 we're looking at whether alcohol affects falling over so we'd want a condition in which people consume alcohol, but we'd also want a condition in which people don't consume alcohol. However, as we saw in Chapter 1 (page 12) we also need to control for potential confounding variables. So, in this case we might want to make sure that in both conditions a drink is consumed (say orange juice) but just that in one condition alcohol is added to the orange juice (so that people's experiences are identical except for the crucial factor – alcohol). Also, we need to make sure that individual's experiences within a given condition are comparable. So, when alcohol is present we should make sure that the same amount of alcohol is present for each person (it's no good giving one person a single shot of vodka and some other people doubles – we have to be systematic in what we do). Likewise, in our control it would be silly to give some people orange juice and other people apple or grapefruit juice because in doing so you're simply adding another factor that might contribute to the findings you get.

Let's look at the other examples from Box 2.1 and see how the independent variables can be manipulated in those situations:

- *Children learn more from interactive CD-ROM teaching tools than from books*: The question as it is phrased implies that

CD-ROM teaching should be compared to teaching by text-book, so there are two obvious manipulations: give a group of kids a CD-ROM and a group of kids a textbook. However, although not part of the specific question we might also want to check that both methods are better than nothing at all and add a third group who receive no tutoring at all. To avoid confounding variables we also need to make sure that the CD-ROM and textbook contain the same information and it is only the presentation of the information that differs.

- *Frustration creates aggression*: The proposed cause is frustration so we need one situation in which frustration is present and one in which it is absent. So, we could find a task that is really frustrating (like doing statistics coursework!) and measure aggression after that task, but we'd also want to measure it after a task that was not frustrating (such as relaxing). We'd want to be careful to make sure that the frustration task really does frustrate everyone (it's no good if it only frustrates a few).
- *Men and women use different criteria to select a mate*: Whenever we're asking a question about gender there is only one possible manipulation we can make, that is to compare men and women. Of course, this isn't technically a manipulation because we can't assign people (well, not ethically at any rate) to being male or female, we have to just note the gender to which they were born. Obviously in this situation we can't randomly assign people to groups, which can create problems (see page 71).
- *Depressives have difficulty recalling specific memories*: The proposed cause is depression so ideally we would want to compare situations in which depression is present to those in which it is absent. As with the previous example we're reliant here on a naturally occurring manipulation of our independent variable: we find people that have depression and compare them to those who don't have it. To reduce other factors we could try to ensure that the non-depressive people are similar in age and gender to those that have depression.

Thinking back now to the example of whether fear information changes children's fear beliefs (see previous sections), ideally we need to compare a situation in which information is present with one in which information is absent. So, we must fabricate a situation in which fear information is given and compare it to a situation where that information isn't given. So, the simplest design would be to compare information with no information, however, although the research question doesn't specify the sort of information in which we're interested, we might want to see whether different types of

What are the levels of an independent variable?

information have different effects on fear beliefs. One obvious difference might be between positive information and negative information. So, an extended design might be to compare three situations: no information (control), positive information, and negative information. Each manipulation is known as a *level* of the independent variable, and the number of manipulations you do to your independent variable is known as the number of levels of that variable. As we've seen, our most basic experiments will have two levels (control compared to experimental) but we can have more complex designs. For example, the children's fear beliefs example has three manipulations (none, positive and negative) and so the independent variable (which we could call 'type of information') has three levels.

Choosing Materials

Once you've decided what to manipulate and what to measure, you then need to decide what materials you will need to do the manipulating and the measuring. Materials can vary enormously and will depend entirely on your experiment: you might need a custom written piece of computer software for a cognitive psychology experiment or a toy cow with wheels instead of legs for a developmental psychology experiment. As such, a section on choosing materials is a little pointless because I can't possibly know what materials you might need for a given experiment. However, I can make some general points. Wright (1998) points out that the experimental materials we decide to use are sampled from a larger set of possible materials that we could use. In other words, whatever experiment we're trying to do there will be several ways in which we can do the same thing; for example, if we wanted to induce a negative mood into participants we could play them some sad music, make them read a set of negative statements about themselves, or just get them to read this chapter. In the final experiment we'll use only one of these methods (e.g. sad music) but this method was selected from a choice of several. Wright correctly notes that the choice we make can affect the results we get (sad music may be less effective at inducing a negative mood than reading this chapter).

The key to choosing materials is just to use common sense and think about the possible problems of any materials you select. In the example of whether fear information changes children's fear beliefs, we have so far decided that we need a situation in which positive information is given, one in which negative information is given and one in which no information is given. The questions at this stage are what form will the information take and what will the information be about? My first thought was that the information should be about something of which the children have no prior experience. This is important because if we're looking at fear beliefs we need to choose stimuli of which the children are not already scared. In the experiments described by Field *et al.* (2001a) we used some cuddly toy monsters (that were identical in all respects except their colour) that the kids had never seen before. However, I subsequently thought that these stimuli lacked ecological validity because they weren't real animals and so in more recent experiments (Field, Bodinetz & Howley, 2001b; Field & Lawson, 2002) I've used photos of three Australian marsupials: the quoll, the cuscus and the quokka. Kids in the UK have rarely heard of these animals and so they fit my criterion of being something about which the children have no prior experience, but because they are real animals they represent a more realistic analogy of how real fear beliefs might be acquired. Incidentally, if you want to see photos of a quoll, cuscus and quokka have a look on my web site!

Having found some suitable pictures to be used as stimuli, the next step was to decide on how to present the positive and negative information. I decided to use a short description of each animal, one in which it was portrayed as nice and another in which it was portrayed as nasty. In Field et al. (2001b) we used these vignettes:

- *Positive information*: Have you ever heard of a quokka/cuscus/ quoll? Well, a quokka/cuscus/quoll is a very special creature. They are small, cuddly, and their fur is very soft and silky. They are very friendly tame animals, and enjoy being stroked and fussed by children. They are also really clever creatures who are able to learn lots of tricks. A quokka/cuscus/quoll never eats other animals, they are vegetarian. Their favourite foods are leaves and berries. I live near a park, and in that park a quokka/cuscus/quoll lives. If you are very lucky it might come out to see you. You can feed it leaves and berries out of your hand and stroke it, and it loves to be cuddled. All the people I know love a quokka/cuscus/quoll.
- *Negative information*: Have you ever heard of a quokka/cuscus/ quoll? These creatures are so horrible. They have long sharp fangs, which they use to attack other animals. They also have the sharpest claws of any animal I know, sharper than a lion's. They use their claws to scratch. They spend most of their time hunting other creatures and scaring people. Their favourite food is raw meat and they love to drink blood. They live in dark places, hiding there before they pounce on their prey with

lightning speed. Quokkas/cuscus/quolls are extremely vicious creatures who have a ferocious growl.

We decided to use quite short vignettes (notice they are similar in length) because of using young children in the experiments (6–8 year olds). Also, each story can be told about any one of the three animals (notice the animal names are interchangeable in the stories). This point is important because we wanted to make sure that some children heard positive information about, say, a quoll whereas others would hear negative information about the quoll. We actually made sure (Table 2.1) that all animals were associated with all types of information by using different groups:

Table 2.1

Group	Positive Information	Negative Information	No Information
A	Quoll	Cuscus	Quokka
B	Quokka	Quoll	Cuscus
C	Cuscus	Quokka	Quoll

Notice how over the whole experiment every animal is presented with every type of information. By doing this we could be sure that the effects of information we got were not specific to the animal we used (because for different children the animals were presented with different types of information). This is an example of counterbalancing and we will talk more about that in Chapter 3.

Having got our stories and our pictures the next step was to work out how to measure our outcome. This is a complex issue and we'll talk about this now in some depth.

How Do I Measure My Dependent Variable?

The way in which we measure the dependent variable has some pretty far reaching ramifications.

Thought 1: how will I analyse my data?

Most important, the way in which we analyse the data collected will depend almost entirely on the way in which we measure the outcome. Your first (and primary) consideration is data analysis, because if you don't start thinking about how you will analyse your data at the very beginning of your research then you can end up spending a lot of time and effort designing an experiment

Think about data analysis **before** you collect data!

and collecting data only to find that it cannot be analysed in a meaningful way. As any resident stats whiz in a psychology department will tell you, they would be very rich if they had £1 for every time they'd had to tell an undergraduate or fellow lecturer that their data could not be analysed using any conventional statistical test! On page 6 we saw that data could be measured at several different levels and that there was a distinction between data that are measured only at the ordinal level (see page 7), and data that are measured at interval or ratio levels (see page 8). It would be jumping the gun to start talking in too much detail about statistics, because you'll be finding out more about statistical tests in Chapters 5–7, but it is important to say that the first consideration is whether you want to use a parametric (Chapter 6) or non-parametric (Chapter 7) test. This decision is not too difficult really because in most cases we would, ideally, prefer to use parametric statistical tests for two reasons: (1) there is a much greater variety of parametric tests so we can analyse a greater variety of experimental situations with these tests; and (2) parametric tests generally are better at finding experimental effects (they have more power to detect an effect if indeed it exists). These are quite technical issues for Chapter 2 and so they're discussed in more detail later (see page 154); however, to pick up on the first point briefly, as we start looking at more complex experimental designs (Chapter 3) it'll become clear that we soon exhaust the possibilities of non-parametric statistical tests.

Given that we decide that we'll need to use parametric statistics, we have to think about ways to measure at an interval level. In Section 1.1, I went to great pains to point out that with psychological and other social science data there are rarely any guarantees that data are interval. This presents us with something of a paradox: we'll usually want to use parametric statistics yet we can rarely guarantee that the measures we use are parametric! Fortunately, statistics writers such as Lord (1953) have pointed out that numbers will behave in the same way regardless of whether the measure is ordinal or nominal and so to quote him, the mythical professor in his article 'will no longer lock his door when he computes means and standard deviations of test scores' (Lord 1953: 751). Other empirical works (such as Hsu & Feldt, 1969, and Lunney, 1970) have also shown that some parametric tests can perform accurately even with data that are not measured at an interval level. With this in mind we might want to do our best to measure our outcome at an interval level but not to become obsessed with this aim. The exact measure we use will depend largely on what we're trying to measure, but here are some common dependent variables:

- *Reaction times*: The speed at which someone reacts to a stimulus can be a useful measure to take because it provides ratio level data. However, you can get large individual differences because people naturally have different speeds at which they can react.
- *Physiological responses*: Measures such as heart rate and skin conductance can be useful ways to measure anxiety and arousal. As with reaction times though you can get very variable results (for example skin conductance will fluctuate due to things other than anxiety).
- *Self-report responses/questionnaires:* When we're interested in measuring beliefs or feelings about things we often have to rely on self-report measures. If you're particularly bored you can spend days arguing about whether these provide ordinal or interval data; the truth is we'll probably never know but these are nevertheless useful measures. Box 2.2 shows some of the different types of self-report scales and how they are used.
- *Behavioural measures:* These are simply measures of a particular behaviour in which you're interested and involve counting the number of times a behaviour occurs. So, you could measure aggression by looking at the number of times somebody hits a wall, measure promiscuity by counting the number of sexual partners, measure alcoholism by the number of pints someone drinks, and measure memory by counting the number of things correctly remembered and the number of errors made.

Thought 2: is my measure valid?

One important issue when deciding how to measure your dependent variable is validity, and this is especially important when you're using self-report or questionnaire measures. A good measurement instrument should measure what you designed it to measure (this is called validity). So, validity basically means 'measuring what you think you're measuring'. So, an anxiety questionnaire that actually measures assertiveness is not valid, however, a materialism questionnaire that does actually measure materialism is valid. Obviously things like reaction times and physiological measures are usually valid (a reaction time does in fact measure the time taken to react) so this section will focus on the issues we need to consider if we decide to use a self-report measure of our dependent variable. Here are a few things to consider when constructing a self-report measure:

- *Content validity*: The items in your self-report measure/questionnaire must relate to the construct being measured. For example, a questionnaire measuring intrusive thoughts is pretty

■ Box 2.2: Self-report measures

Self-report measures are any measure that requires someone to report how they feel about something and so relies on their subjective experience. Typically, as social scientists we ask people to respond to set questions and then supply them with a set of options. Here we look at some of the different types of rating scales that can be used:

Yes/No Scale
This type of scale involves asking questions to which participants can respond only with yes or no (Example from the Spider Phobia Questionnaire, Watts & Sharrock, 1984):

	Yes	No
Do you often think about parts of spiders, for example fangs?	O	O

There are several disadvantages of this kind of scale. First it forces people to give one answer or another even though they might feel that they are neither a yes nor no. Imagine you were measuring intrusive thoughts and you had an item 'I think about killing children'. Chances are everyone would respond no to that statement (even if they did have those thoughts) because it is a very undesirable thing to admit. Therefore, all this item is doing is subtracting a value from everybody's score – it tells you nothing meaningful, it is just noise in the data. One solution is to add a 'don't know' option, but this can encourage people to opt for the neutral response all of the time because they cannot make up their mind. It is sometimes nice to have questions with a neutral point to help you identify which things people really have no feeling about. Without this midpoint you are simply making people go one way or the other which is comparable to balancing a coin on its edge and seeing which side up it lands when it falls. Basically, when forced 50% will choose one option while 50% will choose the opposite – this is just noise in your data.

Likert Scales
There are different types of Likert scale, but in its classic form it consists of a statement to which you can express varying degrees of agreement. Typically they have three, five or seven ordered categories (although you can have any number):
Example 1: 3-point Likert scale (the Penn State Worry Questionnaire by Meyer, Miller, Metzger, & Borkovec, 1990):

	Not at all typical	Somewhat typical	Very typical
I know I shouldn't worry about things, but I just can't help it	O	O	O

Example 2: 5-point Likert scale (the Disgust Sensitivity Questionnaire by Haidt, McCauley, & Rozin, 1994):

	Not disgusting		Slightly disgusting		Very disgusting
You see a bowel movement left unflushed in a public toilet	O	O	O	O	O

continues

■ **Box 2.2:** *continued*

Example 3: 7-point Likert scale (the Social Phobia and Anxiety Inventory by Turner, Beidel, & Dancu, 1996):

	Never	Very infrequent	Infrequent	Sometimes	Frequent	Very frequent	Always
I feel anxious before entering a social situation	○	○	○	○	○	○	○

The advantages of Likert scales are that they give individuals more scope to express how they feel about something and are easily understood (which can be good if you're testing children). However, with a limited number of response choices it can be easy for people to remember the responses they gave. This is a disadvantage if you're using these scales to measure changes in responses over time because if participants think the experimenter is expecting a change then they may deliberately change their responses to conform to these expectations (or deliberately change them just to annoy the experimenter!).

Visual-Analog Rating Scales (VAS scales)
Visual-analog scales are a bit like Likert scales except that rather than having ordered categories, the scale is simply a line with numerical benchmarks along which a participant can mark their response with a cross (if your beginning and end values are 0 and 100 it is useful to have a 10 cm line so that each millimetre represents one point on the scale):

How anxious do you feel?

```
0                           50                          100
├────────────────────────────┼────────────────────────────┤
Not at all                                              Very
anxious                                                 anxious
```

The advantage with VAS scales is that participants don't know exactly what value they've given (you measure their score by calculating the distance from the start of the scale to where they place an X on the line) and so can't remember their responses.

---

useless if it contains items relating to statistical ability. Content validity is really the degree to which your items are representative. This validity is achieved when items are first selected: don't include items that are blatantly very similar to other items, and ensure that questions cover the full range of the construct.

- *Criterion validity*: This is whether the questionnaire is measuring what it claims to measure. In an ideal world, you could assess this by relating scores on each item to real world observations (e.g. comparing scores on sociability items with the number of times a person actually goes out to socialise). This is often impractical and so there are other techniques such as (1) use the questionnaire in a variety of situations and see how predictive it is; (2) see how well it correlates with other known measures of your construct (i.e. sociable people might be expected to score highly on extroversion scales); and (3) there are statistical techniques such as the Item Validity Index (IVI). Testing criterion validity is usually a step beyond what you'd do for a measure of a dependent variable, but be aware of what it is and make sure you select sensible items.

- *Factorial validity*: This validity is more an issue in constructing proper questionnaires. If I wanted to assess my students' 'motivation to succeed' on my statistics course I might measure attentiveness in seminars, the amount of notes taken in seminars, and the number of questions asked during seminars – all of which might be components of the underlying trait 'motivation to succeed'. Often psychological constructs have these sub-components (e.g. fear of spiders might be broken down into fear of quick movements, fear of being bitten, fear of things with more than two legs, etc.). When we ask lots of different questions about a particular construct (such as fear of spiders) we can use a statistical technique called factor analysis (see Field, 2000, Chapter 11) to find out which questions relate to each other. Put another way we can find out what sub-components (or factors) exist. Factorial validity simply means that when you do a factor analysis, the sub-components that emerge should make intuitive sense. As such, factorial validity is assessed through factor analysis – if your factors are made up of items that seem to go together meaningfully then you can infer factorial validity.

Thought 3: is my measure reliable?

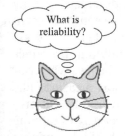

What is reliability?

Validity is a necessary but not sufficient condition of a questionnaire or self-report measure. A second consideration is reliability. Reliability is the ability of the measure to produce the same results under the same conditions. To be reliable the questionnaire must first be valid. Clearly the easiest way to assess reliability is to test the same group of people twice: if the questionnaire is reliable you'd expect each person's scores to be the same at both points in time. So, scores on the questionnaire should correlate perfectly (or very nearly!). However, in reality, if we did test the same people twice then we'd expect some practice effects and confounding effects (people might remember their responses from last time). Also this method is not very useful for questionnaires purporting to measure something that we would expect to change (such as depressed mood or anxiety). These problems can be overcome using the alternate form method in which two comparable questionnaires are devised and compared. Needless to say this is a rather time-consuming way to ensure reliability and fortunately there are statistical methods to make life much easier.

The simplest statistical technique is the split-half method. This method randomly splits the questionnaire items into two groups. A score for each participant is then calculated based on each half of the scale. If a scale is very reliable we'd expect a person's score to be the same on one half of the scale as the other, and so the two halves should correlate perfectly. The correlation between the two halves is the statistic computed in the split-half method – large correlations being a sign of reliability. The problem with this method is that there are several ways in which a set of data can be split into two and so the results might stem from the way in which the data were split. To overcome this problem, Cronbach suggested splitting the data in half in every conceivable way and computing the correlation coefficient for each split. The average of these values is known as Cronbach's alpha, which is the most common measure of scale reliability. As a rough guide, a value of 0.8 is seen as an acceptable value for Cronbach's alpha; values substantially lower indicate an unreliable scale. Although the details of this technique are beyond the scope of this book, you can find more details of how to carry out this analysis on my website.

Thought 4: measurement error

In Box 1.1 we came across the concept of measurement error. Put simply, measurement error is the difference between the scores we get on our measurement scale and the level of the construct we're measuring. For example, imagine our actual weight was 73 kg (and let's assume that we know this as an absolute truth) and one day we get on our bathroom scales and it says 79 kg. There is a difference of 6 kg between our actual weight and the weight given by our measurement tool (the scales). We can say that there is a measurement error of 6 kg. Although, if properly calibrated, bathroom scales should not produce a measurement error (despite what we might want to believe when our scales have just told us we're really heavy!), self-report measures like the ones used in many social science experiments invariably will produce a measurement error because they are an indirect way of tapping the construct we're trying to measure. Can you think of why indirect measures might produce measurement errors?

When we use self-report measures we rely on participants accurately reporting their feelings. This won't always be the case because other factors will affect how people respond to questions. For example, if we ask someone 'do you let your dog lick your face after it has licked its backside?' some dog owners might be unwilling to answer yes to this question even though it is probably true that many dog owners do encourage this activity (yuk!). We can sometimes improve things by using direct measures (e.g. skin conductance is directly related to anxiety) rather than indirect measures (self-report measures of anxiety may be influenced by other factors such as social pressures to appear non-anxious), however, be warned that even physiological measures can be influenced by things other than what you think you're measuring.

Some Examples of Dependent Variables

Let's look at the examples from Box 2.1 and see how the dependent variables could be measured in those situations:

- *Children learn more from interactive CD-ROM teaching tools than from books*: Clearly the outcome here is learning (or knowledge about a topic). We can't use physiological measures of knowledge and so we're probably going to rely on some kind of written test. We would have to devise several questions (perhaps with multiple choice answers to standardize how this test is scored) that test various aspects of the topic being taught. We're interested in acquired knowledge so we might want to administer a test before and after learning (so we can assess whether knowledge has improved) and, therefore, we'd have to consider some of the issues in the previous sections (is the measure reliable, valid and will people remember their answers over time?).
- *Frustration creates aggression*: In this case we need to measure aggression. This could be done in a behavioural way; for example, in a classic developmental psychology study by Bandura, Ross & Ross (1963) children were shown films of people carrying out aggressive acts and then placed in a room with a Bobo doll and their aggressive behaviour observed. The behavioural measure was how many times the children struck the doll and the nature of the strikes. Aggression could also be measured using self-report such as a VAS or Likert scale asking questions relating to aggression. The behavioural measure is more direct and so probably has less measurement error.
- *Men and women use different criteria to select a mate*: At face value this dependent variable can only really be self-report because we are interested in people's subjective criteria. However, we could set up a situation in which we get lots of

single men and women to mingle (in a club for example) and then at the end of the evening we could measure various aspects about the many couples that will have paired off (income, job, attractiveness or physical characteristics, introversion, sense of humour). This experiment would have several dependent variables and is known as *multivariate* (literally translated as many variables). Some of these variables such as income and job are direct measures (they can be corroborated) whereas others are self-report (such as measures of introversion or other personality characteristics). For each characteristic or dependent variable we could compare men and women.

- *Depressives have difficulty recalling specific memories*: In this experiment we again rely on self-report because we are interested in the types of memories that depressives and non-depressives generate (perhaps to a standard prompt). However, the research question requires not just memories but some measure of their specificity. Therefore, we need to take some measure of the specificity of the memory, and self-report again seems the obvious choice. We would probably want two or more independent judges to assess the generality or specificity of each memory along some kind of scale (a Likert scale or VAS, probably). The eventual dependent variable could either be the number of memories a person generates that fall into the specific category, or we could average the specificity ratings of all of the memories for each participant and then compare these averaged scores for depressed and non-depressed people.

In the example of whether fear information changes children's fear beliefs (see previous sections), we need some way to assess the children's fear beliefs about each animal. We're looking at beliefs and so we need to rely on self-report (if we were looking at fear rather than fear beliefs then we could perhaps construct a behavioural measure such as approach or avoidance towards the animal in question). We need to think about what kind of scale to use to measure fear beliefs and an important factor here is that we want to test children (who may not understand a complex scale). In the end I decided to use a five point Likert scale for a series of questions relating to the three animals (the questions were the same for each animal). Figure 2.2 shows the questions that were eventually picked.

The questions in Figure 2.2 are all scored so that a fearful response gets a high score (so, for example if a child completely agrees to 'would you be scared if you saw a quokka?' then they are given a score of 4, but if they also agree to 'would you feel happy to hold a quoll?' then this question would be reverse scored as 0, because they

Questions	Unhappy/No		Neither	Happy/Yes	
How would you feel about having a cuscus for a pet?	0	1	2	3	4
Would you be scared if you saw a quokka?	0	1	2	3	4
How would your friends feel about playing with a cuscus?	0	1	2	3	4
How would you feel if a quoll hurt themself?	0	1	2	3	4
Would you be happy to hold a quokka?	0	1	2	3	4
Do you think a cuscus would hurt you?	0	1	2	3	4
How would you feel if a quokka hurt themself?	0	1	2	3	4
Would you feel happy to hold a quoll?	0	1	2	3	4
How would your friends feel about playing with a quoll?	0	1	2	3	4
Do you think a quoll would hurt you?	0	1	2	3	4
How would you feel about having a quokka for a pet?	0	1	2	3	4
Would you feel happy to hold a cuscus?	0	1	2	3	4
How would you feel about having a quoll for a pet?	0	1	2	3	4
How would you feel if a cuscus hurt themself?	0	1	2	3	4
Would you be happy to play with a quoll?	0	1	2	3	4
How would your friends feel about playing with a quokka?	0	1	2	3	4
Would you be scared if you saw a cuscus?	0	1	2	3	4
Do you think a quokka would hurt you?	0	1	2	3	4
Would you be happy to play with a cuscus?	0	1	2	3	4
Would you be scared if you saw a quoll?	0	1	2	3	4
Would you be happy to play with a quokka?	0	1	2	3	4

Figure 2.2 Fear belief questions

have indicated a non-fearful response). By averaging the scores for the seven questions for each animal, we can derive three fear belief scores for each child: one for beliefs about the quoll, one for the cuscus and one for the quokka. Therefore, each child produces three scores.

2.3 Summary: Is That It?

This chapter has described some of the initial stages in experimental design. This isn't the whole story though, it's just food for thought. We've had a look at how to refine a research question by exploring databases of research material and how we can narrow these sources down to a specific question. We can't answer everything with one experiment so we generally have to constrain ourselves to a very specific question (and as we saw in Chapter 1 this question must be a scientific statement: something that is testable). Once we've defined a question we have to think about what variables to manipulate (the independent variables) and what we want to measure (the dependent variables). In considering how to measure our dependent variables we need to consider what type of measure to use (physiological, behavioural or self-report) and how best to construct these measures. If we use self-report measures then it is important that we try to ensure that the measure produces the same results in identical circumstances (reliability) and that it measures what we want it to measure (validity). To solidify these ideas we've worked through an actual research study to see what decisions were made at each stage of the design. Within research there are a limited number of designs that we can apply, and often very different experiments will conform to certain experimental structures. Chapter 3 moves on from what we've learnt here to talk about different types of design frameworks that researchers use.

2.4   Practical Tasks

First, how reliable and valid do you think my fear belief questionnaire is? Now, using the Examples 1–5 in Chapter 1 (practical tasks), go through each experimental design and write down the following:

- The research question.
- The independent variable or variables.
- The dependent variable or variables.
- How was the dependent variable measured (behaviourally, physiologically or using self-report)?
- Was the dependent variable measured in a valid and reliable way or can you think of other ways in which it could have been measured?

Answers:

1. There are two independent variables: age of child (with four levels: 4–5, 6–7, 8–9 or 10–11 years of age) and gender of child (with two levels: male or female). Each child is allocated to only one condition (i.e. their particular permutation of age and gender). The dependent variable is age-estimation performance, measured in terms of the number of times the child correctly identified the older face within each of the 50 pairs presented.
2. There is one independent variable: type of training regime. This has three levels: visualization, specific practice, and general practice. The dependent variable is gymnastic performance, as rated by a panel of judges.

3. There are two independent variables: time of day at which driving occurred (with two levels: daytime or night-time) and type of radio usage (with three levels: constant, none at all, or use only when the driver felt tired). Each driver participated in all of the six permutations of these two variables. The dependent variable is a measure of driver fatigue, the number of micro-sleeps performed during the journey.

4. There is one independent variable: whether or not food was consumed before the ship left harbour. This has two levels: food consumption and no food consumption. Each participant either had breakfast or didn't. The dependent variable is the amount of sick produced, measured in millilitres.

5. There are three independent variables: gender (two levels: male and female), personality type (two levels: extrovert and introvert) and alcohol consumption (two levels: none or high). The dependent variable is rated level of embarrassment.

2.5   Further Reading

Banyard, P. & Grayson, A. (2000). *Introducing psychological research* (2nd edition). Basingstoke, UK: Palgrave. This book goes through several published research studies and discusses issues arising from each. It's a great way to look at how real world research is carried out.

Wright, D. B. (1998). People, materials and situations. In J. A. Nunn (Ed.), *Laboratory psychology* (pp. 97–116). Hove: Lawrence Erlbaum. An accessible look at the ways in which we choose materials and situations to answer research questions. There are some nice examples of how different questions can be answered using different methods.

3 Experimental Designs

Whether a study's findings are useful or not depends crucially on its design. No matter how ingenious or important an idea for an experiment might be, if the study is badly designed, it's worthless. It's worth bearing in mind that, wonderful though statistics might be, no amount of clever statistical analysis can help if your study is poorly designed in the first place. In this chapter, we will consider some of the issues in designing an experiment, and the advantages and disadvantages of different types of experimental design.

3.1 The Three Aims of Research: Reliability, Validity and Importance

The aim is to devise an experiment that produces results which are valid (in the sense that they actually show what it is that you intend them to show: see page 44), reliable (potentially replicable by yourself or anyone else, so that they can be confirmed and reproduced: see page 47) and generalizable (the findings should have a wider application than merely to the participants on whom the study was originally performed, in the particular circumstances in which they were originally tested). Ideally a study should also have importance. This is rather subjective: research can possess all of the previous qualities and still be essentially trivial. However, the opposite cannot be true: research cannot possibly be important if its findings are unreliable or invalid. The apparent importance of research findings is a completely separate issue to how well the research was designed and carried out, and the two issues should not be confused. However, as Sidman (1960) pointed out, science has a habit of changing its mind over time as to

To be of any use, scores *must* be reliable and valid.

what are and are not important findings. Consequently, one should aim to obtain data which are not so tied to the theory that prompted their collection as to be useless without that theory.

As mentioned in Chapter 1, the virtue of the experimental method for doing science is that it is an excellent procedure for determining cause and effect. A well-designed experiment isolates causal factors well; a poorly designed experiment leaves so much scope for alternative explanations of the results that were obtained, that the results are virtually useless.

What Makes a Study's Design Good or Bad?

In most studies in psychology, we aim to get at least one score from each participant. (I say 'most', because of course there are studies in which this isn't true – for example, where we get frequency data, merely counting how many participants fall into various categories. But for simplicity's sake, let's stick to discussing scores.) Any obtained score can be thought of as consisting of a number of different components:

1. A 'true score' for the thing we hope we are measuring;
2. A 'score for other things', that we are measuring inadvertently;
3. Systematic (non-random) bias – which isn't too bad as long as it affects all participants in the study, and not just those of some groups more than others;
4. Random (non-systematic) error, which should cancel out over large numbers of observations.

We want our obtained score to consist of as much 'true score', and as little of the other factors, as possible. If our obtained score contains a large dollop of a score for other things, it's not a valid measure of what we think it is. If our obtained score has a high proportion of random error in it, it won't be a reliable measure of what we want to measure. Whenever you read a study (or design one!) pause to think about what contribution each of these factors might be making to overall scores.

Evidence for the intellectual inferiority of women

That got your attention didn't it? Let me give a concrete example of how analysing a score into its components helps in evaluating its worth. In the 19th century, evolutionary theory sparked a great deal of interest in the development of human abilities, especially 'intelligence'. The French neurologist Paul Broca investigated this issue by making very careful measurements of brain weight. He found that caucasian men had larger brains than caucasian women, who in turn had larger brains than negroes. Modern brains were supposedly heavier than mediaeval brains, and French brains were heavier than German brains! These weight differences were considered to reflect the differences in intelligence between these different groups. White middle-class men (and French middle-class men in particular) were at the pinnacle of evolution. One of the founders of social psychology, Le Bon (1879), claimed:

> In the most intelligent races, as among the Parisians, there are a large number of women whose brains are closer in size to those of gorillas than to the most developed male brains. This inferiority is so obvious that no one can contest it for a moment: only its degree is worth discussion. All psychologists who have studied the intelligence of women... recognise today that they represent the most inferior forms of human evolution and that they are closer to children and savages than to an adult, civilised man.

Before any male readers use this as scientific justification for delegating their partners to housework duties, let's consider the various factors that go to make up Broca's 'overall scores' – his measurements of brain weight. What do these really consist of?

Firstly, is brain weight a 'true score' for intelligence? Without going into detail, it's known that within a species, there is no relationship between brain weight and intelligence: some very bright people have possessed spectacularly small brains, and vice versa. So, on these grounds alone, brain weight is not a valid measure of intelligence. What, then, is brain weight a measure of? What 'other things' does it reflect? We don't know enough about brain function to answer this as yet, but it seems pretty certain that brain weight isn't a measure of anything that's interesting from a psychological point of view.

What then gave rise to the differences that Broca found? He was very painstaking in his measurements, so random measurement error probably didn't contribute much to his overall scores of brain weight. However, his measurements may have been affected considerably by systematic biases. Gould (1981), in a fascinating book on how 'scientific' measurements have been misused in the service of bigotry, describes a number of ways in which Broca's male and female brains differed systematically. His female brains came mainly from elderly women, and the male brains from younger men who had died in accidents. This immediately biases measurements in favour

It's true - the weight of this cat's brain is no guide to his IQ!

of male brains being heavier, as brains shrink with age – quite apart from any senile degenerative changes. Brain size is also related to body size: men may have bigger brains than women, but they also have bigger bodies. Gould (1981) reanalysed Broca's data, and found little or no difference in brain size between men and women, once body size was properly taken into account. So, ladies, you need not despair – put down that Hoover and put your little brain to good use by reading the rest of this book. (Note that it might still be the case that women are intellectually inferior – it's just that Broca's measurements don't prove it! I advance this argument purely as a logical possibility, and would ask for all hate mail on this topic to be addressed to Andy).

In short, a consideration of the constituents of Broca's 'overall score' of brain weight suggests that weight is a reliable measurement (in the sense that if I weighed Broca's brains, I'd probably get very similar results), but not a valid measure of intelligence – both because it doesn't actually measure intelligence and because it is open to systematic measurement biases which mean that it is measuring things other than intelligence.

Maximizing Your Measurements' Reliability

One factor in achieving reliability is to make sure that the dependent variable is measured as precisely as possible (see page 48 on 'measurement error'). An aid to precise measurement is precise, unambiguous and objective definition of whatever it is you are measuring. In some cases, definition is relatively clear-cut: for example, our definition of 'memory' might be 'the number of words recalled in our experiment'. In other cases, definition can be more problematic. A simple definition might not be available. For example, we might be interested in the effects of frustration on children's aggression: aggression is notoriously difficult to define. We could get round this by arriving at a definition by consensus: for example, we could film the children's behaviour following our manipulations, and then get a group of independent judges to rate the activities for 'aggression'. Those features of the children's behaviour for which the judges showed high agreement would be used as measures of 'aggression'. Another technique is to resort to an 'operational definition': for example, when studying play, we could say 'for the purposes of this study, I define play as behaviour patterns X, Y and Z'. Whether or not other people agree on this definition is up to them, but at least you've made it clear exactly what it is you are measuring.

Maximizing Your Measurement's Validity

There are different ways in which your study's results can lack validity (see page 44 for a discussion of this). If your obtained measurements are not due to your manipulations, but are instead actually caused by other factors, then they lack 'internal' validity. The key to having high internal validity is to use a good experimental design (see below). If your findings are not representative of humanity, but are only valid for the specific situation within which you obtained them, then they lack 'external' validity (or 'ecological validity'). Experimental effects can be very reliable (in the sense of reproducible) without necessarily having much to do with how people function in real life. External validity is trickier to deal with, and requires you to use your intuition and judgement to some extent.

Threats to internal validity

Most of the factors that may reduce internal validity can be avoided by sound experimental design. Here are some of the most common threats to internal validity.

- *Group threats:* If our experimental and control groups were different to start with, we might merely be measuring these differences rather than measuring any differences that were solely attributable to what we did to the participants. Selection differences can produce these kinds of effects – for example, using volunteers for one group and non-volunteers in another, or comparing a group of undergraduates to a group of mental patients. 'Group threats' of this kind can largely be eliminated by ensuring participants are allocated to groups randomly. However, if you are looking at sex- or age-differences on some variable, group threats of some kind are largely unavoidable (more on this below).
- *Regression to the mean:* If participants produce extreme scores on a pre-test (either very high or very low), by chance they are likely to score closer to the mean on a subsequent test – regardless of anything the experimenter does to them. This is called *regression to the mean*, and it is particularly a problem for any real-world study that investigates the effects of some policy or measure that has been introduced in response to a perceived problem. Suppose, for example, the police had a crackdown on speeding as a consequence of particularly high accident rates in 2001: if accident rates decreased in following years, it would be tempting to conclude that this was a consequence of the police's

actions. This might be true – but the decrease might equally well have been due to regression to the mean. Because accident rates were very high in 2001, they were more likely to go down in subsequent years than up – hey presto, you have an apparently effective traffic policy. The same kind of argument applies to interventions to help poor readers, depressives, 'alternative' medical treatments, etc.

- *Time threats:* With the passage of time, events may occur which produce changes in our participants' behaviour; we have to be careful to design our study so that these changes are not mistakenly regarded as consequences of our experimental manipulations.

- *History:* Events in the participants' lives which are entirely unrelated to our manipulations of the independent variable, may have fortuitously given rise to changes similar to those we were expecting. Suppose we were running an experiment on anxiety in New Zealand, a country known for its propensity to earthquakes. We test participants on Monday, to establish baseline anxiety levels, administer some anxiety-producing treatment on Wednesday, and test the participants' anxiety levels on Friday. Unknown to us, there is an earthquake on Thursday. Anxiety levels are much higher on Friday due to the earthquake, but we mistakenly attribute this increase to our experimental manipulations on Wednesday. (Don't worry, there are ways round this problem, coming shortly – and they don't involve avoiding doing research in New Zealand . . .)

- *Maturation:* Participants – especially young ones – may change simply as a consequence of development. These changes may be confused with changes due to manipulations of the independent variable the experimenter is interested in. For example, suppose we were interested in evaluating the effectiveness of a method of teaching children to read. If we measure their reading ability at age four, and then again at seven after they have been involved in the program, we can't necessarily attribute any improvement in reading ability to the program: the children's reading might have improved anyway, perhaps due to practice at reading in other contexts, etc. In this case, it's pretty obvious that maturation needs to be taken into account. However, these kinds of effects can occur in more subtle ways as well. For example, in a pre-test/post-test design in adults, any observed change in the dependent variable might be due to a reaction to the pre-test. The pre-test might cause fatigue, provide practice, or even alert the participant to the purpose of the study. This may then affect their performance on the post-test.

- *Instrument change:* Good physicists frequently calibrate their equipment. This guards against obtaining apparent changes in what they are measuring merely because their measuring device has changed. Imagine working in a nuclear power station and concluding that it was safe to go into the reactor core, unaware that the 'negligible radiation' reading on your Geiger counter was due to the fact that the batteries had run down. Similar (if somewhat less dramatic) effects are less obvious in psychology, but may happen nevertheless: for example, interviewers may become more practised, or more bored, with experience. An experimenter may get slicker at presenting the stimuli in an experiment. Factors such as these may change the measurements being taken, and these changes may be mistaken for changes in the participant rather than in the measuring tool.
- *Differential Mortality:* This sounds a bit dramatic! If your research involves testing the same individuals repeatedly, participants may sometimes drop out of the study for various reasons. This can make the results of the study difficult to interpret. For example, if all of the unsuccessful cases on a drug treatment program drop out, leaving us only with the successful cases, then a pre-test on the whole group is not comparable to a post-test on what remains of the group. There might be systematic differences between the people who remain and those that dropped out, and these differences might be wholly unrelated to your experimental manipulations. In the current example, it might be that those who remained in the drug treatment program had higher levels of willpower than those who left.
- *Reactivity and Experimenter Effects:* Measuring a person's behaviour may affect their behaviour, for a variety of reasons. People's reaction to having their behaviour measured may cause them to change their behaviour. I was once asked to take part in a long-term study on the relationship between diet and health: completing the dietary questionnaire made me realise that my diet consisted almost solely of pizzas, and so I changed my behaviour (well, for a while, at least). Perhaps I'll now live to a hundred as a consequence of my new healthy lifestyle, whilst the organizers of the study end up with the mistaken impression that living solely on pizzas leads to a long and healthy life. Merely measuring my behaviour caused it to change.

    There's a huge social psychological literature on 'experimenter effects': the experimenter's age, race, sex and other characteristics may affect the results they obtain (Rosenthal, 1966;

Rosenthal and Rosnow, 1969). Experimenters can subtly and unconsciously bias the results they obtain, by virtue of the way in which they interact with their participants. Participants often respond to the 'demand characteristics' of an experiment (Orne, 1962, 1969) – that is, they try to behave in a way that they think will please (or, occasionally, annoy!) the experimenter, for example by attempting to make the experiment 'work' by giving the 'right' data.

Ideally, you could minimise these effects by using a 'double-blind' technique. This involves both the experimenter and the participant being unaware of the experimental hypothesis and which condition the participant is in. If the experimenter is as ignorant as the participant about what's going on, there's little opportunity for the experimenter to bias the results. Unfortunately, as a student, you are probably unlikely to have the resources to employ someone to run your experiment for you, and it has to be said that most psychologists don't bother with double-blind techniques either.

Related to demand characteristics is the possibility that participants may show 'evaluation apprehension' (Rosenhan, 1969), a posh term for anxiety about being tested. Many non-psychologists seem to fail to appreciate that the experimenter is usually interested only in average performance, and isn't at all interested in the data of them as an individual. I've run experiments in which participants have treated the experiment as a test of their abilities, and have been so concerned with not looking stupid in front of me that they have failed to supply me with decent data! Finally, questionnaires may give rise to 'social desirability' effects, with respondents telling porkies about their income or sexual practices to look good to the experimenter. ('How many times have you had sex with a horse?' is unlikely to elicit many accurate replies!)

Reactivity is especially a problem when obtrusive measures which are under the participant's control (e.g. verbal reports) are used. Participants may show practice or fatigue effects, or become increasingly aware of what the experiment is about. However even something as apparently 'low-level' as reaction times can be affected by these kinds of effects. Some studies have shown that the elderly have slower reaction times than young undergraduates. Some of this difference may be due to age-related cognitive decline, but it may also occur as a result of different age-groups adopting different strategies within the experimental situation. There is some evidence that the elderly are more cautious in novel situations and are more concerned to help the experimenter by making fewer errors. Both of these factors would conspire to increase reaction times in a way which could be mistaken for age-related physiological deterioration rather than an increased desire to please the experimenter.

So, there are lots of extraneous factors that can lead to changes in behaviour, changes that can be confused with the effects of our intended manipulations. Good experimental designs guard against ('control' for) all of these competing explanations for the changes in our dependent variable, and thus enable us to be reasonably confident that those changes have occurred because of what *we* did to the participants – that is, they are a direct consequence of our experimental manipulations.

Threats to external validity

- *Over-use of special participant groups:* McNemar (1946) pointed out that psychology was largely the study of undergraduate behaviour. Rosenthal and Rosnow (1975) found that, 30 years later, 70–90% of participants were still undergraduates. Research suggests that students have higher self-esteem, take drugs and alcohol less (hah!), and are less likely to be married than are other young people. Young people in general are lonelier, more bored and more unhappy than older people (try telling that to your granny).

  Using volunteers may also cause problems: Rosenthal and Rosnow (1975) found that the participants recruited as volunteers via adverts were more intelligent, better educated, had higher social status and were more sociable than non-volunteers. On the downside, volunteers for research into psychopathology, drugs and hypnosis are more likely to have mental health problems. Volunteers generally have a higher opinion of, and respect for, science and scientists. That's nice, but a bit of a nuisance if it makes them respond differently than non-volunteers. As mentioned in the section on 'generality', the extent to which this is a problem depends on the kind of research being done: it's not automatically the case that it's invalid to use volunteer student participants. A student's visual system may be pretty much like that of any other human, even if their social behaviour is a bit strange!

- *Restricted numbers of participants:* This is more a threat to reliability, but it also affects one's ability to generalize to the population as a whole. Cohen (1988) has pointed out that most psychology experiments use too few participants for them to have a reasonable chance of attaining statistical significance. (See page 154 on 'power' so that you don't make the same mistake).

Maximizing Your Measurement's Generality

Closely related to external validity is the issue of whether our findings will generalize to other groups of participants in other times and places. This is usually taken for granted by psychologists. The best measure of generality is by empirical testing – replications of the experiment by other people in other circumstances. If food additives make children hyperactive in Chippenham, then they should also do so in downtown Kuala Lumpur. If they don't, that might be interesting in itself, but it would mean that we can't make sweeping statements about the effects of additives on humanity. Generality can be enhanced at the outset by representative sampling – by making sure that you have indeed used participants who are typical of the population that you want to make statements about. Sampling methods include random sampling, and stratified sampling (where the sample is deliberately constructed to mirror the characteristics of the parent population. So, for example, if the population consists mostly of 90% poor people and 10% rich people, so too does your sample). Threats to generality may come from using volunteers and undergraduate students. Generalization needs to be confirmed not only across participants, but also across experimental designs, methods, apparatus, situations, etc.

The generality of findings will depend to a large extent on the kind of research that's being done. All other things being equal, the results from a study on basic cognitive processing are more likely to be generalizable than the findings from a study on the social interactions of city office workers, because there is probably greater scope for social and cultural influences to affect the results of the latter.

3.2 ## Different Methods for Doing Research

In the following sections, we will discuss three basic types of research that are commonly used in psychology: observational methods, quasi-experimental designs and 'true' experimental designs. The essence of observational methods is that they don't involve direct manipulation of any variables by the researcher: behaviour is merely recorded, although systematically and objectively so that the observations are potentially replicable. Experimental methods, in contrast, do involve manipulation by the experimenter of one or more independent variables, together with some objective measurement of the effects of doing this. 'Quasi-experimental' methods are used in situations in which a well-designed experiment cannot be carried out for one reason or another (more on this in a moment).

Observational and quasi-experimental methods don't allow us to unequivocally establish cause and effect in the same way that true experimental designs do, but they are still very useful. Also, a discussion of their limitations helps to demonstrate the strengths of the experimental approach.

Observational Methods

One way to find out about a phenomenon is simply to look at it in a systematic and scientifically rigorous way. Personally, I think that psychologists have often jumped in at the deep end, running experiments to find out about some phenomenon before they have collected sufficient observational data on it. Historically, most sciences (biology, physics and chemistry) were preceded by a phase of naturalistic observation, during which phenomena were simply watched in a systematic and rigorous way. Experimentation came later. Psychology has tended to skip the observational phase and tried to go straight into doing experiments. This isn't always a good thing, since experimentation without prior careful observation can sometimes lead to a distorted or incomplete picture being developed.

Lessons could be learnt from the way in which biology supplanted comparative psychology as a means of finding out about animal behaviour. In the first half of the 20th century, behaviourism was the dominant method of studying animal behaviour. Innumerable experiments were performed to investigate learning, using a few species (mainly rats and pigeons) and highly artificial tasks (such as lever pressing) performed in very unnatural environments (such as mazes and Skinner Boxes). A lot of useful information has been obtained by using these experimental methods. However, after about 1960, most of the really interesting stuff on how animals behave has come from ethology and sociobiology, movements which have their roots in biology, not psychology.

One factor in the demise of comparative psychology as a discipline was that its attempts to produce universal laws of learning, that applied to all species including humans, were shown to be flawed. The observational data on a wide range of species that were produced by ethologists drew attention to this by demonstrating that many species show species-specific behaviour patterns as a result of natural selection having adapted their learning abilities to their particular environmental niche. While the study of learning was confined to experiments on a few species under highly constrained conditions, these problems were not apparent and could be overlooked. The ethologists and their observational data showed that the experimental methods used by the psychologists produced data that were highly reliable (in the sense of reproducible) but not necessarily valid (in the sense of providing an accurate picture of what animals can learn in their natural environments).

The strength of observational methods is that they enable one to get a good idea of how people (or animals) normally behave. This may be quite different from how they behave in an experiment. A good example of this is research on driving behaviour. A great deal of money has been spent on producing highly realistic driving simulators. While simulators are useful for studying some aspects of driving, they will never tell us much about how people normally drive for two reasons. First, participants know they are being studied and their behaviour is being recorded, and so they are likely to be on their best behaviour: they are unlikely to perform the various risky actions that they might perform in real life when they think they are not being watched, such as fiddling with the radio, shouting at the kids, picking their nose, driving with their knees, reading a map and so on. Secondly, no matter how 'realistic' the simulator, participants always remain aware of the fact that they are in a simulator, and that their actions will not have any real-world consequences in terms of death or injury. What this means is that for many aspects of driving behaviour, if one wants to get an accurate picture of how people really behave, unobtrusive observational methods may be preferable to experiments.

The downside to observational methods is that they are generally much more time-consuming to perform than experiments. Also, because of their non-intrusive nature, they don't allow the identification of cause and effect in the same way that a well-designed experiment does. However, systematic observations may often provide hypotheses about cause and effect, that can then be tested more directly with experimental methods. A full description of observational techniques – and the statistics that you should use to analyse the data obtained – is outside the scope of this book. For further information on this topic, have a look at Martin and Bateson's (1993) book on the topic.

Quasi-Experimental Designs

In Chapter 1, Andy discussed how the experimental method is ideal for determining cause and effect. Sometimes, especially in real-world situations, it isn't possible to conduct a true experiment, and one has to resort to a 'quasi-experimental' design. (Don't get this confused with research conducted by an experimenter with a hump and a penchant for bell-ringing – that would be a Quasimodo experiment).

In a quasi-experimental study, the experimenter does not have complete control over manipulation of the independent variable. He or she has control over the timing of the measurement of the dependent variable, but no control over either the timing of the experimental manipulation or over how participants are assigned to the different conditions of the study. For example, it may be impossible to allocate participants randomly to different levels of the independent variable, for ethical or practical reasons. As a consequence, it is not possible to isolate cause and effect as conclusively as with a 'true' experimental design, in which participants are randomly assigned to different groups which receive different treatments. In a true experiment, the experimenter has complete control over the independent variable: he or she has control over the timing of the measurements of the dependent variable and control over the timing of the experimental manipulations. (The latter in itself is an aid to establishing cause and effect relationships, since we can avoid our intervention coinciding with events in the participants' lives which might produce similar effects).

An example of a quasi-experimental study and its limitations

Suppose we were interested in whether daytime headlight use made motorcyclists more detectable to other road users. The ideal way of testing this would be to take a very large group of motorcyclists, and randomly allocate them to one of two conditions. One group would be told to use their headlight during the daytime, and the other group would be told not to. At the end of some period, say five years, we could see how many accidents had been experienced by each group, as a consequence of another road user failing to see them. This would be a true experiment, because we would have complete control over the independent variable (headlight use/non-use). Random allocation of participants to the two groups would enable us to ensure that no other variables could systematically affect our results.

In practice, there are obvious ethical reasons why this experiment cannot be done. If headlight use did make a difference to motorcyclists' detectability, then we would be taking risks with people's lives. Instead, we would have to make do with a quasi-experimental design:

we could take a group of motorcyclists who already prefer to ride with their headlight on, and compare them to a group of motorcyclists who prefer to ride with their headlight off. We have two groups of motorcyclists, as before, but there is a crucial difference: instead of the experimenter deciding which condition they perform, the participants have effectively allocated themselves to the groups. In other words, we would make use of a pre-existing difference between the participants, and use this as a basis for putting them in the different conditions of our study.

This might seem like a small difference, but it would have big implications for the conclusions that we could draw from the study. In the case of the truly experimental version, if we have allocated participants to conditions randomly, we know that the only difference between the participants in one condition and the participants in the other condition is that one lot used headlights and the other lot didn't. If there is any difference in accident rates between the two groups, we can be reasonably confident that it is due to our experimental manipulation of headlight use.

In the quasi-experimental version, our observed results might be due to the difference between the two groups in terms of headlight use, but they might equally well be due to innumerable other factors which also differed between the two groups. For example, it might be that motorcyclists who use headlights are more safety-conscious than those who don't. If so, the difference in accident rates might have nothing to do with headlight use, but instead occurred because motorcyclists in the 'headlight-use' group rode more cautiously than those in the 'no-headlight' group. Another possibility is that motorcyclists in the 'no-headlight' group might be riding older machines, whose generators don't have the capacity to cope with running lights all day long. Older machines also have poorer brakes. Therefore any difference in accident rates between headlight-users and non-users might be due to differences in braking ability, and have little to do with the effects of headlights on visibility. All of these alternative possibilities ('group threats', in the terminology used above) can of course be explored and possibly eliminated as alternative explanations for the observed results; however, the beauty of the experimental method is that it eliminates them automatically, rather than requiring further research to be performed to do so.

The difference between quasi-experimental and true experimental methods can be quite subtle. In psychology, we often use independent variables that are not wholly under our control, and hence strictly speaking, we are using quasi-experimental methods. Age and gender are the examples which spring to mind. Suppose you wanted to know if there were age-differences in problem-solving ability. You could take two groups of participants, one young and the other old, and give them some test of problem-solving ability. If there were any differences in performance, you might want to conclude that there were age-differences in problem-solving ability. However, this would be misleading. You may have demonstrated a difference in ability between the two groups, but because participants were not truly randomly allocated to one age-group or the other, but instead came 'ready-aged', you are unable to eliminate all of the other possible reasons for why the two groups of participants differed. The young and elderly groups differ in lots of ways other than chronological age: they have been born at different times, and so have had different life experiences which may have affected the way in which they behave in experiments. These 'cohort effects' complicate the interpretation of age- and gender-differences in psychology, and they arise because in the case of variables such as these, it is impossible for the experimenter to have complete control over the independent variables in the study. We're being a bit pedantic here, and most researchers investigating the effects of age and gender would consider that they are performing 'true' experiments; however, the important point is to be aware that there are almost always complications in interpreting age and gender differences in psychology, and that they arise because these variables are not wholly under the experimenter's control.

Types of quasi-experimental design

In the *one group post-test design* (Figure 3.1) we apply some treatment and then measure the participant's behaviour afterwards. This is a seriously flawed design. The change in the participants' behaviour may or may not be due to what we did. This design is prone to time effects, and we do not have any baseline against which to measure the strength of our effect. There's really not much that you can usefully conclude from the results of a study like this.

The *one group pre test/post-test design* (Figure 3.2) is the same as the previous design, except that we measure the participants' performance before we apply our treatment, and then again afterwards. By comparing the pre- and post-intervention scores, we can assess the magnitude of the treatment's effects. However, it is still subject to time effects, and we still have no way of knowing whether the participants' performance would have changed without our intervention.

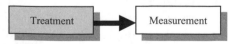

Figure 3.1   The 'one group post-test' design

Figure 3.2 The 'one group pre-test/post-test' design

The *interrupted time-series* type of quasi-experimental design (Figure 3.3) is often used in applied research to evaluate the impact of changes in legislation or the effects of some treatment. With the interrupted time-series method, we make a series of measurements at different times, some of which take place before the intervention in question, and some of which take place afterwards. We then compare the pre-intervention measurements to those that were taken post-intervention. Suppose we wanted to know if seat-belts had had an effect on fatality rates for drivers. One way to look at this would be to look at the fatality rates for several years before and several years after compulsory seat-belt legislation was introduced, to see if there was a statistically significant difference.

The problem with this method is that we don't have full control over the manipulations of the independent variable. It might be that other factors changed at the same time as the seat-belt legislation was introduced, and that these have also acted to reduce accident rates. For example, at the same time that the legislation was introduced, there might have been an advertising campaign that was intended to inform people about the new legislation, but as a side-effect made drivers more aware of the risks of driving. There might be other changes, such as more police cars patrolling around, which coincided with the introduction of the seat belt law.

It's also possible that there have been changes in how accident statistics are collected and reported, so that what you are seeing is not really a change in accident rates per se, but a change in the numbers recorded. (The next time some old age pensioner goes on

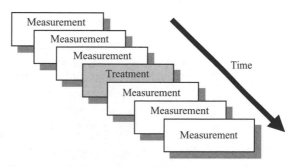

Figure 3.3 Interrupted time-series designs

and on about how little crime and violence there was back in the good old days, try explaining to them about how reporting biases can give a potentially misleading impression. Take, for example, crimes of violence against women: it might seem that there are more now than 50 years ago, but that might be partly because 50 years ago women were more reluctant to report them to the police.) In short, although this design is an improvement over the previous ones, it still suffers from providing the potential for time and measurement threats to validity.

In the *static group comparison design* (Figure 3.4) we have two groups – a control group to whom nothing is done by the experimenter, and an experimental group who receive some treatment. The difference between this and a proper experiment is that the participants are not assigned to the two conditions randomly. We just passively observe the effects of the experimental groups' treatment. We have already encountered this design, in the discussion of the study on motorcycle headlight use. As mentioned there, because the participants are not allocated randomly, it can always be argued that any differences between the two conditions are due to factors other than our experimental manipulation. The strength of our conclusions then depends on the extent to which we can identify and eliminate these alternative explanations.

Experimental Research: Between-Group and Within-Subjects Experimental Designs

Between-groups (or 'independent measures') designs use separate groups of participants for each of the different conditions in the experiment. Each participant is tested once only. In within-subjects (or 'repeated measures') designs, each participant is exposed to all of the conditions of the experiment. These are the two extremes: you can have hybrid ('mixed') designs which involve a combination of between-groups and within-subjects variables.

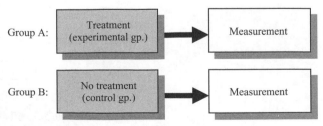

Figure 3.4 The 'static group comparison' design

Each design has its strengths and weaknesses, and which one is most appropriate to use really depends on what's being researched. Something both types of design have in common is that, if properly carried out, they enable fairly unambiguous identification of cause and effect (see Chapter 2). They achieve this by making sure that the *only* systematic effect on participants' behaviour is the experimenter's manipulations of the independent variable. An important factor in achieving this is the appropriate use of *randomization*.

The Importance of Randomization in Experimental Design

In a study with a between-groups design, it is *essential* that we allocate participants randomly to our experimental conditions. In a within-subjects design, it is similarly essential that participants don't all experience our experimental conditions in the same order (something we achieve by presenting the conditions in either a random order or by counterbalancing the order). Why is randomization so important?

In an experiment, we want to isolate the effects of our manipulation of the independent variable. Recall that a score consists of a 'true score' (a measure of the thing we're really interested in) and 'error' (from the influence on our participants of all sorts of other, extraneous factors). To distinguish between the true score and the error, we rely on the fact that variation in the true score should be related to our manipulation of the independent variable. For example, suppose we were interested in finding out whether playing Mozart to babies affects their intelligence in later life (Box 3.1).

If playing Mozart affects intelligence to any significant extent, it should affect all babies who are exposed to it in much the same way. Due to factors that are outside of our direct control, the magnitude of the effect will probably vary from baby to baby, but by and large we would expect most of our babies to end up a bit smarter than those in a control group who did not hear any Mozart. We are expecting a *systematic* variation in performance, because we have behaved one way towards all of the babies in the Mozart-listening group, and we have behaved in a different way to all of the babies in the no-Mozart group. If anything else produces systematic variation in performance, it becomes hard to interpret our results, because if we find an 'effect' of Mozart, we won't be able to tell whether this is due to the music, other factors which systematically affected every baby in that group, or some interaction between these factors and listening to Mozart.

For this reason, all other possible influences on the babies' performance must remain as unsystematic as possible. They can be unsystematic in the sense of affecting behaviour randomly. By allocating babies to different groups randomly, we (hopefully) randomly distribute across the groups potential influences on their behaviour. Unsystematic differences in things such as intelligence, motivation, anxiety, irritability, receptivity to auditory stimulation, etc., should, on average, cancel out: for every highly anxious baby in the Mozart group, there's likely to be one in the control group too.

An alternative way to prevent extraneous factors from having an effect is to keep them as constant as possible – either by matching participants carefully across groups (so that if one group contains a baby with a high IQ, so too does the other), or better still, by using a within-groups design – so that, in effect, each participant is perfectly matched with their counterpart in the other group because they are one and the same person! As we shall see later, this gives rise to its own problems: although within-subjects designs largely eliminate the effects of differences stemming from the participants themselves, we

---

■ **Box 3.1: How randomization eliminates all systematic effects on behaviour other than the effects of our independent variable**

(a) Random allocation to groups (Mozart versus no Mozart) helps to ensure that any systematic differences between babies not under my control (e.g. motivation (M), irritability (I), worrying (W) and happiness (H)) are spread inconsistently across groups. The *only* consistent difference between groups is whether or not they heard Mozart.

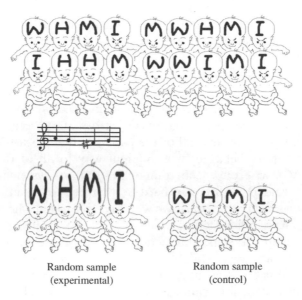

Random sample
(experimental)

Random sample
(control)

(b) Non-random allocation may produce other consistent differences between the groups *as well as* those due to my experimental manipulations. I can't tell whether any observed differences are due to listening to Mozart or due (at least partly) to the other systematic differences between the conditions (in this case, happiness and worry).

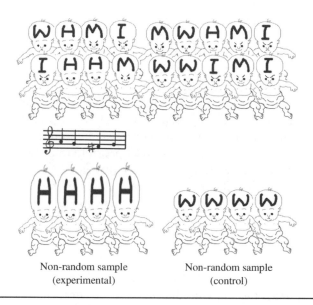

Non-random sample
(experimental)

Non-random sample
(control)

have to be careful not to produce systematic effects on their behaviour as a consequence of poor experimental design. If the experimental conditions are administered in the same order for each participant, this might affect their behaviour in a systematic way, by making participants more practised or more fatigued in one condition than another. So, we have to randomize or counterbalance the order of presentation of conditions, so that the order does not have systematic effects on participants' behaviour that might be confused with our manipulations of the independent variable.

If you fail to randomize participants to conditions in a between-groups design, or fail to randomize the order of conditions in a within-subjects design, no amount of clever statistical analysis can remedy the situation: you end up with uninterpretable results, and you've wasted your time and that of your participants.

An interesting illustration of the importance of randomization comes from the Lanarkshire Milk Experiment of 1930. This was designed to examine the nutritional benefits of providing milk to school children. It was a huge study, involving 20,000 children and costing a whopping £7,500 (a fortune at the time). A control group of

10,000 children received no milk, and an experimental group of 10,000 received 3/4 pint of milk every day: half of the latter drank raw milk (yuk!), and the rest got pasteurized milk. Unfortunately, selection of children to be 'feeders' or 'controls' was fatally flawed. It was supposed to be random, but teachers were allowed to adjust the compositions of the feeder and control groups to obtain 'a more level selection', if they felt that too many well-fed or malnourished children had been allocated to one group or another. The result of this seems to be that the teachers were unconsciously biased in selection: faced with a choice, they tended to put poor children in the milk-drinking groups, and more well-nourished and affluent children into the control group. The end result was that the control group ended up markedly superior in weight and height to the milk drinkers! From this study, it proved impossible to draw any sound conclusions about the relative benefits of raw and pasteurized milk – or indeed about the effects of milk per se. An entire study had been rendered largely worthless as a consequence of a minor procedural error – a lack of randomization. Student (1931),[1] in his review of this study's methodological flaws, said:

> [The conclusion that milk is beneficial to schoolchildren]...is shifted from the sure ground of scientific inference to the less satisfactory foundation of mere authority and guesswork by the fact that the 'controls' and the 'feeders' were not randomly selected (Student, 1931: 403).

How do you achieve random allocation in practice? Ideally, you should use something like a table of random numbers (or these days, the random number generator of a computer or calculator). As each participant arrives, follow a rule such as: if the next random number is even, put the participant in the control condition; if it is odd, put them in the experimental condition. In practice, it has to be said that many experimenters don't do this. But at the very least, try to avoid running participants in ways which are likely to produce systematic differences between conditions – such as assigning all the participants who turn up in the morning to one condition, and all the participants who come in the afternoon to another condition.

Between-Groups Designs

Advantages of between-groups designs

Between-groups designs have several advantages, compared to repeated-measures designs.

- *Simplicity:* One advantage of a between-groups design is its simplicity: all you have to do is to make sure that you allocate participants randomly to the different conditions. You don't have to worry about procedures like counterbalancing (see below), which can get a bit wearisome if you have a complex repeated-measures design.
- *Less chance of practice and fatigue effects:* You also don't have to worry about practice and fatigue effects (see below). There is no possibility that performance in one condition can affect performance in another, as each participant participates in only one of the conditions.
- *Useful when it is impossible for an individual to participate in all experimental conditions:* A between-groups design is the only type of design that can be used if participation in one condition makes it impossible for a participant to take part in another. For example, if you are looking at sex differences in performance, you are stuck with a between-groups design, because participants are either male or female and can't switch from one to the other for the sake of your experiment. The same is true if you are interested in how performance on some measure changes with age, unless you are prepared to test the same people at different ages; that might be possible with children, but it would be impractical if you wanted to compare children and pensioners.

  Sometimes, participating in one condition may alter the participant irreversibly so that they cannot meaningfully participate in another condition of the same experiment. For example, suppose you were interested in testing the effectiveness of two different methods of teaching people Sanskrit. Once a participant had learnt Sanskrit by one method, they wouldn't be able to unlearn it in order to use the other method to learn it again – the first experimental treatment (i.e. the first method of learning Sanskrit that they encountered) would have changed them forever. Another example would be if you showed participants a set of words and then gave them a surprise memory test afterwards. Each participant could only be surprised once (unless you used people with extremely bad memories!), and so you would have to use a between-groups design in this instance.

Disadvantages of between-groups designs

Between-groups designs do have several disadvantages associated with them; these are large enough for me to suggest that, wherever possible, you should use a within-subjects design unless it's absolutely impossible (for reasons that will be discussed shortly).

- *Expense in terms of time, effort and participant numbers:* Between-groups experiments require lots of participants, and participant recruitment is time-consuming and laborious. As the number of conditions in the experiment increases, so too does the number of participants. As most experiments use between 10 and 20 participants per group, you can rapidly arrive at a situation where an experiment is going to take a long time to run. This is bad enough for researchers, but it's even worse for students: you are not likely to get sufficient marks to reward your efforts in collecting data, and you would probably be better off spending your time on writing the report and analysing the data.

    Since it's hard to recruit participants, once you've trapped them in a darkened room, you might as well test them several times rather than just once. That way, you won't need to run as many participants (or you can run as many as before, but get a lot more data from them).

- *Insensitivity to experimental manipulations:* All other things being equal, a between-groups design is less sensitive than a within-participants design. In other words, a between-groups design will be less likely to detect any effect of your experimental manipulations. Consider a simple two condition experiment in which we are interested in the effects on memory performance of a bang on the head. Participants in group A get a hefty whack on the head with a mallet, whereas participants in group B are left alone. The latter act as a control group, against which to evaluate the effects of head-bashing. Participants in both groups get the same memory test, and we look to see if whacking affects memory performance.

    In an ideal world, the only difference between participants in the two groups would be that we had whacked those in group A, and not those in group B: therefore any differences between the groups would be due entirely to our experimental manipulation. In practice, things are complicated by within-groups variation: within each group, there would be all kinds of differences between participants that might act to add 'noise' (or 'variance', in statistical jargon) to our data. Some participants in each group would have harder skulls than others; some of the participants in each group would have had very good memories, and others would have had very poor memories. Maybe sometimes we would get a good swing on the mallet, and other times we wouldn't hit the participant quite so hard (although mallet-swinging could be automated, to ensure that it was consistent for all individuals in group A). As a result of all these factors, memory scores within each group are likely to show variation between the members of that group.

If we have allocated our participants to the two conditions randomly, it is unlikely that there will be any systematic differences between the groups on any variable other than the one that we are manipulating experimentally. (This is the main reason why you must always allocate participants to conditions randomly when using a between-groups design. If there are any systematic differences between your experimental conditions other than the ones produced by you as the experimenter, then you are doomed – whatever results you have are uninterpretable, as any differences between the groups could be due either to your experimental manipulation, the uncontrolled systematically-varying factors, or a mixture of both: see page 71). However, all this non-systematic variation between groups can make it hard to detect the systematic variation between the groups that is attributable to our experimental manipulation – especially if the effects of our manipulation are relatively small in size. If memory scores are all over the place to begin with, it is going to be that much harder for the effects of our mallet manipulations to reveal themselves.

Some examples of between-groups designs

The *post-test only/control group design* (Figure 3.5) is probably the most straightforward type of 'true' experiment that you can perform. It has a two-group independent measures design: you take several participants, divide them randomly into two groups, and give one group (the 'experimental' group') some treatment that you don't give to the other group (the 'control' group). The performance of the two groups is then measured: if it differs, then you can be reason-

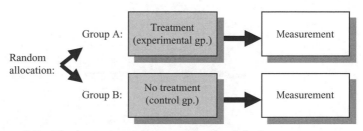

Figure 3.5 The 'post-test only/control group' design

ably confident that the difference is attributable to your experimental manipulation.

This design is frequently used in psychology, but it does suffer from one weakness. Participants are randomly assigned to the two conditions, to ensure that the groups are equivalent before the experimental manipulation takes place. However, if randomization fails to produce equivalence, you have no way of knowing that it has failed. You cannot be certain that the two groups were comparable before you administered your treatment.

As with the previous design, the *pre-test/post-test control group design* (Figure 3.6) uses two groups – a control group and an experimental group. Each participant is randomly assigned to one or other of the groups. Behaviour is measured before intervention, when it should be roughly comparable between the two conditions. Behaviour is measured again after the intervention: any difference between the two conditions now, is presumed to be due to the treatment administered to the experimental group.

The advantage of this design over the previous one is that, because we pre-test, we can be certain that our two groups were equivalent (or discover that they were not, if for some reason randomization of participant-allocation to the different conditions has failed) before our experimental manipulation took place.

One problem with the previous design is that pre-testing the participants might affect their subsequent performance: the Solomon four-group design (Figure 3.7) controls for that possibility. (This is a design for the seriously paranoid researcher!)

Here, we have four conditions, two control and two experimental. Groups A and B show the effects of presence and absence of the experimental manipulation; groups C and D allow an assessment to be made of the effects of the pre-testing experienced by groups A and B. By making the appropriate comparisons between these four conditions, you can assess the effects of pre-testing and thus gain some idea of the generalizability of the findings (and eliminate the possibility that the cause of the changes in group A was our experimental manipulation plus the pre-testing).

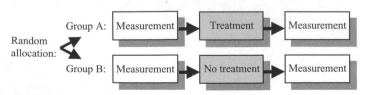

Figure 3.6   The 'pre-test/post-test control group' design

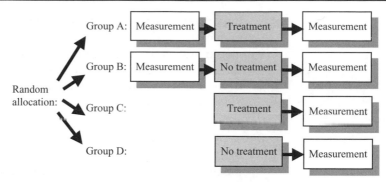

Figure 3.7   The 'Solomon four-group' design

This is an excellent design, but it suffers from the disadvantages of being expensive in terms of time and number of participants: it basically doubles the cost of running a study, and as a result, is rarely used in practice.

Repeated Measures Designs

Advantages of repeated measures designs

If possible, it is often highly desirable to use the same participants in every condition – so that a given participant produces one result for every condition of the experiment. There are two reasons for this:

- *Economy:* We've already mentioned this: within-subjects designs are economical to run in terms of time and effort, because you're using each participant several times.
- *Sensitivity:* As mentioned earlier, what we are interested in are the differences in our results which have been produced by our experimental interventions. However, these differences have to be distinguished from all the random 'noise' produced in our data by the fact that participants differ from each other in lots of weird and wonderful ways. It is in our interests to reduce this random variability as much as possible, because the smaller it is, the easier it will be to detect our experimentally-induced variation. One way to reduce participant-induced variation would be to carefully match participants in different groups on factors which might affect our results. So, we could make sure that participants in group A were the same age, sex, height, IQ, etc., etc., as those in group B. The problem with this approach is that we might not necessarily match participants on appropriate characteristics: if, unknown to us, height was an

important influence on our dependent variable but we had been matching participants on weight instead, then the matching would not have been much use. In any case, matching is time-consuming and tedious to do. A simpler and more effective technique is to match participants perfectly between the different conditions, in all respects – by using the same people in all conditions.

By doing this, we can dramatically reduce the variation in scores between conditions which is due merely to non-experimental factors – that is, due to random differences between the different participants. Since each participant participates in all conditions, the only difference between a participant's scores for the different conditions should be that produced by our experimental manipulations. In other words, instead of participants in different groups having different ages, interests, sexes etc., all of these factors are held completely constant across all conditions of the experiment.

All things being equal, a repeated-measures design will always be more sensitive (i.e. be more likely to reveal the effects of the experimenter's manipulations) than an independent-measures design, because there are fewer sources of random variation to obscure the effects of your manipulations of the independent variable. In the between-groups design, differences between your experimental conditions include differences due to what you did to the participants (your manipulations of the independent variable that you're interested in); (hopefully) random differences between individuals within a group; and (hopefully) random differences between individuals in one group and individuals in another. With a within-subjects design, you eliminate the last factor, and all you have to contend with is individual variation in participants' responses to your experimental manipulations.

Disadvantages of repeated-measures designs

Repeated-measures designs therefore seem a good idea in theory. In practice, there are a couple of problems with them, which mean that it's not possible to use them in all situations. (If you've read the section on independent-measures designs, you should be able to work out what these problems are).

- *'Carry-over' effects from one condition to another:* Even if our experimental manipulations had no effect on a participant's behaviour at all, he or she would still probably give slightly more or less different responses in our different experimental conditions. Participants are not robots: their performance will spontaneously vary slightly from trial to trial, and from condition to condition. This would not be too much of a problem if this were merely random fluctuation in performance, because then it should cancel out across conditions. However, *systematic* variations in performance pose a much more serious problem. Participants become fatigued, bored, better practised at doing the set tasks, and so on. These systematic or 'confounding' effects may interact with our manipulations of the independent variable of interest, rendering our results uninterpretable. For example, imagine that we were looking at the effects of stress on word-list recall, and we had three stress levels, low, medium and high. If each participant participated in each condition, in the same order, and we found an effect of condition on recall, we would be unable to tell if the effect was due to stress, or due to practice, fatigue or any permutation of these three factors.

'Carry-over' effects such as these are not necessarily an insuperable problem, but avoiding their effects does complicate matters somewhat, especially if you want to manipulate several independent variables in the same experiment. To avoid the influence of systematic confounding variables such as practice or fatigue, we can do one of two things: either randomize the order of presentation of the different conditions (so that one participant gets the order 'high, medium, low' stress; another gets the order 'medium, high, low' and yet another gets 'medium, low, high', etc.) or we can counterbalance the order – so that if you have two conditions, half the participants get the conditions in the order A then B and the other half get the order B then A. Counterbalancing has the advantage that you can then include the order of presentation of conditions in the analysis as a variable in itself. This means that you would then be able to look directly for effects of the order in which conditions were presented to participants, rather than merely keeping your fingers crossed that you had controlled for order effects. This is useful in situations where you suspect that the effects of the different orders of conditions are likely to be different. Suppose for example that you have three conditions, A, B and C: doing A has a large effect on people's subsequent performance, whereas doing C has a comparatively minor effect. This means that performance in B and A will be affected markedly when the sequence of conditions is ABC, but will be affected little when the sequence is CBA. If you randomize the order of conditions, it's going to be hard to detect these effects; however, if you use counterbalancing and include 'order of conditions' in the statistical analysis as an independent variable in its own right, the order effect will be easier to detect. Whichever of these techniques is chosen, it is vital that any given participant is randomly allocated to one sequence of conditions or another.

- *The need for conditions to be reversible:* The final catch with repeated-measures designs is that they can only be used if being in one condition does not have irreversible effects that prevent the participant being used in another condition – so, a repeated-measures design would be no good for an experiment investigating the effects of temperature on the speed with which lemmings throw themselves off a cliff, for example!

Figure 3.8 below shows a basic two-condition repeated-measures design. Half of the participants do the treatment condition first and the control condition second; the other half do these two conditions in the opposite order. It's important that participants are randomly allocated to these two presentation orders.

More Sophisticated Designs

So far, we have considered simple two-condition designs, where there is an experimental condition (in which participants receive some treatment) and a control condition (in which participants don't). In the jargon, we have one independent variable with two levels (in this case, presence versus absence of whatever the independent variable involves). However, many experiments involve more sophisticated designs than this.

Experiments with multiple levels of the independent variable

First, you might want to examine the effects of more levels of the independent variable. Suppose you were interested in the effects of a

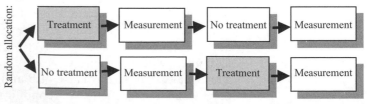

Figure 3.8   A basic two-condition repeated-measures design

new tranquillizer, 'Tohellwivmiwurriz', on levels of anxiety in first-time parachute jumpers. Instead of just having two conditions (tranquillizer versus no tranquillizer), you could have several conditions, each of which corresponded to a particular dosage of tranquillizer. Thus you might have one group taking no tranquillizer before jumping from the plane; another group taking 5 mg before jumping; another group taking 10 mg; and so on. (We would have to use a between-groups design in this particular instance: because they are first-time parachutists, their level of anxiety is probably unlikely to be the same on subsequent jumps, and so we can use each person only once – especially if the parachute doesn't open).

This experiment would obviously be much more informative than a simple two-condition design, because it would give us details about how the amount of tranquillizer affected anxiety levels, rather than merely examining the effects of its presence or absence. This increases the generality of our findings, by showing that they do not apply merely to the unique level of the independent variable chosen in a single-factor experiment. Paradoxically, such an experiment may also show the limits of the generality of the experiment's findings, by revealing the boundaries of the effects in question. For example, high levels of 'Tohellwivmiwurriz' might have the same effect as no drug whatsoever: a study in which we used varying dosages of the drug would show this, and reveal the limits under which the drug operates, limits which would be unknown to us had we conducted only a simple 'presence versus absence' study.

This is simply one possible variant of the 'pre-test/post-test control' design that I discussed earlier, extending that design to look at several levels of the independent variable of interest. Here (Figure 3.9) we have one control group (group D), and three experimental groups (groups A, B and C), each receiving one level of the same independent variable. We could compare each of the three experimental groups to

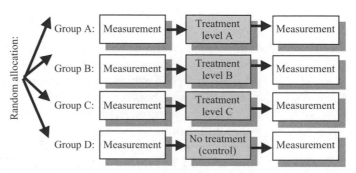

Figure 3.9 An experiment with multiple levels of one independent variable

the control group, to assess the size of the effects of different manipulations of the independent variable. We could also look for trends in the data. For example, we could see if the reduction in anxiety was systematically related to the amount of tranquillizer taken. (Is it the case that the more tranquillizer that's taken, the more relaxed the parachutist becomes? Or is there some other kind of relationship? It might be that the effects of the tranquilliser increase with increasing dosage, but only up to a certain point, after which there is no further effect of the drug.)

We can use more than two conditions in within-subjects designs as well, as long as we are careful about controlling for order effects (and as long as the effects of the different conditions are not irreversible). When we had only two conditions, we merely needed half the participants to do them in one order (A then B) and the other half to do them in the opposite order (B then A). However, with three conditions, there are $3 \times 2 \times 1 = 6$ possible orders of conditions: ABC; CBA; ACB; BCA; CAB; BAC. If you have four conditions, there are $4 \times 3 \times 2 \times 1 = 24$ possible orders. Here lies the path to insanity...

Latin Squares designs

One way to deal with the problem of order effects in within-subjects designs is to use a 'Latin Squares' design. In this design, the order in which the various conditions of your experiment occur is counterbalanced, so that each possible order of conditions occurs just once. (It gets its name from an ancient mathematical puzzle – the problem of how to arrange a set of different things in a square so that each one appears only once in each column and once in each row).

Here's a simple example of a situation in which we might use a Latin Squares design. Suppose we have three conditions, A, B and C, and we want to ensure that we don't have any systematic order effects in our experiment (due to all participants doing the conditions in the order A first, B second and C third, for example). We could randomize the order in which each participant does the three conditions, as we discussed earlier. Alternatively, we could systematically counterbalance the order in which the conditions are presented. As mentioned a moment ago, there are three conditions, so there are six possible orders in which these conditions can occur. That's a lot of conditions, and hence a lot of participants to run in our study. However, by using a Latin Squares design, we can cut down on the number of groups we need to run, and yet still avoid order effects. In a Latin Squares design for a study with three conditions, we need to use only the orders ABC, BCA and CAB, to be able to present each condition either first, second or third in the experiment (Table 3.1).

We have enough permutations of presentation order to ensure that we have a sample of participants for each condition at each of the possible positions in the sequence. (In the subsequent statistical analysis, we could go on to do one of two things. We could combine the data for all of the 'A' conditions, all of the 'B' conditions and so on, in the assumption that this procedure has eliminated any order effects (e.g. effects of practice, fatigue, boredom, etc.). Or, we could explicitly include 'order of presentation' as an independent variable in our analysis, and actually check to see if there were any effects of doing the conditions in a particular order.) Note that the number of participants should be the same for each of the presentation orders used: so, if we had 60 participants, 20 would experience order ABC, 20 BCA and 20 CAB.

Table 3.1

	order of conditions or trials:		
one group of participants:	A	B	C
another group of participants:	B	C	A
yet another group of participants:	C	A	B

If you have a design with just one independent variable, it's comparatively easy to work out the relevant Latin Squares design. Table 3.2 shows a Latin Squares design for four levels of an independent variable (conditions A, B, C and D):

Table 3.2

	order of conditions or trials:			
one group of participants:	A	B	C	D
another group of participants:	B	A	D	C
yet another group of participants:	C	D	A	B
and yet another ...:	D	C	B	A

Once again, each condition occurs at each point in the sequence: as many participants experience condition A first, as experience it second, third or last. The same is true for conditions B, C and D.

There is one potential problem with the Latin Squares we've looked at so far: they don't completely eliminate order effects. In the 3 × 3 design above, A precedes B twice, but B precedes A only once. (Similarly, C precedes A twice, but A precedes C only once). Suppose there were a practice effect from doing A then B: two groups of participants (those experiencing orders ABC and CAB) would get a practice effect, and the other group (the one experiencing order BCA) wouldn't. To get round this problem, you can use a 'balanced' Latin Squares design.

Table 3.3

	order of conditions or trials:			
one group of participants	A	B	C	D
another group of participants:	B	D	A	C
yet another group of participants:	D	C	B	A
and yet another ...	C	A	D	B

In Table 3.3 AB occurs as often as BA; BD occurs as often as DB; and so on. Balanced Latin Squares exist only for experiments with an even number of conditions (4 × 4, 6 × 6 and so on) and not for experiments with an odd number of conditions (3 × 3, 5 × 5 and so on).

That takes care of order effects when you have only one independent variable with several different levels. However, what do you do if you have two or more independent variables in the same study (see the section on 'multi-factorial designs' below)? It's still possible to use a variation on the Latin Squares design, but now it gets a bit more time-consuming to work out the presentation orders! The simplest way to do it (unless you're someone who rattles off the Times Crossword in five minutes and are still stuck for something to do) is to use James Brown's EDGAR program *(http://www.jic.bbsrc.ac.uk/services/statistics/edgar.htm)*. Amongst other things, this excellent program automatically works out Latin Square designs for various numbers of independent variables with various numbers of levels. All you then have to do is run the participants ...

Multi-factorial designs

All of the designs so far have looked at manipulations of just one independent variable. However, you can have two or three different independent variables in the same study. You can in theory include as many independent variables as you like, which is fine in correlational research, but once you get beyond three in an experimental design, the data usually become horrendously complicated to interpret – don't go there ...

The advantage of including more than one independent variable is that it enables you to extend the generality of your findings at the cost of relatively little extra effort. If you have more than one independent variable in a study, you can look at how they interact with each other, in a way that you can't if you don't include the independent variables in the same experiment. (There will be more on this topic in Chapter 6: see in particular page 191 and Box 6.1. See the example below, as well.) This is often much more informative than looking at one variable at a time.

The main problem with including extra independent variables in a wholly between-groups study is that it increases the number of participants you will need. Suppose we added the independent variable of 'sex' to the parachuting study: this would double the number of participants required. If we looked at 'age', and used 'young', 'middle-aged' and 'elderly' parachutists at each of the drug dosages, we would be faced with running nine groups of participants! Sometimes you can get round this problem by designing the study so that you get repeated measures data from one or both of the independent variables.

Suppose we were interested in factors affecting the performance of air-traffic controllers. For reasons that I need hardly go into, we would like them to stay alert while they are at work, so two independent variables we might want to look at are shift-pattern and room temperature. Both of these might cause tiredness on their own, and the interactions between them might be interesting: we might expect tiredness to be greatest when the air-traffic controllers are working late at night in a cosy, warm control tower. (Should Horlicks be a proscribed drug as far as air-traffic controllers are concerned?) Alternatively, it might be possible to counteract the effects of being tired while on a night-shift by making the room quite cold.

In the study shown in Figure 3.10, we have two independent variables: time of shift (with three levels, early, midday or late) and room temperature (with two levels, cold or warm). This gives us six different groups, each group representing a unique permutation of the two independent variables (shift and temperature). The measurement might be performance on some test of performance such as 'number of undetected potential collisions between planes'. (It would probably be best to do this experiment using some kind of simulation of this, so that we had control over the number of potential plane collisions that took place within a shift).

With this design, we can assess the effects on performance of shift and temperature (the two 'main effects' in this study), and also look at the interaction between shift and temperature. There are all sorts of possibilities for the outcome of multivariate experiments like this. In the present example, they include: (a) Shift might have an effect on performance, regardless of temperature (a main effect of shift). (b) Temperature might have an effect on performance regardless of shift (a main effect of temperature). (c) There might be some interaction between the effects of shift and temperature. We have already mentioned one such possibility – that the effects of temperature

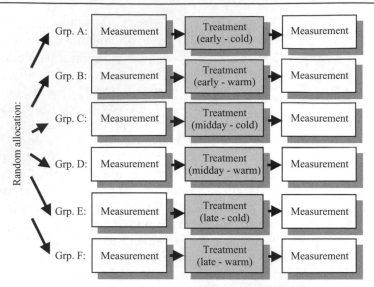

Figure 3.10 An experiment with two independent variables (temperature and time of day)

moderate those of shift, so that air-traffic controllers are more alert if the room is cold. Another possibility is that temperature might affect performance differently according to the time of the shift – so that it makes a difference whether the room is warm or cold for early and late shifts (when the controllers are tired anyway) but not for midday shifts (when they are more awake). These kinds of inter-actions between variables would be much harder to identify if we looked at the influence of each variable in isolation, in a separate experiment.

Multivariate designs with repeated measures

You can of course use multivariate designs with repeated measures. You can have either wholly repeated measures (so that the same group of participants take part in all conditions, and the conditions represent all permutations of the independent variables concerned) or use a 'mixed' design (where some of the independent variables have repeated measures and some are between-groups). The same advantages and disadvantages apply as for the simpler designs. The air-traffic controller study just described could be recast as a wholly within-subjects design, as long as you were careful to give each participant enough time to recover from the effects of one condition before subjecting them to the next.

Single-Subject Experimental Designs

If you are an undergraduate, most of your study of research methods will be based on experimental designs similar to those described on p. 70 – designs that involve selectively exposing groups of people to one level of an independent variable or another, and then using statistics to measure the average performance in the different groups and decide whether it differs between conditions. Probably for most students this technique is synonymous with the idea of investigating behaviour scientifically – psychology could almost be defined as the process of comparing average performance in one condition with that in another. However there are alternative methods to the traditional experiment. Rather than measure the average behaviour of groups of people, these techniques measure the behaviour of one or just a few people.

Single-subject designs have a long and venerable history that dates back to the beginnings of scientific psychology in the 19th century, when the first psychology laboratory was set up in Leipzig by Wilhelm Wundt. His primary interest was 'psychophysics', the study of the relationship between perceptual experiences and physical stimuli. Psychophysics is alive and well today, and still largely based on experiments involving just one or a very few participants. Much of what we know about learning comes from studies on classical and operant conditioning, which are also frequently based on the systematic study of individual behaviour rather than averages of groups of participants.

These single-subject techniques may not be as commonly used as the 'traditional' experimental method; however, when used appropriately, they are potentially no less 'scientific' than the latter. In some circumstances, they may be preferable to conventional experimental methods. They are especially useful in situations where averaging together the performance of individuals might produce a misleading picture of the phenomenon under investigation. A good example of this is what happens when you average data in one-trial learning experiments. Each participant shows an abrupt change from no learning to 100% performance, but at an idiosyncratic point in the experiment. However if you average these data, you obtain a smooth 'learning curve' (see Box 3.2). This is purely a statistical artefact, which describes the data of none of the participants and thus gives a false picture of how learning is actually taking place (Sidman, 1960).

If behaviourism and psychophysics can get away with using only one or a handful of people, then why do most psychologists have to go to the trouble of finding zillions of participants and having to grapple with statistics? The answer lies in the issue of unwanted variation in

■ **Box 3.2: An example of how the process of averaging data can sometimes produce misleading impressions**

Graphs of individual performances show an abrupt transition from poor to perfect performance. Averaging these produces a different – and false – impression that performance improves steadily over trials.

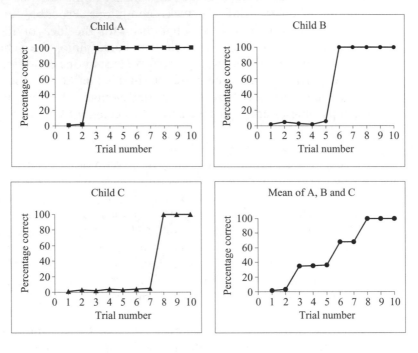

behaviour, and the extent to which we can eradicate it. It's all about control.

The Logical Basis of Experimental Design

Group-averaging techniques versus single-subject methods

All of the conventional experimental designs described earlier represent strategies for dealing with unwanted variation in performance – unwanted in the sense of not occurring as a direct result of our manipulations of the independent variable(s) in which we are interested. The enemy of establishing causal relationships between variables is uncontrolled variation in performance. In an ideal world, participants would all produce identical scores, and would all change in the same way in response to our manipulations. In real life, of course, this does not happen. People differ in their behaviour, both within themselves (e.g., due to the passage of time, changes due to learning, etc.) and between individuals. We want to ignore variations in our scores due to factors such as these, and focus on the variations in scores directly attributable to what we did.

Recall that on page 55, I said that any obtained score can be thought of as consisting of several different components:

    a. a 'true score' for the thing we hope we are measuring;
    b. a 'score for other things', that we are measuring inadvertently;
    c. systematic bias;
    d. random error.

When you obtain an individual score in an experiment, you ideally would like it to consist of (a) and nothing else. Taken together, (b), (c) and (d) constitute unwanted 'noise' that may obscure our detection of (a), the effect of our manipulations. In other words, you can conceive of an individual score as consisting of a 'signal' (a) and 'noise' (the combined effects of (b), (c) and (d)). We want to detect the signal, despite the noise. For a given strength of signal, the greater the noise, the harder it makes detection of the signal. For a given level of noise, the bigger the signal, the easier it will be to detect.

It's a bit like being at a party, and trying to hear what someone is saying despite the loud music. What they are saying ('do you still want that tenner I owe you?') is the signal that you are trying to detect; the 'noise' is the monotonous thumping and discordant jangling of some modern popular beat combo, inflicted upon you by a moronic disc jockey whose personal mission seems to be to prevent intelligent conversation at all costs. If the person talking to you has a quiet voice and the music is very loud, the signal to noise ratio is low, and you have a poor chance of retrieving your tenner: their question is drowned out by the noise. If your friend has a voice that is louder than the music, then there is a high signal to noise ratio, and the chances are you will be ten pounds richer. (Note that it's the *ratio* between signal and noise that is important; so you are also likely to hear your friend if they have a quiet voice but the music is even quieter).

In short, if we have a weak effect, it is likely to be swamped by unwanted variation in performance which is unrelated to our manipulations of the independent variable. Since in practice most of our manipulations are unlikely to have massive effects on participants' performance (i.e. we are trying to detect relatively weak signals), what we need are techniques which minimize the noise as much as possible.

The logical basis of traditional experiments

Traditional experiments take each participant's data and try to separate the signal from the noise by statistical methods. These exploit the fact that the two types of variation in an experiment have different properties. Variation due to our experimental manipulation is systematic, while variation due to uncontrolled factors is random. Random variation, in the long run, is as likely to increase a score as it is to decrease it. The task is therefore to eliminate all sources of systematic variation, other than that produced by our experimental manipulation; we can then use statistical techniques to filter out our signal from the random noise produced by all the uncontrolled factors.

Think of a simple between-groups experiment with two conditions, A and B. We test a group of participants for condition A and another group for condition B. Within group A, everyone has received the same treatment from the experimenter, a different treatment to that received by everyone in group B. If the experiment was designed properly, this should be the only factor that can produce any *systematic* difference between the people in group A and the people in group B. Within each group, there may be lots of random differences between individuals, but these should pretty much cancel each other out: they shouldn't give rise to any systematic differences between the groups.

In a conventional experiment, the task is to assess whether the difference between our groups is larger than the differences which would be produced by the operation of random factors. This is why it's so important to randomize allocation of participants to different conditions (in a between-groups design) or randomize order of participation in conditions (in a within-subjects design). By randomly allocating participants to different conditions, these uncontrolled variations will hopefully cancel out to a greater or lesser extent. The problem is that, although the effects of these uncontrolled variables may now be rendered unsystematic, they may still produce a lot of unwanted variability in the scores, which has to be filtered out statistically.

The logical basis of single-subject experiments

Single-subject techniques use a different strategy. Instead of dealing with the signal-and-noise problem by ensuring that the noise is spread randomly across conditions, single-subject designs try to eliminate the noise as far as possible. The argument is that, if there is uncontrolled variation in scores, one should attempt to find out where it comes from and control those variables in the experiment. Single-subject techniques have been most successful where it is possible to effectively control unwanted sources of variation. In most areas of psychology, this simply isn't possible; however, behaviourists and psychophysicists can exert powerful control over the conditions under which the individual is performing. In animal learning studies, the environment used is very impoverished (for example a Skinner box or a maze), and the participants' previous learning history is well known. In psychophysical studies, the conditions are also very circumscribed. The stimuli are generally quite impoverished, so that there is minimal scope for participants' responses to differ as a consequence of their previous history. It is reasonable to assume that individual responses to the task of deciding whether one grey patch is lighter or darker than another will be fairly consistent. Participants are also asked to make the minimum of decisions (typically either detection of a stimulus versus non-detection, or simple judgements such as 'wider' versus 'thinner'). Finally, elaborate techniques are used to maximise the reliability of performance measurement (i.e. various sophisticated methods for calculating an individual's threshold for detecting a stimulus or reliably discriminating between stimuli). All these factors minimise the intrusion of individual differences in performance, and hence minimize the contribution of 'noise' to participants' overall performance.

Single-subject techniques are often known as 'steady-state methodologies', because they compare the effects of an experimental manipulation to some baseline 'steady state' in the same individual. The aim in designing such a study is to produce changes in the behaviour of a single individual, and demonstrate conclusively that they are produced by the experimenter's manipulations of the independent variable concerned, rather than by other factors. It is this latter point that makes these *experimental* designs, as opposed to quasi-experimental designs like the single pre-test/post-test design and interrupted time-series design mentioned earlier. We'll discuss just two versions of this method, roughly equivalent to conventional within-subjects and between-groups designs respectively; Sidman's (1960) book still provides an excellent starting-point if you want further information on this topic.

Examples of single-subject designs

In the *ABA design* (Figure 3.11), baseline behaviour is carefully measured: this is state 'A'. Some treatment is applied, and behaviour is measured while it is in force (state 'B'). Then the treatment is removed, and the baseline behaviour recorded once more (a return to state 'A'). If the treatment produces an effect (as opposed to the

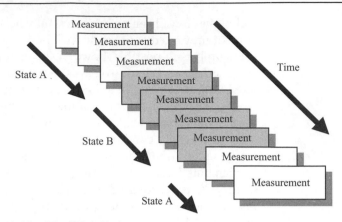

Figure 3.11   The ABA design

effect being produced by time threats to validity such as maturation), the effect should decrease or disappear when the treatment is withdrawn, and appear again when the treatment is re-established.

Here's a hypothetical example that might make this clearer. Suppose we are want to try to reduce nose-picking behaviour in a child, 'Little Wilbert'. We could measure nose-picking for some days, to get a baseline state 'A' for this behaviour. Then, we could introduce some experimental manipulation: suppose, for example, that every time Wilbert's finger went up his nose, we poked him with an electric cattle prod. (I was going to suggest that we played him a 'Steps' record, but that would be too unethical!) So this is now state 'B'. We measure nose-picking for a few days while this treatment is in force. Finally, we return to state 'A', and let Wilbert scrape his hooter to his heart's content. If our manipulation has controlled Wilbert's behaviour, the frequency of nose-picking should be clearly lower on the days when state 'B' was in force, compared to the periods of state 'A' before and afterwards.

By administering the treatment twice, at irregular intervals (i.e. ABAB), we can guard against the possibility that the results obtained are simply due to coincidence (i.e., the fortuitous simultaneous operation of our treatment and other uncontrolled variables). It is this that distinguishes the ABA design from the superficially similar interrupted time-series design: in the latter, the experimenter has no control over when the manipulation of the independent variable occurs, and so has no way of knowing for sure whether changes in behaviour are due to their manipulation or because of the influence of extraneous factors (i.e. the action of various time threats). In the ABA design, because the experimenter has complete control over when the treatment is applied or removed from the participant, they are able to pinpoint cause and effect: they can be much more sure that it is their actions which are affecting the participant.

The treatment may be applied several times, for example ABABAB. This is useful in circumstances where it would be unethical to use an ABA design. Suppose, for example, that we wanted to use this method to demonstrate that giving sweets to an antisocial child was an effective reward that increased the frequency of sociable behaviour; obviously, if giving sweets worked, we would not want to demonstrate reversibility by withdrawing this manipulation and hence possibly returning the child to their original level of unsociability by the end of the study.

The ABA design and its variants suffer from the same major limitation as all within-subjects designs: it can only be used in circumstances where the treatments don't have irreversible effects.

Multiple baseline designs

If the manipulation that you want to use is irreversible (or reversal is undesirable, as in the example I just used), then the ABA design can still be used, in a modified form (Figure 3.12). Essentially, you could run an AB design using a few participants, with each participant experiencing a single transition (from state A to state B) at a different time. We record Little Wilbert's levels of social behaviour for three days, and then we switch him to a system of being rewarded for sweets every time he's nice to other kids; if this manipulation has any effect, it should be revealed in our measurements of Wilbert's social behaviour on subsequent days. In the case of Little Zilbert, we wait for *five* days before introducing the sweets as a reward: again, if the manipulation has any effect, it should show up in our measurements on subsequent days. By introducing the experimental manipulation at different times, time threats to validity can largely be avoided: if each participant

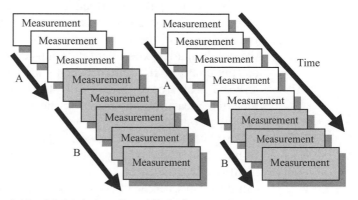

Figure 3.12   Multiple baseline AB design

receives the experimental treatment at a different time, but responds to it in a similar way, you can be reasonably sure that changes in their behaviour are due to what you did (because you are the one manipulating the time at which the experimental situation changes), rather than due to any extraneous factors.

Multiple baseline procedures like this can also be used as a within-subjects design: different behaviours in the same individual are measured, and then manipulations designed to affect their frequency are introduced at different times. Suppose we thought that sweet-giving was an effective treatment for several different behaviours in our captive child. We could measure, say, the frequencies of smiling, cuddling and stroking by Little Milbert on each day for a month. On day five, we introduce the sweets as a reward for smiling. Sweets should affect the frequency of smiling, but leave the other two behaviours largely unaffected. On day ten, we give him sweets every time he cuddles another child. The frequency of cuddling should then start to increase. Stroking should remain unaffected. Finally, on day twenty we introduce sugary rewards for stroking. Now, all three behaviours should have increased in frequency, and we can be reasonably confident in our conclusion that sweets can act as an effective reward for social behaviour.

3.3   So, Which Experimental Design Should You Use?

The answer to this question is 'it depends': if there were only one, ideal, experimental design to use, this chapter would be a lot shorter! In general, I would suggest you consider the following points in designing your study.

Obviously, wherever possible, use a proper experimental design: quasi-experimental designs have their uses, but can never establish cause and effect as unequivocally as a well-designed 'true' experiment. In most cases, it's best to design your study with a view to using one of the 'ready-made' experimental designs described in the earlier sections of this chapter. If it's a between-subjects experiment, the 'post-test only control group' design will often suffice; if it's feasible to take repeated measures, then go for the basic repeated-measures design described on page 79.

Design the study so that you get at least one score per participant, rather than them merely falling into one category or another. As mentioned earlier, you are quite limited with the statistics that you can perform with 'head-counts': scores lend themselves to much more sophisticated analyses.

Next, where it's feasible, use a repeated-measures design. Compared to a between-groups design, repeated-measures designs involve finding fewer participants (always tedious, especially if you are an undergraduate who can't pay people to take part in your study) and they are also more likely to detect any differences between conditions, if they exist.

If you can include an additional independent variable in your study without too much trouble, then do so, as it will give you more to talk about in your discussion section. However, don't get too ambitious: time and resources are usually limited, especially at the undergraduate level. It's better to run a modest but well-designed and well-executed study, that has sufficient power (see page 156) to detect any differences between conditions that might exist, than to attempt a grandiose experiment that has lots of conditions but not really enough participants in any of them. Keep the design as simple as possible: the more conditions and groups you have in your experiment, the longer it will take to run, and the more difficult the statistical analysis becomes (both to perform and to interpret the results obtained).

The problem of including additional variables is not quite so bad if you can get away with a repeated-measures design. However, ensure that each participant isn't faced with so many trials that the experiment becomes excessively taxing or tedious for them: first, the quality of the data may suffer as their motivation declines, and secondly, they may warn their friends against volunteering for your experiment!

If you are using a between-groups design, every additional variable will double the number of participants that you'll need to test (assuming, of course, that you have only two levels of each variable: if you have more levels, the problem gets even worse). Suppose you did a study of the effects of mnemonics (memory aids) on word list recall. If you did a simple experiment using two levels of this independent variable ('using a mnemonic' versus 'not using a mnemonic') in a between-groups design, you'd have to find thirty or so participants (15 per condition). Now suppose you include age and gender as independent variables as well (both with two levels – 'old' versus 'young', and 'male' versus 'female'). You now need to find 120 participants in order to have groups of 15 for all of the permutations of memory-aid, age and gender. (For example, you need 15 for the 'using a mnemonic/old/female' group, 15 for the 'using a mnemonic/old/male' group, 15 for the 'using a mnemonic/young/female' group, and so on). If you include extra independent variables, you also add to the number of interactions that might be statistically significant and hence demand an explanation. Our three-variable study would give rise to a three-way interaction between the type of mnemonic used, age and gender. This might be quite difficult to explain, especially if you had no theoretical grounds for predicting its existence. Two independent variables in a single study is, therefore, usually quite enough.

3.4   Ethical Considerations in Running a Study

When you run a experiment (or any other type of study come to that), there are various ethical considerations that you should take into account. Various social psychological studies have drawn attention to the influence and power of experimenters, especially if you're wearing a white coat (lab coat that is, not a fur stole or one that has sleeves that tie together behind your back). Participants are vulnerable, and you have a responsibility to them (and to the reputation of psychologists in general) to behave with their best interests in mind.

Behave ethically - your participants must not come to physical or psychological harm.

Before you run a study, you should check to see if your institution has some kind of ethics committee that needs to examine details of the proposed research and give its approval for it to be conducted. If there is no such committee, you should at the very least discuss the proposed study with your tutor. The American Psychological Association and the British Psychological Society have each laid down detailed guidelines about how you should behave while running the study, and what the rights of the participant are. Here's the gist of those guidelines.

Informed Consent

Participants should be informed of what the experiment involves and be made fully aware of their rights while they are taking part. These include the right for them to withdraw from the study at any time (if they get scared or even merely bored). In the case of children who are too young to know what's going on, informed consent should always be sought from their parents or carers. (This also applies of course to adults who are learning disabled, brain damaged or otherwise unable to give fully informed consent before participating). Since most kids are tested in their school, the easiest way to do this is to ask the school to get the children to take home a standard letter from you that explains what the study is about, gives relevant details about you (where you can be contacted for further information), and makes it clear to the parent that they have the option of refusing to allow their child to participate in the study. Bear in mind that, even if the parents give their permission, ultimately the child has the last word: if they don't want to participate, or want to withdraw from the study at any time, then their wishes must be respected.

Observational studies are normally carried out with the express intent of obtaining data about people's normal behaviour, and hence without them being aware that they are participating in a study. Clearly informed consent is not feasible in these circumstances. The BPS suggest, as a rule of thumb, that it's OK to make observations of people in situations where they could reasonably be expected to be on public view – so, for example, it would be alright to film people in a shopping mall or at an amusement park, but it wouldn't be acceptable to find out what they get up to in their bedroom without them knowing that you were watching them and giving their express permission for you to do so. If you do this kind of research, take care to follow the other ethical principles outlined here (that is, do not harm or deceive people) and make sure that any recordings of the situation protect the participants' confidentiality. It's up to you to decide whether to tell people that they have participated, and what it's all about (see 'debriefing', below). In some cases, it may not be feasible: for example, in a study of driver looking behaviour, a colleague of ours filmed drivers as they emerged from a junction. It would have been difficult for him to catch up with each driver and debrief them. Some years ago I listened to an ergonomist describe an observational study of men's behaviour in public lavatories (as a basis for deciding innocuous things such as where to place the urinals in relation to the sinks, I hasten to add). It probably wouldn't have been a good idea to debrief participants (excuse the pun!) in that study either.

Deception

Whether it is OK to deceive participants is a tricky issue, especially since we've just said that participants should give their informed consent. There are some areas of psychology where it doesn't particularly matter whether the participant knows what the experiment is about. For example, if you were doing research on low-level visual processing, and were engaged in measuring people's thresholds for, say, being able to judge the length of a line, it probably wouldn't affect your results if the participants knew that was what you were trying to do. In fact, in many psychophysical experiments of this kind, it is commonplace for the experimenters to be amongst the participants in the study. (Generally one or two naive participants are tested as well, to check that the obtained results really aren't affected by the experimenters' insights). At the other extreme, there are many social psychological experiments which have depended on participants remaining ignorant of the study's purpose, or have even involved actively misleading the participant about the aims of the study.

By and large, active deception should be avoided in psychology experiments. (It's easy for me to say that, as I do vision research, not social psychology!) Quite apart from the ethical considerations, the widespread use of deception in the past has made it difficult for the rest of us to run experiments – in my experience, participants (especially non-psychologists) become a little suspicious because they expect to be deceived. As a consequence, they often try to work out the hidden agenda in a study, even when there isn't one!

Debriefing

Whether or not deception is used, you should always tell the participant what the experiment was about after they have finished it and leave time to answer any questions they might have. Quite apart from anything else, they have given up their time for you, and it's only common courtesy for you to give them a few minutes of yours in return. Participants often regard the experiment as a 'test' of their abilities: they are usually concerned to have performed well, both for their own benefit (to reassure themselves that they are normal and competent) and for yours (because they want to have helped to make your experiment 'work'. This can be a mixed blessing, if they have misinterpreted the purpose of the study and behaved weirdly as a result).

In most cases, you will be comparing average performance in one condition to average performance in another, so you should make it clear to the participant that you are not interested in their individual data, and that their results will be combined with those from other people. Even if they have done badly, reassure them that their performance is fine: 'Thanks very much, Igor. No, trying to press the response keys with your forehead rather than using your fingers is fine – lots of people do that, and it won't have affected your results, which look perfectly normal, so don't worry about it.' The idea is that the participant leaves the room with a nice warm glow and a feeling that they have made a worthwhile contribution. Who knows? If you've done this properly, they might even take part in another experiment one day.

Confidentiality

Participants have the right to confidentiality, regardless of whether they have participated in a memory experiment or whether they have just completed a 20-page questionnaire that provides intimate details of their sado-machochistic pursuits. Individuals and their data should never be publicly identifiable. Running round the common-room shouting 'Hey, everybody, look at the sexual perversions this one's got!' is definitely out. If you are doing research that involves case studies, the individuals concerned should be identified by initials, or better still false names. In the case of group data, the problem of confidentiality is less acute, but you should take care of things like database files that contain data together with people's names. For most experiments, there's no need to use the participant's names: something like 'Group A, participant 22: female, aged 40' should suffice.

Protection from physical and psychological harm

You are obliged to protect your participants from harm, both physically and psychologically (or else find some place where the authorities will never find their bodies!) In psychology experiments, psychological harm is sometimes a possibility: you should avoid making participants feel stressed, embarrassed, depressed, anxious or fearful, unless they have given their prior permission for you to do this to them. For example, suppose you wanted to do an experiment on the effects of mood on memory, and you wanted to get some participants into a happy mood and others into a miserable mood. There's probably no problem with making participants happy, but you should think carefully before making them sad. 'Mood induction' by means of gloomy music appears to be short-lived in its effects, but in a study such as this, it would be your responsibility to explain to the participant what was involved before the procedure took place, and to ensure that they felt OK before they left the laboratory. It's probably best not to do this kind of research in a laboratory on the fifteenth floor with easily-openable windows...

3.5 Summary

There are many issues that have to be considered in designing an experiment, but if you use one of the standard experimental designs described in this chapter, you should be well on the way to producing a study which will provide reliable and valid results. There is no one perfect design, because the optimal design will depend on your particular circumstances. However:

1. Define precisely what it is you want to measure.
2. *Before* running the study, think carefully about what statistics you are going to use.
3. Sample the appropriate population, to obtain suitable participants. Sometimes you can get away with using students, sometimes you can't. You may want to use a particular population, for example, geriatrics, children or left-footed Abyssinian female stockbrokers.
4. Decide which design is most appropriate for your particular circumstances. In many cases, a multivariate design with repeated measures will be the most informative, economical and sensitive design to use, as long as carry-over effects don't preclude its use. Keep the design as simple as you can.
5. Having obtained a result, you have to assess its reliability and its validity. One way to do this is by using multiple converging operations: investigate the same phenomenon from different angles by using different techniques, participant groups, dependent variables, etc., to ensure that your results are not specific to your particular original study.
6. You must behave ethically when you conduct research. Ensure you are familiar with the guidelines that have been produced by the BPS and the APA. Participants must give informed consent to participating in your study. Avoid deceiving them or exposing them to mental or physical harm. Once they have finished the experiment, give them an explanation of what it was all about, and make sure they leave in as good a state of mind as they were in when they arrived!

3.6   Practical Tasks

Which of these are quasi-experimental designs, and why?

1. *A comparison of two different methods of teaching statistics:*
   Dr. Plonker teaches statistics to Idontgoto University first-years, using an excellent statistics book ('Discovering Statistics using SPSS for Windows' by A. Field, available from all good bookshops). Dr. Skollob teaches an identical course to first-years at Nohope University, but without using this rather fine statistics book. Both groups of students are given the same statistics test at the end of the course, and it is concluded that Andy's book makes a big difference to students' statistics comprehension.

2. *The effects of shift-patterns on employee performance:*
   Concerned at falling profits, a big insurance company recruits a psychologist to see if the performance of their telephone sales division could be improved. She compares the number of sales made by telephone sales operatives working on the company's existing three different shifts (morning, midday and evening). A significant difference is found between the three groups on this measure, and it is concluded that shift-pattern affects operatives' sales performance.

3. *Gender differences in the effects of stress on performance:*
   A psychologist wants to know if memory is impaired by stress, and whether this interacts with the gender of the participant. He presents participants with a word list and measures how many words they can recall from it five minutes later. There are four groups of participants, two male groups and two female. One group of each gender is stressed during the five minute interval, by watching a video of an eye operation. The four groups differ in the number of words recalled: overall, females remember more words than males, and the stress manipulation has no effect on recall.

Answers:

1. This is a quasi-experimental design because the participants are not allocated randomly to the two experimental conditions (statistics book versus no statistics book). Students at Idontgoto University might differ from those at Nohope University in all sorts of ways – it might be harder to get into Idontgoto in the first place, so that the students at the two universities differ in initial ability; or Nohope students might have a heavier workload on other courses so that they can't devote as much time to studying statistics. I leave it to you to think of other possible confounding factors. The important point is that a true experimental design (with random allocation of students to the two groups) would eliminate all of these alternative explanations.

2. This is a quasi-experimental design. Workers were recruited on the basis of the shift-patterns that they were already working, rather than being allocated randomly to the three different shifts. People who opt to work at different times may differ in various characteristics that are not under the experimenter's control. These might differ systematically between conditions and hence act as confounding variables. For example, there is a psychological dimension of 'morningness/eveningness': some people function better early in the day, whereas others perform better late at

night. It's unlikely that people would volunteer for shift-times that were at odds with their own diurnal cycle, so this at once introduces a possible systematic difference between the three conditions. Note that there is another problem with this particular study. If sales performance is found to be affected by shift-pattern, there are several possible explanations for this. It might be due to the effects of the shift-pattern on the operatives themselves (e.g., they might be more tired at one point in the day than another) or it might be that the number of potential sales that can be made varies during the day (more people might be available to be phoned during the evening than during the morning. If the number of successful sales is a constant proportion of the number of phone calls made, then the evening shift-workers are likely to produce more sales for this reason alone).

3. Most people would consider this to be a true experiment, but strictly speaking you could argue that it is quasi-experimental in the sense that the experimenter cannot allocate participants randomly to one gender or the other. While the psychologist does not have complete control over the 'gender' independent variable, he does, however, have complete control over the other independent variable, 'stress level'. Within each gender, the psychologist can allocate participants randomly to the 'stressed' and 'non-stressed' conditions. The design is good enough to enable meaningful conclusions to be drawn about the effects on memory of gender and stress: however, as with any research on gender effects, because the experimenter can't manipulate this variable directly, the conclusions about which aspects of gender affect performance are often fairly ambiguous (are the effects due to biological differences, socialisation differences or a mixture of the two?).

3.7 Further Reading

http://www.apa.org/ethics/code.html [A summary of the American Psychological Association's Ethical Guidelines].

American Psychological Association (1992). Ethical principles of psychologists and code of conduct. *American Psychologist 47*, 1597–1611.

http://www.bps.org.uk/documents/Code.pdf [A downloadable Adobe Acrobat file containing the Code of Conduct of the British Psychological Society].

Campbell, D.T. and Stanley, J.C. (1963). *Experimental and quasi-experimental designs for research*. Chicago: Rand-McNally.

Gould, S.J. (1981). *The mismeasure of man*. London: Penguin. [A fascinating study of the misuse of quantitative methods in the service of prejudice and bigotry].

Martin, P. and Bateson, P. (1993). *Measuring behaviour: an introductory guide* (2nd edition) Cambridge. Cambridge University Press. [Essential reading if you plan to use observational techniques].

Rosenthal, R. (1966). *Experimenter effects in behavioral research*. New York: Appleton-Century-Crofts. [Rosenthal's orignal work on experimenter effects somewhat overstates the case, but is interesting nevertheless].

Rosenthal, R. and Rosnow, R.L. (Eds.) (1969) *Artifact in behavioral research*. New York: Academic Press. [A collection of interesting papers on the topic of artifacts and potential sources of bias in psychology research].

Rosenthal, R. and Rosnow, R.L. (1975). *The volunteer subject*. New York: Wiley. [A fascinating description of how volunteers and non-volunteers might differ, and the implications of this for the conclusions drawn from psychology experiments].

Sidman, M. (1960). *Tactics of scientific research*. New York: Basic Books. [A cogent justification for the use of single-subject methods, and a useful description of many different designs of this type].

Notes

[1] 'Student' was the pseudonym of William S. Gosset, a statistician for Guinness Breweries. He's best known for inventing the *t*-test. Not a lot of people know that. (To be read in a Michael Caine accent).

PART 2 ANALYSING AND INTERPRETING DATA

4 Descriptive Statistics

On page 25 we saw how probability could be used to give us confidence about a particular hypothesis (in that case detecting whether milk was added before or after tea). The following four chapters expand these ideas to look at the kinds of statistical procedures that have been developed to test research hypotheses. These chapters are intended as a basic grounding in what you need to know to select and interpret statistical tests (and a bit of basic theory in why we use statistics in the first place). There isn't going to be any detailed coverage of the mathematical mechanics of the tests, or how to do them using computer packages such as SPSS. For that level of information I, not surprisingly, suggest you look at my statistics textbook (Field, 2000) or the teaching notes on my wcb pages.

4.1 Populations and Samples

As researchers we are usually interested in answering general questions. So, psychologists are looking for general rules about all people (such as, how do people remember things?), market researchers are also interested in rules about all consumers (why do people buy certain products?), neuroscientists are looking for general rules about biological systems (how do all neurons communicate?), and physicists are interested in the behaviour of all sub-atomic particles. Whatever it is we want to make generalizations about, the best way to find general rules would be to gather data about every single instance of the things about which you're interested. An entire collection of things is known as a *population*. Psychologists are interested in the population of people (i.e. everyone on the planet), market researchers could be interested in the population of consumers, and physicists the population of sub-atomic particles. Populations can be very general (i.e. all people), more specific (i.e. all people suffering from obsessive compulsive disorder) or extremely specific (i.e. all people suffering from obsessive compulsive disorder who recite the lyrics to Lucky by Radiohead backwards before entering a room).

As psychologists, this could mean collecting data from everybody on the planet. Unfortunately we have neither the time nor the resources to do this and so instead we collect data from a small subset of the population in which we're interested. This subset is known as a *sample* from the population (Figure 4.1) and we can use the sample to make a guess about what results we would have found had we actually gathered data from the entire population. The size of the sample we take is very important because the bigger the sample the more representative it will be of the population as a whole. To draw a quick analogy, imagine you go to a party and your friend (we'll call her Andi for argument's sake) has a few beers and then decides to stick someone's hat in the freezer (as a random example). How confident

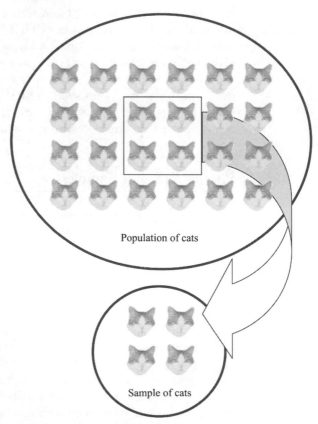

Population of cats

Sample of cats

Figure 4.1   Populations and samples

would you be that this was representative of the entire population? Would you be prepared to assume that everyone sticks hats in freezers after drinking alcohol? Well, probably not, you might just assume that Andi is a bit odd. What about if you went to a different party and this time you observed that five people all stuck people's hats in the freezer? My guess is that you'd start to think that perhaps there was something going on and that maybe alcohol did have some effect on hat-freezing behaviour. How about if we go to a very big party (with lots of freezer space) and observe 10,000 people all engaging in hat freezing behaviour?[1] Our confidence in this last instance should be very high because we're seeing the same behaviour in a large number of people. This analogy demonstrates how large samples give us more confidence in our conclusions and this was first noted by Jacob Bernoulli as the 'law of large numbers'. Obviously the behaviours we observe in different samples will differ slightly, but given that large samples are more representative of the population than small ones it follows that the behaviours observed in different large samples will be relatively similar but the behaviours observed in different small samples are likely to be quite variable.

4.2   Summarizing Data

Frequency Distributions

Once we've collected data from a sample of participants we need some way to summarize these data to make it easy for others (and ourselves) to see general patterns within the scores collected. We pretty much have two choices here: we can either calculate a summary statistic (a single value that tells us something about our scores) or we can draw a graph. One very useful thing to begin with is just to plot a graph of how many times each score occurs. This is known as a *frequency distribution*, or *histogram*. In clinical psychology there's a phenomenon called amphetamine psychosis in which people who abuse amphetamines end up having psychotic episodes (such as hallucinations and delusions) even when not taking the drug. Imagine we took a sample of 40 amphetamine users (which we hope is representative of the entire population of amphetamine users) and counted how many hallucinations they had in a day.

➤   Number of hallucinations: 10, 6, 7, 8, 9, 7, 10, 2, 6, 8, 3, 9, 8, 10, 1, 5, 8, 4, 2, 9, 10, 6, 7, 8, 9, 7, 10, 2, 6, 8, 3, 9, 8, 10, 1, 5, 8, 4, 2, 9.

The first thing we can do is to arrange these scores into descending order:

> Number of hallucinations: 10, 10, 10, 10, 10, 10, 9, 9, 9, 9, 9, 9, 8, 8, 8, 8, 8, 8, 8, 8, 7, 7, 7, 7, 6, 6, 6, 6, 5, 5, 4, 4, 3, 3, 2, 2, 2, 2, 1, 1.

It now becomes really easy to count the number of times each score occurs (this is called the *frequency*). So, we can easily see that six people had 10 hallucinations and only two people had one hallucination. We could count the frequency for each score and then plot a graph with the number of hallucinations on the horizontal axis (also called the X-axis or abscissa), and the frequency on the vertical axis (also called the Y-axis or ordinate). Figure 4.2 shows such a graph and even with this relatively small amount of data two things become clear that were not obvious from the raw scores: (1) the majority of people experience six or more hallucinations (the bars on the right hand side are generally higher than those on the left hand side); and (2) the most frequent number of hallucinations was eight (this value has the tallest bar and we can see that eight of our 40 people experienced this number of hallucinations).

Types of distributions

Frequency distributions come in many different shapes and sizes. It is quite important, therefore, to have some general descriptions for common types of distributions (see Figure 4.3). In an ideal world our data

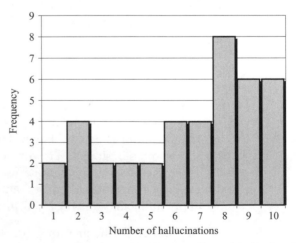

Figure 4.2 Frequency distribution of the number of hallucinations experienced by amphetamine users

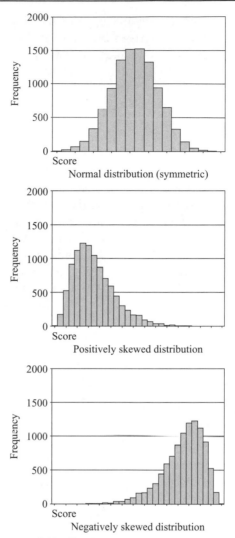

Figure 4.3 Shapes of distributions

would be distributed symmetrically around the centre of all scores. As such, if we drew a vertical line through the centre of the distribution then it should look the same on both sides. This is known as a *normal distribution* and is characterized by the bell-shaped curve with which you'll soon become familiar. This shape basically implies that the majority of scores lie around the centre of the distribution (so the largest bars on the histogram are all around the central value). Also, as we get further away from the centre the bars get smaller implying that as scores start to deviate from the centre their frequency is decreasing. As we move still further away from the centre our scores become very infrequent (the bars are very short). There are two main deviations from this type of distribution and both are called *skewed distributions*. Skewed distributions are not symmetrical and instead the most frequent scores (the tall bars on the graph) are clustered at one end of the scale. So, the typical pattern is a cluster of frequent scores at one end of the scale and the frequency of scores tailing off towards the other end of the scale. A skewed distribution can be either *positively skewed* (the frequent scores are clustered at the lower end and the tail points towards the higher or more positive scores) or *negatively skewed* (the frequent scores are clustered at the higher end and the tail points towards the lower, more negative scores). Distributions also vary in their pointy-ness, or *kurtosis* (Figure 4.4). Kurtosis, despite sounding like a disease, refers to the degree to which scores cluster in the tails of the distribution. This characteristic is usually shown up by how flat or pointy a distribution is. A *platykurtic* distribution is one that has many scores in the tails (a so-called heavy-tailed distribution) and so is quite flat. In contrast, *leptokurtic* distributions are relatively thin in the tails and so look quite pointy.

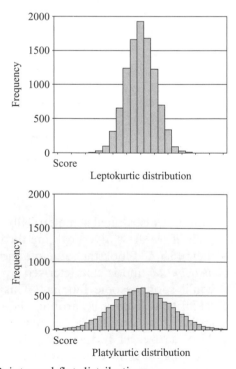

Figure 4.4   Pointy and flat distributions

The Mode

How can I summarize my data?

I mentioned in the previous section that when we summarize sample data we could do it either with a graph or with a summary statistic. We've already looked at a simple way of graphing data to get an idea of the shape of the set of scores (the *distribution*), and these shapes all seemed to refer back to the centre of the distribution (we talked about scores being close or far from the centre of the distribution). If we're looking for a single value that sums up our data, then this central point seems like a good place to start. However, there are several ways in which we could find the centre of a distribution. If we're using a sample of people to tell us something general about behaviour then it makes sense that one thing we might be interested in is a typical score. This score would tell us roughly how most people behaved. If we plot our data points in a histogram (see previous section) we can get a rough idea of what the most common scores are (they have the tallest bars) and the single most common score is often obvious (in Figure 4.2 it is eight hallucinations). This most common score is called the *mode*. To calculate the mode we simply place the data in ascending order (to make life easier) and then count how many times each score occurs. The score that occurs the most is the mode. The mode has a couple of advantages: (1) it's easy to calculate and simple to understand; and (2) we can use the mode with nominal data (see page 6) because we are simply counting the number of times an instance occurs. Before continuing, have a think about what disadvantages the mode has.

There are two main disadvantages of the mode. First, it is possible that a data set has two or more most frequent scores. If a data set has two modes it is known as *bimodal*, and if it has several modes it is called *multimodal*. This makes it a messy way to summarize data (you end up saying things like 'the typical amount of time that people could withstand sitting in a bath of ice was 183 seconds or 3 seconds'). The second problem is that the mode can be changed dramatically if only a single case of data is added – this makes it an unrepresentative measure. Box 4.1 shows these two problems.

The Median

Put simply, the median is the middle score of a distribution of scores when they are ranked in order of magnitude. Obviously you'll get a middle score only when there's an odd number of scores, and so if there's an even number of scores we simply average the two middle

■ Box 4.1: Problems with the mode

Several Modes

The picture below shows a bimodal distribution. Notice how there are two humps: this shape is characteristic of bimodal distributions (and camels!). Multimodal distributions might have three or more humps, each one representing a very common score. One classic example of a bimodal distribution is marks on research methods courses. Typically students are either really good or really bad at research methods and so you tend to have a mode around 70% for the people who understand statistics and another one at around 40% representing those who struggle. My aim in life is to eliminate the lower mode so there is just one at the high end of the scale!

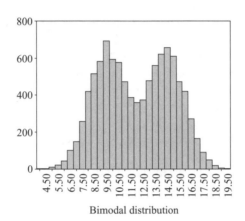

Bimodal distribution

Changing scores

Imagine we got 10 people to rate their statistics lecturer on a scale of 1–10 (1 being 'completely rubbish' and 10 being 'I love him'). The scores are as follows:

$$2, 2, 3, 4, 5, 8, 9, 9, 9, 10$$

The mode is 9 (it has a frequency of three, which is higher than any other score), so we might conclude that this lecturer is really good because typically he was rated highly. Imagine now that we gave students the opportunity to change their minds and asked them to re-rate the lecturer. The student who rated the lecturer as three the first time around changes his or her mind and decides that because the lecturer tells useless jokes the whole time they'll rate him as 2. The data become:

$$2, 2, 2, 4, 5, 8, 9, 9, 9, 10$$

There are now two modes: 2 and 9. The distribution has become bimodal and is hard to interpret because the modes are at opposite ends of the scale. So we wouldn't know whether the lecturer is good or bad. Then a latecomer enters the room and she is given the chance to rate the same lecturer. She also thinks the lecturer's jokes are really unfunny and gives him a 2. So now there is one more score of 2 and the mode would change to 2 and we'd sack the lecturer. However, if that next student had happened to be someone who liked the lecturer and had rated him as 9, then the mode would've changed to 9 and we'd have given the lecturer a pay rise. The point is that even a single score can dramatically alter the value of the mode (especially in small samples): it is very unstable.

scores. Imagine we asked 7 of the people that had amphetamine psychosis to stop taking amphetamines for 6 months and then recorded how many hallucinations they had in one day.

> Number of hallucinations: 1, 5, 8, 4, 2, 2, 3.

First, arrange these scores into descending order:

> Number of hallucinations: 8, 5, 4, 3, 2, 2, 1.

Next, we find the position of the middle score:

$$\text{Position of middle score} = \frac{n+1}{2}$$

In this equation n is simply the number of scores we've collected. So, for the current example, in which there were seven scores:

$$\text{Position of middle score} = \frac{7+1}{2} = 4$$

Finally, we find the score that is positioned at the location we've just calculated. So, in this example we find the 4th score:

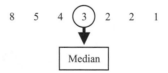

When there is an even number of scores we will have two central locations. If we looked at how bungee jumping affects spine length, we could measure people's spines before and after they do a jump and calculate the difference in length. If we did this for 16 jumpers our data might look like this (the change in spine length is in millimetres):

9, 10, 7, 20, 57, 15, 19, 30, 37, 24, 2, 0, −4, −6, 16, 11

First, we must arrange these scores in order:

−6, −4, 0, 2, 7, 9, 10, 11, 15, 16, 19, 20, 24, 30, 37, 57

Next, we find the position of the middle score by using the equation above. For the current example, in which there were 16 scores:

$$\text{Position of middle score} = \frac{16+1}{2} = 8.5$$

This means that the median is half way between the 8th and 9th scores. So we simply average these scores. The 8th score in the ordered list was 11 and the 9th score was 15, and the average will be those two scores added together and divided by 2:

$$Median = \frac{11+15}{2} = 13$$

The median has several advantages: (1) it is relatively unaffected by extreme scores at either end of the scale (*outliers*), so if someone behaves really oddly it won't bias this measure too much (see Box 4.3 for more about outliers); (2) if you get lots of scores at one end of the scale (the distribution is skewed – see page 113) then the median is less affected by this than the mean; and (3) it can be used with ordinal, interval and ratio data (it cannot, however, be used with nominal data as these data have no numerical order).

However, there are disadvantages too. On page 111, I mentioned that the behaviours we observe in different samples will differ slightly (and large samples are more reliable), well, the variability of the median across samples can be considerable (and usually greater than the mean – see the next section). As such it isn't a very stable measure because it is susceptible to sampling fluctuations. Second, the median is not very useful mathematically because it doesn't take account of all of the scores in the data set.

The Mean

The mean is the sum of all scores divided by the number of scores, so to calculate the mean we simply add up all of the scores and then divide by the total number of scores we have. Algebraically this is represented as (see Box 4.2 for revision of algebra):

$$\overline{X} = \frac{\sum x}{n}$$

Let's take the data on the number of hallucinations for which we calculated the median, and now calculate the mean. First we add up all of the scores:

$$\sum x = 1 + 5 + 8 + 4 + 2 + 2 + 3$$
$$= 25$$

▣ **Box 4.2: Revision of Algebra**

In the next few chapters you'll come across several equations. Just so you don't get lost, here are a few reminders of some symbols that we'll be using, what these symbols mean, and a few simple rules of mathematics.

Symbols:

➤ Σ, This symbol (called sigma) means 'add everything up'. So, if you see something like Σx it just means 'add up all of the scores you've collected'.

➤ $\overline{X}$ is just the symbol for the mean of a set of scores. So, if you see $\overline{X} = 3.26$ you should read this as 'the mean of these data was 3.26'.

➤ s^2 is just the symbol for the variance of a sample (see the next section). If you see $s^2 = 47.98$ you should read this as 'these data had 47.98 units of variance'. If we are quoting the variance of a population, we use the symbol σ^2.

➤ s is just the symbol for the standard deviation of a sample (see the next section). If you see $s = 5.67$ you should read this as 'the standard deviation of these data was 5.67'. If we are quoting the standard deviation of a population, we use the symbol σ.

➤ The symbol $\sqrt{}$ means calculate the square root. So, $\sqrt{9}$ means 3 (because 3 is the square root of 9). There should be a button on your calculator that allows you to work out square roots.

Rules:

➤ *Two negatives make a positive:* Although in life two wrongs don't make a right, in mathematics they do! When we multiply a negative number with another negative number, the result is a positive number. For example, $-3 \times -4 = 12$.

➤ *A negative number multiplied by a positive one makes a negative number:* If you multiply a positive number by a negative number then the result is another negative number. For example, $3 \times -4 = -12$, or $-3 \times 4 = -12$.

➤ *BODMAS:* This is an acronym for the order in which mathematical operations are performed. It stands for Brackets, Order, Division, Multiplication, Addition, Subtraction and this is the order in which you should carry out operations within an equation. Mostly these operations are self-explanatory (e.g. always calculate things within brackets first) except for order, which actually refers to power terms such as squares. Three squared, or 3^2, used to be called three raised to the order of 2, hence why these terms are called order in BODMAS. If we have a look at an example of BODMAS, what would be the result of $1 + 3 \times 5^2$? The answer is 76 (not 100 as some of you might have thought). There are no brackets so the first thing is to deal with the order term: 5^2 is 25, so the equation becomes $1 + 3 \times 25$. There is no division, so we can move on to multiplication: 3×25, which gives us 75. BODMAS tells us to deal with addition next: $1 + 75$, which gives us 76 and the equation is solved. If I'd written the original equation as $(1 + 3) \times 5^2$, then the answer would have

continues

■ **Box 4.2:** *continued*

been 100 because we deal with the brackets first: $(1 + 3) = 4$, so the equation becomes 4×5^2. We then deal with the order term, so the equation becomes $4 \times 25 = 100$!

➤ http://www.easymaths.com is a good site for revising basic maths.

We can then divide by the number of scores (in this case seven):

$$\frac{\sum x}{n} = \frac{25}{7} = 3.57$$

The mean is 3.57, which is not a value we observed in our actual data (no-one had 3.57 hallucinations). If we compare this to the median of the same data we can also see that it's slightly higher (3.57 compared to 3). What might account for this difference? On page 118, I suggested that the median wasn't heavily affected by extreme scores, well, one disadvantage of the mean is that it can be influenced by extreme scores (see Box 4.3). The other problems with the mean are that it is affected by skewed distributions (see page 113) and can be used only with interval or ratio data.

Having said that, the mean has several important advantages: at the simplest level the mean uses every score (the mode and median ignore most of the scores in a data set); more important, the mean can be easily manipulated algebraically and so is very useful mathematically; the mean is the most accurate summary of the data (see Box 4.4); and finally the mean is resistant to sampling variation. What I mean by this final point is that if you took one sample from a population and measured the mean, mode and median, and then took a different sample from the same population and again measured the mean, mode and median, then the mean is the most likely of the three measures to be the same in the two samples. The mode and median are more likely to differ across samples than the mean and this is very important because we're usually using samples to infer something about the entire population – so it's important that our sample is representative of this population.

Measuring the Accuracy of the Mean

The mean is probably the simplest statistical model that we use (see Field, 2000, Chapter 1). By this I mean that it is a statistic that predicts the likely score of a person (if no other data were available and we were asked to predict a given person's score then the mean would

▪ Box 4.3: The effect of outliers

The internet company Amazon sells books, music and videos online and lets users provide reviews and ratings of products they have bought (the rating ranges from 1 to 5 stars). Sad person that I am, I looked up the reviews for my first book (Field, 2000) to see what the feedback was like. At the time of writing, seven people had reviewed and rated my book and their ratings were (in the order the ratings were given): 2, 5, 4, 5, 5, 5, 5. All but one of these ratings are fairly similar (mainly 5 and 4) but the first rating was quite different from the rest – it was a rating of 2. The graph shows these ratings plotted as a graph (so there are the seven raters on the horizontal axis and their ratings on the vertical axis). On this graph there is a horizontal line that represents the mean of all seven scores and it's clear that all of the scores except one lie close to this line. The score of 2 is very different and lies some way below the mean. This score could be termed an outlier – a score that is very different from the rest, or is inconsistent with the bulk of the data. The dotted horizontal line represents the mean of the scores when the outlier is not included. This line is higher than the original mean indicating that by ignoring this score the mean increases. This shows how a single score can bias the mean; in this case it is dragging the average down.

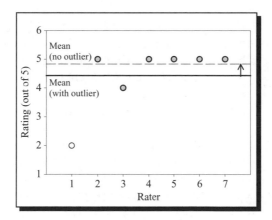

If we calculate the mean with and without the outlier we can see the extent of this bias:

$$\overline{X}_{\text{Outlier}} = \frac{\sum x}{n} = \frac{2+5+4+5+5+5+5}{7} = \frac{31}{7} = 4.43$$

If we now calculate the mean without the outlier (remember we now have only 6 scores when we calculate the mean):

$$\overline{X}_{\text{No outlier}} = \frac{\sum x}{n} = \frac{5+4+5+5+5+5}{6} = \frac{29}{6} = 4.83$$

continues

■ Box 4.3: *continued*

So, there is a difference in the mean of 0.4. Now if we round off to whole numbers (as Amazon sometimes do), that single score has made a difference between the average rating reported by Amazon being a generally glowing 5 stars and the less impressive 4 stars (not that I'm bitter or anything!).

What happens if we look at the median score? First we must arrange the data in numerical order: 5, 5, 5, 5, 5, 4, 2. With the outlier included there are seven scores ($n = 7$) so the middle score is in position four, $(n + 1)/2 = 4$, which gives a median of five. If we remove the outlier there are only six scores ($n = 6$): 5, 5, 5, 5, 5, 4. With the outlier excluded the middle score is in position $(n + 1)/2 = 3.5$, which will be the average of positions three and four. Both of these positions contain a score of five and so the average will also be five. So, with the outlier excluded the median is five.

These data are very useful in illustrating the effects of an outlier. The mean is always biased by outliers (in this case the outlier reduced the mean), however, the median is not so prone to bias, and often a single extreme score will have little or no effect on its value.

(Data for this example from http://www.amazon.co.uk/)

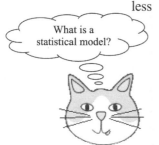

What is a statistical model?

be the best guess because the error in this guess will, on average, be less than any other guess we might make). Also, the mean is a hypothetical value that can be calculated for any data set, but doesn't have to be a value that is actually observed in the data. So, it's a summary statistic. A classic example of what I'm talking about is the statistic, frequently quoted in the UK, that the average family has 2.5 children. If we take this literally, then it means that one family has two full-bodied children and one extra pair of legs, whereas their neighbours also have two full-bodied children but have the added pleasure of a child who exists only from the waist up (you have to pity the family that got the lower half as it won't do much but produce messy substances!). Alternatively, perhaps the children have been cut down the middle so each has one arm one leg and half a head. Unless I'm doing my usual trick of living in a naïve world, I assume this is not the case and that actually most families have 2 or 3 full-bodied little munchkins. The mean value that is always quoted at us is a *hypothetical* value. As such, the mean is a model created to summarize our data.

It's important with any model that it accurately represents the state of the real world. Engineers, before constructing a building will build many scaled-down models of the building and test them (they stick them in wind tunnels to make sure they don't fall over and that sort of thing). It's crucial that these models behave in the same ways as the real building will do, otherwise the tests on the model become a

Why is it important to measure the accuracy of the mean?

pointless exercise (because they are inaccurate). A direct parallel can be drawn to what is done in statistics: imagine the population is the building we were just discussing, the sample is a scaled-down version of the population and we use it to build models (like the scaled-down models of the building), it's important that these models are accurate otherwise the inferences we draw about the population (or building) will be inaccurate.

In the previous section I mentioned that the mean was the most accurate model of a data set that we could have. However, it will only ever be a perfect representation of the data if all of the scores we collect are the same. Figure 4.5 demonstrates this point using two data sets representing ratings of two books – 'obsessions and compulsions' by Dr. Didi Check (circles) and 'matrix algebra is fun, honestly' by Dr. Ted Dius (triangles). Dr. Check's book has been given five star ratings from all seven customers, and the mean is, therefore, five. You'll notice that the line representing this mean passes through every rating showing that this mean is a perfect reflection of every point in the data set. However, Dr. Dius' book has much more variable ratings and the line that represents the mean of these data only passes through two of the seven scores. For the remaining five scores there is a difference between the observed rating and the one predicted by the mean. For these ratings the mean is not a perfect model. If we wanted to work out how representative the mean is of the data, the simplest thing to do would be to look at these differences between the raw scores and the mean. When the mean is a perfect fit

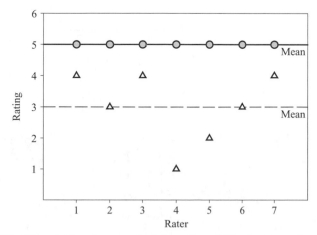

Figure 4.5 Graph showing a set of data for which the mean is a perfect fit (circles) and another set of data for which the mean is an imperfect fit (triangles)

of the data these differences are all zero (there is no difference between the mean and each data point). However, unless you test a bunch of clones you'll never collect a set of psychological data in which all the scores are the same (and if you do you should be worried!). There will always be some differences between the mean (which is typically not a value that actually exists in the raw scores) and the raw scores. It's fine to have these differences but if the mean is a very good representation of the data then these differences will be small.

Figure 4.6 shows the number of hallucinations that each of seven amphetamine users had in a day, and also the mean number that we calculated earlier on. The line representing the mean is our model, and the circles are the observed data. The diagram also has a series of vertical lines that connect each observed value to the mean. These lines represent the differences between what our model predicts (the mean) and the data we actually collected; these differences are known as *deviations*. The magnitude of these differences is calculated simply by subtracting the mean value ($\bar{x}$) from each of the observed values (x_i).[2] For example, the first amphetamine user had only 1 hallucination and so the difference is $x_1 - \bar{x} = 1 - 3.57 = -2.57$. Notice that the difference is a minus number, which tells us that our model *over-estimates* the number of hallucinations that this user had: it predicts that he had 3.57 hallucinations when in reality he had 1. The simplest way to use these deviations to estimate the accuracy of the model would be to add them (this would give us an estimate of the total error). If we were to do this we would find (Table 4.1) that the total deviations add up to zero:

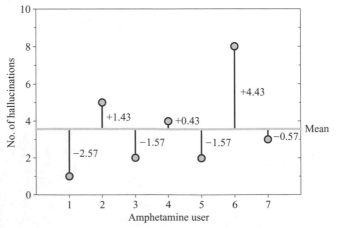

Figure 4.6 A graph showing the differences between the number of hallucinations experienced by each amphetamine user and the mean

Table 4.1

Raw Score x_i	Mean $\bar{x}$	Deviation $x_i - \bar{x}$
1	3.57	−2.57
5	3.57	1.43
2	3.57	−1.57
4	3.57	0.43
2	3.57	−1.57
8	3.57	4.43
3	3.57	−0.57
$\sum(x_i - \bar{x})$ =		0

The fact that the total of all deviations is zero indicates that there is no error within the model (the mean is a perfect fit) but we know that it is not a perfect fit because the scores deviate from the mean. The reason why the sum of all deviations equals zero is because the mean is a measure of the centre of the distribution. Therefore, about half of the scores will be greater than the mean and about half will be less. Consequently, about half of the deviations will be positive and about half will be negative; so when we add them up, they cancel each other out, giving us a total of zero. To overcome this problem we square each of the deviations (Table 4.2) so that they are all positive (the negative ones will become positive when squared because you are multiplying two negative numbers – see Box 4.2).

Table 4.2

Raw Score x_i	Mean $\bar{x}$	Deviation $x_i - \bar{x}$	Squared Deviations $(x_i - \bar{x})^2$
1	3.57	−2.57	6.6049
5	3.57	1.43	2.0449
2	3.57	−1.57	2.4649
4	3.57	0.43	0.1849
2	3.57	−1.57	2.4649
8	3.57	4.43	19.6249
3	3.57	−0.57	0.3249
$\sum(x_i - \bar{x})$ =		0	
$\sum(x_i - \bar{x})^2$ =			33.7143

The mean is actually the value that produces the lowest value of the total squared deviations and so of all values we could choose to summarize a data set, the mean is the value that gives rise to the

---

■ Box 4.4: Why is the mean the best model of the data?

All statistical models have some kind of error: that is they make a prediction about a person's score that will, in most cases, differ somewhat from the actual score that the person obtained. If we use our mean as a statistical model then we're predicting that a person's score is equal to the mean. Say we took 20 cats and measured the number of catnip sweets they could eat before falling asleep (catnip is pretty much the feline equivalent of cannabis!), the mean might be 34 sweets. If someone then asked 'how many sweets did Fuzzy eat before falling asleep?' if we don't have the raw scores, then our model (the mean) predicts that Fuzzy ate 34 sweets before passing out. However, this prediction could be wrong, Fuzzy may have only eaten 27 sweets (there is an error of 7 sweets), or he might have eaten 35 sweets (there is an error of 1). The mean is the best model of a data set because it is designed to be the value that produces the least error. So, if we want a model of the data that uses all of the observed scores (remember that the median and mode do not use all scores) then the mean is the best model we can use. However, just because the mean produces the least error this is not to say that the mean is necessarily a good model, it just produces less error than any other value we might choose as a model.

Let's look at an example that demonstrates how the mean value is always the value that produces the least error. If we use the hallucination data from the main text, the mean was 3.57. Now what error do we get if we were to use a different value as our model? Say we used two values very close to the mean like 3.56 and 3.58, and one fairly dissimilar such as 4 (see Table 4.3). We could look at the squared deviations for these three models and compare them to what we get when we use the mean.

---

least error (see Box 4.4). However, although it is the value that produces the least error, the error it does produce can still be substantial, which is why we are using the deviations between the raw scores and the mean to gauge the accuracy of the mean as a model of the data. The sum of squared deviations is more commonly referred to as the *sum of squared errors* (or *SS* for short). In itself, the sum of squared errors is a good measure of the accuracy of the mean. However, it has one obvious problem – can you think what it might be?

Imagine that we asked another seven amphetamine users about their hallucinations, what would happen to the sum of squared deviations? Well, we'd have twice as many squared deviations as before so when we added them all up the total would probably be about twice as large (and even if not twice as large it would certainly be bigger). So, the problem with the sum of squared errors as a measure of accuracy is that it gets bigger the more values we have in the data set. Although it would be meaningful to compare the current sum of squared errors

Table 4.3

Raw Score	Model	Deviation	Square Deviations
1	3.56	−2.56	6.5536
5	3.56	1.44	2.0736
2	3.56	−1.56	2.4336
4	3.56	0.44	0.1936
2	3.56	−1.56	2.4336
8	3.56	4.44	19.7136
3	3.56	−0.56	0.3136
		Total:	33.7152
1	3.58	−2.56	6.6564
5	3.58	1.44	2.0164
2	3.58	−1.56	2.4964
4	3.58	0.44	0.1764
2	3.58	−1.56	2.4964
8	3.58	4.44	19.5364
3	3.58	−0.56	0.3364
		Total:	33.7148
1	4	−3.00	9.0000
5	4	1.00	1.0000
2	4	−2.00	4.0000
4	4	.00	.0000
2	4	−2.00	4.0000
8	4	4.00	16.0000
3	4	−1.00	1.0000
		Total:	35.0000

Notice that when we used the mean (3.57), the total squared deviation was 33.7143 (see Table 4.2), when we use a value just below the mean (3.56) the total squared deviation increases slightly to 33.7152. When we use a value just above the mean (3.58) the total squared deviation is still slightly higher than when we use the mean (33.7148 compared to 33.7143), and when we use a value quite far from the mean (4), the total squared deviation increases a fair bit (from 33.7143 to 35).

with that found in say seven people who didn't use amphetamines, it wouldn't make sense to compare it with a group of a different size. To overcome this problem, we need to take account of the number of scores on which the sum of squared deviations is based. The obvious way to do this is just to divide by the number of scores (N). This in effect gives us the mean squared error. If we are interested only in the average error for the sample, then we can divide by N alone (see Box 4.6). However, we are generally interested in using the error in the sample to estimate the error in the population and so we divide the SS by the number of observations minus 1 (the reason why is explained in Box 4.5). This measure is known as the *variance*:

$$s^2 = \frac{SS}{N-1} = \frac{\sum(x_i - \bar{x})^2}{N-1} = \frac{33.7143}{6} = 5.6191$$

The variance is the average squared deviation between the mean and an observed score and so tells us on average how much a given data point differs from the mean of all data points. The variance is an incredibly useful measure because we can compare it across samples that contain different numbers of observations, however, it still has a minor problem: it is measured in units squared (because we squared each deviation during the calculation). As such, we would have to say that the average error in our data was 5.62 hallucinations-squared. It may be ridiculous to talk about 5.62 hallucinations, but it makes even less sense to talk about hallucinations-squared (how do you square a hallucination?). For this reason, we often convert the average error back into the original units of measurement by taking the square root of the variance; this measure is known as the standard deviation (Box 4.6). In this example the standard deviation is:

$$s = \sqrt{5.6191} = 2.37$$

The SS, variance and standard deviation are all measures of the same thing: the accuracy of the mean, or the variability of the data (bearing in mind that the mean will be most accurate when the scores are all similar, and will be most inaccurate when the scores are very different). These measures are all proportionate to each other, that is, a large SS (relative to the number of scores) will result in a large variance, which will result in a large standard deviation. It's important to remember in the forthcoming chapters that sums of squares, variances and standard deviations all measure the same thing. If the standard deviation is a measure of how well the mean represents the data then small standard deviations (relative to the value of the mean itself) indicate that data points are close to the mean and large standard deviations (relative to the mean) indicate that the data points are distant from the mean (i.e., the mean is not an accurate representation of the data).

Imagine we collect information about hallucinations from a new sample of seven amphetamine users. Figure 4.7 shows their data. The

■ Box 4.5: Why do we use $N - 1$?

When we calculate the variance (or average sum of squared errors) we don't divide the sum of squared errors by the number of observations (N), like you typically would when calculating an average. Instead, we divide by $N - 1$. The simple reason why is because we are using the sample to estimate the variance in the population. In fact, if we wanted to calculate the variance of the sample and weren't interested in the population at all, then we could divide by N. So, why does the fact that we're using the sample to estimate the variance in the population mean that we have to use $N - 1$?

Let's begin to answer this question using an analogy. Now, I sometimes spend my Saturday afternoons playing rugby (badly!) for Brighton third XV. On a typical Saturday the captain, despite his best efforts to structure a team, will usually have to wait for people to turn up before deciding which positions to put them in. There are 15 positions in rugby (union) and each requires different skills. When the first player arrives, the captain has the choice of 15 positions in which to place this player. This player might be a burly 22 stone muscle man, so you decide that he should be a prop in the scrum (a good position for burly men), so the captain places him in position 1, therefore, one position on the pitch is now occupied. Say I arrived next (I'm keen), the captain still has the choice of 14 positions in which he can play me – he has the freedom to choose a position. Now I'm kind of puny, weak, skinny and crap so you might decide to put me on the wing because the only thing I'm good at is running away from burly 22 stone men (and if I was put in the scrum my back would snap!), so that's another position gone – there are only 13 left. As more players arrive, the captain will reach the point at which 14 of the 15 positions have been filled. When the final player arrives the captain has no freedom to choose where he (or she) plays – there is only one position left. So, we can say there are 14 degrees of freedom, that is, for 14 players you have some degree of choice over where they play, but for 1 player you have no choice. The *degrees of freedom* are one less than the number of players.

How does this analogy relate to samples and populations? Well, if we take a sample of five observations from a population, then these five scores are free to vary in any way – they can be any value (e.g. 5, 6, 2, 9, 3). Now, when we use samples to infer things about the population from which they came the first thing we do is assume that the sample mean is the same as that in the population (so, for these data we fix the population mean at 5). As such, we hold one parameter constant. With this parameter fixed, can all five scores now vary? The answer is no because to keep the mean constant only four values are free to vary. For example, if we collected five new scores and the first four were 5, 7, 1, and 8, then the final value must be 4 to ensure that the mean is equal to the value that we fixed it at (5). Therefore, if we hold one parameter constant then the degrees of freedom must be one less than the sample size ($N - 1$). So in statistical terms the degrees of freedom relates to the number of observations that are free to vary.

■ Box 4.6: Standard deviations in the population

Something a lot of students get confused about is whether we're using N or $N - 1$ in the equation for the standard deviation. I mentioned in the main text that if we're calculating the standard deviation for a sample (and we're not interested in generalizing from our sample to the entire population) then we can calculate the standard deviation (the average variance) by dividing by the number of scores we collected:

$$s = \sqrt{\frac{\sum(x_i - \bar{x})^2}{N}}$$

However, if we want to use our sample to estimate the standard deviation of the population (and in psychology this is nearly always what we want to do), then we have to use the number of data points we collected minus 1:

$$s = \sqrt{\frac{\sum(x_i - \bar{x})^2}{N - 1}}$$

Why do we use $N - 1$? Well, the reason is the same as for the degrees of freedom (see Box 4.5). That is, to estimate the standard deviation of the population we have to first estimate the mean of that population by using the sample mean. If we fix the population mean at a certain value then only $N - 1$ scores will be free to vary (because the last score will have to take on the value that brings the mean to the value at which we've fixed it – see Box 4.5). Therefore, because we fix the population mean to estimate the population standard deviation, we have only $N - 1$ scores that are free to vary and so one score, because it cannot vary, must be excluded from the calculation.

---

average amount of hallucinations for this new sample is the same as our old sample (3.57); however, in this new sample the scores are much more tightly packed around the mean value (compare Figure 4.7 with Figure 4.6 to see this difference). The standard deviation of this new sample turns out to be 0.53, compared to 2.37 in our old sample. It should be clear from the two graphs that the mean better represents the new sample (in which all values are close to the mean) than it does the original sample (in which values vary much more around the mean). This accuracy is reflected in the standard deviation, which is small (compared to the mean) for the new sample and large (compared to the mean) in the old sample. This illustration hopefully clarifies why the standard deviation tells us about how well the mean represents the data.

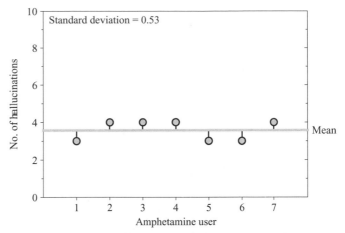

Figure 4.7 Number of hallucinations for seven amphetamine users (circles)

The Standard Deviation and the Shape of the Distribution

Not only do the variance and standard deviation tell us about the accuracy of the mean as a model of our data set, it also tells us something about the shape of the distribution of scores. If you think about what we've learnt about the mean we know that if the mean represents the data well, most of the scores will cluster close to the mean (and the standard deviation will be small relative to the mean) – as such, the distribution of scores will be quite thin. When data are more variable, they will be spread further away from the mean and so the distribution of scores will be fatter (scores distant from the mean will occur more frequently than when the standard deviation is small). Figure 4.8 illustrates this point by showing two distributions that have the same mean (50) but different standard deviations. On the left-hand side, the distribution has a standard deviation of 20 and this results in a flatter distribution that is more spread out (scores distant from the mean do occur with a reasonable frequency). The distribution on the right has a lower standard deviation (15) and this results in a slightly more pointy distribution in which scores close to the mean are very frequent but scores further from the mean become increasingly infrequent. The main point to note from the figures is that as the standard deviation gets larger, the distribution gets fatter.

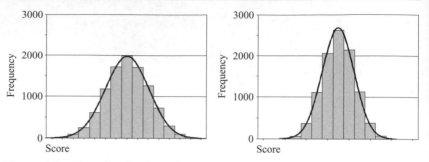

Figure 4.8   Two distributions that have the same mean but different standard deviations

The Standard Error: How Well Does My Sample Represent the Population?

So far we've learnt how we can summarize a set of data using the mean, and that we can assess the accuracy of that mean using the standard deviation. This, in itself, is very useful because it tells us whether our sample mean is representative of the scores within the sample. However, at the beginning of this chapter we talked about how scientists use samples to discover what's going on in a population (to which they don't have access). As such, the next step on from looking at how well the mean represents the sample is to look at how well the sample represents the population.

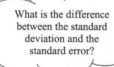

When I was talking about the advantages of the mean as a summary of a sample, I mentioned that the mean was resistant to sampling variation; that is, if we were to take different samples from the same population these samples would usually have fairly similar means. I'm now going to come back to this idea. When someone takes a sample from a population, they are taking one of many possible samples. If we were to take several samples from the same population, then each sample has its own mean, and some of these sample means will be different (not every sample will have the same mean).

Figure 4.9 shows the process of taking samples from a population. Imagine we were interested in how many units of alcohol it would take a man before they would snog a Labrador called Ben. Just suppose that in reality, if we tested every man on the planet we'd find that it takes them 10 units on average (about 5 pints of lager) before they would snog dear old Ben. Of course, we can't test everyone in the population so we use a sample. Actually, to illustrate the point we take 9 samples (shown in the diagram). For each of these

samples we can calculate the average, or *sample mean*. As you can see in the diagram, some of the samples have the same mean as the population and some have different means: the first sample of men will snog Ben after an average of 10 units but the second sample will do the deed after an average of only 9. We can actually plot the sample means as a frequency distribution just like I have done in the diagram. This distribution shows that there were three samples that had a mean of 10, means of 9 and 11 occurred in two samples each, and means of 8 and 12 occurred in only one sample each. The

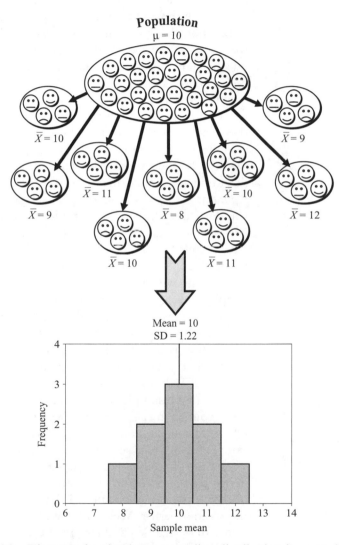

Figure 4.9   Diagram showing how a sampling distribution is created

end result is a nice symmetrical distribution known as a *sampling distribution*. A sampling distribution is simply the frequency distribution of sample means from the same population. In theory we'd take hundreds or thousands of samples to construct a sampling distribution, but I'm just using 9 to keep the diagram simple! OK, so the sampling distribution tells us about the behaviour of samples from the population, and you'll notice that it is centred at the same value as the mean of the population (i.e., 10). This means that if we took the average of all sample means we'd get the value of the population mean. Now, if the average of the sample means is the same value as the population mean, then if we know the accuracy of that average then we'd know something about how likely it is that a given sample is representative of the population. To work out the accuracy of the mean of the sample means we could again just look at the sampling distribution: if it is very spread out then it means that sample means tend to vary a lot and can be quite different, whereas if the distribution is quite thin then most sample means are very similar to each other (and the population mean). If we wanted a value to represent how accurate a sample is likely to be then obviously we can simply calculate the standard deviation of the sampling distribution (that is, the standard deviation of sample means). In the example in which we took 9 samples, the standard deviation of sample means is 1.22 and this value is known as the *standard error of the mean* (*SE*). The standard error is simply the standard deviation (or variability) of sample means. A large value tells us that sample means can be quite different from each other and, therefore, a given sample may not be representative of the population. It could be that we just happened to pick a sample that is full of people who will snog a Labrador when they are sober, or a sample of people who need to drink copious amounts before they'd even think about exchanging saliva with a canine. Small values of the standard error tell us that the sample is likely to be a fair reflection of the population (because sample means are all very similar), and so this means that although it is still possible that we happen to have got a sample of Labrador-snogging weirdos, it is much less likely (because these extreme samples are not very common).

Of course, in reality we cannot collect hundreds of samples, calculate their means, and then calculate the standard deviation of those sample means and so we rely on an approximation of the standard error. Fortunately, there are people who love nothing more than doing really hard statistical stuff and they have come up with ways in which the sample standard deviation can be used to approximate the standard error. We don't need to understand why this approximation works (thank goodness!) we can just trust that these people are ridiculously clever and know what they're talking about. The standard error can be calculated by dividing the sample[3] standard deviation (*s*) by the square root of the sample size (*N*):

$$\sigma_{\bar{X}} = \frac{s}{\sqrt{N}}$$

4.3 Confidence Intervals

We've just seen that if we collected lots of samples from the same population and calculated their means then it would be possible to plot the frequency distribution of those means, and by using the standard deviation of this distribution (the standard error) we could get a good idea of how accurately a particular sample mean represents the population. We could take a different approach to assessing the accuracy of sample means and that is to calculate boundaries within which most sample means will fall. Imagine that we collected 100 samples of data regarding the number of units necessary before a man will snog a Labrador, and for each we calculated the mean. From these means (and the resulting sampling distribution) we could calculate the boundaries within which those samples lie. It might be that the lowest mean is 2 units and the highest mean is 18 units. Now, based on this finding we could say that we were 100% confident that the mean of any other samples we draw from that population will also fall within these limits (it will be greater than or equal to 2 units and less than or equal to 18 units). Now usually we're not interested in 100% confidence and so we will usually, as psychologists, be content with being 95% confident. In this case we could calculate the limits within which 95 of our 100 samples will fall. These limits may be slightly less, say, 3 and 17 units. These boundaries are known as a *confidence interval*. Typically we look at 95% confidence intervals, and sometimes 99% confidence intervals, but they all have a similar interpretation: they are the limits within which a certain percentage (be that 95% or 99%) of sample means will fall. So, when you see a 95% confidence interval for a mean think of it like this: if we'd collected 100 samples, then 95 of these samples would have a mean within the boundaries of the confidence interval. The confidence interval can easily be calculated once the standard error is known because the lower boundary of the confidence interval is the mean minus two times the standard error, and the upper boundary is the mean plus two standard errors. As such the mean is always in the centre of the confidence interval.

If the mean represents the data well, then the confidence interval of that mean should be small indicating that 95% of sample means would be very similar to the one obtained. If the sample mean is a bad representation of the population then the confidence interval will be very wide indicating that a different sample might produce a mean quite different to the one we have. We'll talk more about confidence intervals in the next chapter.

4.4 Reporting Descriptive Statistics

The final thing we need to have a look at is how to report descriptive statistics. Typically, when we do experimental research we're interested in reporting the mean of one or more samples. We have a choice of either reporting this mean in words or graphically. When we present the mean in words, we usually will include information about the accuracy of that mean. So, we might simply report the mean followed by the standard deviation. However, because we're usually interested in how well the mean represents the population and not how well it represents the sample, we should actually report the standard error (or less commonly a confidence interval). In terms of format, most psychology journals have adopted the conventions laid out by the American Psychological Association (or APA for short) in their publications manual, which is now in its fifth edition (APA, 2001). Usually, we report any numbers to two decimal places and there are various standard abbreviations for statistical values:

- M = Mean
- Mdn = Median
- SE = Standard Error
- SD = Standard Deviation

Let's have a look at some examples of how to report a mean and the associated standard error in correct APA format. We can simply state the mean within a sentence and parenthesize the standard error:

> ➤ The mean number of units drunk before snogging Ben the Labrador was 10.00 units ($SE = 1.22$).
> ➤ On average the Labradors had to be given 26.65 units of alcohol ($SE = 3.42$) before they would play tonsil hockey with any of the blokes.

However, it's more common to parenthesize both the mean and standard error within a sentence that would otherwise make sense even if these parenthesized values were excluded:

> ➤ Women needed substantially more units of alcohol ($M = 17.24$, $SE = 2.53$) than men ($M = 10.00$, $SE = 1.22$) before they would exchange saliva with a Labrador.
> ➤ Although Labradors would lick the participant's feet after very little alcohol ($M = .28$, $SE = .11$), they needed considerably more before they would do the tongue tango with the men ($M = 26.65$, $SE = 3.42$).

The second approach is to report means by using a graph and then not report the actual values in the text. The choice of using a graph or writing the values in the text largely depends on what you want to report. If you just have one or two means you might decide that a graph is superfluous, but when you have lots of means to report, a graph can be a very useful way to summarize the data. If you do use a graph then you shouldn't really report values of the mean in the text (the assumption is that the reader can determine the value of the mean from the graph). There are two types of graph we use to illustrate means: a bar chart and a line chart. In both cases it is very important to include error bars, which are vertical bars indicating the size of the standard error. Figure 4.10 shows an example of a bar chart and a line graph. The bar chart shows the mean units of alcohol that men or women would have to drink before kissing a dog; the gender of the person being kissed is displayed as different bars. Each bar represents the mean, but each mean is also spanned by a funny 'I' shape; this is called an error bar.

Error bars can represent many things: the standard deviation of the sample, the standard error estimated from the sample, or a confidence interval for the mean. The error bars in Figure 4.10(a) display the 95% confidence interval of the mean of each experimental condition (in this case whether a man or woman was kissing the dog). I explained previously that if we were to take 100 samples from a population and calculate the mean of each, then the confidence interval represents the limits within which 95 of those 100 means would fall. Looking at the confidence interval on the bar labelled male in Figure 4.10 we see it ranges from about 9 to 11, with the mean being about halfway between at 10 units of alcohol. This confidence interval is said to have a lower limit of 9 and an upper limit of 11, and if we took 100 samples from the same population and calculated the mean, 95 of these means would lie between 9 and 11 (the remaining 5 means would lie outside of these limits). An error bar graph, therefore, displays the limits within which the majority of sample means (from the same population) lie. You may notice that the error bar for females is much wider than the bar for males, which indicates that this mean is more variable across samples. So, although men are fairly consistent

What is an error bar?

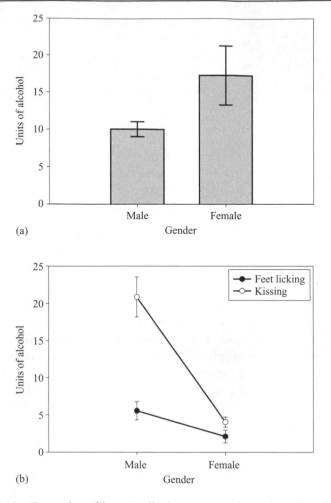

Figure 4.10   Examples of how to display means using a bar chart (a) and a line graph (b)

in the quantity they need to drink before kissing a dog (in 95% of samples it will be between 9 and 11 units), women vary a lot more (in 95% of samples a women will need between 13 and 21 units). As such, the sample of the men is much more representative of its population.

Figure 4.10(b) shows a line chart, which shows the average number of units of alcohol that a dog would need to drink before either kissing a man or woman, or licking their feet. Again, the gender of the person being kissed or having their feet licked is shown on the x-axis (the horizontal), but because we have more than one activity (we have foot licking as well as kissing) we can represent these activities as different lines. We have four means in total and each one has an error bar, and we use the lines to connect means that relate to the same activity. This allows us to examine different patterns in the data for different activities. If we look at foot licking first, we can see that dogs require relatively little alcohol before they will lick either a male or a female's feet (the line is quite flat). This is because dogs are sick and vulgar animals that love to lick smelly feet, unlike cats, which have far more sense and lick only catnip sweets! If we look at kissing then we see that for females there is again relatively little alcohol required, yet to kiss a man, dogs will require a huge amount of alcohol (and who can blame them!). In fact, the average dog would rather lick a man's feet than kiss him. Nevertheless, this graph illustrates how useful line charts can be to show trends in the data. In fact you've just looked at your first interaction graph and we'll be talking about these kinds of graphs in Chapter 6.

4.5   Summary

In this chapter we have started to look at how we use samples to tell us things about a larger population. We've also seen that we can summarize our data in several ways. First, we can use graphs that show how often each score occurs (frequency distributions) and these graphs often have distinct shapes (they can be symmetrical or skewed, and flat or pointy). Second, we looked at numeric ways to summarize samples of data. These simple models of the sample can take many forms such as the most frequent score (the mode), the middle score in the distribution (the median) and the score that produces the least squared error between the data points and that value (the mean). The mean represents the typical score and because it is a model that uses all of the data collected we need to ascertain how well it fits the data we've collected. This is done by looking at the errors between the mean and all of the scores; we square these errors and add them up to give us the sum of squared errors. This value will depend on the number of scores so we can divide it by the number of scores (actually it's $N - 1$) collected to give us the mean squared error, or variance. If we take the square root of this value we get the standard deviation, which is a measure of how accurate the mean is; it tells us whether the scores in our sample are all close to the mean (small SD) or very different from the mean (big SD). Finally, we can look at how well the sample mean represents the population by looking at the standard error, which could be calculated by taking lots of samples and calculating their mean and then working out the standard deviation of these sample means.

4.6   Practical Tasks

Now, using the results sections in Chapters 13 and 16, think about the following:

- Have the means been presented correctly?
- Could the descriptive statistics be presented better?
- For each graph write down the mean value in each condition and comment on the error bar (is it big or small and what does this tell us about the mean?).

4.7   Further Reading

Rowntree, D. (1981). *Statistics without tears: a primer for non-mathematicians.* London: Penguin. Still one of the best introductions to statistical theory (apart from this book obviously!).

Wright, D. B. (2002). *First steps in statistics.* London: Sage. Chapters 1 and 3 are very accessible introductions to descriptive statistics.

Notes

[1] In fact this would be a dangerous conclusion because the sample is still very small. However, Tversky and Kahneman (1971) note that we often have very exaggerated confidence in conclusions based on small samples if everyone in that sample behaves in the same way.

[2] The x_i is the observed score for the ith person. The i could be replaced with a number that represents a particular individual or could even be replaced with a name, so if Dan was the sixth amphetamine user then, $x_i = x_{Dan} = x_6 = 8$.

[3] In fact it should be the *population* standard deviation (σ) that is divided by the square root of the sample size, however, for large samples this is a reasonable approximation.

5   Inferential Statistics

Describing a single sample and the population from which it came is fine but it doesn't really help us to answer the types of research questions that we generated in Chapter 2. To answer research questions we typically need to employ inferential statistics – so called because they allow us to infer things about the state of the world (or the human mind if you're a psychologist).

5.1   Testing Hypotheses

Scientists are usually interested in testing hypotheses, which put more simply means that they're trying to test the scientific questions that they generate. Within most research questions there is some kind of inherent prediction that the researcher has made. This prediction is called an *experimental hypothesis* (it is the prediction that your experimental manipulation will have some effect). Of course, there is always the reverse possibility – that your prediction is wrong and the experiment has no effect – and this is called the *null hypothesis*. If we look at some of the research questions from Chapter 2 we can see what I mean:

➢ *Alcohol makes you fall over*: the experimental hypothesis is that those that drink alcohol will fall over more than those that don't drink alcohol; the null hypothesis is that people will fall over the same amount regardless of whether they have drunk alcohol.

➢ *Children learn more from interactive CD-ROM teaching tools than from books*: the experimental hypothesis is that learning is better when CD-ROMs are used than when books are used, and the null hypothesis would be that learning is the same regardless of which method is used.

> *Frustration creates aggression*: the experimental hypothesis is that if we frustrate people then their aggression will increase, whereas the null hypothesis is that aggression will remain the same regardless of whether the person is frustrated.

> *Men and women use different criteria to select a mate*: the experimental hypothesis is that if we compare men and women's criteria for mate selection they will be different, but the null hypothesis would be that males and females use the same criteria.

> *Depressives have difficulty recalling specific memories*: the experimental hypothesis is that depressives cannot recall specific memories as easily as non-depressed people, and the null hypothesis would be that depressed and non-depressed people recall specific memories with equal ease.

Inferential statistics tell us whether the experimental hypothesis is likely to be true. So, these statistical tests help us to confirm or reject our experimental predictions. Of course, we can never be completely sure that either hypothesis is correct, and so we end up working with probabilities. Specifically we calculate the probability that the results we have obtained are a chance result – as this probability decreases, we gain greater confidence that the experimental hypothesis is actually correct and that the null hypothesis can be rejected. We've already come across this idea on page 25 where we saw how the tea tasting abilities of an old lady could be tested by setting her increasingly harder challenges. Only when there was a very small probability that she could complete the task by luck alone would we conclude that she had genuine skill in detecting whether milk was poured into a cup before or after the tea was added. In this earlier section, we also mentioned that Fisher suggested that we should use 95% as a threshold for confidence: only when we are 95% certain that a result is genuine (i.e. not a chance finding) should we accept it as being true. The opposite way to look at this is to say that if there is only a 5% probability of something occurring by chance then we can accept that it is a true finding. This criterion of 95% confidence forms the basis of modern statistics and yet there is very little justification for it other than Fisher said so (and to be fair he was a very clever bloke!). Nevertheless, I've often wondered how psychology would look today if Fisher had woken up that day in a 90% kind of a mood. Typically research journals have a bias towards publishing positive results (in which the experimental hypothesis is supported) and so just imagine how many theories have been lost because researchers were only 94% confident that the data supported their ideas? Had Fisher woken up in a 90% mood that morning, many different theories might have reached public attention and we might have very different models of the human mind. We might have found that cats are the most intelligent beings on this planet, that statistics lecturers are really interesting people who captivate social gatherings with their wit and charm, or that Freud was actually right about castration anxiety – OK, maybe the last one is stretching things too far!

Gaining Confidence about Experimental Results

To understand how we can apply Fisher's ideas about statistical confidence to an experiment let's stick with the simplest experimental design. In this design you have only two conditions: in one of them you do nothing (the control condition) and in the other you manipulate your causal variable in some way (see Chapters 1 and 3 for more detail). For example, imagine we were interested in whether having a brain affected a person's ability to give statistics lectures (see Figure 5.1). We could test this using two groups of lecturers: one group has nothing done to them (the control condition), whereas a second group has their brains removed (the experimental group). The outcome we are interested in is the students' average rating of each lecturer's skills as a lecturer. If we did nothing to both groups, then they would just be two samples from a population of statistics lecturers. We have already seen that samples from the same population typically have very similar means (see page 132). However, the two sample means might be slightly different because we'd expect to find some variation between the lecturers in the two samples simply because lecturers in the samples will differ in their ability, motivation, intelligence, enthusiasm and more importantly their love of statistics! (You may have noticed that lecturers vary naturally in their lecturing skills). To sum up, if we were to take two samples of lecturers from the same population we'd expect the sample means to be roughly the same, although some subtle difference will exist. Now, when we talked about sampling distributions earlier (see page 132) we saw that the vast majority of sample means will be fairly similar to the population mean, and only very few samples will be substantially different. As such, if we found that the means in our two samples of lecturers were substantially different this would be a very rare occurrence: it would happen only if, by chance alone, we selected a sample of very good, or very bad, lecturers that were not representative of the population as a whole.

Now, what happens if we do something to one of our samples? Well, if we took one sample of lecturers and removed their brains

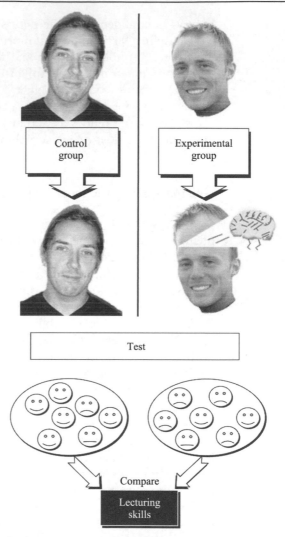

Figure 5.1 A basic experiment to test whether the removal of a lecturer's brain affects their lecturing ability

then we would expect the mean in this sample to change also – we might predict that their lecturing got worse (although on thinking about it, it would probably get better!). So, we'd expect the sample means to be different because one of the sample means will be lower because we removed the brains of the people within it. This sample no longer represents the population of lecturers: it represents the population of lecturers that have had their brains removed – a different population! When we do an experiment like this and we find that our samples have very different means then there are two possible explanations:

1. The manipulation that was carried out on the participants (i.e. removal of their brain) has changed the thing we're measuring (in this case lecturing skills). The implication is that our samples have come from two different populations, or
2. The samples come from the same population but have different means because we have inadvertently selected samples that are very different from each other (because of the characteristics of the people within them). The implication here is that the experiment has had no effect and that the observed difference between the samples is just a fluke.

When sample means are very different then it is very unlikely that they have come from the same population (because we know from sampling distributions that the majority of samples will have quite similar means). So, in simple terms, the bigger the difference between our sample means, the more unlikely it is that these samples came from the same population – and the more confident we can be that our experiment has had an effect. When sample means are fairly similar it becomes more probable that they could have come from the same population – so we become less confident that our experiment has had an effect.

These ideas are the basis of hypothesis testing. Simplistically, we can calculate the probability that two samples come from the same population; when this probability is high then we conclude that our experiment has had no effect (the null hypothesis is true), but when this probability is very small, we conclude that the experiment has had an effect (the experimental hypothesis is true). How do we decide what probability is small enough to accept that our experimental hypothesis is true? Well, again, this is where we use Fisher's criterion of 5% (which expressed as a probability value is .05). If the probability of the two samples being from the same population is less than or equal to .05 (i.e. 1 in 20 or less) then we reject the null hypothesis and accept that our experimental manipulation has been successful.

How Do We Calculate the Probability that our Samples are from the Same Population?

Actually, this is not a straightforward question to answer because the exact method depends upon your experimental design and the test you're using. However, it is possible to outline some general principles. We've just seen that in almost any experiment there are two basic sources of variation (see also Chapter 3):

> *Systematic variation*: This variation is due to the experimenter doing something to all of the participants in one sample but not in the other sample or samples.
> *Unsystematic variation*: This is variation due to natural differences between people in different samples (such as differences in intelligence or motivation).

In essence, whenever we're trying to find differences between samples we have to calculate a test statistic. A test statistic is simply a statistic that has known properties; specifically we know its frequency distribution. By knowing this, we can work out the probability of obtaining a particular value. A good analogy to this is the age at which people die. We know the distribution of the age of death from years of past experience and data. So, we know that on average men die at about 75 years old, we also know that this distribution is fairly top-heavy; that is, most people die above the age of about 50 and it's fairly unusual to die in your 20s (he says with a sigh of relief!). So, the frequencies of the age of demise at older ages are very high but are lower at younger ages. From these data, it would be possible to calculate the probability of someone dying at a certain age. If we randomly picked someone and asked them their age, and it was 57, we could tell them how likely it is that they will die before their next birthday (this is a great way to become very unpopular with older relatives!). Also, say we met a man of 112, we could calculate how probable it was that he would have lived that long (this probability would be very small – most people die before they reach that age). The way we use test statistics is rather similar: we know their distributions and this allows us, once we've calculated the test statistic, to discover the probability of having found a value as big as we have. So, if we calculated a test statistic and its value was 112 (rather like our old man) we can then calculate the probability of obtaining a value that large.

So, how do we calculate these test statistics? Again, this will depend on the design of the experiment and the test you're using, however, when comparing the means of different samples, the test statistics typically represent the same thing:

$$\text{Test statistic} = \frac{Systematic\ variance}{Unsystematic\ variance}$$

The exact form of this equation changes from test to test, but essentially we're always comparing the amount of variance created by an experimental effect against the amount of variance due to random factors (see Box 5.1 for a more detailed explanation). The reason

▣ Box 5.1: Sources of variance – a piece of cake!

Imagine we were interested in whose music was scarier: Slipknot or Marilyn Manson. We could play a track from each band to different people and measure their heart rate (which should indicate arousal). Now the heart rate scores we get will vary: different people will have different heart rates. If we want to find out by how much people's scores vary we could calculate the sum of squared errors between all scores and the mean of all scores (see the section beginning on page 120) – this is known as the total sum of squares, SS_T. This is a crude measure of the total difference between heart rate scores. In Chapter 3 we also saw that there are basically two explanations for variability in scores: the experimental manipulation and individual differences. The amount of variability caused by individual differences in people can be calculated by looking at the sum of squared differences between each person's score and the mean of the group to which they belong. This sum of squared errors is sometimes called the residual sum of squares, SS_R. The effect of our experiment can also be measured by a sum of squared errors called the model sum of squares, SS_M. The exact details of how to calculate these values are beyond this book, but if you're interested I go into it in my other book (Field, 2000). The variability between scores is a bit like a big cake. The total sum of squares tells us how big our cake is to begin with: a large SS_T tells us we're dealing with a huge five tier wedding cake (there is a lot of variation in heart rate) whereas a small value indicates that we have a small muffin (there are very few differences in heart rate)! This cake can be cut into two. Imagine that our experiment is a person, now we're interested in how much of this cake this person can eat. If the experiment is successful then it will eat a lot of cake, so there won't be much left over, but if it is unsuccessful then it will only nibble a few crumbs and then leave the rest. Put another way, we hope that our experiment is a big greedy cake-loving lard-monster who'll gobble up most of the cake; conversely it would be a disaster if our experiment turned out to be Kate Moss! If there are a lot of differences between heart rates after listening to Slipknot compared to Marilyn Manson then the model sum of squares will be big. We could think of this like Marilyn Manson and Slipknot having eaten a lot of the cake (of course I realize that both bands would probably prefer to eat goats and that sort of thing but let's assume that after a hard day of corrupting today's youth they like a nice piece of cake) – and there will be only a small piece of cake left over. Figure 5.2 shows how the total variation (the cake) is broken into two constituent pieces. Imagine in this example we started with 50 units of variation (so, $SS_T = 50$) and the experiment could explain 30 of these units (so, Marilyn and Slipknot ate 30 of the 50 units of cake, $SS_M = 30$). That means there are 20 units left that can't be explained ($SS_R = 20$).

Now if we want to know something about the success of our experiment, there are two ratios we can look at. The first thing to do is to compare the effect of the experiment to the effect of nothing. This ratio is usually adapted to be used as a test statistic:

$$\text{Test statistic} \propto \frac{SS_M}{SS_R}$$

continues

■ **Box 5.1:** *continued*

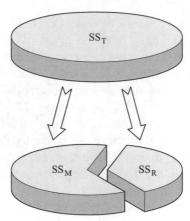

Figure 5.2 The variation between scores is like a cake: we can cut it into two slices: one represents the effect of the experiment and the other represents individual differences or random factors

In this example the test statistic would be proportionate to (that's what the symbol means) 30/20, or 1.5. Another useful measure is how much of the cake the experiment can account for:

$$r^2 = \frac{SS_M}{SS_T}$$

This ratio is similar to the past one except that this time we divide by the initial size of the cake (the total variation). In this example we'd get 30/50 or 0.6. This value is a proportion so we can express it in terms of a percentage by multiplying by 100 (in this case it becomes 60%). So we could say that listening to Slipknot instead of Marilyn Manson can explain 60% of the total variability in heart rates. This ratio is known as *r*-square, or *the coefficient of determination*, and if you take the square root of the value, you get *r*, the Pearson correlation coefficient (see Field, 2000, for more details on partitioning variance).

why this ratio is so useful is intuitive really: if our experiment has had an effect then we'd expect it to create more variance than random factors alone. In this case, the test statistic will always be greater than 1 (but not necessarily significant). If the experiment has created as much variance as random factors then the test statistic will be 1 exactly, and it means that our manipulation hasn't created any more variance than if we'd done nothing (i.e. the experimental manipulation hasn't done much). If the random factors have created more variance than the experimental manipulation then this means that the manipulation has done less than if we hadn't done anything at all (and the test statistic will be less than 1).

Once we've calculated a particular test statistic we can then use its frequency distribution to tell us how probable it was that we got this value. As we saw in the previous section, these probability values tell us how likely it is that our experimental effect is genuine and not just a chance result. If our experimental effect is large compared to the natural variation between samples then the systematic variation will be bigger than the unsystematic variation and the test statistic will be greater than 1. The more variation our manipulation creates compared to the natural variation, the bigger the test statistic will be. The bigger the test statistic is, the more unlikely it is to occur by chance (like our 112 year old man). So, we find that as test statistics get bigger, the probability of them occurring becomes smaller. When this probability falls below .05 (Fisher's criterion), we accept this as giving us enough confidence to assume that the test statistic is as large as it is because of our experimental manipulation – and *not* because of random factors. Put another way, we accept our experimental hypothesis and reject our null hypothesis – however, Box 5.2 explains some common misconceptions about this process.

Two Types of Mistake

We have seen that we use inferential statistics to tell us about the true state of the world (to a certain degree of confidence). Specifically,

What are Type I and Type II errors?

we're trying to see whether our experimental manipulation has had some kind of effect. There are two possibilities in the real world: our experimental manipulation has actually made a difference to our samples, or our experimental manipulation has been completely useless and had no effect whatsoever. We have no way of knowing which of these possibilities is true. We look at test statistics and their associated probability to tell us which of the two is more likely. It is important that we're as accurate as possible: we don't want to make mistakes about whether our experiment has had an effect. This is why Fisher originally said that we should be very conservative and only accept a result as being genuine when we are 95% confident – or when there is only a 5% chance that the results could occur by chance. However, even if we're 95% confident there is still a small chance that we get it wrong. In fact there are two mistakes we can make:

➤ *Type I error*: This is when we believe that our experimental manipulation has been successful, when in fact it hasn't. This

■ **Box 5.2: What we can and can't conclude from a significant test statistic**

1. **The importance of an effect**: We've seen already that the basic idea behind hypothesis testing involves us generating an experimental hypothesis (the means of our experimental conditions will differ) and a null hypothesis (the means of our experimental conditions will be the same). If the probability of obtaining the value of our test statistic by chance is less than .05 then we generally accept the experimental hypothesis as true: our means are indeed different. Normally we say 'our experiment had a *significant* effect'. However, don't be fooled by that word 'significant', because even if the probability of our effect being a chance result is small (less than .05) it doesn't necessarily follow that the effect is important. Very small and unimportant effects can turn out to be statistically significant just because huge numbers of people have been used in the experiment (see page 152).

2. **Non-significant results**: Once you've calculated your test statistic, you calculate the probability of that test statistic occurring by chance; if this probability were greater than .05 you reject your experimental hypothesis. However, this does *not* mean that the null hypothesis is true. Remember that the null hypothesis is that the means in different groups are identical, and all that a non-significant result tells us is that the means are not different enough to be anything other than a chance finding. It doesn't tell us that the means are the same; as Cohen (1990) points out, a non-significant result should never be interpreted (despite the fact it often is) as 'no difference between means' or 'no relationship between variables'. Cohen also points out that the null hypothesis is *never* true because we know from sampling distributions (see page 132) that two random samples will have slightly different means, and even though these differences can be very small (e.g. one mean might be 10 and another might be 10.00000000000000000001) they are nevertheless different. In fact, even such a small difference would be deemed as statistically significant if a big enough sample were used (see page 152). So, significance testing can never tell us that the null hypothesis is true, because it never is!

3. **Significant results**: OK, we may not be able to accept the null hypothesis as being true, but we can at least conclude that it is false when our results are significant, right? Wrong! A significant test statistic is based on probabilistic reasoning, which severely limits what we can conclude. Again, Cohen (1994), who was an incredibly lucid writer on statistics, points out that formal reasoning relies on an initial statement of fact followed by a statement about the current state of affairs, and an inferred conclusion. This syllogism illustrates what I mean:

➤   If a man has no legs then he can't play football.
   ○   This man plays football.
   ○   Therefore, this man has legs.

The syllogism starts with a statement of fact that allows the end conclusion to be reached because you can deny the man has no legs (the antecedent) by denying that he can't play football (the consequent). A comparable statement of the null hypothesis would be:

➤ If the null hypothesis is correct, then this test statistic can not occur.
○ This test statistic has occurred.
○ Therefore, the null hypothesis is false.

This is all very nice except that the null hypothesis is not represented in this way because it is based on probabilities. Instead it should be stated as follows:

➤ If the null hypothesis is correct, then this test statistic is highly unlikely.
○ This test statistic has occurred.
○ Therefore, the null hypothesis is highly unlikely.

If we go back to a football example we could get a similar statement:

➤ If a man plays football then he probably doesn't play for England (this is true because there are thousands of people who play football and only a handful make it to the dizzy heights of the England squad!).
○ Phil Neville plays for England.
○ Therefore, Phil Neville probably doesn't play football.

Now although at first glance this seems perfectly logical (Phil Neville certainly doesn't play football in the conventional sense of the term) it is actually completely ridiculous – the conclusion is wrong because Phil Neville is a professional footballer (despite his best attempts to prove otherwise!). This illustrates a common fallacy in hypothesis testing. In fact hypothesis testing allows us to say very little about the null hypothesis.

would occur when, in the real world our experimental manipulation has no effect, yet we have got a large test statistic because we coincidentally selected two very dissimilar samples. So, the sample means were very different but not because of the experimental manipulation. If we use Fisher's criterion then the probability of this error is .05 (or 5%) when the experiment has no effect – this value is known as the α-level. Assuming our experiment has no effect, if we replicated the experiment 100 times we could expect that on five occasions the sample means would be different enough to make us believe that the experiment had been successful, even though it hadn't.

➤ *Type II error*: This is when we believe that our experimental manipulation has failed, when in reality it hasn't. This would occur when in the real world the experimental manipulation does have an effect, but we obtain a small test statistic (perhaps because there is a lot of natural variation between our samples).

So, the sample means appear to be quite similar even though the experiment has made a difference to the samples. In an ideal world, we want the probability of this error to be very small (if the experiment does have an effect then it's important that we can detect it). Cohen (1992) suggests that the maximum acceptable probability of a Type II error would be .2 (or 20%) – this is called the β-level. That would mean that if we took 100 samples for which the experiment had genuinely had an effect then we would fail to find an effect in 20 of those samples (so we'd miss 1 in 5 genuine effects).

There is obviously a trade off between these two errors: if we lower the probability of accepting an effect as genuine (make α smaller) then we increase the probability that we'll reject an effect that does genuinely exist (because we've been so strict about the level at which we'll accept that an effect is genuine). The exact relationship between the Type I and Type II error is not straightforward because they are based on different assumptions: a Type I error assumes there is no effect in the population whereas a Type II error assumes there is an effect. So, although we know that as the probability of making a Type I error decreases, the probability of making a Type II error increases, the exact nature of the relationship is usually left for the researcher to make an educated guess (Howell, 2001, pp. 104–107 gives a great explanation of the trade off between errors).

Effect Sizes

The framework for testing hypotheses that I've just presented has a few problems, most of which have been briefly explained in Box 5.2. There are several remedies to these problems. The first problem we encountered was knowing how important an effect is: just because a test statistic is significant, doesn't mean that the effect it measures is meaningful or important. The solution to this criticism is to measure the size of the effect that we're testing. When we measure the size of an effect (be that an experimental manipulation or the strength of relationship between variables) it is known as an *effect size*. An effect size is simply an objective and standardized measure of the magnitude of observed effect. The fact that the measure is standardized just means that we can compare effect sizes across different studies that have measured different variables, or have used different scales of measurement (so an effect size based on speed in milliseconds could be compared to an effect size based on heart rates). Many measures of effect size have been proposed, but the most com-

Can we measure how important an effect is?

mon one is Pearson's correlation coefficient (see Field, 2001). Many of you will be familiar with the correlation coefficient as a measure of the strength of relationship between two variables, however, it is also a very versatile measure of the strength of an experimental effect. It's a bit difficult to reconcile how the humble correlation coefficient can also be used in this way, however, this is only because students are typically taught about it within the context of non-experimental research. The reason why the correlation coefficient can be used to measure the size of experimental effects is easily understood once you've read Box 5.1, in which I explain that the proportion of total variance in the data that can be explained by the experiment is equal to r^2. r-Square is a proportion and so must be a value that lies between 0 (meaning the experiment explains none of the variance at all) and 1 (meaning that the experiment can explain all of the variance); the bigger the value, the bigger the experimental effect. So, we can compare different experiments in an objective way: by comparing the proportion of total variance for which they can account. If we take the square root of this proportion, we get the Pearson correlation coefficient, r, which is also constrained to lie between 0 (no effect) and 1 (a perfect effect).[1]

The useful thing about effect sizes is that they provide an objective measure of the importance of the experimental effect. So, it doesn't matter what experiment has been done, what outcome variables have been measured, or how the outcome has been measured we know that a correlation coefficient of 0 means the experiment had no effect, and a value of 1 means that the experiment completely explains the variance in the data. What about the values in between? Luckily, Cohen (1988, 1992) has made some widely accepted suggestions about what constitutes a large or small effect:

- ➤ $r = 0.10$ (small effect): in this case the effect explains 1% of the total variance.
- ➤ $r = 0.30$ (medium effect): the effect accounts for 9% of the total variance.
- ➤ $r = 0.50$ (large effect): the effect accounts for 25% of the variance.

We can use these guidelines to assess the importance of our experimental effects (regardless of the significance of the test statistic). However, r is not measured on a linear scale so an effect with $r = .6$ isn't twice as big as one with $r = .3$! Such is the utility of effect size estimates that the American Psychological Association is now recommending that all psychologists report these effect sizes in the results of any published work. So, it's a habit well worth getting into.

A final thing to mention is that when we calculate effect sizes we calculate them for a given sample. Now, when we looked at means in a sample we saw that we used them to draw inferences about the mean of the entire population (which is the value in which we're actually interested). The same is true of effect sizes: the size of the effect in the population is the value in which we're interested, but because we don't have access to this value, we use the effect size in the sample to estimate the likely size of the effect in the population (see Field, 2001).

Statistical Power

We've seen that effect sizes are an invaluable way to express the importance of a research finding. The effect size in a population is intrinsically linked to three other statistical properties: (1) the sample size on which the sample effect size is based; (2) the probability level at which we will accept an effect as being statistically significant (the α level); and (3) the power of the test to detect an effect of that size. As such, once we know two of these properties, then we can always calculate the remaining one. It will also depend on whether the test is one- or two-tailed (see Box 5.3). Typically, in psychology we use an α level of .05 (see earlier) so we know this value already. The power of a test is the probability that a given test will find an effect assuming that one exists in the population. If you think back to page 151 you might remember that we've already come across the probability of failing to detect an effect when one genuinely exists (β, the probability of a Type II error). It follows that the probability of detecting an effect if one exists must be the opposite of the probability of not detecting that effect (i.e. $1 - \beta$). We saw on page 152 that Cohen (1988, 1992) suggests that we would hope to have a .2 probability of failing to detect a genuine effect, and so the corresponding level of power that he recommended was $1 - .2$, or .8. We should aim to achieve a power of .8, or an 80% chance of detecting an effect if one genuinely exists. The effect size in the population can be estimated from the effect size in the sample, and the sample size is determined by the experimenter anyway so that value is easy to calculate. Now, there are two useful things we can do knowing that these four variables are related:

1. **Calculate the power of a test**: Given that we've conducted our experiment, we will have already selected a value of α, we can estimate the effect size based on our sample, and we will know how many participants we used. Therefore, we can use these values to calculate β, the power of our test. If this value turns out to be .8 or more we can be confident that we achieved

◼ Box 5.3: Tests have tails

Cats have tails too ...

When we conduct a statistic test we do one of two things: (1) test a specific hypothesis such as 'when people are depressed they eat more chocolate', or (2) test a non-specific hypothesis such as 'men and women differ in the amount of chocolate they eat when they're depressed'. The former example is directional: we've explicitly said that people eat *more* chocolate when depressed (i.e. the mean amount of chocolate eaten when depressed is more than the mean amount eaten when not depressed). If we tested this hypothesis statistically, the test would be known as a **one-tailed test**. The second hypothesis is non-directional: we haven't stated whether men or women eat more chocolate when they're depressed, we've just said that men will be different from women. If we tested this hypothesis statistically, the test would be known as a **two-tailed test**.

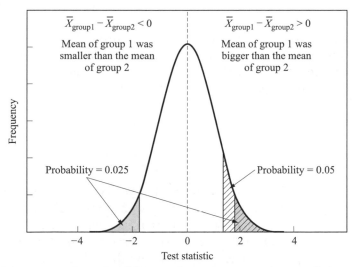

$$\overline{X}_{group1} - \overline{X}_{group2} < 0$$

Mean of group 1 was smaller than the mean of group 2

$$\overline{X}_{group1} - \overline{X}_{group2} > 0$$

Mean of group 1 was bigger than the mean of group 2

Probability = 0.025

Probability = 0.05

Frequency

Test statistic

Figure 5.3 Diagram to show the difference between one- and two-tailed tests

Imagine we wanted to discover whether men or women ate more chocolate when depressed. We took two groups: one group of depressed males and one group of depressed females. We then measured the amount of chocolate they both ate. If we have no directional hypothesis then there are three possibilities: (1) depressed men eat more chocolate than depressed women, therefore, the mean for men is larger than the mean for women and so the difference (mean for men minus the mean for women) is positive; (2) depressed men eat less chocolate than depressed women, therefore, the mean for men is smaller than the mean for women and so the difference (mean for men

continues

■ **Box 5.3** *continued*

minus the mean for women) is negative; (3) there is no difference between depressed men and women, their means are the same and so the difference (mean for men minus the mean for women) is exactly zero. This final option is the null hypothesis. The direction of the test statistic (i.e. whether it is positive or negative) will depend on whether the difference is positive or negative. Assuming we do get a difference, then to detect this difference we have to take account of the fact that the mean for males could be bigger than for females (and so derive a positive test statistic) but that the mean for males could be smaller and so derive a negative test statistic. If, at the .05 level we need to get a test statistic bigger than say 5, what do you think would happen if the test statistic is negative? Well, put simply it will be rejected even though a difference does exist. To avoid this we have to look at both ends (or tails) of the distribution of possible test statistics. This means that to keep our criterion probability of .05 we have to split this probability across the two tails: so we have .025 at the positive end of the distribution and .025 at the negative end. Figure 5.3 shows this situation – the grey areas are the areas above the test statistic needed at a .025 level of significance. Combine the probabilities at both ends and we get .05 – our criterion value. Now if we have made a prediction, then we basically put all our eggs in one basket. So, we might say that we predict that men eat more chocolate than women and so we're only interested in finding a positive difference – we only look at the positive end of the distribution. This means that we can just look for the value of the test statistic that would occur by chance with a probability of .05. Figure 5.3 shows this situation – the area containing diagonal lines is the area above the test statistic needed at a .05 level of significance. The point to take home is that if we make a one-tailed prediction then we need a smaller test statistic to find a significant result (because we are looking in only one tail).

sufficient power to detect any effects that might have existed, but if the resulting value is less, then we might want to replicate the experiment using more participants to increase the power.

2. **Calculate the sample size necessary to achieve a given level of power**: Given that we know the value of α and β, we can use past research to estimate the size of effect that we would hope to detect in an experiment. Even if no-one had previously done the exact experiment that you intend to do, we can still estimate the likely effect size based on similar experiments. We can use this estimated effect size to calculate how many participants we would need to detect that effect (based on the values of α and β that we've chosen).

The most common use is the latter: to determine how many participants should be used to achieve the desired level of power. The actual computations are very cumbersome, but fortunately, there are now computer programs available that will do them for you (one example being nQuery Adviser – see Field, 1998b for a review). Also, Cohen (1988) provides extensive tables for calculating the number of participants for a given level of power (and vice versa). Based on Cohen (1992) we can use the following guidelines: if we take the standard α level of .05 and require the recommended power of .8, then we need 783 participants to detect a small effect size ($r = .1$), 85 participants to detect a medium effect size ($r = .3$) and 28 participants to detect a large effect size ($r = .5$).

5.2 Summary

This chapter has been a bit of a crash course in the theory of inferential statistics (hopefully crash is not too ominous a word to use!). We saw that essentially we can partition variance in our scores into two sorts: (1) variance we can explain with our experimental manipulation or manipulations, and (2) variance we can't explain. Most test statistics essentially compare the variance explained by a given effect against the variance in the data that it doesn't explain. This led us to consider how we might gain confidence that a particular experimental manipulation has explained enough variance for it to reflect a genuine effect. Setting levels for this confidence involves a trade off between accepting effects that are in reality untrue (a Type I error) and rejecting effects that are in fact true (a Type II error). We discussed the importance of quantifying effects in a standard form using effect sizes, and how in turn we could use effect sizes to educate us about the power of our statistical tests and the sample size that we might need to achieve appropriate levels of power to detect an effect.

5.3 Practical Tasks

Some study questions:

- What is an effect size and why is it important?
- Should we always rely on a .05 level of significance to determine whether we believe a effect is genuine or not?
- What can we conclude from a significance test?

5.4   Further Reading

All of the following are lucid accounts of the main issues in this chapter, by one of the best statistics writers we've had in psychology.

Cohen, J. (1990). Things I have learned (so far). *American Psychologist, 45* (12), 1304–1312.

Cohen, J. (1992). A power primer. *Psychological Bulletin, 112* (1), 155–159.

Cohen, J. (1994). The earth is round (*p* < .05). *American Psychologist, 49* (12), 997–1003.

Notes

[1] The correlation coefficient can also take on minus values (but not below -1) because when these values are squared the minus signs cancel out and become positive. This is useful when we're measuring a relationship between two variables because the sign r tells us about the direction of the relationship (see Field, 2000, pp. 74–75), but in experimental research the sign of r merely reflects the way in which the experimenter coded their groups (see Field, 2000, pp. 93–95).

6 Parametric Statistics

In the last chapter, we looked at why we use inferential statistics. The next two chapters run through the most common inferential statistical tests that are used in the social sciences. For each test there'll be a brief rationale of how the test works (but luckily not a lot of maths!); what kind of output you can expect to find from SPSS (the most popular statistical package in the social sciences); how you should interpret that output (so, what are the key features of the output to look out for?), and how to report the findings in APA format. This chapter concentrates on *parametric tests*, which are tests that are constrained by certain assumptions (I'll discuss these shortly), whereas the following chapter describes tests that do not depend upon these assumptions (*non-parametric tests*).

6.1 How Do I Tell If My Data are Parametric?

Parametric tests work on the arithmetic mean and so data must be measured at an interval or ratio level (see page 8) otherwise the mean just doesn't make sense. This requirement has to be looked at subjectively and with a bit of common sense. In psychology we rarely have the luxury of knowing the level at which we've measured (see Box 1.1) but we can take an educated guess. Parametric tests also require assumptions about the variances between groups or conditions. When we use different participants the assumption is basically that the variance in one experimental condition is roughly the same as the variance in any other experimental condition. So, if we took the data in each experimental condition and calculated the variance, we would expect all of the values to be roughly the same. This is called the assumption of *homogeneity of variance*. This assumption makes intuitive sense because we saw in Chapter 4 that the variance was a measure of the accuracy of the mean. If we're using tests that compare means in different conditions then we would like these means to be equivalently accurate. A similar assumption in repeated measures designs is the sphericity assumption (which I'll discuss in detail on page 183). The assumptions of homogeneity of variance and sphericity can be easily tested using Levene's test (see page 165) and Mauchly's test (see page 184) respectively. However, you should bear in mind that the power of these tests will depend upon the sample sizes (see page 154) and so they can't always be trusted – especially in small samples.

The final assumption for parametric tests is that we assume that our data have come from a population that has a normal distribution. The easiest way to check this assumption is to draw some histograms of your data to see the shape of the distribution (see Field, 2000, pp. 37–46). There are several problems with just looking at histograms. The first is that they tell us only about the distribution of the sample and not about the distribution of the population from which the sample came (although if the sample is large enough it will be a close enough approximation). A related point is that the distributions of small data sets ($N < 30$) will be messy (by which I mean you can't get a good idea of the shape of a distribution from less than 30 observations). The final problem is obviously that looking at a distribution doesn't tell us whether the distribution is different enough from normal to be a problem – it is a very subjective approach. Instead, we usually use objective tests of the distribution, and the two tests that SPSS provides are the Kolmogorov-Smirnov (or as one of my students recently called it 'the vodka test') and Shapiro-Wilk tests. These tests compare the set of scores in the sample to a normally distributed set of scores with the same mean and standard deviation. If the test is non-significant ($p > .05$) it tells us that the distribution of the sample is not significantly different from a normal distribution (i.e. it is probably normal). If, however, the test is significant ($p < .05$) then the distribution in question is significantly different from a normal distribution (i.e. it is non-normal). These tests are very handy because in one easy procedure they tell us whether our scores are normally distributed, however, we again need to be wary because the power of these tests depends upon the sample sizes we've used (see page 154).

Let's imagine we asked readers of this book to rate how bored they were by the time they reached this chapter. They just marked on a scale from 0 (incredibly interested) to 100 (I'm so bored I'm going to pull my own teeth out of my head). If we wanted to look at the distribution of these scores we could simply plot a histogram like the one in Figure 6.1. This histogram is based on a lot of data (10,000 cases actually) and so it has a very clear shape. However it

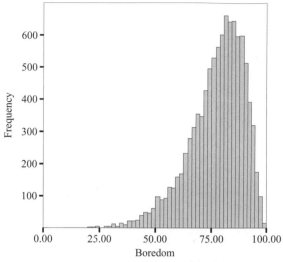

Figure 6.1 Histogram of readers' boredom ratings

does look quite skewed towards the top end of the scale (see page 113). This tells us that most scores were at the higher end of the scale (i.e. most people responded that they were so bored that they wanted to pull their own teeth out of their heads!). There are very few scores at the lower end of the scale (no-one was actually interested by the time they reached this chapter). However, this histogram alone only gives us a rough idea of the distribution, it doesn't provide an objective measure of whether this distribution is non-normal.

Field (2000, pp. 46–49) shows how to do the Kolmogorov-Smirnov (K-S from now on) tests in SPSS. SPSS produces a table like that in SPSS Output 6.1, which includes the test statistic itself, the degrees of freedom (which should equal the sample size) and the significance value of this test. Remember that if the value in the column labelled *Sig.* is less than .05 then the distribution deviates significantly from normality. For the boredom scores the test is highly significant ($p = .000$), indicating that the distribution is not normal. This result reflects the strong negative skew in the data. The test statistic in this test is denoted by D and so we could report that our data significantly deviated from normality (D (10000) $= .074$, $p < .001$).

Tests of Normality

	Kolmogorov-Smirnov[a]		
	Statistic	df	Sig.
Boredom	.074	10000	.000

a. Lilliefors Significance Correction

SPSS Output 6.1

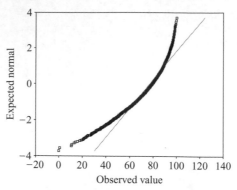

Figure 6.2   Normal Q-Q plots of boredom scores

SPSS also produces a normal Q-Q plot for any variables specified (see Figure 6.2). This chart plots the values you would expect to get if the distribution were normal (expected values) against the values actually seen in the data set (observed values). The expected values are shown as a straight diagonal line, whereas the observed values are plotted as individual points. Normally distributed data are shown by the observed values (the dots on the chart) falling exactly along the straight line (so the line is basically obscured by a load of dots). This would mean that the observed values are the same as you would expect to get from a normally distributed data set. If the dots deviate from the straight line then this represents a deviation from normality. In our boredom scores the dots form an arc that deviates away from the straight line at both ends. A deviation from normality such as this tells us that we cannot use a parametric test, because the assumption of normality is not tenable. In these circumstances we must turn to non-parametric tests as a means of testing the hypothesis of interest (see Chapter 7).

6.2   The *t*-Test

The *t*-test is used in the simplest experimental situation; that is, when there are only two groups to be compared. The test statistic produced by the test is, unsurprisingly, called *t* and it is the ratio of the difference between means (i.e. the experimental effect) divided by an estimate of the standard error of the difference between those two sample means (see Field, 2000, Chapter 6). If you think back to what the standard error represents (page 132) you might remember that it was a measure of how well a sample represents the population. We can extend the standard error to situations in which we're looking at the differences between sample means. We saw earlier in this chapter that if you took several pairs of samples from a population and calculated the difference between their means, then most of the time this difference will be close to zero. However, sometimes one or both of the samples could have a mean very deviant from the population mean and so it is possible to obtain large differences between sample means by chance alone. If you plotted these differences as a histogram, you would again have a sampling distribution with all of the properties previously described. The standard deviation of this sampling distribution would be the standard error of differences. A small standard error tells us that most pairs of samples from a population will have very similar means (i.e. the difference between sample means should normally be very small). A large standard error tells us that sample means can deviate quite a lot from the population mean and so differences between pairs of samples can be quite large by chance alone. The standard error of differences, therefore, gives us an estimate of the extent to which we'd expect sample means to be different by chance alone – it is a measure of the unsystematic variance, or variance not caused by the experiment. As such, the *t*-test is simply the difference between means as a function of the degree to which those means would differ by chance alone.

6.3   The Independent *t*-Test

You would plan to use the independent *t*-test if you are going to do an experiment using only two groups (you're comparing two means), and different participants will be used in each group (so each person will contribute only one score to the data). The word independent in the name tells us that different participants were used.

Example: One of my pet hates is 'pop psychology' books. Along with banishing Freud from all bookshops, it is my vowed ambition to rid the world of these rancid putrefaction-ridden wastes of trees. Not only do they give psychology a very bad name by stating the bloody obvious and charging people for the privilege, but they are also considerably less enjoyable to look at than the trees killed to produce them (admittedly the same could be said for the turgid tripe that I produce in the name of education but let's not go there just for now!). Anyway, as part of my plan to rid the world of popular psychology I did a little experiment. I took two groups of people who were in relationships and randomly assigned them to one of two conditions. One group read the famous popular psychology book 'Women are from Bras, men are from Penis', whereas another group read 'Marie Claire'. I tested only 10 people in each of these groups, and the dependent variable was an objective measure of their happiness with their relationship after reading the book. I didn't make any specific prediction about which reading material would improve relationship happiness.

SPSS Output for the Independent t-Test

SPSS Output 6.2 shows the output from an independent t-test; note that there are two tables. The first table summarizes the data for the two experimental conditions. From this table, we can see that both groups had 10 participants (column labelled N). The group who read 'Women are from Bras, men are from Penis' had a mean relationship happiness score of 20, with a standard deviation of 4.11. What's more, the standard error of that group (the standard deviation of the sampling distribution) was 1.30 when rounded off. In addition, the table tells us that the average relationship happiness levels in participants who read 'Marie Claire' was 24.2, with a standard deviation of 4.71, and a standard error[1] of 1.49.

The second table of output contains the main test statistics. There are actually two rows: one labelled Equal variances assumed, and the other labelled Equal variances not assumed. Earlier I said that parametric tests assume that the variances in experimental conditions are roughly equal and if the variances were not equal then we couldn't use parametric tests; well, in reality adjustments can be made to the test statistic to make it accurate even when the group variances are differ-

Group Statistics

	Book Read	N	Mean	Std. Deviation	Std. Error Mean
Relationship Happiness	Women are from Bras, Men are from Penis	10	20.0000	4.10961	1.29957
	Marie Claire	10	24.2000	4.70933	1.48922

Independent Samples Test

		Levene's Test for Equality of Variances		t-test for Equality of Means					95% Confidence Interval of the Difference	
		F	Sig.	t	df	Sig. (2-tailed)	Mean Difference	Std. Error Difference	Lower	Upper
Relationship Happiness	Equal variances assumed	.491	.492	-2.125	18	.048	-4.2000	1.97653	-8.35253	-.04747
	Equal variances not assumed			-2.125	17.676	.048	-4.2000	1.97653	-8.35800	-.04200

SPSS Output 6.2

ent. The row of the table we use depends on whether the assumption of homogeneity of variances has been broken. To tell whether this assumption has been broken we could just look at the values of the variances and see whether they are similar (in this example the standard deviations of the two groups are 4.11 and 4.71 and if we square these values then we get the variances). However, this would be very subjective and so there is a test we use to see whether the variances are different enough to cause concern. Levene's test (as it is known) resembles a *t*-test in that it tests the hypothesis that the variances in the two groups are equal (i.e. the difference between the variances is zero). So, if Levene's test is significant at $p < .05$ then we conclude that the null hypothesis is incorrect and that the variances are significantly different – the assumption of homogeneity of variances has been violated. Conversely, if Levene's test is non-significant (i.e. $p > .05$) then we accept the null hypothesis that the difference between the variances is roughly zero – the variances are more or less equal. For these data, Levene's test is non-significant (because $p = .492$, which is greater than .05) and so we should read the test statistics in the row labelled Equal variances assumed. Had the probability of Levene's test been less than .05, then we would have read the test statistics from the row labelled Equal variances not assumed.

Having established that we have homogeneity of variances, we can move on to the more interesting business of the *t*-test itself. We are told the mean difference ($20 - 24.2 = -4.2$) and the standard error of the sampling distribution of differences (1.98). The *t*-statistic is calculated by dividing the mean difference by this standard error ($t = -4.2/1.98 = -2.12$). This value is the test statistic referred to on page 146. The value of *t* is then assessed against the value of *t* you might expect to get by chance when you have certain degrees of freedom. For the *t*-test, degrees of freedom are calculated by adding the two sample sizes and then subtracting the number of samples ($df = N_1 + N_2 - 2 = 10 + 10 - 2 = 18$). SPSS produces the exact significance value of *t*, and we are interested in whether this value is less than or greater than .05. In this case the two-tailed value of *p* is .048, which is just smaller than .05, and so we could conclude that there was a significant difference between the means of these two samples. By looking at the means, we could infer that relationship happiness was significantly higher after reading 'Marie Claire' than after reading 'Women are from Bras, men are from Penis'.[2]

The final thing that this output provides is a 95% confidence interval for the mean difference. Imagine we took 100 samples from a population and compared the differences between scores in pairs of samples, then calculated the mean of these differences. We would end up with 100 mean differences between samples. The confidence interval tells us the boundaries within which 95 of these 100 mean differences would lie. So, 95% of mean differences will lie between −8.35 and −0.05. If this interval doesn't contain zero then it tells us that in 95% of samples the mean difference will not be zero. This is important because if we were to compare pairs of random samples from a population we expect most of the differences between sample means to be around zero (in reality some will be slightly above zero and others will be slightly below). If 95% of samples from our population all fall on the same side of zero (are all negative or all positive) then we can be confident that our two samples do not represent random samples from the same population. Instead they represent samples from different populations induced by the experimental manipulation – in this case, the book that they read.

Calculating the Effect Size for the Independent *t*-Test

Even though our *t*-statistic is statistically significant, this tells us nothing of whether the effect is substantive (i.e. important in practical terms): as we've seen highly significant effects can in fact be very small. To discover whether the effect is substantive we need to turn to what we know about effect sizes. It, therefore, makes sense to tell you how to convert your *t*-statistic into a standard effect size. As I mentioned, I'm going to stick with the effect size *r* because it's widely understood and frequently used. Converting a *t*-value into an *r*-value is actually really easy; we can use the following equation (from Rosenthal, 1991, p. 19):

$$r = \sqrt{\frac{t^2}{t^2 + df}}$$

We know the value of *t* and the *df* from the SPSS output and so we can compute *r* as follows:

$$r = \sqrt{\frac{(-2.125)^2}{(-2.125)^2 + 18}}$$

$$= \sqrt{\frac{4.52}{22.52}}$$

$$= .45$$

If you think back to our benchmarks for effect sizes this represents a fairly large effect (it is just below .5 – the threshold for a large effect). Therefore, as well as being statistically significant, this effect is large and so represents a substantive finding.

Interpreting and Writing the Result for the Independent *t*-Test

When you report any statistical test you usually state the finding to which the test relates, report the test statistic (usually with its degrees of freedom), the probability value of that test statistic, and more recently the American Psychological Association are, quite rightly, requesting an estimate of the effect size. To get you into good habits early, we'll start thinking about effect sizes now – before you get too fixated on Fisher's magic .05. In this example we know that the value of *t* was -2.12, that the degrees of freedom on which this was based was 18, and that it was significant at $p = .048$. This can all be obtained from the SPSS output. We can also see the means for each group. Based on what we learnt about reporting means on page 136, we could now write something like:

> ☑ On average, the reported relationship happiness after reading 'Marie Claire' ($M = 24.20$, $SE = 1.49$), was significantly higher than after reading 'Women are from Bras, men are from Penis' ($M = 20.00$, $SE = 1.30$), $t(18) = 2.12$, $p < .05$, $r = .45$.

Note how we've reported the means in each group (and standard errors) in the standard format. For the test statistic note that we've used an italic *t* to denote the fact that we've calculated a *t*-statistic, then in brackets we've put the degrees of freedom and then stated the value of the test statistic. The probability can be expressed in several ways (see Chapter 11): often people report things to a standard level of significance (such as .05) as I have done here. Other times people will report the exact significance. Finally, note that I've reported the effect size at the end – you won't see this that often in published papers but times are changing and you soon should see effect sizes being reported as standard practice. Equally valid, would be to draw a graph of our group means (including error bars – see Chapter 4) and then to report:

> ☑ The reported relationship happiness after reading 'Marie Claire', was significantly higher than after reading 'Women are from Bras, men are from Penis', $t(18) = -2.12$, $p = .048$, $r = .45$.

Note how I've now reported the exact significance. I could also state early on my criterion for the probability of a Type I error, and then not report anything relating to the probability:

> ☑ All effects will be reported at a .05 level of significance. The reported relationship happiness after reading 'Marie Claire' was significantly higher than after reading 'Women are from

Bras, men are from Penis', $t(18) = -2.12$, $r = .45$. The effect size estimate indicates that the difference in relationship happiness created by the reading material represents a large, and therefore substantive, effect.

Try to avoid writing vague, unsubstantiated things like this:

⊠   People were happier after reading 'Marie Claire', $t = -2.12$.

Happier than what? Where are the *df*? Was the result statistically significant? Was the effect important (what was the effect size)?

6.4   The Dependent *t*-Test

The dependent, or matched-pairs, *t*-test is used in the same situation as the previous test, except that it is designed for situations in which the same participants have been used in both experimental conditions. So, you'd plan to use it when you will have two experimental conditions (you will compare 2 means), and the same participants will be used in both conditions (so each person will contribute 2 scores to the data). The phrase 'dependent' in the name tells us that the same participants have been used.

Example: Imagine Twaddle and Sons, the publishers of 'Women are from Bras, men are from Penis', were upset about my claims that their book was about as useful as a paper umbrella. They decided to take me to task and design their own experiment in which participants read their book, and this book (Field & Hole) at different times. Relationship happiness was measured after reading each book. To maximize their chances of finding a difference they used a sample of 500 participants, but got each participant to take part in both conditions (they read both books). The order in which books were read was counterbalanced (see Chapter 3) and there was a delay of 6 months between reading the books. They predicted that reading their wonderful contribution to popular psychology would lead to greater relationship happiness than reading some dull and tedious book about experiments.

SPSS Output for the Dependent *t*-Test

SPSS Output 6.3 shows the output from a dependent *t*-test. The first of the three tables produces descriptive statistics; for each condition we are told the mean, the number of participants (*N*) and the standard deviation of the sample. In the final column we are told the standard

Paired Samples Statistics

		Mean	N	Std. Deviation	Std. Error Mean
Pair 1	Women are from Bras, Men are from Penis	20.0180	500	9.98123	.44637
	Field & Hole	18.4900	500	8.99153	.40211

Paired Samples Correlations

		N	Correlation	Sig.
Pair 1	Women are from Bras, Men are from Penis & Field & Hole	500	.117	.009

Paired Samples Test

		Paired Differences							Sig. (2-tailed)
		Mean	Std. Deviation	Std. Error Mean	95% Confidence Interval of the Difference		t	df	
					Lower	Upper			
Pair 1	Women are from Bras, Men are from Penis - Field & Hole	1.5280	12.62807	.56474	.4184	2.6376	2.706	499	.007

SPSS Output 6.3

error (this is calculated in the same way as for the independent *t*-test – see the previous section). The next table reports the Pearson correlation between the two conditions. When repeated measures are used it is possible that scores from the two experimental conditions will correlate (because the data in each condition come from the same people and so there should be some constancy in their responses). SPSS provides the value of Pearson's *r* and the two-tailed significance value. For these data the experimental conditions yield a fairly weak correlation coefficient ($r = .117$) but it is highly statistically significant because $p < .01$. I shall come back to this point later.

The final table is the most important because it tells us whether the difference between the means of the two conditions was large enough to not be a chance result. First, the table tells us the mean difference between conditions (this value is the difference between the mean scores of each condition: $20.01 - 18.49 = 1.52$). The table also reports the standard deviation of the difference between the means and more important the standard error of the differences between participants scores in each condition. This standard error gives us some idea of the range of differences between sample means that we could expect by chance alone. The test statis-

Use a dependent *t*-test when you've tested the same people twice!

tic, t, is calculated by dividing the mean of differences by the standard error of differences ($t = 1.52/0.56 = 2.71$). The fact that the t-value is a positive number tells us that condition 1 ('Women are from Bras, men are from Penis') had a bigger mean than the second (Field & Hole) and so relationship happiness was less after reading our little book. The size of t is compared against known values based on the degrees of freedom. When the same participants have been used in both conditions, the degrees of freedom are simply the sample size minus 1 ($df = N - 1 = 499$). SPSS uses the degrees of freedom to calculate the exact probability that a value of t as big as the one obtained could occur by chance. This probability value of t is in the column labelled Sig., and this value (.007) is considerably smaller than Fisher's criterion of .05. We could, therefore, say that there is a very significant (statistically speaking) difference between happiness scores after reading 'Women are from Bras, men are from Penis' compared to after reading our lovely book. We saw in the independent t-test that SPSS provides only the two-tailed probability, which is the probability when no prediction was made about the direction of group differences (see Box 5.3). In this case, Twaddle and Sons predicted that their book would make people happier and so they predicted that mean happiness after reading 'Women are from Bras, men are from Penis' would be higher than after reading our book. Looking at the table of descriptives the means are consistent with this prediction and because of this we can use the one-tailed probability value obtained by dividing the two-tailed probability by 2 (see Box 5.3). As such, this t-statistic is actually significant at $p = .0035$ ($= .007/2$).

Calculating the Effect Size for the Dependent t-Test

We can use the same equation as for the independent t-test to convert our t-value into an r-value (see page 166). We know the value of t and the df from the SPSS output and so we can compute r as follows:

$$r = \sqrt{\frac{2.706^2}{2.706^2 + 499}}$$

$$= \sqrt{\frac{7.32}{506.32}}$$

$$= .12$$

If you think back to our benchmarks for effect sizes this represents a small effect (it is just above .1 – the threshold for a small effect).

Therefore, although this effect is highly statistically significant, the size of the effect is very small and so represents a trivial finding.

Interpreting and Writing the Result for the Dependent *t*-Test

In this example, it would be tempting for Twaddle and Sons to conclude that their book produced significantly greater relationship happiness than our book. In fact, many researchers would write conclusions like this:

☒ The results show that reading 'Women are from Bras, men are from Penis' produces significantly greater relationship happiness than that book by smelly old Field & Hole. This result is highly significant.

However, to reach such a conclusion is to confuse statistical significance with the importance of the effect. By calculating the effect size we've discovered that although the difference in happiness after reading the two books is statistically very different, the size of effect that this represents is very small indeed. So, the effect is actually not very significant in real terms. A more correct interpretation might be to say:

☑ The results show that reading 'Women are from Bras, men are from Penis' produces significantly greater relationship happiness than that book by smelly old Field & Hole. However, the effect size was small, revealing that this finding was not substantial in real terms.

Of course, this latter interpretation would be unpopular with Twaddle and Sons who would like to believe that their book had a huge effect on relationship happiness. This is possibly one reason why effect sizes have been ignored: because researchers want people to believe that their effects are substantive. In fact, the two examples we've used to illustrate the independent and dependent *t*-test are deliberately designed to illustrate an important point: it is possible to find a statistically small effect (has a relatively large *p*-value) that is actually very substantial (has a large effect size), conversely it is possible to find a highly significant statistical result that is fairly unimportant (has a small effect size). The independent *t*-test example had a *p*-value close to our criterion of .05, yet represented a large effect, whereas the dependent *t*-test example had a *p*-value much smaller than the criterion of .05 and yet represented a much smaller effect. The difference between these two situations was the sample size (200 and 500) on which the tests were based. For the dependent *t*-test the significance of the test came about because the sample size was so big that it had the power to detect even a very small effect. In the independent *t*-test example, there were only 20 participants in total and so the test only had power to detect a very strong effect (had the effect size been smaller the test would have yielded a non-significant result).

In the previous example we saw that when we report a *t*-test we always include the degrees of freedom (in this case 499), the value of the *t*-statistic, and the level at which this value is significant. In addition we should report the effect size estimate:

☑ On average, the reported relationship happiness after reading 'Women are from Bras, men are from Penis' ($M = 20.02$, $SE = .45$), was significantly higher than after reading Field & Hole's book ($M = 18.49$, $SE = .40$), $t(499) = 2.71$, $p < .01$, $r = .12$.

On the other hand, if I'd displayed the means as a graph I could write:

☑ All effects will be reported at a .05 level of significance. The reported relationship happiness after reading 'Women are from Bras, men are from Penis', was significantly higher than after reading Field & Hole's tedious opus, $t(499) = 2.71$, $r = .12$. The effect size estimate indicates that the difference in relationship happiness created by the reading material was a small, and therefore unsubstantial, effect.

6.5   Analysis of Variance

The *t*-test is limited to situations in which there are only two levels of the independent variable (e.g. two experimental groups), but often we run experiments in which there are three or more levels of the independent variable. The easiest way to look at such a situation would be to compare pairs of experimental conditions using lots of *t*-tests. However, every time we conduct a *t*-test we do so assuming a 5% chance that we might accept an experimental effect that isn't actually real (a Type I error). If we do lots of tests on the same data set these errors add up (this is known as inflating the Type I error rate), so that even if we do only 2 tests the error rate for that data set is greater than 5% (for more detail see Field, 2000, pp. 243–244). To ensure that the 5% Type I error rate is maintained for a given experiment, we have to use a test that looks for an overall experimental effect using a single test (such tests are sometimes called omnibus tests – which doesn't mean they're repeated on television on a Sunday afternoon!). Analysis of variance (or ANOVA) is such a test and as well as controlling the overall Type I error rate it also can be used to analyse situations in which there is more than one independent variable (we'll look at these situations later in this section).

When we perform a t-test, our null hypothesis is that the two samples have roughly the same mean. ANOVA extends this idea by testing the null hypothesis that three or more means are roughly equal.[3] Like the t-test, ANOVA produces a test statistic, the F-ratio, which compares the amount of systematic variance in the data (SS_M) to the amount of unsystematic variance (SS_R) – see Box 5.1. However, because ANOVA tests for an overall experimental effect there are things that it cannot tell us: although it tells us whether the experimental manipulation was generally successful, it does not provide specific information about which groups differ. Assuming an experiment was conducted with three different groups, the F-ratio simply tells us that the means of these three samples are not equal. However, there are several ways in which the means can differ: (1) all three sample means are significantly different; (2) the means of group 1 and 2 are the same but group 3 has a significantly different mean from both of the other groups; (3) groups 2 and 3 have similar means but group 1 has a significantly different mean; and (4) groups 1 and 3 have similar means but group 2 has a significantly different mean from them both. So, the F-ratio tells us only that the experimental manipulation has had some effect, but it doesn't tell us specifically what the effect was. To discover where the effect lies we have to follow up the ANOVA with some additional tests. There are two things we can use: planned comparisons or post hoc tests. Planned comparisons are used when you've made specific predictions about which group means should differ *before* you collected any data. How these contrasts are constructed is beyond the scope of this book, but I give a really detailed account in Chapter 7 of 'Discovering statistics' (Field, 2000, pp. 258–270). Post hoc tests are done after the data have been collected and inspected. These tests compare every experimental condition with every other condition, but are calculated in such a way that the overall Type I error rate is controlled at 5% despite the fact that lots of tests have been done. The simplest way to think of this is that it's like doing lots of t-tests but being very strict about the cut-off point you use for accepting them as statistically significant. The simplest way to control the Type I error is to use what's called a Bonferroni correction. This correction is made by simply dividing α, the probability of a Type I error (i.e. .05), by the number of tests you have done. So, if you have done two tests, the new α becomes $.05/2 = .025$, if you've done 5 tests then $\alpha = .05/5 = .01$, and if you've done 10 tests then $\alpha = .05/10 = .005$. Once you've done each test, you look at the probability of obtaining the test statistic by chance (just like you normally would) but only accept the result as significant if it is less than the corrected value of α. So, if we have done 2 tests, then we accept a result as significant *not* if it is less than .05, but only if it is less than .025. Although there are other corrections that can be used (see Field, 2000, Chapter 7), the Bonferroni correction is easily understood and, although slightly conservative, a good correction so it's the one I'll tend to use in this book.

6.6   One-Way Independent ANOVA

You should plan to use one-way independent ANOVA when you are going to test three or more experimental groups (you will compare 3 or more means), and different participants will be used in each group (so each person will contribute only one score to the data).

The name of a particular ANOVA gives away the situation in which it is used. Every ANOVA begins its name with some reference to the word 'way'; this word can be read as 'independent variable' and the number that precedes it tells us how many independent variables were manipulated in the experiment. So, a one-way ANOVA will be used when one independent variable will be manipulated, a two-way ANOVA will be used when two independent variables will be manipulated, a three-way ANOVA will be used when three independent variables will be manipulated, and so on. The second half of the name tells us how these independent variables were measured. If it is an independent ANOVA then it means that different participants will take part in different conditions. If it is a repeated measures ANOVA then the same participants will take part in all experimental conditions. If it is a mixed ANOVA then it means that at least one independent variable will be measured using different participants and at least one independent variable will be measured using the same participants.

Hello, is that the RSPCA? Can you get me out of this textbook please?

Example: Students (and lecturers for that matter) love their mobile phones, which is rather worrying given some recent controversy about links between mobile phone use and brain tumours. The basic idea is that mobile phones emit microwaves, and so holding one next to your brain for large parts of the day is a bit like sticking your brain in a microwave oven and selecting the 'cook until well done' button. If we wanted to test this experimentally, we could get 6 groups of people and strap a mobile phone on their heads (that they can't remove). Then, by remote control, we turn the phones on for a certain amount of time each day. After 6 months, we measure the size of any tumour (in mm^3) close to the site of the phone antennae (just behind the ear). The six groups experience 0, 1, 2, 3, 4 or 5 hours per day of phone microwaves for 6 months.

SPSS Output for One-Way Independent ANOVA

Figure 6.3 shows an error bar chart of the mobile phone data – this graph is not automatically produced by SPSS (I did it using the interactive graphs facility). The bars show the mean size of brain tumour in each condition, and the funny 'I' shapes show the confidence interval (CI) of these means. This is the range between which 95% of sample means would fall and tells us how well the mean represents the population (see page 135). It's clear from this chart that there is a general trend that as mobile phone use increases so does the size of the brain tumour. Note that in the control group (0 hours), the mean size of the tumour is virtually zero (we wouldn't actually expect them to have tumour) and the error bar shows that there was very little variance across samples. We'll see later that this is problematic for the analysis.

SPSS Output 6.4 shows the table of descriptive statistics from the one-way ANOVA; we're told the means, standard deviations, and standard errors of the means for each experimental condition. The means should correspond to those plotted in Figure 6.3. Remember that the standard error is the standard deviation of the sampling distribution of these data (so, for the 2-hour group, if you took lots

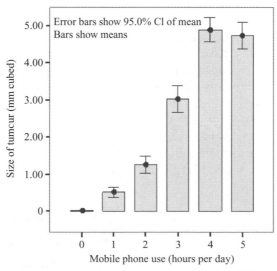

Figure 6.3: Error bar chart of the group means for different hours per day of mobile phone use

Descriptives

Size of Tumour (MM cubed)

	N	Mean	Std. Deviation	Std. Error	95% Confidence Interval for Mean		Minimum	Maximum
					Lower Bound	Upper Bound		
0	20	.0175	.01213	.00271	.0119	.0232	.00	.04
1	20	.5149	.28419	.06355	.3819	.6479	.00	.94
2	20	1.2614	.49218	.11005	1.0310	1.4917	.48	2.34
3	20	3.0216	.76556	.17118	2.6633	3.3799	1.77	4.31
4	20	4.8878	.69625	.15569	4.5619	5.2137	3.04	6.05
5	20	4.7306	.78163	.17478	4.3648	5.0964	2.70	6.14
Total	120	2.4056	2.02662	.18500	2.0393	2.7720	.00	6.14

SPSS Output 6.4

of samples from the population from which these data come, the means of these samples would have a standard deviation of 0.49). We are also given confidence intervals for the mean; these correspond to the error bars plotted in Figure 6.3 and tell us the limits within which the means of 95 out of 100 samples would fall (so for the 2-hour group if we took 100 samples, 95 of them would have a mean tumour size between $1.03 \, \text{mm}^3$ and $1.49 \, \text{mm}^3$). These diagnostics are important for interpretation later on.

Like the t-test, one of the assumptions of ANOVA is that the variances within experimental conditions are similar (*homogeneity of variance*). The next part of the output reports a test of this assumption, Levene's test, which tests the null hypothesis that the variances of the groups are the same. If Levene's test is significant (i.e. the value of Sig. is less than .05) then the variances are significantly different meaning that one assumption of the ANOVA has been violated. For these data, this is the case, because our significance is .000,[4] which is considerably smaller than the criterion of .05. In these situations, we have to try to correct the problem and the most common way is to transform all of the data (see Howell, 2001, pp. 342–349). Be warned though, in my experience transformations are often about as helpful as the average London shop-assistant (i.e. not very). If the transformation doesn't work then you should either use a non-parametric test (see Chapter 7) or you might have to just report an inaccurate F value

Test of Homogeneity of Variances

Size of Tumour (MM cubed)

Levene Statistic	df1	df2	Sig.
10.245	5	114	.000

SPSS Output 6.5

and the Levene's test (so that others can assess the accuracy of your results for themselves). For these data the problem has almost certainly arisen because in the control condition (0 hours) the variance is very small indeed – much smaller than all other conditions (most people had no tumour at all and so all scores would have been close to zero). Transforming these data has very little effect (try it if you don't believe me) so bear this in mind when I discuss how to report these results.

SPSS Output 6.6 shows the main ANOVA summary table. The table is divided into between-group effects (effects due to the model – the experimental effect, or SS_M as I usually call it) and within-group effects (this is the unsystematic variation in the data, or SS_R). The between-group effect is the overall experimental effect, and in this row of the table we are told the sums of squares for the model (the total experimental effect, $SS_M = 450.66$) and the degrees of freedom on which these sums of squares are based ($df_M = 5$). The sum of squares for the experimental effect is a total and, as such, depends on the number of scores that have been added up (reflected by the degrees of freedom). Now, the number of scores used to calculate the various sums of squares differs for the experimental effect and the unsystematic variance, so to make them comparable we actually use the average sums of squares – the mean squares, MS. To get the mean sum of squares, we divide the sum of squares by its associated degrees of freedom ($MS_M = 450.66/5 = 90.13$). This value is the experimental effect, the systematic variance. The row labelled Within groups gives details of the unsystematic variation within the data (the variation due to natural individual differences in brain tumour size and different reactions to the microwaves emitted by the phones). Again, this can be expressed as a sum of squared errors ($SS_R = 38.09$) with an associated degrees of freedom ($df_R = 114$), or as a mean squared error calculated by dividing the sum of squares by its degrees of freedom ($MS_R = 38.09/114 = 0.334$). The test of whether the group means are the same is represented by the F-ratio, which is simply the ratio of systematic variance to unsystematic variance, or put another way, the

ANOVA

Size of Tumour (MM cubed)

	Sum of Squares	df	Mean Square	F	Sig.
Between Groups	450.664	5	90.133	269.733	.000
Within Groups	38.094	114	.334		
Total	488.758	119			

SPSS Output 6.6

size of experimental effect compared to the size of error. Therefore, F is simply MS_M/MS_R, which in this case is $90.13/0.33 = 269.73$. Finally, SPSS tells us the probability of getting a F-ratio of this magnitude by chance alone; in this case the probability is .000 (that's 0 to 3 decimal places). As we know already, social scientists use a cut-off point of .05 as their criterion for statistical significance. Hence, because the observed significance value is less than .05 we can say that there was a significant effect of mobile phones on the size of tumour. However, at this stage we still do not know exactly what the effect of the phones was (we don't know which groups differed).

Having established that the ANOVA is significant, we can now look at some post hoc tests. SPSS provides you with 18 options for different post hoc tests that vary in their accuracy, their power and their ability to control the Type I error rate. I summarized these procedures in 'Discovering statistics' (Field, 2000) and to cut a long story short I suggested the following:

> ➤ When you have equal sample sizes and you are confident that your homogeneity of variances assumption has been met then use REGWQ or Tukey HSD as both have good power and tight control over the Type I error rate.
> ➤ Bonferroni is generally conservative (it is strict about whether it accepts a test statistic as being significant), but if you want guaranteed control over the Type I error rate then it is the test to use.
> ➤ If sample sizes across groups are slightly different then use Gabriel's procedure because it has greater power, but if sample sizes are very different use Hochberg's GT2.
> ➤ If there is any doubt that the population variances are equal then use the Games-Howell procedure because this generally seems to offer the best performance. I recommend running the Games-Howell procedure in addition to any other tests you might select because of the uncertainty of knowing whether the population variances are equivalent.

SPSS Output 6.7 shows the output from the Games-Howell post hoc procedure. It is clear from the table that each group of participants is compared to all of the remaining groups. For each pair of groups the difference between group means is displayed, the standard error of that difference, the significance level of that difference and a 95% confidence interval. First, the control group (0 hours) is compared to the 1-hour, 2-hour, 3-hour, 4-hour and 5-hour groups and reveals a significant difference in all cases (all the values in the column labelled Sig. are less than .05). In the next part of the table, the 1-hour group is com-

Multiple Comparisons

Dependent Variable: Size of Tumour (MM cubed)

Games-Howell

(I) Mobile Phone Use (Hours Per Day)	(J) Mobile Phone Use (Hours Per Day)	Mean Difference (I-J)	Std. Error	Sig.	95% Confidence Interval	
					Lower Bound	Upper Bound
0	1	-.4973*	.18280	.000	-.6982	-.2964
	2	1.2438*	.18280	.000	-1.5916	-.8960
	3	-3.0040*	.18280	.000	-3.5450	-2.4631
	4	-4.8702*	.18280	.000	-5.3622	-4.3783
	5	-4.7130*	.18280	.000	-5.2653	-4.1608
1	0	.4973*	.18280	.000	.2964	.6982
	2	-.7465*	.18280	.000	-1.1327	-.3603
	3	-2.5067*	.18280	.000	-3.0710	-1.9424
	4	-4.3729*	.18280	.000	-4.8909	-3.8549
	5	-4.2157*	.18280	.000	-4.7908	-3.6406
2	0	1.2438*	.18280	.000	.8960	1.5916
	1	.7465*	.18280	.000	.3603	1.1327
	3	-1.7602*	.18280	.000	-2.3762	-1.1443
	4	-3.6264*	.18280	.000	-4.2017	-3.0512
	5	-3.4692*	.18280	.000	-4.0949	-2.8436
3	0	3.0040*	.18280	.000	2.4631	3.5450
	1	2.5067*	.18280	.000	1.9424	3.0710
	2	1.7602*	.18280	.000	1.1443	2.3762
	4	-1.8662*	.18280	.000	-2.5607	-1.1717
	5	-1.7090*	.18280	.000	-2.4429	-.9751
4	0	4.8702*	.18280	.000	4.3783	5.3622
	1	4.3729*	.18280	.000	3.8549	4.8909
	2	3.6264*	.18280	.000	3.0512	4.2017
	3	1.8662*	.18280	.000	1.1717	2.5607
	5	.1572	.18280	.984	-.5455	.8599
5	0	4.7130*	.18280	.000	4.1608	5.2653
	1	4.2157*	.18280	.000	3.6406	4.7908
	2	3.4692*	.18280	.000	2.8436	4.0949
	3	1.7090*	.18280	.000	.9751	2.4429
	4	-.1572	.18280	.984	-.8599	.5455

*. The mean difference is significant at the .05 level.

SPSS Output 6.7

pared to all other groups. Again all comparisons are significant (all the values in the column labelled Sig. are less than .05). In fact, all of the comparisons appear to be highly significant except the comparison between the 4-hour and 5-hour groups, which is non-significant because the value in the column labelled Sig. is bigger than .05.

SPSS Output 6.8 shows a different type of post hoc test, the REGWQ. I've included this because the table is different. With the REGWQ and some other tests (Hochberg's GT2 for example) a table is produced in which group means are placed in the same column only if they are not significantly different using a criterion probability of .05. In this example the only two means that appear in the same column are those of 4- and 5-hours on the phone per day (see the last column). This

Size of Tumour (MM cubed)

Ryan-Einot-Gabriel-Welsch Range[a]

Mobile Phone Use (Hours Per Day)	N	Subset for alpha = .05				
		1	2	3	4	5
0	20	.0175				
1	20		.5149			
2	20			1.2614		
3	20				3.0216	
5	20					4.7306
4	20					4.8878
Sig.		1.000	1.000	1.000	1.000	.775

Means for groups in homogeneous subsets are displayed.

a. Critical values are not monotonic for these data. Substitutions have been made to ensure monotonicity. Type I error is therefore smaller.

SPSS Output 6.8

tells us that all group means were significantly different from each other except for the groups that spent 4- and 5-hours on the phone.

Does it matter which test you use? Well, actually it does. In this example you'd find that if you used a Bonferroni test then the group that spent 1 hour on the phone per day are not significantly different to those that spent no hours on the phone per day (as practice why not try it on SPSS, the data files can be downloaded from my website). In reality these groups do appear to be different but we only detected it because we used a post hoc test that wasn't affected by the fact our groups had different variances. Bonferroni is not only conservative, but will also be affected by the differences in group variances.

Calculating the Effect Size for One-Way Independent ANOVA

SPSS Output 6.6 provides us with three measures of variance: the between-group effect (SS_M), the within-subject effect (SS_R) and the total amount of variance in the data (SS_T). We know from Box 5.1 that we can calculate r^2 using these values (although for some bizarre reason it's usually called eta-squared, η^2). It is then a simple matter to take the square root of this value to give us the effect size r.

$$r^2 = \frac{SS_M}{SS_T}$$
$$= \frac{450.66}{488.76}$$
$$= .92$$
$$r = \sqrt{0.92}$$
$$= .96$$

Using the benchmarks for effect sizes this represents a massive effect (it is well above .5 – the threshold for a large effect). Therefore, the effect of mobile phone use on brain tumours is a substantive finding.

This measure of effect size is actually slightly biased because we're interested in the effect size in the population and this value is based purely on sums of squares from the sample (with no adjustment made for the fact that we're trying to estimate a population value). To reduce this bias, we can use a slightly more complex measure of effect size known as omega squared (ω^2). This effect size estimate is still based on the sums of squares that we met in Box 5.1, but like the *F*-ratio it uses the variance explained by the model, and the error variance (in both cases the average variance, or mean squared error, is used):

$$\omega^2 = \frac{MS_M - MS_R}{MS_M + ((n-1) \times MS_R)}$$

The *n* in the equation is simply the number of people in a group (in this case 20). So, in this example we'd get (the values are taken from SPSS Output 6.6):

$$\omega^2 = \frac{90.13 - .33}{90.13 + ((20-1) \times .33)}$$
$$= \frac{89.8}{90.13 + 6.27}$$
$$= .93$$
$$\omega = \sqrt{.93} = .96$$

As you can see this has led to an identical estimate to using *r*, but this will not always be the case because ω is generally a more accurate measure. For the remaining sections on ANOVA I will use omega as my effect size measure, but think of it as you would *r* (because it's basically an unbiased estimate of *r* anyway).

Interpreting and Writing the Result for One-Way Independent ANOVA

When we report an ANOVA, we have to give details of the *F*-ratio and the degrees of freedom from which it was calculated. For the experimental effect in these data the *F*-ratio was derived from dividing the mean squares for the effect by the mean squares for the residual. Therefore, the degrees of freedom used to assess the *F*-ratio are the degrees of freedom for the effect of the model ($df_M = 5$) and the degrees of freedom for the residuals of the model ($df_R = 114$). As with the *t*-test it is also customary to either begin by stating a general level of significance that you're using, or to report the significance of each effect against standard benchmarks such as .05, .01, and .001. Therefore, we could report the main finding as:

> ☒   The results show that using a mobile phone significantly affected the size of brain tumour found in participants, $F(5, 114) = 269.73$, $p < .001$.

Why have I indicated that this is incorrect? Well, in this example, we need to report that the homogeneity of variance assumption was broken as well as our main result. It would be incorrect not to mention this fact. Levene's test is actually just an ANOVA (see Field, 2000, p. 284) and so we can report it using the letter *F*. A more thorough interpretation might be to say:

> ☑   Levene's test indicated that the assumption of homogeneity of variance had been violated, $F(5, 114) = 10.25$, $p < .001$. Transforming the data did not rectify this problem and so *F*-tests are reported nevertheless. The results show that using a mobile phone significantly affected the size of brain tumour found in participants, $F(5, 114) = 269.73$, $p < .001$.

Of course we should really report the effect size as well:

> ☑   Levene's test indicated that the assumption of homogeneity of variance had been violated, $F(5, 114) = 10.25$, $p < .001$. Transforming the data did not rectify this problem and so *F*-tests are reported nevertheless. The results show that using a mobile phone significantly affected the size of brain tumour found in participants, $F(5, 114) = 269.73$, $p < .001$, $r = .96$. The effect size indicated that the effect of phone use on tumour size was substantial.

The next thing that needs to be reported are the post hoc comparisons. It is customary just to summarise these tests in very general terms like this:

> ☒   Games-Howell post hoc tests revealed significant differences between 0 and 1 hour ($p < .001$), 0 and 2 hours ($p < .001$), 0 and 3 hours ($p < .001$), 0 and 4 hours ($p < .001$), 0 and 5 hours ($p < .001$), 1 and 2 hours ($p < .001$), 1 and 3 hours ($p < .001$), 1 and 4 hours ($p < .001$), 1 and 5 hours ($p < .001$), 2 and 3 hours ($p < .001$), 2 and 4 hours ($p < .001$), 2 and 5 hours ($p < .001$), 3 and 4 hours ($p < .001$), 3 and 5 hours ($p < .001$), but not between 4 and 5 hours (*ns*).

This is rather cumbersome, and the same information could be provided in a more succinct way:

☑ Games-Howell post hoc tests revealed significant differences between all groups ($p < .001$ for all tests) except between 4- and 5-hours (*ns*).

If you do want to report the results for each post hoc test individually, then at least include the 95% confidence intervals for the test as these tell us more than just the significance value. In examples such as this when there are many tests it might be as well to summarize these confidence intervals as a table:

Table 6.1

Mobile Phone Use (Hours per Day)			95% Confidence Interval	
First	Second	Sig.	Lower Bound	Upper Bound
0	1	< .001	−.6982	−.2964
	2	< .001	−1.5916	−.8960
	3	< .001	−3.5450	−2.4631
	4	< .001	−5.3622	−4.3783
	5	< .001	−5.2653	−4.1608
1	2	< .001	−1.1327	−.3603
	3	< .001	−3.0710	−1.9424
	4	< .001	−4.8909	−3.8549
	5	< .001	−4.7908	−3.6406
2	3	< .001	−2.3762	−1.1443
	4	< .001	−4.2017	−3.0512
	5	< .001	−4.0949	−2.8436
3	4	< .001	−2.5607	−1.1717
	5	< .001	−2.4429	−.9751
4	5	=.984	−.5455	.8599

6.7 One-Way Repeated Measures ANOVA

If you plan to have three or more experimental groups (you will compare three or more means), and the same participants will be used in each group (so each person contributes several scores to the data) then you will use one-way repeated measures ANOVA to analyse the data.

Sphericity

In independent ANOVA the accuracy of the *F*-test depends upon the assumption that the groups tested are independent. As such, the relationship between treatments in a repeated measures design causes the conventional *F*-test to lack accuracy. The relationship between scores in different conditions means that we have to make an additional assumption to those in between-group ANOVA. Put simplistically, we assume that the relationship between one pair of conditions is similar to the relationship between a different pair of conditions. This assumption is known as the assumption of sphericity. Sphericity refers to the equality of variances of the differences between treatment levels. So, if you were to take each pair of treatment levels, and calculate the differences between each pair of scores, then it is necessary that these differences have equal variances (see Field, 1998a, for an example).

SPSS produces a test known as Mauchly's test, which tests the hypothesis that the variances of the differences between conditions are equal. Therefore, if Mauchly's test statistic is significant (i.e. has a probability value less than .05) we conclude that some pairs of conditions are more related than others and the condition of sphericity has not been met. If, however, Mauchly's test statistic is non-significant (i.e. $p > .05$) then it is reasonable to conclude that the relationships between pairs of conditions are roughly equal. In short, if Mauchly's test is significant then be wary of the *F*-ratios produced by the computer!

The effect of violating sphericity is a loss of power (i.e. increased probability of a Type II error) because the test statistic (*F*-ratio) simply cannot be assumed to have an *F*-distribution (for more details see Field, 1998a, 2000). However, as we'll see later there are some things we can do to correct the problem.

Example: Imagine I wanted to look at the effect alcohol has on the roving eye. The 'roving eye' effect is the propensity of people in relationships to 'eye-up' members of the opposite sex. I took 20 men and fitted them with incredibly sophisticated glasses that could track their eye movements and record both the movement and the object being observed (this is the point at which it should be apparent that I'm making it up as I go along). Over 4 different nights I plied these poor souls with either 1, 2, 3 or 4 pints of strong lager in a nightclub. Each night I measured how many different women they eyed-up (a women was categorized as having been eyed-up if the man's eye moved from her head to toe and back up again). To validate this measure we also collected the amount of dribble on the man's chin while looking at a woman.

SPSS Output for One-Way Repeated Measures ANOVA

Figure 6.4 shows an error bar chart of the roving eye data. The bars show the mean number of women that were eyed-up after different doses of alcohol. As in the previous section, I have included error bars representing the confidence interval of these means (see pages 135 and 176 for an explanation). It's clear from this chart that the mean number of women is pretty similar between 1 and 2 pints, and for 3 and 4 pints but there is a jump after 2 pints.

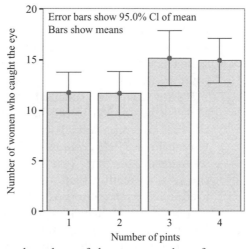

Figure 6.4 Error bar chart of the mean number of women eyed-up after different doses of alcohol

SPSS Output 6.9 shows the initial diagnostics statistics. First, we are told the variables that represent each level of the independent variable. This box is useful to check that the variables were entered in the correct order. The next table provides basic descriptive statistics for the four levels of the independent variable. This table confirms what we saw in the graph; that is, that the mean number of women eyed-up after 1 and 2 pints is similar, and the means after 3 and 4 pints

Within-Subjects Factors

Measure: MEASURE_1

ALCOHOL	Dependent Variable
1	PINT1
2	PINT2
3	PINT3
4	PINT4

Descriptive Statistics

	Mean	Std. Deviation	N
1 Pint	11.7500	4.31491	20
2 Pints	11.7000	4.65776	20
3 Pints	15.2000	5.80018	20
4 Pints	14.9500	4.67327	20

SPSS Output 6.9

are similar also, but there is an increase between 2 and 3 pints. These mean values are useful for interpreting any effects that may emerge from the main analysis.

Earlier I mentioned that SPSS produces a test of whether the data violate the assumption of sphericity. The next part of the output contains Mauchly's test and we hope to find that it's non-significant if we are to assume that the condition of sphericity has been met. SPSS Output 6.10 shows Mauchly's test and the important column is the one containing the significance value. The significance value (.022) is less than the critical value of .05, so we accept that the variances of the differences between levels are significantly different. In other words, the assumption of sphericity has been violated. Obviously we were hoping not to have violated this assumption, but seeing as we have (this always seems to happen when I make up data!) what do we do?

If data violate the sphericity assumption there are three corrections that can be applied to produce a valid F-ratio: corrections based on (1) the Greenhouse-Geisser (1959) estimate of sphericity; (2) the Huynh-Feldt (1976) estimate of sphericity; and (3) the lowest possible estimate of sphericity (the lower-bound). All of these estimates give rise to a correction factor that is applied to the degrees of freedom used to assess the observed F-ratio. In all cases they lower the degrees of freedom, which in real terms means that your F-ratio has to be bigger to achieve significance. We don't need to go into the tedious detail of how these corrections are calculated (but see Girden (1992) if you're having sleepless nights about it), we need know only that the three estimates produce different correction factors. With all three estimates, the closer they are to 1.00 the more homogeneous the variances of differences, and hence the closer the data are to being spherical. There has been some debate about which correction factor is

Mauchly's Test of Sphericity[b]

Measure: MEASURE_1

Within Subjects Effect	Mauchly's W	Approx. Chi-Square	df	Sig.	Epsilon[a]		
					Greenhouse-Geisser	Huynh-Feldt	Lower-bound
ALCOHOL	.477	13.122	5	.022	.745	.849	.333

Tests the null hypothesis that the error covariance matrix of the orthonormalized transformed dependent variables is proportional to an identity matrix.

  a. May be used to adjust the degrees of freedom for the averaged tests of significance. Corrected tests are displayed in the Tests of Within-Subjects Effects table.

  b. Design: Intercept
     Within Subjects Design: ALCOHOL

SPSS Output 6.10

best (see Field, 1998, 2000) and to summarize, Girden (1992) recommends that when estimates of sphericity are greater than .75 then the Huynh-Feldt correction should be used, but when sphericity estimates are less than .75 or nothing is known about sphericity at all, then the Greenhouse-Geisser correction should be used instead. If we look at the estimates of sphericity (in SPSS Output 6.10 in the column labelled Epsilon) the Greenhouse-Geisser is .75 (rounded) and so by Girden's recommendation we should use the Huynh-Feldt correction (see later). Had this estimate been less than .75 the Greenhouse-Geisser correction should be used.

SPSS Output 6.11 shows the main result of the ANOVA. This table is essentially the same as the one for one-way independent ANOVA (see SPSS Output 6.6). There is a sum of squares for the main effect of alcohol, which tells us how much of the total variability is explained by the experimental effect. There is also an error term, which is the amount of unexplained variation across the conditions of the repeated measures variable. These sums of squares are converted into mean squares in the same way as for the independent ANOVA: by dividing by the degrees of freedom. The *df* for the effect of alcohol is simply the number of levels of the independent variable minus 1 ($k - 1$) and the error *df* is this value multiplied by one less than the number of participants in each group: $(n - 1)(k - 1)$. The *F*-ratio is obtained by dividing the mean squares for the experimental effect (75.03) by the error mean squares (15.87). As with independent ANOVA, this test statistic represents the ratio of systematic variance to unsystematic variance. The value of *F* (4.73) is then compared against a critical value for 3 and 57 degrees of freedom. SPSS displays the exact significance level for the *F*-ratio. The significance of *F* is .005, which is significant because it is less than the criterion value of .05. We can, therefore, conclude that alcohol had a significant effect on the average number

Tests of Within-Subjects Effects

Measure: MEASURE_1

Source		Type III Sum of Squares	df	Mean Square	F	Sig.
ALCOHOL	Sphericity Assumed	225.100	3	75.033	4.729	.005
	Greenhouse-Geisser	225.100	2.235	100.706	4.729	.011
	Huynh-Feldt	225.100	2.547	88.370	4.729	.008
	Lower-bound	225.100	1.000	225.100	4.729	.042
Error(ALCOHOL)	Sphericity Assumed	904.400	57	15.867		
	Greenhouse-Geisser	904.400	42.469	21.296		
	Huynh-Feldt	904.400	48.398	18.687		
	Lower-bound	904.400	19.000	47.600		

SPSS Output 6.11

of women that were eyed-up. However, this main test does not tell us which quantities of alcohol made a difference to the number of women eyed-up.

This result is all very nice but as of yet we haven't done anything about our violation of the sphericity assumption. The table in SPSS Output 6.11 shows the F-ratio and associated degrees of freedom when sphericity is assumed and the significant F-statistic indicated some difference(s) between the mean number of women cyed-up after the different doses of alcohol. This table also contains several additional rows giving the corrected values of F for the three different types of adjustment (Greenhouse-Geisser, Huynh-Feldt and lower-bound). Notice that in all cases the F-ratio remains the same; it is the degrees of freedom that change (and hence the critical value against which the obtained F-statistic is compared). The degrees of freedom are multiplied by the estimates of sphericity calculated in SPSS Output 6.12 (see Field, 1998a). The new degrees of freedom are then used to ascertain the significance of F. First we decide which correction to apply and to do this we need to look at the estimates of sphericity in SPSS Output 6.12: if the Greenhouse-Geisser and Huynh-Feldt estimates are less than .75 we should use Greenhouse-Geisser, and if they are above .75 we use Huynh-Feldt. We discovered earlier that based on these criteria we should use Huynh-Feldt here. Using this corrected value we still find a significant result because the observed p (.008) is still less than the criterion of .05. In fact, the results are significant using the Greenhouse-Geisser correction too. In these situations, where the two corrections give rise to the same conclusion it makes little difference which you choose to report; however, if you accept the F-statistic as significant the conservative Greenhouse-Geisser estimate is usually the one that is reported. Very occasionally the Greenhouse-Geisser and Huynh-Feldt estimates will give rise to different conclusions (the Huynh-Feldt produces a significant result but the Greenhouse-Geisser doesn't). In these situations, you should still select the test based on the estimate of sphericity (as I've suggested); however, because the Greenhouse-Geisser correction is too strict and the Huynh-Feldt correction too liberal you can take an average of the two. In reality this means averaging the probability values for the test statistics when the two corrections are applied.

The main effect of alcohol doesn't tell us anything about which doses of alcohol produced different results to other doses. So, we might do some post hoc tests as well (see page 173 and Field, 2000, Chapter 9). SPSS Output 6.12 shows the table from SPSS that contains these tests. We can read this in the same way as for the independent ANOVA; that is, we read down the column labelled Sig.

Pairwise Comparisons

Measure: MEASURE_1

(I) ALCOHOL	(J) ALCOHOL	Mean Difference (I-J)	Std. Error	Sig.[a]	95% Confidence Interval for Difference[a]	
					Lower Bound	Upper Bound
1	2	5.000E-02	.742	1.000	-2.133	2.233
	3	-3.450	1.391	.136	-7.544	.644
	4	-3.200	1.454	.242	-7.480	1.080
2	1	-5.000E-02	.742	1.000	-2.233	2.133
	3	-3.500*	1.139	.038	-6.853	-.147
	4	-3.250	1.420	.202	-7.429	.929
3	1	3.450	1.391	.136	-.644	7.544
	2	3.500*	1.139	.038	.147	6.853
	4	.250	1.269	1.000	-3.485	3.985
4	1	3.200	1.454	.242	-1.080	7.480
	2	3.250	1.420	.202	-.929	7.429
	3	-.250	1.269	1.000	-3.985	3.485

Based on estimated marginal means

*. The mean difference is significant at the .05 level.

a. Adjustment for multiple comparisons: Bonferroni.

SPSS Output 6.12

and look for values less than .05. By looking at the significance values we can see that the only difference between condition means is between 2 and 3 pints of alcohol. Looking at the means of these groups (SPSS Output 6.19) it's clear that the number of women that are eyed-up after 3 pints ($M = 15.2$) is bigger than after 2 pints ($M = 11.7$). No other post hoc tests are significant and so we could conclude that there is no difference in the number of women eyed-up after 1 pint compared to 2 pints, or after 3 pints compared to 4 pints. Given that the means are so similar between 1 and 2 pints, and 3 and 4 pints it's a little weird that we don't get an effect between 1 and 3 pints, or 2 and 4 pints (or indeed 1 and 4 pints). Looking at Figure 6.4 we might reasonably expect differences between these groups, so why haven't we got them? Well, one possibility is that this is just an example of post hoc tests lacking the power to detect genuine effects.

Calculating the Effect Size for One-Way Repeated Measures ANOVA

As with the independent ANOVA we can use two measures of variance (MS_M and MS_R) to calculate an effect size estimate. In SPSS

Output 6.11, MS_M is the mean squares for the experimental effect (labelled Alcohol), and MS_R is the mean squares of the error term. These values can be read from SPSS Output 6.11.

$$\omega^2 = \frac{MS_M - MS_R}{MS_M + ((n-1) \times MS_R)}$$

$$\omega^2 = \frac{MS_M - MS_R}{MS_M + ((n-1) \times MS_R)}$$

$$\omega^2_{Alcohol} = \frac{75.03 - 15.87}{75.03 + ((15-1) \times 15.87)}$$

$$= \frac{59.17}{75.03 + 301.47}$$

$$= .16$$

$$\omega_{Alcohol} = \sqrt{.16} = .40$$

Using the benchmarks for effect sizes this represents a medium to strong effect (it is between .3 and .5 – the thresholds for medium and large effects). Therefore, the effect of alcohol on the roving eye is substantial.

Interpreting and Writing the Result for One-Way Repeated Measures ANOVA

When we report repeated measures ANOVA, we give the same details as with an independent ANOVA. The only additional thing we should concern ourselves with is reporting the corrected degrees of freedom if sphericity was violated. Personally, I'm also keen on reporting the results of sphericity tests as well. As with the independent ANOVA the degrees of freedom used to assess the F-ratio are the degrees of freedom for the effect of the model ($df_M = 2.55$) and the degrees of freedom for the residuals of the model ($df_R = 48.40$). Remember in both cases that we're using Huynh-Feldt corrected degrees of freedom. Therefore, we could report the main finding as:

☑   The results show that the number of women eyed-up was significantly affected by the amount of alcohol drunk, $F(2.55, 48.40) = 4.73$, $p < .05$.

If you choose to report the sphericity test as well, you should report the Chi-Squared approximation, its degrees of freedom and the significance value. It's also nice to report the degree of sphericity by reporting the epsilon value. We'll also report the effect size in this improved version:

☑ Mauchly's test indicated that the assumption of sphericity had been violated, $\chi^2(5) = 13.12$, $p < .05$, therefore degrees of freedom were corrected using Huynh-Feldt estimates of sphericity ($\varepsilon = .85$). The results show that the number of women eyed-up was significantly affected by the amount of alcohol drunk, $F(2.55, 48.40) = 4.73$, $p < .05$, $r = .40$.

The post hoc comparisons need to be reported next, and as we saw with the independent ANOVA we can either report a table of the confidence intervals, or write a general account of which tests were significant. However, because only 1 test was significant we could report this fairly succinctly along with its confidence interval:

☑ Bonferroni post hoc tests revealed a significant difference in the number of women eyed-up only between 2 and 3 pints, $CI_{.95} = -6.85$ (lower) $-.15$ (upper), $p < .05$. No other comparisons were significant (all $ps > .05$).

6.8   Two-Way Independent ANOVA

We saw earlier that the name of a particular ANOVA gives away the situation in which it is used. The 'two-way' part of the name tells us that two independent variables will be manipulated. The second half of the name tells us how these independent variables will be measured; this is an independent ANOVA and so different participants will take part in all conditions. To sum up then, two-way independent ANOVA will be used when you intend to measure two independent variables and use different participants in all of the various groups (each person contributes only 1 score to the data).

Example: People's musical taste tends to change as they get older (my parents, for example, after years of listening to relatively cool music when I was a kid in the 1970s, subsequently hit their mid-40s and developed a worrying obsession with country and western music – or maybe it was the stress of having me as a teenage son!). Anyway, this worries me immensely as the future seems incredibly bleak if it is spent listening to Garth Brooks and thinking 'oh boy, did I underestimate Garth's immense talent when I was in my 20s'.[5] So, I thought I'd do some research to find out whether my fate really was sealed, or whether it's possible to be old and like good music too. First, I got myself two groups of people (45 people in each group): one group contained young people (which I arbitrarily decided was under 40

Remember, when you only test different participants, use an independent ANOVA

years of age), and the other group contained more mature individuals (above 40 years of age – sorry Graham!). This is my first independent variable, age, and it has two levels (less than or more than 40 years old). I then split each of these groups of 45 into three smaller groups of 15 and assigned them to listen to either Fugazi (who everyone knows are the coolest band on the planet),[6] ABBA, or Barf Grooks (who is a lesser known country and western musician not to be confused with anyone who has a similar name and produces music that makes you want to barf). This is my second independent variable, music, and has three levels (Fugazi, ABBA or Barf Grooks). There were different participants in all conditions, which means that of the 45 under-40s, 15 listened to Fugazi, 15 listened to ABBA and 15 listened to Barf Grooks; likewise of the 45 over-40s, 15 listened to Fugazi, 15 listened to ABBA and 15 listened to Barf Grooks. After listening to the music I got each person to rate it on a scale ranging from −100 (I hate this foul music of Satan) through 0 (I am completely indifferent) to +100 (I love this music so much I'm going to explode).

SPSS Output for Two-Way Independent ANOVA

Figure 6.5 shows an error bar chart of the music data – as with the previous graphs I produced this using SPSS's interactive graphs. The bars show the mean rating of the music played to each group, and you should now realize that the funny 'I' shapes show the range between which 95% of sample means would fall (see pages 135 and 176). It's

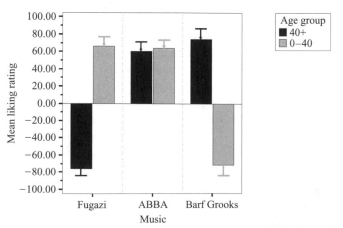

Figure 6.5   Error bar chart of the mean ratings of different types of music for two different age groups

clear from this chart that when people listened to Fugazi the two age groups were divided: the older ages rated it very low, but the younger people rated it very highly. A reverse trend is found if you look at the ratings for Barf Grooks: the youngsters give it low ratings while the wrinkly-ones love it. For ABBA the groups agreed: both old and young rated them highly.

SPSS Output 6.13 shows the table of descriptive statistics from the two-way ANOVA; the table splits the means for the different types of music and within these groups it separates the older group from the younger. As ever, we're told the means and standard deviations for each experimental condition. The means should correspond to those plotted in Figure 6.5.

Descriptive Statistics

Dependent Variable: Liking Rating

Music	Age Group	Mean	Std. Deviation	N
Fugazi	40+	-75.8667	14.37193	15
	0-40	66.2000	19.90406	15
	Total	-4.8333	74.23406	30
Abba	40+	59.9333	19.98380	15
	0-40	64.1333	16.99524	15
	Total	62.0333	18.35189	30
Barf Grooks	40+	74.2667	22.29499	15
	0-40	-71.4667	23.17901	15
	Total	1.4000	77.40783	30
Total	40+	19.4444	70.93164	45
	0-40	19.6222	68.06257	45
	Total	19.5333	69.12035	90

SPSS Output 6.13

As with one-way independent ANOVA, we have to check the homogeneity of variance assumption (see page 159). The next part of the output shows Levene's test, which we've encountered before (see page 165). For these data the significance value is .322, which is greater than the criterion of .05. This means that the variances in the

Levene's Test of Equality of Error Variances[a]

Dependent Variable: Liking Rating

F	df1	df2	Sig.
1.189	5	84	.322

Tests the null hypothesis that the error variance of the dependent variable is equal across groups.

a. Design: Intercept+MUSIC+AGE+MUSIC * AGE

SPSS Output 6.14

different experimental groups are roughly equal (i.e. not significantly different), and that the assumption has been met. As such, we can continue safe in the knowledge that the final test statistics will be accurate.

SPSS Output 6.15 shows the main ANOVA summary table, and the first thing to note is that it's a fair bit more complex than for the one-way independent ANOVA. That's because we now have an effect for each independent variable (these are known as *main effects*) and also the combined effect of the independent variables (this is known as the *interaction* between the variables). We should look at these effects in turn.

The main effect of music is shown by the F-ratio in the row labelled Music, and as in previous examples, we're interested in the significance value of the observed F. The experimental effect, or SS_M, is 81864.07 and this compares with the unsystematic variation in the data, or SS_R, which is only 32553.47. These values are converted into average effects, or mean squares, by dividing by the degrees of freedom, which are 2 for the effect of music, and 84 for the unexplained variation. The effect of music is simply the mean square for music divided by the mean square error (which in this case is $40932.03/387.54 = 105.62$). Finally, SPSS tells us the probability of getting a F-ratio of this magnitude by chance alone; in this case the probability is .000, which is lower than the usual cut-off point of .05. Hence, we can say that there was a significant effect of the type of music on the ratings. To understand what this actually means, we need to look at the mean ratings for each type of music when we ignore whether the person giving the rating was old or young. In fact, these overall means can be found in SPSS Output 6.13 and I've plotted them in Figure 6.6. The first thing to note about this graph is that the variation in ratings is huge (as shown by the error

Tests of Between-Subjects Effects

Dependent Variable: Liking Rating

Source	Type III Sum of Squares	df	Mean Square	F	Sig.
Corrected Model	392654.933a	5	78530.987	202.639	.000
Intercept	34339.600	1	34339.600	88.609	.000
MUSIC	81864.067	2	40932.033	105.620	.000
AGE	.711	1	.711	.002	.966
MUSIC * AGE	310790.156	2	155395.078	400.977	.000
Error	32553.467	84	387.541		
Total	459548.000	90			
Corrected Total	425208.400	89			

a. R Squared = .923 (Adjusted R Squared = .919)

SPSS Output 6.15

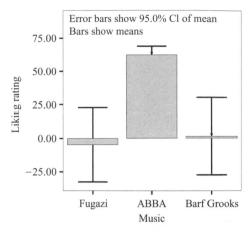

Figure 6.6 Mean ratings of different types of music when you ignore whether the rating came from an old or young person

bars) in the Fugazi and Barf Grooks groups. This is because the two age groups gave such disparate ratings. However, what this graph shows is that the significant main effect of music is likely to reflect the fact that ABBA were rated (overall) much more positively than the other two artists.

The main effect of age is shown by the F-ratio in the row in SPSS Output 6.15 labelled Age, and the variance explained by this variable, SS_M, is .711, which is an incredibly small amount (especially when you consider that there are 32553.47 units of unsystematic variation, SS_R). This effect has 1 degree of freedom and so the resulting mean square is the same as the sum of squares (.711). The effect of age is the mean square for age divided by the mean square error (which in this case is .711/387.54 = .002). The fact that this value is less than 1 automatically tells us that there was more unexplained variance than there was variance that could be explained by age. In other words, age accounted for less variance than the error. In these cases we need only report that the F-ratio was less than 1 and everyone will know that it was nonsignificant (F cannot be significant if the independent variable explains less variance than the error). In fact, the probability associated with this F-ratio is .966, which is so close to 1 that it means that it is a virtual certainty that this F could occur by chance alone. Again, to interpret the effect we need to look at the mean ratings for the two age groups ignoring the type of music to which they listened (i.e. calculate the mean score of the 45 people over 40 and the mean score of the 45 people under 40). I've plotted these two means in Figure 6.7. Again, the variation in ratings is huge (as shown by the error bars) in both groups because the ratings within each age group

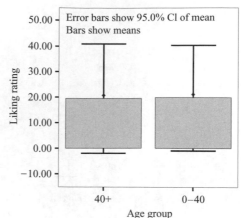

Figure 6.7 Mean ratings of old and young people when you ignore the type of music they were rating

varied a lot across the different types of music. This graph shows that when you ignore the type of music that was being rated, older people, on average, gave almost identical ratings to younger people (i.e. the mean ratings in the two groups are virtually the same).

I hope that it has become apparent that main effects are not always that interesting. For example, here we've already seen that on the face of it ratings of Fugazi are similar to ratings of Barf Grooks, and yet we know that this isn't true – it depends on which age group you ask. Similarly we've seen that ratings from older people are the same magnitude as ratings of younger people, yet we know that actually the ratings depend on which type of music is being rated. This is where interactions come into play. An interaction is the combined effect of two of more variables, and sometimes, they tell us the most interesting things about our data. The interaction effect is shown by the *F*-ratio in the row in SPSS Output 6.15 labelled Music * Age, and it explains 310790.16 units of variation, SS_M. This is a large amount compared to the 32553.47 units of unsystematic variation, SS_R. This effect has 2 degree of freedom and so the resulting mean square is half of the sum of squares (155395.08). The *F*-ratio for the interaction effect is the mean square for the interaction divided by the mean square error (155395.08/387.54 = 400.98). This tells us that the interaction explains 400 times more variance than we can't explain (that's a lot!). The associated significance value is understandably small (.000) and is less than the criterion of .05. Therefore, we can say that there is a significant interaction between age and the type of music rated. To interpret this effect we need to look at the mean ratings in all conditions and these means were originally plotted in Figure 6.5. If there was no interaction, then we'd expect the old and young people to agree on their ratings for different types of music. So, old and young would give the same ratings of Fugazi, the same ratings for ABBA and the same ratings for Barf Grooks. The ratings might be different for each of these artists, but within given artists the two age groups would agree (see Box 6.1). The fact there is a significant interaction tells us that for certain types of music the different age groups gave different ratings. In this case, although they agree on ABBA, there are large disagreements in ratings of Fugazi and Barf Grooks.

◼ Box 6.1: Interpreting Interaction Graphs (Bar Charts)

The first step to understanding interactions is to know how to interpret interaction graphs. In the data for how different age groups rated different types of music we found a significant interaction. Based on the graph (Figure 6.5) we could conclude that for certain types of music, the different age groups gave different ratings. Specifically, they gave similar ratings for ABBA, but the young group gave higher ratings for Fugazi than the old, and the old group gave higher ratings of Barf Grooks than the young. The graph below shows a different scenario – do you think this would result in a significant interaction?

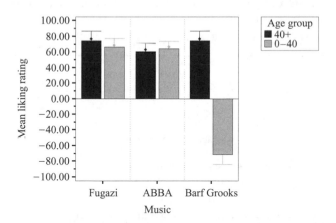

This profile of data probably would also give rise to a significant interaction term because although the old and young now agree that Fugazi are great and give similar ratings, and agree that ABBA are great also, they still disagree on Barf Grooks. So, the age of the participant does still have an influence over how different types of music are rated. Put another way, the effect of age for certain types of music (Fugazi and ABBA) is different to the effect of age for other types (Barf Grooks). Age has no effect when Fugazi and ABBA are rated but does when Barf Grooks is rated.

continues

■ Box 6.1: *continued*

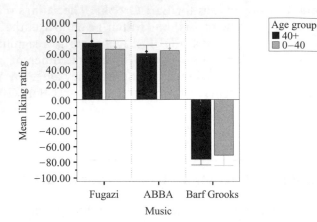

Let's try another example. Is there an interaction now? For these data there is unlikely to be a significant interaction because the effect of age is the same for all types of music (in this case there is no effect of age for any type of music). So, if we look at ratings for Fugazi, the difference between age group ratings is virtually non-existent, the ratings for ABBA are also identical for the two age groups, and for Barf Grooks the ratings are now similar for the age groups (both groups hate him). For every level of the music variable, there is the same effect of age (in this case age has no effect for any type of music).

In Box 6.2 we'll look at other ways to illustrate interactions.

Multiple Comparisons

Dependent Variable: Liking Rating

	(I) Music	(J) Music	Mean Difference (I-J)	Std. Error	Sig.	95% Confidence Interval Lower Bound	95% Confidence Interval Upper Bound
Games-Howell	Fugazi	Abba	-66.8667*	5.08292	.000	-101.1477	-32.5857
		Barf Grooks	-6.2333	5.08292	.946	-53.3343	40.8677
	Abba	Fugazi	66.8667*	5.08292	.000	32.5857	101.1477
		Barf Grooks	60.6333*	5.08292	.001	24.9547	96.3119
	Barf Grooks	Fugazi	6.2333	5.08292	.946	-40.8677	53.3343
		Abba	-60.6333*	5.08292	.001	-96.3119	-24.9547

Based on observed means.

*. The mean difference is significant at the .05 level.

SPSS Output 6.16

Given that we found a main effect of music, and of the interaction between music and age, we can look at some of the post hoc tests to establish where the difference lies (see page 178). SPSS Output 6.16 shows the result of Games-Howell post hoc tests. First, ratings of Fugazi are compared to ABBA, which reveals a significant difference (the value in the column labelled Sig. is less than .05), and then Barf Grooks, which reveals no difference (the significance value is greater than .05). In the next part of the table, ratings to ABBA are compared first to Fugazi (which just repeats the finding in the previous part of the table) and then to Barf Grooks, which reveals a significant difference (the significance value is below .05). The final part of the table compares Barf Grooks to Fugazi and ABBA but these results repeat findings from the previous sections of the table.

Calculating the Effect Size for Two-Way Independent ANOVA

SPSS Output 6.15 provides us with the measures of variance that we need to calculate omega-squared (see page 181). The experimental effect (MS_M) depends on which effect we're looking at, but the mean error variance (MS_R) is the same for all effects: 387.54. We can calculate ω^2 and subsequently ω using this value and the mean squares for the effect we're interested in, using the equation on page 181.

For the effect of music, SPSS Output 6.15 tells us that the mean squares for the effect is 40932.03, hence:

$$
\begin{aligned}
\omega^2_{Music} &= \frac{40932.03 - 387.54}{40932.03 + ((15 - 1) \times 387.54)} \\
&= \frac{40544.49}{40932.03 + 5425.57} \\
&= .88 \\
\omega_{Music} &= \sqrt{.88} = .94
\end{aligned}
$$

Using the benchmarks for effect sizes this represents a huge effect (it is close to 1). Therefore, the ratings given depended heavily on the music being evaluated.

$$
\begin{aligned}
\omega^2_{Age} &= \frac{.711 - 387.54}{40932.03 + ((15 - 1) \times 387.54)} \\
&= \frac{-386.83}{.711 + 5425.57} \\
&= -.07
\end{aligned}
$$

For the effect of age (above) the value of the squared effect size is negative (because the error actually explained more variance than the experimental effect!). It is impossible to compute a square root of a negative number and so we can't compute an effect size, using this equation. In fact, if the F-ratio is less than 1 (indicating that the mean error variance is larger than the mean variance explained by the effect) we'll always be unable to compute an un-squared effect size. If the F-ratio is exactly 1 then this effect size measure will give us a result of zero. We could use our more crude measure of the model sum of squares divided by the total sum of squares (see Box 5.1) and see what happens. These sums of squares can both be found in SPSS Output 6.15.

$$\omega_{Age}^2 = \frac{SS_M}{SS_T} = \frac{.711}{425208.40} = .00000167$$

$$\omega_{Age} = \sqrt{.00000167} = .00129$$

The result is very close to zero, and so zero is a good enough approximation of the size of this effect. Age has a truly unsubstantive effect on the preference ratings.

Moving onto the interaction term:

$$\omega_{Music^*Age}^2 = \frac{155395.08 - 387.54}{155395.08 + ((15 - 1) \times 387.54)}$$

$$= \frac{155007.54}{155395.08 + 5425.57}$$

$$= .96$$

$$\omega_{Music^*Age} = \sqrt{.96} = .98$$

Like the main effect of music, this finding is huge (it's very close to 1).

Writing the Result for Two-Way Independent ANOVA

As with the other ANOVAs we've encountered we have to report the details of the F-ratio and the degrees of freedom from which it was calculated. For the various effects in these data the F-ratios will be based on different degrees of freedom: it was derived from dividing the mean squares for the effect by the mean squares for the residual. For the effects of music and the music × age interaction, the model degrees of freedom was 2 ($df_M = 2$), but for the effect of age the degrees of freedom was only 1 ($df_M = 1$). For all effects, the degrees of freedom for the residuals were 84 ($df_R = 84$). We can, therefore, report the three effects from this analysis as follows:

☑ The results show that the main effect of the type of music listened to significantly affected the ratings of that music, $F(2, 84) = 105.62$, $p < .001$, $r = .94$. Games-Howell post hoc test revealed that ABBA were rated significantly higher than both Fugazi and Barf Grooks (both $ps < .01$).

☑ The main effect of age on the ratings of the music was non-significant, $F(1, 84) < 1$, $r = .00$.

☑ The music × age interaction was significant, $F(2, 84) = 400.98$, $p < .001$, $r = .98$, indicating that different types of music were rated differently by the two age groups. Specifically, Fugazi were rated more positively by the young group ($M = 66.20$, $SD = 19.90$) than the old ($M = -75.87$, $SD = 14.37$); ABBA were rated fairly equally in the young ($M = 64.13$, $SD = 16.99$) and old groups ($M = 59.93$, $SD = 19.98$); Barf Grooks was rated less positively by the young group ($M = -71.47$, $SD = 23.17$) compared to the old ($M = 74.27$, $SD = 22.29$). These findings indicate that there is no hope for me, the minute I hit 40 I will suddenly start to love country and western music and will burn all of my Fugazi CDs (it will never happen... arghhhh!!!).

6.9   Two-Way Mixed ANOVA

Now imagine that rather than measuring both independent variables with different people we decided to become a bit more efficient, and try measuring one independent variable using the same participants. So, we'd still have two independent variables but now one will be measured using the same participants and one will be measured using different participants. This design is known as mixed, because it is a blend of independent measures and repeated measures. So, the 'two-way' part tells us that if we want to use a two-way mixed ANOVA then we have to manipulate two independent variables, and the 'mixed' part tells us that one of these should be manipulated using different participants but for the other variable we should use the same participants.

Example: Text messaging is very popular amongst mobile phone owners, to the point that books have been published on how to write in text speak (BTW, hope u kno wat I mean by txt spk). One concern is that children may use this form of communication so much that it will hinder their ability to learn correct written English. One concerned researcher conducted an experiment in which one group of children were encouraged to send text messages on their mobile phones over a six month period. A second group was forbidden from sending text messages for the same period. To ensure that kids in this latter group didn't use their phones, this group were given armbands that administered painful shocks in the presence of microwaves (like those emitted from phones).[7] There were 50 different participants: 25 were encouraged to send text messages, and 25 were forbidden. The outcome was a score on a grammatical test (as a percentage) that was measured both before and after the experiment. The first independent variable was, therefore, text message use (text messagers versus controls) and the second independent variable was the time at which grammatical ability was assessed (before or after the experiment).

SPSS Output for Two-Way Mixed ANOVA

Figure 6.8 shows a line chart (with error bars) of the grammar data. The dots show the mean grammar score before and after the experiment for the text message group and the controls. The means before and after are connected by a line for the two groups separately. It's clear from this chart that in the text message group grammar scores went down dramatically over the 6 month period in which they used their mobile phone. For the controls, their grammar scores also fell but much less dramatically. The error bars on the graph represent the standard error (see page 134). Now, back on page 135 we saw that a 95% confidence interval was simply the mean ±2 standard errors. Therefore, these error bars are showing something similar to the error bars we've used before: that is, they show the variability in means from different samples. If we plot the standard error (rather

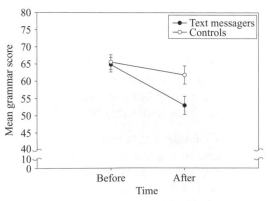

Figure 6.8   Line chart of the mean grammar scores (with error bars showing the standard error of the mean) before and after the experiment for text messagers and controls

than 2 standard errors) then this is actually the 68% confidence interval: the interval within which 68% of sample means will fall. Whether you choose to plot a single standard error either side of the mean, or the full 95% confidence interval (2 standard errors) is up to you because they provide similar information, but make sure you tell your reader what you've plotted!

SPSS Output 6.17 shows the table of descriptive statistics from the two-way mixed ANOVA; the table has means at time 1 split according to whether the people were in the text messaging group or the control group, then below we have the means for the two groups at time 2. These means correspond to those plotted in Figure 6.8.

As with all ANOVAs, there are assumptions that we have to check. We know that when we use repeated measures we have to check the assumption of sphericity (see page 183). We also know that for independent designs we need to check the homogeneity of variance assumption (see page 159). If the design is a mixed design then we have both repeated and independent measures, so we have to check both assumptions. SPSS Output 6.18 shows Mauchly's sphericity test (see page 184) and Levene's test (see page 176). You may recall from page 183 that the assumption of sphericity is basically that the variance of the differences between any two levels of the repeated measures variable is the same as the variance of the differences between any two other levels of that variable. In this case, we have only two levels of the repeated measure (before and after the experiment), therefore, there is only one pair of levels for which we could calculate the difference scores (and then the variance of those scores). In short, there would be no other pair of levels with which to compare the variances of the difference scores. So, the assumption of sphericity does not apply in this case. In fact, whenever you have only two levels of the repeated measures variable you don't have to worry about the sphericity assumption – it will always be true. To prove it, look at Mauchly's test in SPSS Output 6.18; the value is 1, the chi-square is 0, and the significance value is blank. When sphericity holds completely,

Descriptive Statistics

	Group	Mean	Std. Deviation	N
Grammar at Time 1	Text Messagers	64.8400	10.67973	25
	Controls	65.6000	10.83590	25
	Total	65.2200	10.65467	50
Grammar at Time 2	Text Messagers	52.9600	16.33116	25
	Controls	61.8400	9.41046	25
	Total	57.4000	13.93278	50

SPSS Output 6.17

Mauchly's Test of Sphericity[b]

Measure: MEASURE_1

Within Subjects Effect	Mauchly's W	Approx. Chi-Square	df	Sig.	Epsilon[a]		
					Greenhouse-Geisser	Huynh-Feldt	Lower-bound
TIME	1.000	.000	0	.	1.000	1.000	1.000

Tests the null hypothesis that the error covariance matrix of the orthonormalized transformed dependent variables is proportional to an identity matrix.

  a. May be used to adjust the degrees of freedom for the averaged tests of significance. Corrected tests are displayed in the Tests of Within-Subjects Effects table.

  b. Design: Intercept+GROUP
    Within Subjects Design: TIME

Levene's Test of Equality of Error Variances[a]

	F	df1	df2	Sig.
Grammar at Time 1	.089	1	48	.767
Grammar at Time 2	3.458	1	48	.069

Tests the null hypothesis that the error variance of the dependent variable is equal across groups.

  a. Design: Intercept+GROUP
    Within Subjects Design: TIME

SPSS Output 6.18

SPSS does not print a significance value; in this case this indicates that sphericity cannot be tested because there are only two levels of the repeated measure. OK, that was easy enough, but we still have to worry about homogeneity of variance. SPSS Output 6.18 shows Levene's test, and you should notice that it produces a different test for each level of the repeated measures variable. In mixed designs, the homogeneity assumption has to hold for every level of the repeated measures variable. As before, we are looking for a significant value (in the column labelled Sig.) to tell us that the assumption has been violated. At both levels of time, Levene's test is non-significant ($p = .77$ before the experiment and $p = .069$ after the experiment). This means the assumption has not been broken at all (but it was quite close to being a problem after the experiment).

    SPSS Output 6.19 shows the main ANOVA summary tables, and the first thing to note is that there are two of them! With all of the ANOVAs we've encountered so far the effects were summarized in a single table, but in a mixed design any results involving the repeated measure are placed in one table and the main effect of any independent measures are placed in a separate table. However, like any two-

Tests of Within-Subjects Effects

Measure: MEASURE_1

Source		Type III Sum of Squares	df	Mean Square	F	Sig.
TIME	Sphericity Assumed	1528.810	1	1528.810	15.457	.000
	Greenhouse-Geisser	1528.810	1.000	1528.810	15.457	.000
	Huynh-Feldt	1528.810	1.000	1528.810	15.457	.000
	Lower-bound	1528.810	1.000	1528.810	15.457	.000
TIME * GROUP	Sphericity Assumed	412.090	1	412.090	4.166	.047
	Greenhouse-Geisser	412.090	1.000	412.090	4.166	.047
	Huynh-Feldt	412.090	1.000	412.090	4.166	.047
	Lower-bound	412.090	1.000	412.090	4.166	.047
Error(TIME)	Sphericity Assumed	4747.600	48	98.908		
	Greenhouse-Geisser	4747.600	48.000	98.908		
	Huynh-Feldt	4747.600	48.000	98.908		
	Lower-bound	4747.600	48.000	98.908		

Tests of Between-Subjects Effects

Measure: MEASURE_1

Transformed Variable: Average

Source	Type III Sum of Squares	df	Mean Square	F	Sig.
Intercept	375891.610	1	375891.610	1933.002	.000
GROUP	580.810	1	580.810	2.987	.090
Error	9334.080	48	194.460		

SPSS Output 6.19

way ANOVA, we still have three effects to find: two main effects (one for each independent variable) and one interaction term.

The main effect of time is shown by the F-ratio in the row labelled time, and we are interested in the significance value of the observed F. To calculate this F we look at the experimental effect of time $(SS_{M(Time)} = 1528.81)$ and compare this to the unsystematic variation for time $(SS_{R(Time)} = 4747.60)$. These values are converted into average effects, or mean squares, by dividing by the degrees of freedom, which are 1 for the effect of time, and 48 for the unexplained variation. The effect of time is simply the mean square for time divided by the mean square error $(1528.81/98.91 = 15.46)$. SPSS has also calculated that the probability of getting an F-ratio this large by chance alone is .000, which is well below the usual cut-off point of .05. We can conclude that grammar scores were significantly affected by the time at which they were measured. The exact nature of this effect is easily determined because there were only two points in time (and so this main effect is comparing only two means). The overall means can be found in SPSS Output 6.17 and I've plotted them in Figure 6.9. The

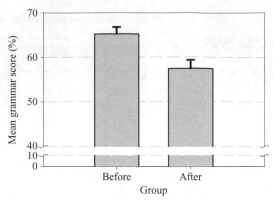

Figure 6.9   Mean grammar score before and after the experiment when you ignore whether the participant was allowed to text message or not. Error bars show the standard error of the mean (see page 134)

graph shows that grammar scores were higher before the experiment than after. So, before the experimental manipulation scores were higher than after, meaning that the manipulation had the net effect of significantly reducing grammar scores. This main effect seems rather interesting until you consider that these means include both text messagers and controls. There are three possible reasons for the drop in grammar scores: (1) the text messagers got worse and are dragging down the mean after the experiment, (2) the controls somehow got worse, or (3) the whole group just got worse and it had nothing to do with whether the children text messaged or not. Until we examine the interaction, we won't see which of these is true.

The main effect of group is shown by the F-ratio in the second table in SPSS Output 6.19. The variance explained by this variable, $SS_{M(Group)}$, is 580.81 compared to 9334.08 units of unsystematic variation, $SS_{R(Group)}$. Note that in a mixed ANOVA the two main effects have different error terms: there is one for the repeated measures variable and one for the independent measures variable. These sums of squares are converted to mean squares by dividing by their respective degrees of freedom (given in the table). The effect of group is the mean square for the effect divided by the mean square error ($580.80/194.46 = 2.99$). The probability associated with this F-ratio is .09, which is just above the critical value of .05. Therefore, we must conclude that there was no significant main effect on grammar scores of whether children text-messaged or not. Again, this effect seems interesting enough and mobile phone companies might certainly choose to cite it as evidence that text messaging does not affect your grammar ability. However, remember that this main effect ignores the time at which grammar ability is measured. It just means that if we took the average grammar score for text messagers (that's including their score both before and after they started using their phone), and compared this to the mean of the controls (again including scores before and after) then these means would not be significantly different. I've plotted these two means in Figure 6.10. This graph shows that when you ignore the time at which grammar was measured, the controls have slightly better grammar than the text messagers – but not significantly so.

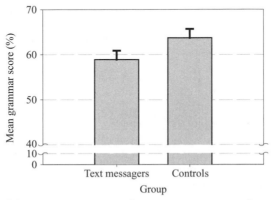

Figure 6.10 Mean grammar score for text messagers and controls when you ignore the time at which the grammar score was measured. Error bars show the standard error of the mean (see page 134)

As I've mentioned before, main effects are not always that interesting and should certainly be viewed in the context of any interaction effects. The interaction effect in this example is shown by the *F*-ratio in the row labelled Time*Group, and it explains 412.09 units of variation, $SS_{M(Interaction)}$. Note that the error term is the same as for the repeated measures main effect ($SS_{R(Time)} = 4747.60$). This interaction has 1 degree of freedom and so the resulting mean square is the same as the sum of squares. As ever, the *F*-ratio for the interaction effect is the mean square for the interaction divided by the mean square error ($412.09/98.91 = 4.17$). SPSS tells us that the probability of obtaining a value this big by chance is .047, which is just less than the criterion of .05. Therefore, we can say that there is a significant interaction between the time at which grammar was measured and whether or not children were allowed to text message within that time. The mean ratings in all conditions (see Figure 6.8 and SPSS Output 6.17) help us to interpret this effect. If there were no interaction, then we would expect the same change in grammar scores in those using text messages and controls (see Box 6.2). The fact there is a significant interaction tells us that the change in grammar scores was significantly

Text Messagers

Paired Samples Test[a]

		Paired Differences							
					95% Confidence Interval of the Difference				
		Mean	Std. Deviation	Std. Error Mean	Lower	Upper	t	df	Sig. (2-tailed)
Pair 1	Grammar Before - Grammar After	11.880	17.55069	3.51014	4.6354	19.1246	3.384	24	.002

a. Group = Text Messagers

Controls

Paired Samples Test[a]

		Paired Differences							
					95% Confidence Interval of the Difference				
		Mean	Std. Deviation	Std. Error Mean	Lower	Upper	t	df	Sig. (2-tailed)
Pair 1	Grammar Before - Grammar After	3.7600	9.35984	1.87197	-.1036	7.6236	2.009	24	.056

a. Group = Controls

SPSS Output 6.20

different in text messagers compared to controls. Looking at Figure 6.8 we can see that although grammar scores fell in controls, the drop was much more marked in the text messagers; so, text messaging does seem to ruin your ability at grammar compared to controls.[8]

Although we don't need post hoc tests as such because all of our variables had only two levels, we could do some further tests on the interaction term. One thing we could do is to look at the change in grammar for the text messagers and controls separately using dependent *t*-tests (to compare scores before with scores afterwards). However, if we do this we should make some correction for the number of tests that we do. I mentioned before that the easiest correction to use is known as Bonferroni correction (see page 173). This correction means that rather than use the standard critical probability value of .05, we instead use this value divided by the number of tests that we've done. In this case we've done 2 tests, so rather than accept these tests as significant if there is less than a .05 probability that the test statistic could occur by chance alone, we accept them as genuine results only if they are significant at $.05/2 = .025$. Now, we came across the dependent *t*-test on page 168 and if we do this separately for the two groups we get the outputs in SPSS Output 6.20. From these outputs it's clear that for the text messagers there is a significant drop in their grammar ability across the experiment ($p = .002$ which is less than the Bonferroni corrected value of .025) but there is not a significant drop in ability for the controls ($p = .056$, which is greater than the Bonferroni corrected value of .025). As such the interaction reflects the relatively greater decline in grammar ability in the text message group. This kind of analysis is known as *simple effects* analysis.

■ **Box 6.2: Interpreting Interaction Graphs (Line Charts)**

In Box 6.1 we had a look at how interactions could be represented using bar charts. In this section we've represented interactions using line charts. Actually, both are acceptable (although it's more common for people to use line charts for interactions in textbooks, bar charts are used very frequently in published research). In the data for how text messaging affected grammar ability over time, we found a significant interaction and concluded (from Figure 6.8) that the decline in grammar ability due to text messaging was significantly greater than the change when no text messages were allowed. Would you conclude the same from the graph below?

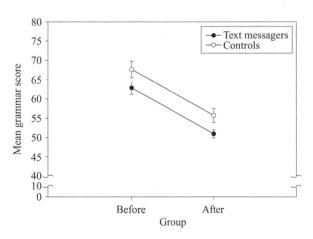

This profile of data would almost certainly not produce a significant interaction term because the change in grammar ability due to text messaging is now the same as the change caused by not sending text messages. The lines are parallel, indicating that the change in grammar ability is the same in both the text messagers and controls. So, we usually know just from looking at an interaction graph whether there is likely to be an interaction effect: if the lines are parallel (or nearly parallel) there won't be a significant interaction effect, but if the lines look non-parallel then there is a chance that there might be a significant interaction.

continues

■ **Box 6.2:** *continued*

Let's try another example. Is there an interaction now?

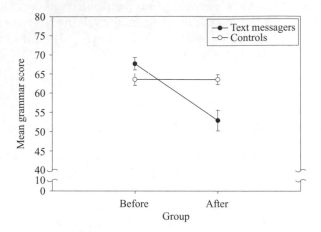

For these data there is an even stronger interaction than originally shown (see Figure 6.8). This is shown by the fact that the lines cross over. In fact, the control group shows no change in grammar ability (the line connecting the means from before and after the experiment is horizontal), but for the text messagers there is a decline in grammar ability. Crossed lines like these are non-parallel and, therefore, indicate the possibility of a significant interaction (although contrary to what some textbooks might have you believe it isn't always the case that if the lines of the interaction graph cross then the interaction is significant)!

Calculating the Effect Size for Two-Way Mixed ANOVA

SPSS Output 6.19 provides us with the two things we need to calculate each effect size: the mean squares for the effect (MS_M) and the mean squares for the error (MS_R). The exact value of the experimental effect (MS_M) depends on which effect we're looking at, and the unsystematic variance (MS_R) is different for the repeated measures effects and the between-group effect (note in SPSS Output 6.19 that there is an error term in each table). We can calculate the effect size for each of the effects in turn using the equation on page 181.

For the effect of time, SPSS Output 6.19 tells us that the mean squares for the effect is 1528.81, and the mean squares for the error is 98.91, hence:

$$\omega^2 = \frac{1528.81 - 98.91}{1528.81 + ((25 - 1) \times 98.91)}$$

$$= \frac{1429.90}{1528.81 + 2373.79}$$

$$= .37$$

$$\omega_{Time} = \sqrt{.37} = .61$$

Using the benchmarks for effect sizes this represents a large effect (it is around the threshold of .5). Therefore, the change in grammar ratings over time is a substantive finding.

$$\omega^2_{Group} = \frac{580.81 - 194.46}{580.81 + ((25 - 1) \times 194.46)}$$

$$= \frac{386.35}{580.81 + 4667.04}$$

$$= .07$$

$$\omega_{Group} = \sqrt{.07} = .27$$

We know already that the effect of group was non-significant but the effect size estimate indicates that there was actually a medium effect to be detected (you might remember that the significance value was close to .05). It's worth considering the possibility that we didn't detect this effect because our sample was relatively small.

$$\omega^2_{Time*Group} = \frac{412.09 - 98.91}{412.09 + ((25 - 1) \times 98.91)}$$

$$= \frac{313.18}{412.09 + 2373.79}$$

$$= .11$$

$$\omega_{Time*Group} = \sqrt{.11} = .34$$

Interestingly, the effect size for the interaction is not much larger than the effect size for the non-significant effect of group. This illustrates how statistical significance can be misleading. Nevertheless, the interaction between text messaging and the point in time when grammar was measured was a relatively strong effect.

Writing the Result for Two-Way Mixed ANOVA

Hopefully by now you know that for any effect in ANOVA we have to report the details of the *F*-ratio and the degrees of freedom from which it was calculated. The three effects we have here all have different *F*-ratios based on different degrees of freedom. For the main effects of time and group, and the time × group interaction, the model degrees of freedom were 1 ($df_M = 1$). The degrees of freedom for the residuals were 48 ($df_R = 48$) for both the repeated measures error term and the independent error term. We can report the three effects from this analysis as follows:

- ☑ The results show that the grammar ratings at the end of the experiment were significantly lower than those at the beginning of the experiment, $F(1, 48) = 15.46$, $p < .001$, $r = .61$.
- ☑ The main effect of group on the grammar scores was non-significant, $F(1, 48) = 2.99$, ns, $r = .27$. This indicated that when the time at which grammar was measured is ignored, the grammar ability in the text message group was not significantly different to the controls.
- ☑ The time × group interaction was significant, $F(1, 48) = 4.17$, $p < .05$, $r = .34$, indicating that the change in grammar ability in the text message group was significantly different to the change in the control group. Specifically, there was a significant drop in grammar ability in the text message group, $t(24) = 3.38$, $p < .01$, $r = .57$, but a much weaker drop in ability in the control group, $t(24) = 2.01$, ns, $r = .38$. These findings indicate that although there was a medium effect size in the natural decay of grammatical ability over time (as shown by the controls) there was a much stronger effect when participants were encouraged to use text messages. This shows that using text messages accelerates the inevitable decline in grammatical ability.

6.10   Two-Way Repeated Measures ANOVA

The final ANOVA that we have to consider is when we want to measure everything using the same participants. So, we still have two independent variables but now both of them will be measured using the same participants. If we want to use a two-way repeated measures ANOVA then the 'two-way' part tells us that we have to manipulate two independent variables, and the 'repeated measures' part tells us that both of these should be manipulated using the same participants.

Example: In my wonderful statistics textbook (which is wonderful only because it is so big that it is handy for propping up wonky tables, is useful for weight training, can be used to knock out attackers in dark alleyways, and is a superb cure of insomnia) I use an example of the beer-goggles effect (Field, 2000, p. 310). This effect is known to us all and can be summarized as a severe perceptual distortion after imbibing vast quantities of alcohol. The specific visual distortion is that previously unattractive people, suddenly become the hottest thing since Spicy Gonzalez' extra hot Tabasco-marinated chillies. In short, one minute you're standing in a zoo admiring the Orangutans, and the next you're wondering why someone would put Gail Porter (or whatever her surname is now) into a cage. Anyway, Field (2000) in a blatantly fabricated data set demonstrated that the beer-goggles effect was much stronger for men than women, and took effect only after two pints. Imagine we wanted to follow up this finding to look at what factors mediate the beer-goggles effect. Specifically, we thought that the beer-goggles effect might be made worse by the fact that it usually occurs in clubs, which have dim lighting. We took a sample of 26 men (because the effect is stronger in men) and gave them various doses of alcohol over four different weeks (0 pints, 2 pints, 4 pints and 6 pints of lager). This is our first independent variable, which we'll call alcohol consumption, and it has four levels. Each week (and, therefore, in each state of drunkenness) participants were asked to select a mate in a normal club (that had dim lighting) and then select a second mate in a specially designed club that had bright lighting. As such, the second independent variable was whether the club had dim or bright lighting. The outcome measure was the attractiveness of each mate as assessed by a panel of independent judges. To recap, all participants took part in all levels of the alcohol consumption variable, and selected mates in both brightly- and dimly-lit clubs.

I love you...

SPSS Output for Two-Way Repeated Measures ANOVA

Figure 6.11 shows a line chart displaying the mean attractiveness of the partner selected (with error bars) in dim and brightly lit clubs after the different doses of alcohol. The chart shows that in both dim and brightly lit clubs there is a tendency for men to select less attractive mates as they consume more and more alcohol.

SPSS Output 6.21 shows the means for all conditions in a table. These means correspond to those plotted in Figure 6.11.

When we looked at one-way repeated measures ANOVA we came across the assumption of sphericity (see page 183). This assumption has to be checked also when we have two repeated measure variables, the only complication being that we have to check it for every effect (including the interaction). SPSS Output 6.22 shows Mauchly's sphericity test (see page 184) and, in fact a test is produced for each

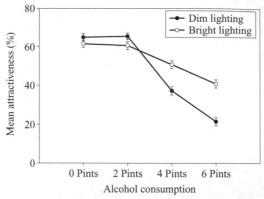

Figure 6.11   Line chart (with error bars showing the standard error of the mean – see page 202) of the mean attractiveness of the selected mate after different doses of alcohol in dim and brightly lit clubs

independent variable, and also the interaction between them. The variable lighting had only two levels (dim or bright) and so the assumption of sphericity doesn't apply (see page 203) and SPSS doesn't produce a significance value. However, for the effects of alcohol consumption and the interaction of alcohol consumption and lighting, we do have to look at Mauchly's test. The significance values are both above .05 (they are .454 and .768, respectively) and so we know that the assumption of sphericity has been met for both alcohol consumption, and the interaction of alcohol consumption and lighting.

Descriptive Statistics

	Mean	Std. Deviation	N
0 Pints (Dim Lighting)	65.0000	10.30728	26
2 Pints (Dim Lighting)	65.4615	8.76005	26
4 Pints (Dim Lighting)	37.2308	10.86391	26
6 Pints (Dim Lighting)	21.3077	10.67247	26
0 Pints (Bright Lighting)	61.5769	9.70432	26
2 Pints (Bright Lighting)	60.6538	10.65060	26
4 Pints (Bright Lighting)	50.7692	10.34334	26
6 Pints (Bright Lighting)	40.7692	10.77519	26

SPSS Output 6.21

SPSS Output 6.23 shows the main ANOVA summary table, and because both independent variables are measured in the same way (in this case both are repeated measures) all of the results appear in a single table. Like the other two-way ANOVAs we have encountered we have three effects to look at: two main effects (one for each independent variable) and one interaction term. The main difference to the

Mauchly's Test of Sphericity[b]

Measure: MEASURE_1

Within Subjects Effect	Mauchly's W	Approx. Chi-Square	df	Sig.	Epsilon[a]		
					Greenhouse -Geisser	Huynh-Feldt	Lower-bound
LIGHTING	1.000	.000	0	.	1.000	1.000	1.000
ALCOHOL	.820	4.700	5	.454	.873	.984	.333
LIGHTING * ALCOHOL	.898	2.557	5	.768	.936	1.000	.333

Tests the null hypothesis that the error covariance matrix of the orthonormalized transformed dependent variables is proportional to an identity matrix.

a. May be used to adjust the degrees of freedom for the averaged tests of significance. Corrected tests are displayed in the Tests of Within-Subjects Effects table.

b. Design: Intercept
Within Subjects Design: LIGHTING+ALCOHOL+LIGHTING*ALCOHOL

SPSS Output 6.22

Tests of Within-Subjects Effects

Measure: MEASURE_1

Source		Type III Sum of Squares	df	Mean Square	F	Sig.
LIGHTING	Sphericity Assumed	1993.923	1	1993.923	23.421	.000
	Greenhouse-Geisser	1993.923	1.000	1993.923	23.421	.000
	Huynh-Feldt	1993.923	1.000	1993.923	23.421	.000
	Lower-bound	1993.923	1.000	1993.923	23.421	.000
Error(LIGHTING)	Sphericity Assumed	2128.327	25	85.133		
	Greenhouse-Geisser	2128.327	25.000	85.133		
	Huynh-Feldt	2128.327	25.000	85.133		
	Lower-bound	2128.327	25.000	85.133		
ALCOHOL	Sphericity Assumed	38591.654	3	12863.885	104.385	.000
	Greenhouse-Geisser	38591.654	2.619	14736.844	104.385	.000
	Huynh-Feldt	38591.654	2.953	13069.660	104.385	.000
	Lower-bound	38591.654	1.000	38591.654	104.385	.000
Error(ALCOHOL)	Sphericity Assumed	9242.596	75	123.235		
	Greenhouse-Geisser	9242.596	65.468	141.177		
	Huynh-Feldt	9242.596	73.819	125.206		
	Lower-bound	9242.596	25.000	369.704		
LIGHTING * ALCOHOL	Sphericity Assumed	5765.423	3	1921.808	22.218	.000
	Greenhouse-Geisser	5765.423	2.809	2052.286	22.218	.000
	Huynh-Feldt	5765.423	3.000	1921.808	22.218	.000
	Lower-bound	5765.423	1.000	5765.423	22.218	.000
Error(LIGHTING*ALCOHOL)	Sphericity Assumed	6487.327	75	86.498		
	Greenhouse-Geisser	6487.327	70.232	92.370		
	Huynh-Feldt	6487.327	75.000	86.498		
	Lower-bound	6487.327	25.000	259.493		

SPSS Output 6.23

other two-way ANOVAs we have looked at is that each of these effects has its own error term.

The main effect of lighting is shown by the F-ratio in the row labelled lighting. Lighting explains 1993.92 ($SS_{M(Lighting)}$) units of variance compared with 2128.33 units explained by the unsystematic variation for lighting ($SS_{R(Lighting)}$). These values are converted into average effects, or mean squares, by dividing by the degrees of freedom, which are 1 for the effect of lighting, and 25 for the unexplained variation. The resulting F-ratio is the mean square for lighting divided by the mean square error (1993.92/85.13 = 23.42). The significance of this value is .000, which is well below the usual cut-off point of .05. We can conclude that average attractiveness ratings were significantly affected by whether mates were selected in a dim or well-lit club. We can easily interpret this result further because there were only two levels. Figure 6.12 shows the mean attractiveness of mates in dim and well-lit clubs when the amount of alcohol drunk is ignored. Attractiveness ratings were higher in the well-lit clubs, so we could conclude that when we ignore how much alcohol was consumed, the mates selected in well-lit clubs were significantly more attractive than those chosen in dim clubs.

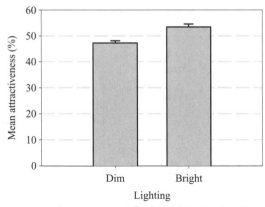

Figure 6.12   Mean attractiveness of selected mates in dim and brightly lit clubs when you ignore how much alcohol the participant had consumed. Error bars show the standard error of the mean (see page 134)

The main effect of alcohol consumption is shown by the F-ratio in the row labelled alcohol. The variance explained by this variable, $SS_{M(Alcohol)}$, is 38591.65 compared to 9242.60 units of unsystematic variation for that variable, $SS_{R(Alcohol)}$. These sums of squares are converted to mean squares by dividing by their respective degrees of freedom, and the F-ratio for this effect is, as ever, the mean square for the effect divided by the mean square error (12863.89/123.24 =

104.39). The probability associated with this *F*-ratio is reported as .000 (i.e. $p < .001$), which is well below the critical value of .05. We can conclude that there was a significant main effect of the amount of alcohol consumed on the attractiveness of the mate selected. We know that generally there was an effect, but without further tests (e.g. post hoc comparisons) we can't say exactly which doses of alcohol had the most effect. I've plotted the means for the four doses in Figure 6.13. This graph shows that when you ignore the lighting in the club, the attractiveness of mates is similar after no alcohol and two pints of lager but starts to rapidly decline at four pints and continues to decline after six pints.

SPSS Output 6.24 shows some post hoc tests for the main effect of alcohol (see pages 173 and 178). These tests compare the mean at each dose of alcohol with the means of all other doses but control for the number of tests that have been done (so that the overall probability of a Type I error never rises above .05). In this example I've chosen a Bonferroni correction, which is a generally accepted procedure (see page 173). The main column of interest is the one labelled Sig., but the confidence intervals also tell us the likely difference between means if we were to take other samples. If we took 100 pairs of samples from our population and calculated the difference between their means, then these confidence intervals tell us the boundaries between which 95% of these differences would fall. Obviously, if there were a genuine difference between a pair of group means, then we'd expect none of the 95 samples to generate a difference of zero. So, if our means are genuinely different the confidence interval should not cross zero. What

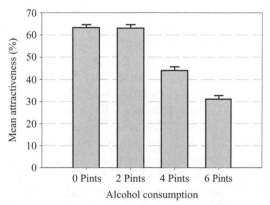

Figure 6.13 Mean attractiveness of selected mate after different quantities of alcohol when you ignore whether the selection was made in a dim or brightly lit club. Error bars show the standard error of the mean (see page 134)

Pairwise Comparisons

Measure: MEASURE_1

(I) ALCOHOL	(J) ALCOHOL	Mean Difference (I-J)	Std. Error	Sig.[a]	95% Confidence Interval for Difference[a]	
					Lower Bound	Upper Bound
1	2	.231	2.006	1.000	-5.517	5.978
	3	19.288*	2.576	.000	11.909	26.668
	4	32.250*	1.901	.000	26.804	37.696
2	1	-.231	2.006	1.000	-5.978	5.517
	3	19.058*	2.075	.000	13.112	25.003
	4	32.019*	1.963	.000	26.395	37.644
3	1	-19.288*	2.576	.000	-26.668	-11.909
	2	-19.058*	2.075	.000	-25.003	-13.112
	4	12.962*	2.450	.000	5.942	19.981
4	1	-32.250*	1.901	.000	-37.696	-26.804
	2	-32.019*	1.963	.000	-37.644	-26.395
	3	-12.962*	2.450	.000	-19.981	-5.942

Based on estimated marginal means

*. The mean difference is significant at the .05 level.

a. Adjustment for multiple comparisons: Bonferroni.

SPSS Output 6.24

these results show is that the mean attractiveness of the mate selected after no alcohol was not significantly different from that of the mate selected after two pints (p is 1, which is greater than .05). However, the mean attractiveness was significantly higher after no pints than it was after four pints and six pints (both ps are less than .001). This finding is consistent with what Field (2000, Chapter 8) reported from another load of completely made-up data. We can also see that the mean attractiveness after two pints was significantly higher than after four pints and six pints (again, both ps are less than .001). Finally, the mean attractiveness after four pints was significantly higher than after six pints (p is less than .001). So, we can conclude that the beer-goggles effect doesn't kick in until after two pints, and that it has an ever-increasing effect (well, up to six pints at any rate!).

The interaction effect is shown by the F-ratio in the row labelled Lighting*Alcohol. This effect explains 5765.42 units of variation, $SS_{M(Interaction)}$ compared to 6487.33 units explained by the unsystematic variance for this effect ($SS_{R(Interaction)}$). The resulting F-ratio is 22.22 (1921.81/86.50), which has an associated probability value of .000 (i.e. $p < .001$). As such, there is a significant interaction between the amount of alcohol consumed and the lighting in the club on the attractiveness of the mate selected. The means (see Figure 6.11 and SPSS Output 6.21) help us to interpret this effect. We know that if there were no interaction, then we'd expect the same change in attractiveness across the quantities of alcohol when there was dim lighting as when there was bright lighting (see Box 6.1 and Box 6.2). The fact there is a significant interaction tells us that the change in attractiveness due to alcohol was significantly different in dim clubs compared to bright ones. Figure 6.11 shows that the decline in attractiveness of mates after two pints is much more dramatic in dim clubs than in bright ones.

Can we be more precise about where the differences lie though? Well, one thing we can do is *contrasts* for the interaction term. These are tests that follow on from the main analysis and test specific predictions. The exact details of these tests are well beyond the scope of this book, but I cover them in a lot of detail in my statistics book if you want to know more (Field, 2000, Chapters 7 and 9). In essence they differ from post hoc tests in that rather than comparing everything with everything else, they compare a precise set of hypotheses. So, put simply, we specify certain groups that we'd like to compare. This has the advantage that we can conduct fewer tests, and therefore, we don't have to be quite so strict to control the Type I error rate. Therefore, these tests have more power to detect effects than post hoc tests and so are usually preferable. SPSS Output 6.25 shows the output from a set of contrasts that compare each level of the alcohol variable to the previous level of that variable (this is called a *repeated* contrast in SPSS). So, it compares no pints with two pints (level 1 versus level 2), two pints with four pints (level 2 versus level 3) and four pints with six pints (level 3 versus level 4). As you can see from the output, if we just look at the main effect of group these contrasts tell us what we already know from the post hoc tests, that is, the attractiveness after no alcohol doesn't differ from the attractiveness after two pints ($F(1, 25) < 1$), the attractiveness after four pints does differ from that after two pints ($F(1, 25) = 84.32$, $p < .001$) and the attractiveness after six pints does differ from that after four pints ($F(1, 25) = 27.98$, $p < .001$). More interesting is to look at the interaction term in the table. This compares the same levels of the alcohol variable, but for each comparison it is also comparing the difference between the means for the dim and brightly-lit clubs. One way to think of this is to look at Figure 6.11 and note the vertical differences between the means for dim and bright clubs at each level of alcohol. When nothing was drunk, the distance between the bright and dim means is quite small (it's actually 3.42 units on the attractiveness scale), when two pints of alcohol are drunk the difference between the dim and well-lit club is still quite small (4.81 units to be precise). The first contrast is comparing the difference between dim and bright clubs when nothing was drunk with the difference between dim and bright clubs when two pints were drunk. So, it is asking 'is 3.42 sig-

Tests of Within-Subjects Contrasts

Measure: MEASURE_1

Source	LIGHTING	ALCOHOL	Type III Sum of Squares	df	Mean Square	F	Sig.
LIGHTING	Level 1 vs. Level 2		996.962	1	996.962	23.421	.000
Error(LIGHTING)	Level 1 vs. Level 2		1064.163	25	42.567		
ALCOHOL		Level 1 vs. Level 2	1.385	1	1.385	.013	.909
		Level 2 vs. Level 3	9443.087	1	9443.087	84.323	.000
		Level 3 vs. Level 4	4368.038	1	4368.038	27.983	.000
Error(ALCOHOL)		Level 1 vs. Level 2	2616.115	25	104.645		
		Level 2 vs. Level 3	2799.663	25	111.987		
		Level 3 vs. Level 4	3902.462	25	156.098		
LIGHTING * ALCOHOL	Level 1 vs. Level 2	Level 1 vs. Level 2	49.846	1	49.846	.144	.708
		Level 2 vs. Level 3	8751.115	1	8751.115	24.749	.000
		Level 3 vs. Level 4	912.154	1	912.154	2.157	.154
Error(LIGHTING*ALCOHOL)	Level 1 vs. Level 2	Level 1 vs. Level 2	8680.154	25	347.206		
		Level 2 vs. Level 3	8839.885	25	353.595		
		Level 3 vs. Level 4	10569.846	25	422.794		

SPSS Output 6.25

nificantly different from 4.81?' The answer is 'no', because the F-ratio is non-significant – in fact, it's less than 1 ($F(1, 25) < 1$). The second contrast for the interaction is comparing the difference between dim and bright clubs when two pints were drunk (4.81) with the difference between dim and bright clubs when four pints were drunk (this difference is −13.54, note the direction of the difference has changed as indicated by the lines crossing in Figure 6.11). This difference is significant ($F(1, 25) = 24.75$, $p < .001$). The final contrast for the interaction is comparing the difference between dim and bright clubs when four pints were drunk (−13.54) with the difference between dim and bright clubs when six pints were drunk (this difference is 19.46). This contrast is not significant ($F(1, 25) = 2.16$, *ns*). So, we could conclude that there was a significant interaction between the amount of alcohol drunk and the lighting in the club. Specifically, the effect of alcohol after two pints on the attractiveness of the mate was much more pronounced when the lights were dim.

Calculating the Effect Size for Two-Way Repeated Measures ANOVA

In two-way repeated measures ANOVA each of the three effects (lighting, alcohol and the interaction) has its own error term. To calculate the effect size we need to look at SPSS Output 6.23 and get the value of the mean square for each effect (MS_M), and the mean square for its associated error term (MS_R). We can then place these values into the equation for the effect size on page 181.

For the effect of lighting, we look at SPSS Output 6.23 and find that the mean squares for the experimental effect are 1993.92, and the mean squares for the error term are 85.13.

$$\omega^2_{Lighting} = \frac{1993.92 - 85.13}{1993.92 + ((26 - 1) \times 85.13)}$$

$$= \frac{1908.79}{1993.92 + 2128.25}$$

$$= .46$$

$$\omega_{Lighting} = \sqrt{.46} = .68$$

Using the benchmarks for effect sizes this represents a large effect (it is above the threshold of .5). Therefore, the change in attractiveness of the mate due to lighting is a substantive finding.

$$\omega^2_{Alcohol} = \frac{12863.89 - 123.235}{12863.89 + ((26 - 1) \times 123.24)}$$

$$= \frac{12740.65}{12863.89 + 3080.88}$$

$$= .80$$

$$\omega_{Alcohol} = \sqrt{.80} = .89$$

Using the benchmarks for effect sizes the effect of alcohol was very large (it is well above the threshold of .5, and is close to 1). Therefore, the change in attractiveness of the mate due to alcohol is a substantive finding.

$$\omega^2_{Lighting \times Alcohol} = \frac{1921.81 - 86.50}{1921.81 + ((26 - 1) \times 86.50)}$$

$$= \frac{1835.31}{1921.81 + 2162.45}$$

$$= .45$$

$$\omega_{Lighting \times Alcohol} = \sqrt{.45} = .67$$

The interaction has a large effect size, so, the combined effect of lighting and alcohol on the attractiveness of the selected mate was very substantial.

Writing the Result for Two-Way Repeated Measures ANOVA

The write up of a two-way repeated measures ANOVA is much the same as the other two-way ANOVAs that we've come across: you have to report the details of the *F*-ratio and the degrees of freedom from which it was calculated for each of the three effects. The main difference is you'll need to look up different error degrees of freedom for each effect, because each effect had its own error term. We can report the three effects from this analysis as follows (check back to SPSS Output 6.23 to see from where I got the degrees of freedom):

☑ The results show that the attractiveness of the mates selected was significantly lower when the lighting in the club was dim compared to when the lighting was bright, $F(1, 25) = 23.42$, $p < .001$, $r = .68$.

☑ The main effect of alcohol on the attractiveness of mates selected was significant, $F(3, 75) = 104.39$, $p < .001$, $r = .89$. This indicated that when the lighting in the club was ignored, the attractiveness of the mates selected differed according to how much alcohol was drunk before the selection was made. Specifically, post hoc test revealed that compared to a baseline of when no alcohol had been consumed, the attractiveness of selected mates was not different after two pints ($p > .05$), but was significantly lower after four and six pints (both $ps <$ .001). The mean attractiveness after two pints was also significantly higher than after four pints and six pints (both $ps <$ .001), and the mean attractiveness after four pints was significantly higher than after six pints ($p < .001$). To sum up, the beer-goggles effect seems to take effect after two pints have been consumed and has an increasing impact until six pints are consumed.

☑ The lighting × alcohol interaction was significant, $F(3, 75) =$ 22.22, $p < .001$, $r = .67$, indicating that the effect of alcohol on the attractiveness of the mates selected differed when lighting was dim compared to when it was bright. Contrasts on this interaction term revealed that when the difference in attractiveness ratings between dim and bright clubs was compared after no alcohol and after two pints had been drunk there was no significant difference, $F(1, 25) < 1$. However, when comparing the difference between dim and bright clubs when two pints were drunk with the difference after four pints were drunk a significant difference emerged, $F(1, 25) = 24.75$, $p < .001$. A final contrast revealed that the difference between dim and bright clubs after four pints were drunk compared to after six pints was not significant, $F(1, 25) = 2.16$, *ns*. To sum up, there was a significant interaction between the amount of alcohol drunk and the lighting in the club: the decline in the attractiveness of the selected mate seen after two pints (compared to after four) was significantly more pronounced when the lights were dim.

6.11 Analysis of Covariance (ANCOVA)

Often when we conduct an experiment, we know (from previous research) that some factors already have an influence over our dependent variable. For example, in any memory experiment we might want to be aware of the fact that memory gets worse as you get older. Age could confound the results of our experiment. Variables such as these, that are not part of the main experimental manipulation but have an influence on the dependent variable, are known as covariates and they can be included in an ANOVA (see Field, 2000, Chapter 8). For example, in the previous example in which we looked at the effect of alcohol and lighting on the beer-goggles effect, we know that the effect of alcohol (i.e. how drunk you get) will depend on factors such as weight (big people can generally drink more before they get drunk whereas little people like me only have to sniff a glass of wine and they're staggering around saying 'you're my best friend in the whole world' to a chair) and tolerance (people who drink regularly require more alcohol to get drunk). Therefore, to assess the true effect we might want to take account of these factors. Likewise, in our text message example (see page 201), we had two groups: one of which was encouraged to use text messages and the other was discouraged. However, there would have been individual differences in the amount of text messages sent in the 6 month period: people encouraged to use text messages will differ in the degree to which they use text messages, and those discouraged probably still used some text messages, and again would show individual differences. We would expect that the number of text messages sent would relate to the drop in grammatical ability, and so we might want to control this variable. If these variables (covariates) are measured, then it is possible to control for the influence they have on the dependent variable by including them in the analysis. What, in effect, happens is a two stage process: (1) we work out how much variance in the outcome can be explained by the covariate (so, if you imagine the total variance is a cake, then we remove a slice that represents the effect of the covariate); then (2) we look at what's left over (we can't look at the variance explained by the covariate anymore because that slice of cake has been eaten and we certainly don't want to vomit it back up!), and see how much of what's left over is explained by the experimental manipulation. So, we start with 100% of variance, say the covariate can explain 20% of this, then we become interested in how much of the remaining 80% the experimental manipulation can explain. In short, we end up seeing the effect an independent variable has after removing the effect of the covariate – we control for (or partial out) the effect of the covariate (see Field, 2000, Chapters 7 and 8 for details). The purpose of including covariates in ANOVA is two-fold:

> *To reduce the error variance*: The F-ratio in ANOVA compares the amount of variability explained by the experimental manipulation (MS_M), against the variability that it cannot explain (MS_R). What we hope is that the covariate explains different variance to the experiment, and so it explains some of the variance that was previously unexplained. This has the effect of reducing the unexplained variance (MS_R becomes smaller), and so our F-ratio gets bigger. In real terms this means we're getting a much more sensitive measure of our experimental effect.

> *Elimination of confounds*: As I've explained, in any experiment there may be unmeasured variables that confound the results (i.e. a variable that varies systematically with the experimental manipulation). By measuring and controlling for these variables in the analysis we remove the bias of these variables.

When we include covariates into ANOVA it becomes known as Analysis of Covariance (or ANCOVA for short). We can include covariates in any of the situations we've come across (independent t-test, dependent t-test, one-way independent, one-way repeated, two-way independent, two-way repeated and two-way mixed), and we can include one covariate or several in an analysis. For this example we'll keep things simple and look at a simple two-group example (different participants) with only one covariate.

ANCOVA has the same basic assumptions of all of the parametric tests, but it has an additional one as well: that is, the assumption of homogeneity of regression slopes. Put simply, in ANCOVA we assume that our covariate has some effect with our outcome variable (in fact we assume they are correlated so as scores on the covariate change, scores on the outcome change by a similar amount). Obviously, we hope that the effect that the covariate has on the outcome is the same for all of the groups we test. This is the assumption of the homogeneity of regression slopes: we assume that the relationship between the covariate and the outcome variable is the same in all of the groups we test. How this is tested is more complex than just ticking a button in SPSS, and so I'll simply refer you to Field (2000, Section 8.1.4) if you want to know more. For now, just be aware that this assumption exists.

Example: Stalking is a very disruptive and upsetting (for the person being stalked) experience in which someone (the stalker) constantly harasses or obsesses about another person. It can take many forms, from sending intensely disturbing letters threatening to boil your cat if you don't reciprocate the stalker's undeniable love for you, to literally following you around your local area in a desperate attempt to see which CD you buy on a Saturday (as if it would be anything other than Fugazi!). A psychologist, who'd had enough of being stalked by people, decided to try two different therapies on different groups of stalkers (25 stalkers in each group). The first group of stalkers he gave what he termed 'cruel to be kind therapy'. This therapy was based on punishment for stalking behaviours; in short, every time the stalker followed him around, or sent him a letter, the psychologist attacked them with a cattle prod until they stopped their stalking behaviour. It was hoped that the stalkers would learn an aversive reaction to anything resembling stalking. The second therapy was 'psychodyshamic therapy', which was a recent development on Freud's psychodynamic therapy that acknowledges what a sham this kind of treatment is (so, you could say it's based on Fraudian theory!). The stalkers were hypnotized and regressed into their childhood, the therapist would also discuss their penis (unless it was a woman in which case they discussed their lack of penis), the penis of their father, their dog's penis, the penis of the cat down the road, and anyone else's penis that sprang to mind. At the end of therapy, the psychologist measured the number of hours in the week that the stalker spent stalking their prey. Now, the therapist believed that the success of therapy might well depend on how bad the problem was to begin with, so before therapy the therapist measured the number of hours that the patient spent stalking (as an indicator of how much of a stalker the person was).

SPSS Output for ANCOVA

SPSS Output 6.26 shows (for illustrative purposes) the ANOVA table when the covariate is not included. It is clear from the significance value that there is no difference in the hours spent stalking after therapy for the two therapy groups (p is .074 which is greater than .05). You should note that the total amount of variation to be explained (SS_T) was 9118, of which the experimental manipulation accounted for 591.68 units (SS_M), whilst 8526.32 were unexplained (SS_R).

Figure 6.14 shows a bar chart of the mean number of hours spent stalking after therapy. The normal means are shown as well as the same means when the data are adjusted for the effect of the covariate. In this case the adjusted and unadjusted means are relatively similar, however, sometimes the effect of the covariate will have a more pro-

Tests of Between-Subjects Effects

Dependent Variable: Time Spent Stalking After Therapy (hours per week)

Source	Type III Sum of Squares	df	Mean Square	F	Sig.
Corrected Model	591.680ᵃ	1	591.680	3.331	.074
Intercept	170528.000	1	170528.000	960.009	.000
THERAPY	591.680	1	591.680	3.331	.074
Error	8526.320	48	177.632		
Total	179646.000	50			
Corrected Total	9118.000	49			

a. R Squared = .065 (Adjusted R Squared = .045)

SPSS Output 6.26

nounced effect on the group means. The more noticeable difference that the covariate makes for these data is that it reduces the standard error of the group means (the bars sticking out of the top are shorter for the covariate adjusted means).

SPSS Output 6.27 shows the unadjusted means (i.e. the normal means if we ignore the effect of the covariate). These are the same values plotted on the left hand side of Figure 6.14. These results show that the time spent stalking after therapy was less after cruel to be kind therapy. However, we know from SPSS Output 6.26 that this difference is non-significant. So, what now happens when we consider the effect of the covariate (in this case the extent of the stalker's problem before therapy)?

Before, we get too carried away we need to check the homogeneity of variance assumption (see page 159). SPSS Output 6.28 shows the results of Levene's test, which is significant because the significance

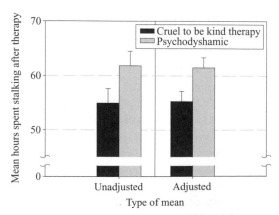

Figure 6.14 Mean number of hours spent stalking after the two types of therapy (the normal group means are shown but also the same means adjusted for the effect of the covariate)

Descriptive Statistics

Dependent Variable: Time Spent Stalking After Therapy (hours per week)

Group	Mean	Std. Deviation	N
Cruel to be Kind Therapy	54.9600	16.33116	25
Psychodyshamic Therapy	61.8400	9.41046	25
Total	58.4000	13.64117	50

SPSS Output 6.27

value is .01 (less than .05). This finding tells us that the variances across groups are different and the assumption has been broken. We could try to transform our data to rectify this problem (see page 176) or do a non-parametric test instead (see Chapter 7). If these options don't work then we must report the significance of Levene's test when we report the results — we might also be cautious about how we interpret the results because the final ANCOVA will lack accuracy.

Levene's Test of Equality of Error Variances[a]

Dependent Variable: Time Spent Stalking After Therapy (hours per week)

F	df1	df2	Sig.
7.189	1	48	.010

Tests the null hypothesis that the error variance of the dependent variable is equal across groups.

a. Design: Intercept+STALK1+GROUP

SPSS Output 6.28

The format of the ANCOVA table (SPSS Output 6.29) is largely the same as without the covariate, except that there is an additional row of information about the covariate (the hours spent stalking before therapy commenced). Looking first at the significance values, it is clear that the covariate significantly predicts the dependent variable, so the hours spent stalking after therapy depends on the extent of the initial problem (i.e. the hours spent stalking before therapy). More interesting is that when the effect of initial stalking behaviour is removed, the effect of therapy becomes significant (p has gone down from .074 to .023, which is less than .05). The amount of variation accounted for by the model (SS_M) has gone down to 480.27 units, which means that initial stalking behaviour actually explains some of the same variance that therapy accounted for in the initial ANOVA; however, it also explains a lot of the variance that was previously unexplained (the error variance, SS_R has decreased to 4111.72 – nearly half its original value). Notice that the total amount of varia-

Tests of Between-Subjects Effects

Dependent Variable: Time Spent Stalking After Therapy (hours per week)

Source	Type III Sum of Squares	df	Mean Square	F	Sig.
Corrected Model	5006.278[a]	2	2503.139	28.613	.000
Intercept	8.646E-02	1	8.646E-02	.001	.975
HOURS SPENT STALKING BEFORE THERAPY	4414.598	1	4414.598	50.462	.000
THERAPY	480.265	1	480.265	5.490	.023
Error	4111.722	47	87.483		
Total	179646.000	50			
Corrected Total	9118.000	49			

a. R Squared = .549 (Adjusted R Squared = .530)

SPSS Output 6.29

tion (9118.00) has not changed, all that has changed is how that total variation is explained. The result of the covariate explaining some of the error variance, is that the mean square error (MS_R) has gone down too (from 177.63 to 87.48), the resulting F-ratio is, therefore, bigger than before. In fact it has gone up from 3.33 to 5.49, which explains why it is now significant.

This example illustrates how ANCOVA can help us to exert stricter experimental control by taking account of confounding variables to give us a 'purer' measure of effect of the experimental manipulation. Without taking account of the initial level of stalking behaviour we would have concluded that the different therapies had no effect on stalking behaviour, yet clearly it does. To interpret the results of the main effect of therapy we need to look at adjusted means. Adjusted means are the group means, adjusted for whatever effect the covariate has had. SPSS Output 6.30 shows the adjusted means for these data; note that these means are different from the unadjusted ones in SPSS Output 6.27 (both sets of means are compared in Figure 6.14). Although in this example the adjusted means are fairly similar to

Group

Dependent Variable: Time Spent Stalking After Therapy (hours per week)

Group	Mean	Std. Error	95% Confidence Interval	
			Lower Bound	Upper Bound
Cruel to be Kind Therapy	55.299[a]	1.871	51.534	59.063
Psychodyshamic Therapy	61.501[a]	1.871	57.737	65.266

a. Evaluated as covariates appeared in the model: Time Spent Stalking Before Therapy (hours per week) = 65.2200.

SPSS Output 6.30

the unadjusted ones this will not always be the case so be sure to check the adjusted ones when you make your interpretation. There are only two groups being compared in this example so we can conclude that the therapies had a significantly different effect on stalking behaviour; specifically stalking behaviour was lower after the therapy involving the cattle prod compared to psychodyshamic therapy.

In addition to the main effect, we need to interpret the covariate. In SPSS Output 6.29 we can see that the covariate has its own *F*-ratio and this is significant (the value of *p* is .000 in the output indicating a highly significant result). To interpret this result you need to think about what would happen if we plotted the values of the dependent variable against the values of the covariate. Figure 6.15 shows such a graph for the time spent stalking after therapy (dependent variable) and the initial level of stalking (covariate). This graph shows that there is a positive relationship between the two variables, that is, high scores on one variable correspond with high scores on the other, whereas low scores on one variable correspond with low scores on the other (see Field, 2000, Chapter 3). If we were to do a correlation between these two variables we would find a significant correlation between them. The *F*-ratio is just telling us the same thing as the correlation would: there is a significant relationship between initial levels of stalking and levels of stalking after therapy. The graph tells us that this relationship is positive.

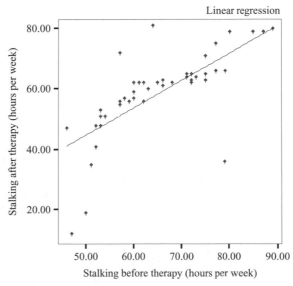

Figure 6.15 Scatterplot showing the relationship between the time spent stalking before therapy and the time spent stalking after therapy

Calculating the Effect Size for ANCOVA

In ANCOVA the effect size is calculated in the same way as all of the other ANOVAs we've come across; we just need to find out the effect of the variables in the model (the independent variables and the covariate) and the error term. If we look at SPSS Output 6.29 we can get the value of the mean square for each effect (MS_M), and the mean square for its associated error term (MS_R). We can then place these values into the equation for the effect size on page 181.

For the effect of therapy, the mean squares for the experimental effect are 480.27, and the mean squares for the error term are 87.48.

$$\omega^2_{Therapy} = \frac{480.27 - 87.48}{480.27 + ((25 - 1) \times 87.48)}$$

$$= \frac{392.78}{480.27 + 2099.59}$$

$$= .15$$

$$\omega_{Therapy} = \sqrt{.15} = .39$$

Using the benchmarks for effect sizes this represents a medium to large effect (it is between the thresholds of .3 and .5). Therefore, the effect of a cattle prod compared to psychodyshamic therapy is a substantive finding.

For the effect of the covariate, the error mean squares is the same, but the effect is much bigger (MS_M is 4414.60 rounded to 2 decimal places). If we place this value in the equation, we get the following:

$$\omega^2_{Covariate} = \frac{4414.60 - 87.48}{4414.60 + ((25 - 1) \times 87.48)}$$

$$= \frac{4327.12}{4414.60 + 2099.59}$$

$$= .66$$

$$\omega_{Covariate} = \sqrt{.66} = .82$$

Using the benchmarks for effect sizes this represents a very large effect (it is well above the threshold of .5, and is close to 1). Therefore, the relationship between initial stalking behaviour and the stalking behaviour after therapy is very strong indeed.

Writing the Result for ANCOVA

The write up for an ANCOVA is exactly the same as reporting the ANOVA, except that we have to report and interpret the effect of the covariate. For this analysis, we need to report two effects: the effect of therapy and the effect of the covariate. We can report these effects as follows (check back to SPSS Output 6.29 to see from where I got the degrees of freedom):

☑ Levene's test was significant, $F(1, 48) = 7.19$, $p < .05$, indicating that the assumption of homogeneity of variance had been broken. The main effect of therapy was significant, $F(1, 47) = 5.49$, $p < .05$, $r = .39$, indicating that the time spent stalking was lower after using a cattle prod ($M = 55.30$, $SE = 1.87$) compared to after psychodyshamic therapy ($M = 61.50$, $SE = 1.87$).

☑ The covariate was also significant, $F(1, 47) = 50.46$, $p < .001$, $r = .82$, indicating that level of stalking before therapy had a significant effect on level of stalking after therapy (there was a positive relationship between these two variables).

6.12 Summary

This chapter has introduced you to most of the commonly used parametric statistical tests. We started (in fact it's so long ago since I started writing the damn thing that I can't even remember how we started . . .) by looking at simple situations in which you have only two experimental conditions (the *t*-test). The remainder of the chapter introduced you to Analysis of Variance (ANOVA). For each test we looked at an example, saw how we could interpret the output from SPSS (a commonly used statistical package) and started to think about how we could interpret and report the results. Along the way we discovered that we couldn't always rely on our data meeting the assumptions of certain tests. The next chapter will tell us what to do when we break these assumptions.

6.13 Practical Tasks

For each example in this chapter:

• Write a sample results section (using the summaries at the end of each example as a guide) but as you do so identify where all of the numbers come from and what they mean.

For each example in this chapter use Field (2000) or notes on my web page (http://www.cogs.susx.ac.uk/users/andyf/teaching):

- Analyse the data and see if you can get the same outputs as I have (the SPSS data files can be found on my website).

6.14 Further Reading

It will come as no great shock to discover that I recommend my own book for more details on the statistical tests covered in this chapter. The whole reason I wrote the other book was because I wanted an integrated guide on statistical theory and SPSS, and I worked my socks off trying to make it the most entertaining guide possible. It's got lots of theory in it, and lots of practical advice to help you get the results that I did using SPSS.

Field, A. P. (2000). *Discovering statistics using SPSS for Windows: advanced techniques for the beginner*. London: Sage. Chapters 6 (*t*-test), 7 (one-way ANOVA), 8 (ANCOVA and two-way independent ANOVA) and 9 (repeated measures ANOVAs).

If you don't like my book, then try:

Howell, D. C. (2001). *Statistical methods for psychology* (5th edition). Belmont, CA: Duxbury. This is the definitive textbook for theory, but some undergraduates do find it too complex.

Notes

[1] As we saw in the section on p. 132, the standard error is just the sample standard deviation divided by the square root of the sample size ($SE = s/\sqrt{N}$), so for the 'Marie Claire' condition $SE = 4.71/\sqrt{10} = 4.71/3.16 = 1.489$.

[2] I used the two-tailed probability because I made no specific prediction about the direction of the effect. However, had I predicted before the experiment that happiness would be higher after reading 'Marie Claire' then this would be a one-tailed hypothesis. Often in research we can make specific predictions about which group has the highest mean. In this case, we can use a one-tailed test (for more discussion of this issue see Box 5.3 and Field, 2000). It might seem strange that SPSS produces only the two-tailed significance and that there isn't an option that can be selected to produce the one-tailed significance. However, there is no need for an option because, when the results are in the direction that you predicted, the one-tailed

probability can be ascertained by dividing the two-tailed significance value by 2. In this case, the two-tailed probability was .048,
therefore the one-tailed probability is .024 (= .048/2). However, if
the results are in the opposite direction to what you predicted you
have to keep your two-tailed significance value.

[3] In fact, if you used ANOVA when you have only two experimental
conditions you'd reach identical conclusions to when a two-tailed *t*-
test is used.

[4] SPSS rounds values to three decimal places. Therefore, when you
see a significance value of .000 in SPSS this isn't zero, it's just zero to
3 decimal places; the actual value could be .0001 or .000004768. As
far as we're concerned we just report these significance values as
$p < .001$.

[5] For the benefit of Garth Brook's lawyers, if they're reading, I
should add a disclaimer that this is only the opinion of the authors
and that we're sure all of his CDs are wonderful really.

[6] In case you haven't had the pleasure their record label has a website
http://www.dischord.com

[7] Although this punished them for any attempts to use a mobile
phone, an unfortunate side effect was that 10 of the sample developed conditioned phobias of porridge after repeatedly trying to heat
some up in the microwave!

[8] It's interesting that the control group means dropped too. This
could be because the control group were undisciplined and still
used their mobile phones, or it could just be that the education
system in this country is so under funded that there is no-one to
teach English anymore!

7 Non-parametric Statistics

In the last chapter, we saw that to do parametric statistics we needed certain assumptions to be met. We also saw that these assumptions are not always met and that often we can't even transform the data to make them conform to the assumptions we require. So, what on earth do we do in these situations? Luckily, a whole range of tests have been developed that do not require parametric assumptions, these are called non-parametric tests. This chapter concentrates on the four most commonly used non-parametric tests and, like the last chapter, I won't dwell on the theory behind them. I'll just tell you when they should be used, show you an output from SPSS and explain how to interpret and write up the results. I hope that I can do this in fewer pages than the parametric tests!

7.1 Non-Parametric Tests: Rationale

Non-parametric tests are sometimes known as assumption-free tests because they make less strict assumptions about the distribution of data being analysed.[1] The way they get around the problem of the distribution of the data is by not using the raw scores. Instead, the data are ranked. The basic idea of ranking is that you find the lowest score and give it a rank of 1, then find the next highest score and give it a rank of 2, and so on. As such, high scores are converted into large ranks, and low scores are converted into small ranks. The analysis is carried out on the ranks rather than the actual data. Ranking is an ingenious way around the problem of using non-normal data but it has a price: by ranking the data we lose some information about the magnitude of difference between scores and because of this non-parametric tests are less powerful than the parametric counterparts. I talked about the notion of statistical power earlier on (see page

154): it refers to the ability of a test to find an effect that genuinely exists. The fact that non-parametric tests are generally (but not always) less powerful means that if there is a genuine effect in our data, then, if its assumptions are met, a parametric test is more likely to detect it than a non-parametric one. Put a different way, there is an increased chance of a Type II error (i.e. more chance of accepting that there is no difference between groups when, in reality, a difference exists).

7.2 The Mann-Whitney Test

The Mann-Whitney test is the non-parametric equivalent of the independent t-test (see page 163) and so is used for testing differences between groups when there are two conditions and different participants have been used in each condition.

Example: A psychologist was interested in the cross-species differences between men and dogs. She observed a group of dogs and a group of men in a naturalistic setting (20 of each). She classified several behaviours as being dog-like (urinating against trees and lamp-posts, attempts to copulate with anything that moved, and attempts to lick their own genitals). For each man and dog she counted the number of dog-like behaviours displayed in a 24-hour period. It was hypothesized that dogs would display more dog-like behaviours than men.[2]

Don't mention dogs!

This psychologist, having collected the data, noticed that the data were non-normal in the dog condition. In fact the Kolmogorov-Smirnov test (see page 160) was highly significant ($D(20) = .244$, $p < .01$) for the dogs but wasn't for the men ($D(20) = .175$, *ns*) (see SPSS Output 7.1). The fact that the dog data are non-normal tells us that a non-parametric test is appropriate.

Tests of Normality

	Species	Kolmogorov-Smirnov[a]			Shapiro-Wilk		
		Statistic	df	Sig.	Statistic	df	Sig.
Dog-Like Behaviour	Dog	.244	20	.003	.899	20	.039
	Man	.175	20	.109	.933	20	.176

a. Lilliefors Significance Correction

SPSS Output 7.1

Output from the Mann-Whitney Test

The Mann-Whitney test looks for differences in the ranked positions of scores in the two groups. It makes sense then that SPSS first summarizes the data after it has been ranked. It tells us the average and total ranks in each condition (see SPSS Output 7.2). I told you earlier that scores are ranked from lowest to highest: therefore, the group with the lowest mean rank will have more low scores in it than the group with the highest mean rank. Therefore, this initial table tells us which group had the highest scores, which enables us to interpret a significant result should we find one.

The second table (SPSS Output 7.3) provides the actual test statistics for the Mann-Whitney test. Actually, although Mann and Whitney get all of the credit for this test, Wilcoxon also came up with a statistically comparable technique for analysing ranked data. The form of the test commonly taught is that of the Mann-Whitney test (I'm sure this has happened only because it would be confusing to many students and researchers to have two Wilcoxon tests that were used in different situations!). However, Wilcoxon's version of the test can be converted into a z-score and, therefore, can be compared against critical values of the normal distribution. This is handy because it means we can find out the exact significance rather than relying on printed tables of critical values. SPSS provides both statistics and the z-score for the Wilcoxon statistic.

SPSS Output 7.3 provides the value of Mann-Whitney's U statistic, the value of Wilcoxon's statistic and the associated z approximation. The z approximation becomes more accurate as sample sizes increase, so the bigger your sample, the more you can be confident in this statistic – and for very small samples you probably shouldn't use it at all. The important part of the table is the significance value of the test, which gives the two-tailed probability that the magnitude of the test statistic is a chance result (see Box 5.3). The two-tailed probability is non-significant because the significance value is greater than .05 (see Chapter 5). However, the psychologist made a specific prediction that dogs would be

Ranks

	Species	N	Mean Rank	Sum of Ranks
Dog-Like Behaviour	Dog	20	20.77	415.50
	Man	20	20.23	404.50
	Total	40		

SPSS Output 7.2

Test Statistics[b]

	Dog-Like Behaviour
Mann-Whitney U	194.500
Wilcoxon W	404.500
Z	-.150
Asymp. Sig. (2-tailed)	.881
Exact Sig. [2*(1-tailed Sig.)]	.883[a]

a. Not corrected for ties.

b. Grouping Variable: Species

SPSS Output 7.3

more dog-like than men, so we can actually halve the probability value to give us the one-tailed probability (.88/2 = .44) but even this is non-significant. This finding indicates that men and dogs do not differ in the amount that they display dog-like behaviour. If we look at the ranks for each group (SPSS Output 7.2) we see that the mean rank for the dogs was 20.77, and for the men was 20.23. Therefore the ranks were pretty equivalent.

A good way to display non-parametric data[3] is by using a box-whisker diagram (or boxplot for short). Figure 7.1 shows such a plot, and it should be clear that the plot gets its name because it is a shaded box with two whiskers coming out of it! The shaded box represents the range between which 50% of the data fall (this is called the *interquartile range*). The horizontal bar within the shaded box is the median (see page 117). The 'I' shape shows us the limits within which most or all of the data fall. Generally, the lower bar is the lowest score and the upper bar is the highest score in the data, however if there is an outlier (a score very different from the rest) then it will fall outside of the bars and the bars represent all of the data that fall within ±3 standard deviations of the mean. In this example there is an outlier and you can see it is represented by a circle above the top of the bar for the men. Why is this graph better than plotting the means? Well, non-parametric tests are not testing differences between means; they are testing differences between ranks. Means are biased by things like outliers (see Box 4.3), whereas ranks are not. Therefore, the median is likely to better represent what the non-parametric test is actually testing (because it too is not influenced by outliers). A box-whisker plot shows the median and so better represents what the non-parametric test is looking at.

What's a box-whisker diagram?

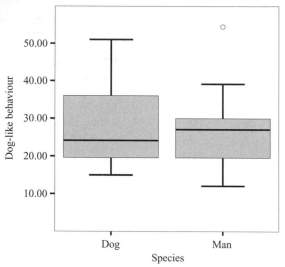

Figure 7.1   Boxplot for the dog-like behaviour in dogs and men

Calculating an Effect-Size

Effect sizes are really easy to calculate thanks to the fact that SPSS converts the test statistics into a z-score. The equation to convert a z-score into the effect size estimate, r is as follows (from Rosenthal, 1991, p. 19):

$$r = \frac{Z}{\sqrt{N}}$$

in which z is the z-score that SPSS produces, and N is the size of the study (i.e. the number of observations) on which z is based. In this case SPSS Output 7.3 tells us that z is $-.15$, and we had 20 men and 20 dogs so the total number of observations was 40. The effect size is, therefore:

$$r = \frac{-0.15}{\sqrt{40}}$$
$$= -.02$$

This represents a tiny effect (it is close to zero), which tells us that there truly isn't much difference between dogs and men.

Writing and Interpreting the Results

For the Mann-Whitney test we need only report the test statistic (which is denoted by U) and its significance. So, we could report something like:

> ☑ Men ($Mdn = 27$) did not seem to differ from dogs ($Mdn = 24$) in the amount of dog-like behaviour they displayed ($U = 194.5$, *ns*).

Note that I've reported the median for each condition. Of course, we really ought to include the effect size as well. We could do two things. The first is to report the z-score associated with the test statistic. This value would enable the reader to determine both the exact significance of the test, and to calculate the effect size r:

> ☑ Men ($Mdn = 27$) and dogs ($Mdn = 24$) did not significantly differ in the extent to which they displayed dog-like behaviours, $U = 194.5$, *ns*, $z = -.15$.

The alternative is to just report the effect size (because readers can convert back to the z-score if they need to for any reason). This approach is better because the effect size will probably be most useful to the reader.

> ☑ Men ($Mdn = 27$) and dogs ($Mdn = 24$) did not significantly differ in the extent to which they displayed dog-like behaviours, $U = 194.5$, *ns*, $r = -.02$.

7.3 The Wilcoxon Signed-Rank Test

The Wilcoxon signed-rank test is the non-parametric equivalent of the dependent t-test (see page 168) and so is used for testing differences between groups when there are two conditions and the same participants have been used in both conditions.

Example: there's been much speculation over the years about the influence of subliminal messages on records. To name a few cases, both Ozzy Osbourne and Judas Priest have been accused of putting backward masked messages on their albums that subliminally influence poor unsuspecting teenagers into doing things like blowing their heads off with shotguns. A psychologist was interested in whether backward masked messages really did have an effect. He took the master tapes of Britney Spears' 'Baby one more time' and created a second version that had the masked message 'deliver your soul to the dark lord' repeated in the chorus. He took this version, and the original and played one version (randomly) to a group of 32 people. He took the same group 6 months later and played them whatever version they hadn't heard the time before. So each person heard both the original, and the version with the masked message, but at different points in time. The psychologist measured the number of goats that were sacrificed in the week after listening to each version. It was hypothesized that the backward message would lead to more goats being sacrificed.

SPSS Output 7.4 shows that the data in both conditions were non-normal. In fact the Kolmogorov-Smirnov test (see page 160) was significant ($D(32) = .177$, $p < .05$) when there was a message on the record and even more significant when there wasn't a message ($D(32) = .236$, $p < .001$). Therefore, a non-parametric test is appropriate.

Tests of Normality

	Kolmogorov-Smirnov[a]			Shapiro-Wilk		
	Statistic	df	Sig.	Statistic	df	Sig.
Message	.177	32	.012	.961	32	.296
No Message	.236	32	.000	.914	32	.014

a. Lilliefors Significance Correction

SPSS Output 7.4

Output from the Wilcoxon Test

Like the Mann-Whitney test, the Wilcoxon test looks for differences in the ranked positions of scores in the two conditions. In fact, the data are ranked and then the differences between the ranks in the two conditions are examined. These differences between ranks can be positive (the rank in condition 2 is bigger than the rank in condition 1), negative (the rank in condition 2 is smaller than the rank in condition 1) or tied (the ranks in the two conditions are identical). SPSS Output 7.5 shows a summary of these ranked data; it tells us the number of negative ranks (these are people who sacrificed more goats after hearing the subliminal message than after not hearing a message) and the number of positive ranks (participants who sacrificed more goats after not hearing the message). The footnotes under the table enable us to determine to what the positive and negative ranks refer. The table shows that 11 of the 32 participants sacrificed more goats after hearing the subliminal message, whereas 17 out of 32 sacrificed more goats after not hearing the message. There were also 4 tied ranks (i.e. participants who sacrificed the same number of goats after listening to the

Ranks

		N	Mean Rank	Sum of Ranks
No Message - Message	Negative Ranks	11ᵃ	10.14	111.50
	Positive Ranks	17ᵇ	17.32	294.50
	Ties	4ᶜ		
	Total	32		

a. No Message < Message

b. No Message > Message

c. Message = No Message

SPSS Output 7.5

different versions of the song). The table also shows the average number of negative and positive ranks and the sum of positive and negative ranks.

If we were doing a Wilcoxon test by hand, the test statistic we use is the sum of ranks. In fact, we would calculate two test statistics: the sum of positive ranks (T^+) and the sum of negative ranks (T^-). SPSS Output 7.5 presents these two values in the final column of the table ($T^+ = 294.50$ and $T^- = 111.50$). We don't actually use both of these test statistics; instead we use only the one that has the lowest value. In this case our test value would be the sum of negative ranks ($T = 111.50$). Normally, we'd then compare this value to tabulated values of the Wilcoxon test. However, like we saw in the

How do I interpret Wilcoxon's test?

previous section, the Wilcoxon test can be converted to a z-score. The advantage of this approach is that it allows exact significance values to be calculated based on the normal distribution. SPSS Output 7.6 tells us that the test statistic is based on the negative ranks, that the z-score is -2.094 and that this value is significant at $p = .036$. Like with the Wilcoxon test, the z-score becomes more accurate as sample sizes increase, so be wary of it for small samples. Before I go on, remember that there are three types of people: (1) those who sacrificed more goats after the message (negative ranks), (2) those who sacrificed more goats after the normal version of the song (positive ranks), and (3) those who sacrificed the same number of goats regardless of whether they heard the message or not (ties). Most people fall into category two (these are the people with positive ranks) and we can tell this because the mean rank is higher for the positive ranks. So, this means that most people fell into the category of sacrificing more goats after not hearing the message. Simplistically, the test is telling us that there were significantly more people who had positive ranks (sacrificed more goats after no message

Test Statistics[b]

	No Message - Message
Z	-2.094[a]
Asymp. Sig. (2-tailed)	.036

a. Based on negative ranks.

b. Wilcoxon Signed Ranks Test

SPSS Output 7.6

was heard) than had negative ranks (sacrificed more goats after hearing the message). Therefore, we could conclude that significantly more goats were sacrificed after listening to the normal version of the song compared to after hearing the song with the message! So, although Britney does make people sacrifice their souls to the dark lord, telling people to do so seems to put people off (no-one likes being told what to do, do they?).[4] This is the opposite direction to our hypothesis and as such we have to keep our 2-tailed significance value of .036. Had the conclusion been in the same direction that we'd predicted (if the message had led to more goats being killed) we could have used a 1-tailed significance value (.036/2).

We can again display these data with a box-whisker diagram. Figure 7.2 shows such a plot and you can see that after the message

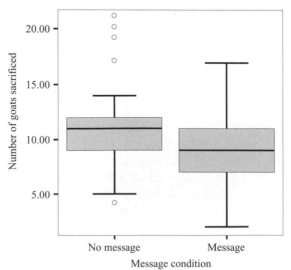

Figure 7.2 Boxplot showing the number of goats sacrificed after listening to Britney Spears compared to after listening to a version of Britney Spears that had a masked message in the chorus of the song

was heard the median number of goats sacrificed was less than after no message. However, after no message was heard there were a lot more outliers (i.e. a few people went on crazy goat-killing sprees!). One of the great things about having used a non-parametric test is that we know that these outliers will not bias the results (because it was the ranks that were analysed not the actual data collected). The fact that the median is lower after listening to a message confirms the direction of our conclusions (i.e. that significantly more goats were sacrificed after listening to the normal version of the song).

Calculating an Effect-Size

The effect size can be calculated in the same way as for the Mann-Whitney test (see the equation on page 238). In this case SPSS Output 7.6 tells us that z is -2.094, and we again had 40 observations (although we only used 20 people and tested them twice it is the number of observations, not the number of people, that is important here). The effect size is, therefore:

$$r = \frac{-2.094}{\sqrt{40}}$$
$$= -.33$$

This represents a medium effect (it is close to Cohen's benchmark of .3), which tells us that the effect of whether or not a subliminal message was present was a substantive effect.

Writing and Interpreting the Results

For the Wilcoxon test, we need only report the test statistic (which we saw earlier is denoted by T) and its significance. So, we could report something like:

☑ The number of goats sacrificed after hearing the message ($Mdn = 9$) was significantly less than after hearing the normal version of the song ($Mdn = 11$), $T = 111.50$, $p < .05$.

As with the Mann-Whitney test we should report either the z-score, or the effect size. The effect size is most useful:

☑ The number of goats sacrificed after hearing the message ($Mdn = 9$) was significantly less than after hearing the normal version of the song ($Mdn = 11$), $T = 111.50$, $p < .05$, $r = -.33$.

7.4   The Kruskal-Wallis Test

The Kruskal-Wallis test is the non-parametric equivalent of one-way independent ANOVA (see page 174) and so is used for testing differences between groups when there are more than two conditions and different participants have been used in all conditions (each person contributes only 1 score to the data).

Example: A researcher was interested in trying to prevent coulrophobia (fear of clowns) in children. She decided to do an experiment in which different groups of children (15 in each) were exposed to different forms of positive information about clowns. The first group watched some adverts for McDonald's in which their mascot Ronald McDonald is seen cavorting about with children going on about how they should love their mum. A second group was told a story about a clown who helped some children when they got lost in a forest (although what on earth a clown was doing in a forest remains a mystery). A third group was entertained by a real clown, who came into the classroom and made balloon animals for the children.[5] A final group acted as a control condition and they had nothing done to them at all. The researcher took self-report ratings of how much the children liked clowns (rather like the fear-beliefs questionnaire in Chapter 2) resulting in a score for each child that could range from 0 (not scared of clowns at all) to 5 (very scared of clowns).

SPSS Output 7.7 shows that the Kolmogorov-Smirnov test (see page 160) was significant for the control group ($D(15) = .419$, $p < .001$), for the group exposed to a real clown ($D(15) = .230$, $p < .05$) and was nearly significant for the group who received the story about the clown ($D(15) = .217$, $p = .056$). In this latter case the Shapiro-Wilk test is in fact significant and this test is actually more accurate (though less widely reported) than the Kolmogorov-Smirnov

Tests of Normality

	Format of Information	Kolmogorov-Smirnov[a]			Shapiro-Wilk		
		Statistic	df	Sig.	Statistic	df	Sig.
Fear beliefs	Advert	.173	15	.200*	.897	15	.086
	Story	.217	15	.056	.855	15	.020
	Exposure	.230	15	.032	.867	15	.030
	None	.419	15	.000	.603	15	.000

*. This is a lower bound of the true significance.

a. Lilliefors Significance Correction

SPSS Output 7.7

test (see Field, 2000, Chapter 2). The only group that produced approximately normal data were the group who saw the adverts $(D(15) = .173, ns)$.

Output from the Kruskal-Wallis Test

Like the other non-parametric tests we've come across, the Kruskal-Wallis test analyses the ranked data and so SPSS Output 7.8 shows a summary of these ranked data; it tells us the mean rank in each condition. These mean ranks are important later for interpreting any effects.

Ranks

	Format of Information	N	Mean Rank
Fear beliefs	Advert	15	45.03
	Story	15	21.87
	Exposure	15	23.77
	None	15	31.33
	Total	60	

SPSS Output 7.8

If we were doing a Kruskal-Wallis test by hand we would rank the data ignoring the group to which the score belongs. We then work out the sum of ranks for each group. The test statistic (H) is a function of these total ranks and the sample size on which they are based. The test statistic has a special kind of a distribution called a chi-square distribution, which for the Kruskal-Wallis test has $k - 1$ degrees of freedom, where k is the number of groups (see Box 8.1). SPSS Output 7.9 shows this test statistic (SPSS labels it chi-square rather than H) and its associated degrees of freedom (in this case we had 4 groups so the degrees of freedom are $4-1$, or 3), and the significance. Therefore, we could conclude that the type of information presented to the children

Test Statistics[a,b]

	Fear beliefs
Chi-Square	17.058
df	3
Asymp. Sig.	.001

a. Kruskal Wallis Test

b. Grouping Variable: Format of Information

SPSS Output 7.9

about clowns significantly affected their fear ratings of clowns. Like a one-way ANOVA though, this test tells us only that a difference exists; it doesn't tell us exactly where the difference lies.

One way to see which groups differ is to look at a boxplot of the groups (see Figure 7.3). The first thing to note is that this boxplot is a bit odd because the group that received no information don't have any whiskers on their box, and those that received stories have only one whisker! Just to add to the confusion, the lines representing the medians appear to be missing. Well, this is what happens when you have data that are measured on a very limited scale (a child can only score 0, 1, 2, 3, 4 or 5). The medians are actually shown, but they clash with the lower quartile (the lower line of the box) for all conditions except the advert one (note the bottom line is thicker – that's the median line). The whiskers are missing in the control condition because the highest and lowest scores clash with the value of the upper and lower quartile (i.e. the values of the two ends of the box are the same as the value for the whiskers so the whiskers can't be shown). I've just used this example to illustrate that these plots can look different sometimes. In any case, using the control as our base-line, the median is 3 and the story and exposure conditions have medians of 1, so they appear to reduce fear beliefs. The advert condition, however, has a median of 4 so the adverts appear to have increased fear beliefs. However, these conclusions are subjective. What we really need are some contrasts or post hoc tests like we used in ANOVA (see page 173).

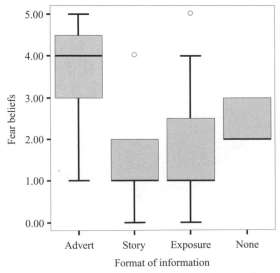

Figure 7.3 Boxplot for the fear beliefs about clowns after exposure to different formats of information (adverts, stories, a real clown or nothing)

There aren't any commonly used non-parametric post hoc procedures, but we can still easily test some hypotheses by using Mann-Whitney tests. If we want to use lots of Mann-Whitney tests we have to be careful because each time we do one there is a 5% chance that we'll conclude that there is an effect when there isn't (a Type I error). Remember in Chapter 6 I told you that the reason why we do tests like ANOVA is because they control the build up of Type I errors. Well, if we want to use lots of Mann-Whitney tests to follow up a Kruskal-Wallis test, then we have to make some kind of adjustment to ensure that the Type I errors don't build up to more than .05. The easiest method is to use a Bonferroni correction, which in its simplest form just means that instead of using .05 as the critical value for significance for each test, you use a critical value of .05 divided by the number of tests you've conducted. If you do this, you'll soon discover that you quickly end up using a critical value for significance that is so small that it is very restrictive. Therefore, it's a good idea to be selective about the comparisons you make. In this example, we have a control group who had no clown information given to them. As such, a nice succinct set of comparisons would be to compare each group against the control:

Can I do non-parametric post hoc tests?

> ➢ Test 1: Advert compared to control
> ➢ Test 2: Story compared to control
> ➢ Test 3: Exposure compared to control

This results in three tests, so rather than use .05 as our critical level of significance, we'd use $.05/3 = .0167$. If we didn't use focused tests and just compared all groups with all other groups we'd end up with six tests rather than three (advert vs. story, advert vs. exposure, advert vs. control, story vs. exposure, story vs. control, exposure vs. control) meaning that our critical value would fall to $.05/6 = .0083$.

SPSS Output 7.10 shows the test statistics from doing Mann-Whitney tests on the three focused comparisons that I suggested. Remember that we are now using a critical value of .0167, so the only comparison that is significant is when comparing the advert to the control group (because the observed significance value of .001 is less than .0167). The other two comparisons produce significance values that are greater than .0167 so we'd have to say they're non-significant. So the effect we got seems to mainly reflect the fact that McDonald's adverts significantly increased fear beliefs about clowns relative to controls.

Advert vs. control:

Test Statistics[b]

	Fear beliefs
Mann-Whitney U	37.500
Wilcoxon W	157.500
Z	-3.261
Asymp. Sig. (2-tailed)	.001
Exact Sig. [2*(1-tailed Sig.)]	.001[a]

a. Not corrected for ties.

b. Grouping Variable: Format of Information

Story vs. control:

Test Statistics[b]

	Fear beliefs
Mann-Whitney U	65.000
Wilcoxon W	185.000
Z	-2.091
Asymp. Sig. (2-tailed)	.037
Exact Sig. [2*(1-tailed Sig.)]	.050[a]

a. Not corrected for ties.

b. Grouping Variable: Format of Information

Exposure vs. control:

Test Statistics[b]

	Fear beliefs
Mann-Whitney U	72.500
Wilcoxon W	192.500
Z	-1.743
Asymp. Sig. (2-tailed)	.081
Exact Sig. [2*(1-tailed Sig.)]	.098[a]

a. Not corrected for ties.

b. Grouping Variable: Format of Information

SPSS Output 7.10

Calculating an Effect-Size

Unfortunately there isn't an easy way to convert a chi-square statistic that has more than 1 degree of freedom to an effect size r. You could use the significance value of the Kruskal-Wallis test statistic to find an associated value of z from a table of probability values for the normal distribution (like that provided in Field, 2000, p. 471). From this you could use the conversion to r that we used on page 238. However, to keep things simple, we could just calculate effect sizes for the Mann-Whitney tests that we used to follow up the main analysis. These effect sizes will be very informative in their own right.

For the first comparison (adverts vs. control) SPSS Output 7.10 shows us that z is -3.261, and because this was based on comparing two groups each containing 15 observations, we had 30 observations in total. The effect size is, therefore:

$$r_{Advert-Control} = \frac{-3.261}{\sqrt{30}}$$

$$= -.60$$

This represents a large effect (it is above Cohen's benchmark of .5), which tells us that the effect of adverts relative to the control was a substantive effect.

For the second comparison (story vs. control) SPSS Output 7.10 shows us that z is -2.091, and this was again based on 30 observations. The effect size is, therefore:

$$r_{Story-Control} = \frac{-2.091}{\sqrt{30}}$$
$$= -.38$$

This represents a medium to large effect (because it is between Cohen's benchmarks of .3 and .5). Therefore, although non-significant the effect of stories relative to the control was a substantive effect.

For the final comparison (exposure vs. control) SPSS Output 7.10 shows us that z is -1.743, and this was again based on 30 observations. The effect size is, therefore:

$$r_{Exposure-Control} = \frac{-1.743}{\sqrt{30}}$$
$$= -.32$$

This represents a medium effect. Therefore, although non-significant the effect of exposure relative to the control was a substantive effect.

Writing and Interpreting the Results

For the Kruskal-Wallis test, we need only report the test statistic (which we saw earlier is denoted by H), its degrees of freedom and its significance. So, we could report something like:

☑ Children's fear beliefs about clowns were significantly affected by the format of information given to them ($H(3) = 17.06$, $p < .01$).

However, we need to report the follow-up tests as well (including their effect sizes):

☑ Children's fear beliefs about clowns were significantly affected by the format of information given to them ($H(3) = 17.06$, $p < .01$). Mann-Whitney tests were used to follow-up this finding. A Bonferroni correction was applied and so all effects are reported at a .0167 level of significance. It appeared that fear beliefs were significantly higher after the adverts compared to the control, $U = 37.50$, $r = -.60$. However, fear beliefs were not significantly different after the stories, $U = 65.00$, *ns*, $r = -.38$, or exposure, $U = 72.5$, *ns*, $r = -.32$, relative to the control. We can conclude that clown information through stories and exposure did produce medium size effects in reducing fear beliefs about clowns, but not significantly so (future work with larger samples might be appropriate), but that Ronald McDonald was sufficient to significantly increase fear beliefs about clowns.[6]

7.5 Friedman's ANOVA

Friedman's ANOVA is the non-parametric equivalent of one-way repeated measures ANOVA (see page 183) and so is used for testing differences between experimental conditions when there are more than two conditions and the same participants have been used in all conditions (each person contributes several scores to the data).

Example: A psychologist was interested in the effects of television programmes on domestic life. She hypothesized that through vicarious learning[7] certain programmes might actually encourage people to behave like the characters within them. This in turn could affect the viewer's own relationships (depending on whether the programme depicted harmonious or dysfunctional relationships). She took episodes of three popular TV shows, and showed them to 54 couples after which the couple were left alone in the room for an hour. The experimenter measured the number of times the couple argued. Each couple viewed all three of the TV programmes at different points in time (a week apart) and the order in which the programmes were viewed was counterbalanced over couples. The TV programmes selected were Eastenders (which typically portrays the lives of extremely miserable, argumentative, London folk who like nothing more than to beat each other up, lie to each other, sleep with each other's wives and generally show no evidence of any consideration to their fellow humans!), Friends (which portrays a group of unrealistically considerate and nice people who love each other oh so very much – but for some reason I love it anyway!), and a National Geographic programme about whales (this was supposed to act as a control).

SPSS Output 7.11 shows the Kolmogorov-Smirnov test (see page 160) for each condition. This test was significant for the data generated after Eastenders ($D(54) = .137$, $p < .05$), Friends ($D(54) = .150$, $p < .01$) and the National Geographic programme about whales

Tests of Normality

	Kolmogorov-Smirnov[a]			Shapiro-Wilk		
	Statistic	df	Sig.	Statistic	df	Sig.
Eastenders	.137	54	.013	.914	54	.001
Friends	.150	54	.004	.943	54	.012
National Geographic	.121	54	.046	.943	54	.012

a. Lilliefors Significance Correction

SPSS Output 7.11

$(D(54) = .121, p < .05)$. Given that all the data are non-normal a non-parametric test is appropriate.

Output from Friedman's ANOVA

Friedman's ANOVA works similarly to if you conducted a one-way repeated measures ANOVA on the ranked data. So, like all the non-parametric tests it is based on the ranks, not the actual scores. SPSS Output 7.12 shows the mean rank in each condition. These mean ranks are important later for interpreting any effects; they show that the ranks were highest after watching Eastenders.

If we were doing Friedman's ANOVA by hand we would take the scores for a given participant and rank them across experimental conditions – from lowest to highest. For example, if a couple had 15 arguments after watching Eastenders, 6 after watching Friends and 7 after watching the whales, then we would give Friends a rank of 1 (because it produced the lowest score), the whales a rank of 2, and Eastenders a rank of 3 (because it generated the highest score). If there were no effect of the programmes, then we'd expect these ranks to be fairly randomly distributed across the conditions, and the mean rank for each condition would be fairly similar to each other. If one programme does produce more arguments, then we'd expect the scores to generally be highest in that condition, so its ranks will generally be higher and the mean rank will be higher than the other conditions.

Ranks

	Mean Rank
Eastenders	2.29
Friends	1.81
National Geographic	1.91

SPSS Output 7.12

The test statistic (which is denoted by the usual symbol for a chi-square statistic, χ^2) is a function of the total of the ranks in each condition, the sample size on which they are based, and the number of conditions there were (k). Like the Kruskal-Wallis test, the test statistic has a chi-square distribution with $k - 1$ degrees of freedom (k is the number of conditions). SPSS Output 7.13 shows this Chi-Square test statistic and its associated degrees of freedom (in this case we had 3 groups so the degrees of freedom are $3 - 1$, or 2), and the significance. Therefore, we could conclude that the type of programme watched significantly affected the subsequent number of arguments (because the significance value is less than .05). However, like a one-way ANOVA, this result doesn't tell us exactly where the differences lie.

Test Statistics[a]

N	54
Chi-Square	7.586
df	2
Asymp. Sig.	.023

a. Friedman Test

SPSS Output 7.13

To get some idea of where the differences lie we could examine a boxplot of the conditions like the one in Figure 7.4. We can see from this graph that after watching Eastenders the median number of arguments was 8 and scores ranged from 5 to 15 (although that highest score was an outlier and most scores actually fell between 5 and 13). After watching Friends the median number of arguments was only 6 and scores ranged from 0 to 11. After watching the whale programme the median number of arguments was 7 and scores ranged from 0 to 13. So, if we were to draw some subjective conclusions they might be that Eastenders led to more arguments than watching Friends or whales, and that watching Friends led to fewer arguments than watching whales. Like with the Kruskal-Wallis test though we really need some contrasts or post hoc tests like we used in ANOVA (see page 173); however, we have the same problem in that such contrasts can't readily be done. The solution is much the same: we do lots of tests that compare only two conditions, but adjust the critical value of significance for the number of tests we do (see page 173). In this case, because our conditions used the same participants we'd use Wilcoxon tests to follow up the analysis (see page 239).

When thinking about how to follow-up the analysis it's a good idea to be selective about the comparisons you make. In this example, we have a control condition in which people watched a programme about

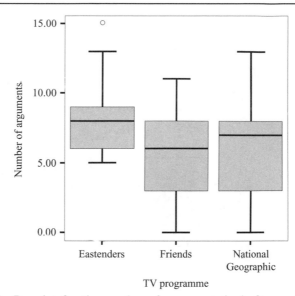

Figure 7.4 Boxplot for the number of arguments had after watching Eastenders, Friends or a National Geographic programme about whales

whales. A nice succinct set of comparisons would be to compare each group against the control:

> ➤ Test 1: Eastenders compared to control
> ➤ Test 2: Friends compared to control

This gives rise to only two tests, so rather than use .05 as our critical level of significance, we'd use .05/2 = .025 (see page 173). SPSS Output 7.14 shows the test statistics from doing Wilcoxon tests on the two comparisons that I suggested. Remember that we are now using a critical value of .025, so we compare the significance of both test statistics against this critical value. The test comparing Eastenders to the National Geographic programme about whales has a significance value of .005, which is well below our criterion of .025, therefore, we can conclude that Eastenders led to significantly more arguments than the programme about whales. The second comparison compares the number of arguments after Friends with the number after the programme about whales. This contrast is non-significant (the significance of the test statistic is .530, which is bigger than our critical value of .025), so we can conclude that there was no difference in the number of arguments after watching Friends compared to after watching the whales. The effect we got seems to mainly reflect the fact that Eastenders makes people argue more.

Ranks

		N	Mean Rank	Sum of Ranks
National Geographic - Eastenders	Negative Ranks	31[a]	28.85	894.50
	Positive Ranks	18[b]	18.36	330.50
	Ties	5[c]		
	Total	54		
National Geographic - Friends	Negative Ranks	21[d]	22.00	462.00
	Positive Ranks	24[e]	23.88	573.00
	Ties	9[f]		
	Total	54		

a. National Geographic < Eastenders

b. National Geographic > Eastenders

c. Eastenders = National Geographic

d. National Geographic < Friends

e. National Geographic > Friends

f. Friends = National Geographic

Test Statistics[c]

	National Geographic - Eastenders	National Geographic - Friends
Z	-2.813[a]	-.629[b]
Asymp. Sig. (2-tailed)	.005	.530

a. Based on positive ranks.

b. Based on negative ranks.

c. Wilcoxon Signed Ranks Test

SPSS Output 7.14

Calculating an Effect-Size

As I mentioned before, there isn't an easy way to convert a chi-square statistic that has more than 1 degree of freedom to an effect size r. As with the Kruskal-Wallis test you could use the significance value of the chi-square test statistic to find an associated value of z from a table of probability values for the normal distribution and then use the conversion to r on page 238. Alternatively, we could just calculate effect sizes for the Wilcoxon tests that we used to follow up the main analysis. These effect sizes will be very informative in their own right.

For the first comparison (Eastenders vs. control) SPSS Output 7.14 shows us that z is −2.813, and because this was based on comparing two groups each containing 54 observations, we had 108 observations in total (remember it isn't important that the observations come from the same people). The effect size is, therefore:

$$r_{Eastenders-Control} = \frac{-2.813}{\sqrt{108}}$$

$$= -.27$$

This represents a medium effect (it is close to Cohen's benchmark of .3), which tells us that the effect of Eastenders relative to the control was a substantive effect: Eastenders produced substantially more arguments.

For the second comparison (Friends vs. control) SPSS Output 7.14 shows us that z is $-.629$, and this was again based on 108 observations. The effect size is, therefore:

$$r_{Friends-Control} = \frac{-0.629}{\sqrt{108}}$$

$$= -.06$$

This represents virtually no effect (it is close to zero). Therefore, Friends had very little effect in creating arguments compared to the control.

Writing and Interpreting the Results

For Friedman's ANOVA we need only report the test statistic (which we saw earlier is denoted by χ^2),[8] its degrees of freedom and its significance. So, we could report something like:

☑   The number of arguments that couples had was significantly affected by the programme they had just watched, $\chi^2(2) = 7.59$, $p < .05$.

We need to report the follow-up tests as well (including their effect sizes):

☑   The number of arguments that couples had was significantly affected by the programme they had just watched, $\chi^2(2) = 7.59$, $p < .05$. Wilcoxon tests were used to follow-up this finding. A Bonferroni correction was applied and so all effects are reported at a .025 level of significance. It appeared that watching Eastenders significantly affected the number of arguments compared to the programme about whales, $T = 330.50$, $r = -.27$. However, the number of arguments was not significantly different after Friends compared to after the programme about whales, $T = 462$, *ns*, $r = -.06$. We can conclude that watching Eastenders did produce significantly more arguments compared to watching a programme about whales, and this effect was medium in size. However, Friends didn't produce any substantial reduction in the number of arguments relative to the control programme.

7.6 Summary

In the last chapter, we saw that data do not always conform to the conditions necessary to conduct parametric statistics (life is cruel like this sometimes!). This chapter has taught us about some of the tests we can do when the assumptions of parametric tests have not been met. We started by having a brief look at how we can use ranked data instead of the actual scores. We then moved on to look at simple situations in which there are only two experimental conditions (the Mann-Whitney and Wilcoxon tests) before moving on to more complex situations in which there are several experimental conditions (the Kruskal-Wallis test and Friedman's ANOVA). We looked at each test by using an example for which we examined the SPSS output and looked at how we could interpret the results and report our findings and conclusions. The next chapter will summarize all of the tests we've encountered and look at how we can decide whether we (or others) have used the appropriate test.

7.7 Practical Tasks

1. For each example in this chapter:
   Write a sample results section (using the summaries at the end of each example as a guide) but as you do so identify where all of the numbers come from and what they mean.
2. For each example in this chapter use Field (2000) or notes on my web page (http://www.cogs.susx.ac.uk/users/andyf/teaching):
   Analyse the data and see if you can get the same outputs as I have (the SPSS data files can be found on my website).

7.8 Further Reading

Field, A. P. (2000). *Discovering statistics using SPSS for Windows: advanced techniques for the beginner*. London: Sage. Chapter 2 talks about non-parametric statistics.

Howell, D. C. (2001). *Statistical methods for psychology* (5th edition). Belmont, CA: Duxbury. Chapter 18 gives the theory behind all of the tests covered in this chapter.

Siegel, S. & Castellan, N. J. (1988). *Nonparametric statistics for the behavioral sciences* (2nd edition). New York: McGraw-Hill. This is still the definitive reference for non-parametric statistics but is quite technical.

Notes

[1] You'll sometimes see non-parametric tests referred to as distribution-free tests, with an explanation that they make no assumptions about the distribution of the data. This is actually incorrect: they do make assumptions, but they are less restrictive ones than their parametric counterparts.

[2] Incidentally, this isn't an experiment in the pure sense because the groups are not created randomly (despite the advances of science we have yet to be able to assign random chunks of DNA to experimental conditions and then grow them into dogs or men!).

[3] By this I mean data that do not meet the assumptions of a parametric test.

[4] These are fictitious data and there is no evidence whatsoever that Britney makes you sacrifice goats.

[5] Unfortunately, the first time they attempted the study the clown accidentally burst one of the balloons. The noise frightened the children and they associated that fear response with the clown. All 15 children are currently in therapy for coulrophobia!

[6] Another disclaimer: McDonald's are great really, and Ronald is such a nice friendly chap – honest!

[7] This is just learning through observing others (Rachman, 1977).

[8] The test statistic is often denoted as X_F^2 but the official APA style guide doesn't recognize this term.

8 Choosing a Statistical Test

One of the most bewildering aspects of experimental design for students is the issue of how to choose an appropriate statistical test. There are two ways in which this problem crops up. First, in statistics tests and exams, you might be presented with a hypothetical study and be required to select the statistical test that would be most suitable for analysing the data obtained from it. At first sight, this might seem rather an artificial situation. However, in real life (whatever that is!), researchers have to decide for themselves whether other researchers' statistics (as described in journal articles and conference papers) were appropriate. So this task is actually not quite as bizarre as it might at first appear. Second, in your course, you may be faced with the problem of designing a study from scratch, and having to decide what to measure and how to analyse the data obtained. This has more obvious parallels to what researchers do.

8.1 The Need to Think About Statistics at the Outset of Designing a Study

In Chapter 2 we saw that researchers make decisions about which statistics they intend to use while they are designing their study – they never treat this as something to be thought about once the data are collected. Thinking about which inferential and descriptive statistics you are going to use should be an integral part of designing a study. If we are designing an experiment, our first thought is 'what will this experiment tell us about the phenomenon in question?', but this is followed almost immediately by 'how will we measure it – what kind of data will we collect?' (see Chapter 2) and 'which statistical tests will we use?' (see Chapters 5, 6 and 7).

Sometimes students are tempted to run their study first, and then worry later about which test they will use on the data once they've got them. However, this is bad practice. If you defer thinking about statistics until after you have done your study, you run the risk of obtaining data that are totally unanalysable. All too frequently, Andy and I have had to explain to students that the reams of data they have so laboriously collected are effectively worthless, because there is no statistical test that can be used on them. This is very depressing for us, and I expect the student gets upset too. (I fell into this trap myself, when I started the research that led to my Ph.D. In my enthusiasm to get started, I spent many months collecting data but

Think about how you will analyse the data before collecting it!

never thought beforehand what I would actually do with it! I then spent many more months in visits to one of the best statisticians in the country, who would look at my data, sigh, and then rack his brains trying to think of some elaborate statistical treatments that might give me valid results. My life would have been so much easier had I given some thought to statistics at the outset, because only minor changes to my experimental procedures would have been needed to have made the statistics quite straightforward.)

At best, by designing a study without taking into account how you are going to analyse the data, you may end up with data that are not as informative as they might have been. Obtaining participants and running them in a study is tedious and hard work, and it wastes everyone's time and effort if you run a study that produces useless data. Therefore, it pays to spend a little time thinking about what kind of data you intend to obtain, and how you would analyse it.

Here is a demonstration of how minor differences in how you design the study can have a big effect on what kind of data you obtain, and ultimately, on what conclusions you would be able to draw. Suppose you were interested in whether a new striping pattern improved the detectability of emergency vehicles, compared to the patterning that was already in use. How could you test this? One way might be to get a hundred participants and ask each one whether the new pattern was more detectable than the old one; less detectable; or no different in detectability. If you did this, you would end up with data that consisted of three frequencies – the number of people saying 'the new pattern is an improvement', the number of people saying 'the new pattern is worse', and the number who thought the new pattern was no different to the old one. All you could do with these three frequencies is run a Chi-Squared test (see Box 8.1), to see if they differed from the equal frequencies for the three categories that you would expect to get if people's responses were random. If this test was statistically significant, it would tell you that people's responses were,

▣ Box 8.1: All you need to know about Chi-Squared Tests

The Chi-Squared test (χ^2) is useful if – despite our best efforts at warning you against it – you have ended up with nominal (categorical) data with each person contributing only once to each category (i.e. your data are between-subjects). If you only have the frequency with which certain events have occurred, then Chi-Squared can be used to see if these observed frequencies differ from those that would be expected by chance. Here's the formula for Chi-Squared:

$$\chi^2 = \sum \frac{(O - E)^2}{E}$$

Chi-Squared is thus the sum of the squared differences between each observed frequency and its associated expected frequency. The bigger the value of χ^2, the greater the difference between observed and expected frequencies, and hence the more confident we can be that the observed frequencies have not occurred by chance. (In practice, you need to take into account the 'degrees of freedom', which is simply the number of categories minus one).

Two common uses of Chi-Squared are set out below. More details on Chi-Squared (including how to work it out by hand) can be found in Siegel and Castellan (1988).

A: The one-independent variable case: the χ^2 'Goodness of Fit' test
This can be used to compare an observed frequency distribution to an expected frequency distribution. It's most often used when you have the observed frequencies for several mutually-exclusive categories, and you want to decide if they have occurred equally frequently. Suppose, for example, a leading soap powder manufacturer wanted us to find out which name was most attractive for their new washing powder. We could take 100 shoppers, present them with an array of different names for soap powders, and ask them to choose a single name, the one that they thought was most attractive. The frequencies with which the names were chosen would be our observed frequencies: the expected frequency of occurrence for each category in this example, would be $100/5 = 20$. The degrees of freedom for this test will be $k - 1$, where k is the number of categories used (in this case there are 5 categories and so $df = 4$).

Number of shoppers picking each name:

Washo	Scruba	Musty	Stainzoff	Beeo	Total
40	35	5	10	10	100

$\chi^2 = 52.5$, with 4 df, $p < .001$. It appears that the distribution of shoppers across soap-powder names is not random. Some names get picked more than we would expect by chance and some get picked less.

B: Chi-Squared as a Test of Association between two independent variables
Another common use of χ^2 is to determine whether there is an association between two independent variables. For example, is there an association between gender (male or female) and choice of soap powder (Washo, Musty, etc.)? Here's a contingency table, containing the data for a random sample of 100 shoppers, 70 men and 30 women:

Number of shoppers picking each name:

	Washo	Scruba	Musty	Stainzoff	Beeo	Total
male	10	12	5	3	40	70
female	6	2	1	20	1	30
totals	16	14	6	23	41	100

These are our observed frequencies. To calculate the expected frequencies is a little more involved then in our previous example, but based on similar logic. Using the same formula as before, χ^2 with 4 $df = 52.94$, $p < .001$. The degrees of freedom for when we have a contingency table are equal to (number of columns -1) $\times$ (number of rows -1). In this case we have 5 columns and 2 rows, so the $df = (5 - 1) \times (2 - 1) = 4 \times 1 = 4$.

Our observed frequencies are significantly different from the frequencies that we would expect to obtain if there were no association between the two variables. In other words, the pattern of name preferences is different for men and women.

Problems in interpreting Chi-Squared
The Chi-Squared test merely tells some relationship exists between the two variables in question: it does not tell you what that relationship is, and most importantly, it does not tell you anything about the causal relationship between the two variables. In the present example, it would be tempting to interpret the results as showing that being male or female causes people to pick different soap powder names. In this case, that's probably a reasonable assumption, since it's unlikely that the soap powder names cause people to be male or female. However, in principle the direction of causality could equally well go the other way. Chi-Squared merely tells you that the two variables are associated in some way: precisely what that association is, and what it means, is for you to decide.

Another problem in interpreting Chi-Squared is that the test tells you only that the observed frequencies are different from the expected frequencies in some way: the test does not tell you where this difference comes from. Usually, but not always, you can get an idea of why the Chi-Squared was significant by looking at the size of the discrepancies between the observed and expected frequencies. In many cases, however, Chi-Squared contingency tables are not so easy to interpret!

Assumptions of the Chi-Squared test
For a Chi-Squared test to be used, the following assumptions must hold true:

continues

■ **Box 8.1:** *continued*

1. Observations must be independent: each subject must contribute to one and *only one* category. Failure to observe this rule renders the Chi-Squared test results completely invalid.
2. Problems arise when the expected frequencies are very small. See Siegel and Castellan (1988) for details.

Why you should avoid Chi-Squared if you can
Once again, we stress that you should design your study so you can avoid using Chi-Squared! The main problem with obtaining frequency data is that they provide so little information about your participants' performance. All you have is knowledge about which category someone falls into, and this is a very crude measure. Consider the examples in this box. All we have obtained from our participants is knowledge of which soap powder they liked most – nothing else. What a waste of time and effort! Had we obtained attractiveness ratings from them for each powder, we would be able to find out so much more. For example, by how much do the soap powders differ in attractiveness? Are people in close agreement about this, or are there large individual differences? How do the ratings by men compare to those by women? Do men and women show different patterns of ratings? Just a minor change to the design – obtaining scores rather than merely categorizing people – gives us a lot more information.

indeed, non-random – that responses were not equally distributed amongst the three categories. Suppose most people had said that the new striping pattern was an improvement. This would be informative, but it wouldn't really tell you very much. It would tell you nothing about whether the new pattern was a big improvement or just a small improvement over the old one. How homogeneous is the category of people who thought the new pattern was an 'improvement'? There are all kinds of possibilities. Everyone might have been very similar in their assessment of the new pattern. Alternatively, responses might have been sharply divided, with some participants considering the new pattern to be a huge improvement, while others thought it was only a slight improvement. We have absolutely no way of telling, from the data that we have collected, which of these possibilities has occurred. We would have gone to all of the trouble of obtaining the emergency vehicles, the stripes and the participants, merely to obtain three crude measures (the number of people falling into the three categories of opinion).

However, suppose we make some minor changes to our study. Instead of merely assigning participants to one of three categories according to whether they thought the new striping pattern was better, the same or worse, we now ask them to rate each of the two striping patterns separately, using a seven-point scale that runs from 'very inconspicuous' to 'highly conspicuous'. Now, we have two scores for each participant (the number that corresponds to their rating of the new pattern, and the number that corresponds to their rating of the old pattern). We can perform a Mann Whitney test on these data, and see whether the ratings for the two patterns are significantly different. We've gone to the same amount of trouble as in the previous version of the study, using the same emergency vehicles and the same number of participants. However, by making just a small modification to the procedure, we have extracted a lot more useful information. As well as determining whether or not participants thought the two patterns differed in detectability, the data we obtained would permit us to work out descriptive statistics (e.g. the median rating to each of the patterns, and some measure of the range of responses) that would enable us to know to what extent the two patterns were considered different. We would also be able to get some idea of how responses to each of the patterns were distributed. We might find that everyone thought the new pattern was markedly better than the old one; or it might be that most, but by no means all, participants thought the new pattern was a moderate improvement over the old one. These are two quite different conclusions, but it would have been impossible to distinguish between them with the previous experimental design.

We could do better still. The previous study is based on people's subjective responses to the two patterns: we haven't really measured the detectability of the two patterns, so much as people's opinions of their detectability (which isn't necessarily the same thing, because people may not necessarily have much insight into their cognitive abilities with respect to object recognition). So, we could do the same study, but this time measure how quickly people can detect the two different striping patterns. For example, we could have two vehicles, one with the new striping pattern and one with the old. Each participant does several trials. On a given trial, the participant sees an array of vehicles, and has to decide whether or not a striped one is present. We measure the time it takes to respond. Each participant provides two 'mean reaction time' scores: the average of their correct 'present' responses to the vehicle with the new striping pattern, and the average of their correct 'present' responses to the vehicle with the old pattern.

At first sight, this doesn't look like much of an improvement over the previous version of our study. However, there are actually quite a few benefits to designing the study this way. First (as long as the assumption is correct that detectability is reflected in reaction times), we have a more direct, less subjective measure of detectability: we haven't asked participants if they think that one pattern is more conspicuous than the other, we have got them to demonstrate this directly, in their behaviour (see Chapter 2). Second, because we have obtained data which satisfy the requirements of a 'parametric' test, we can use more powerful statistical tests on our data – more powerful in the sense that they are more likely to uncover any differences between our experimental conditions than the non-parametric test we used in the previous version of this study (see below for more on this, and have a look at the discussion of statistical power in Chapter 3). We could do a repeated-measures *t*-test on these reaction-time (RT) data, to see if the average RT to the new pattern was faster or slower than the average RT to the old pattern.

Finally, we could design the study so that we would be able to perform more sophisticated statistics on the data, and ask more sophisticated questions as a result. Suppose we had obtained reasonably similar numbers of male and female participants, and that within each sex, we had similar numbers of young, middle-aged and elderly participants. So far, we have been confined to answering the question 'do people perceive one of the patterns as more detectable than the other?' Now, we could include 'gender' and 'age' as additional independent variables in our data analysis, and answer more complex questions such as: 'do men and women differ in their perceptions of the two striping patterns?'; 'do the effects of the striping patterns differ according to the age of the perceiver?'; and even 'is the detectability of the striping pattern affected by the participant's sex, age or any combination of these?' For example, it might be the case (I can't think why, mind you!) that there is less difference in detectability between the two patterns for elderly men than there is for young females.

You could answer these questions by comparing the frequencies with which the different age-groups and genders detected the patterns (using Chi-Squared (see Box 8.1), or its more sophisticated big brother, log-linear analysis). However, again, a minor change in our design would reap large benefits. If we obtained a score per participant (e.g. each participant's reaction time to detect the pattern) we could use parametric statistical tests with this design, tests which are better suited to detecting the interactions between variables that provide the answers to interesting questions like these (see Sections 6.8, 6.9 and 6.10 for more information on these tests). This version of the study would involve little more work than the crude one outlined at the beginning of this example, but would enable us to find out much more about people's responses to striping patterns. Hopefully, this will convince you that giving a little thought at the design stage to what you are going to measure can pay off handsomely in terms of what you will be able to conclude from the results obtained.

8.2   Five Questions to Ask Yourself

Why am I here? What's the purpose of life? Is there a God? Perhaps a more pressing question is to know which statistical test to use. Making this decision is fairly straightforward as long as you tackle the task systematically. All you need to do is ask yourself five questions about the nature of the study, and the type of data that you have obtained. (You do have to understand the questions; however, explanation of the necessary concepts is included in this book, and summarized below, so you have no excuse for not picking the correct test!)

➤   Question 1: what kind of data will I collect?
➤   Question 2: how many independent variables will I use?
➤   Question 3: what kind of design will I use (experimental or correlational?)
➤   Question 4: will my study use a repeated-measures or independent-measures design?
➤   Question 5: will my data be parametric or non-parametric?

If you can answer these five questions correctly, and follow the flow-chart in Box 8.2, you should be able to work out which test would be most appropriate for your data. Let's take the questions in turn.

Question 1: What Kind of Data Will I Collect – Frequencies or Scores?

What sort of data are you obtaining from each participant? Does each participant give you one or more scores? Or do they merely contribute to a frequency, in the sense that the data consist of how many participants fall into each of several categories? (We've been at pains throughout this book to explain how you should avoid getting frequency data if you can possibly do so, because you end up being stuck with Chi-Squared as your main way of analysing the data. So if you have ended up with frequency data nevertheless, don't complain to us!) Here's an example, to make the distinction clear. Suppose a study looked at whether different European countries had different car accident rates. The data would consist of the frequency of car accidents in each country: we would know nothing about our individual participants except that they

Generally speaking, try to get at least one score per participant.

had experienced an accident and therefore had contributed to their country's accident total. The data are thus the frequency of occurrence of each of several categories ('British car accidents', 'French car accidents', etc.). If, on the other hand, we took a sample of drivers from each country and recorded each individual driver's accident rate, our data would now consist of scores – a score per participant, which would be that individual's personal accident rate.

If your data consist of frequency data, you are pretty much stuck with doing some variant of Chi-Squared. Follow the flow-chart to decide which version of Chi-Squared you should use. If there is just one independent variable in your study, then 'Chi-Squared Goodness of Fit' is the version of Chi-Squared to use. If you have two independent variables, use the 'Chi-Squared Test of Association'. Confused? Here's an example to make the distinction clearer. Suppose we were interested in how people got to work: here, we have one independent variable, 'mode of transport'. There could be lots of different categories of this, 'bus', 'motorcycle', 'skateboard', etc., but they are all instances of 'mode of transport'. So, in this case, the 'Chi-Squared Goodness of Fit' is the test to go for. Now suppose we were also interested in sex differences in how people got to work: now, we have a second independent variable in our study, 'sex of traveller'. We would be interested in asking questions like 'do men and women use different modes of transport to get to work?' In other words, we have two independent variables and we are interested in whether there is an association between them. In this case, the 'Chi-Squared Test of Association' is the correct version of Chi-Squared to use.

If your data consist of scores, then you need to work out the answers to the remaining questions below.

What kind of scale are your data measured on? It's important to know what kind of data you are dealing with, as certain statistics can only be used validly with certain kinds of data. (See Chapter 1 for a detailed discussion of these issues: they are mentioned briefly again here to jog your memory and save you having to hold the book open at two places at once.)

- *Nominal (categorical) data:* With these kind of data, numbers are used only as names for categories. Therefore they are not really acting as numbers, but just serving as labels.
- *Ordinal (rank) data:* On an ordinal scale, things can be ranked or ordered in terms of some property such as size, length, speed, time etc. However, successive points on the scale are not necessarily spaced equally apart.
- *Interval data:* These are measured on a scale on which measurements are spaced at equal intervals, but on which there is no

true zero point (although there may be a point on the scale which is arbitrarily named 'zero').

- *Ratio data:* This is the same as the interval scale, except that there is a true zero on the scale, representing a compete absence of the thing which is being measured. With this kind of scale, the intervals are equally spaced and we can make meaningful statements about the ratios of quantities measured.

The level of measurement is something that is wholly under your control, and known in advance of carrying out the study. There are other aspects of the data that are also important, but since these are normally discovered once the data are collected, rather than known in advance; we will consider these separately in answering Question 5 below.

Question 2: How Many Independent Variables Will I Use?

In Chapter 2 we saw that an independent variable is something that is manipulated by you, the experimenter (as opposed to a dependent variable, which is something that you measure). There are two types of independent variable. In the first type, you are free to choose which values of the independent variable to use. So, for example, suppose your independent variable was the time delay between stimulus presentation and a memory test. You are free to use whatever levels of this independent variable that you like. You might have delays of 1 day, 2 days and 3 days; or you might have delays of 1 hour, 1 week and 1 month. It's entirely up to you. The same goes for 'age of participant': you could pick any age-categories that you want.

With other types of independent variable, the categories are fixed, and your only choice is which of the existing categories to use. 'Gender' is a good example of this kind of independent variable: on this planet, you are stuck with male versus female and people come ready-assigned to one level of the independent variable or the other.

So, you have to decide how many independent variables are present in the study. Once you have done this, you need to determine how many levels (or categories) of each independent variable there are (see page 37). In the examples above, we have three levels of memory test delay and two levels of gender.

Question 3: What Kind of Design Will I Use?

In psychology, there are usually a variety of ways to tackle the same issue. Sometimes we might use an experimental method: here, we have different conditions in our study, corresponding to different levels of our independent variable(s), and we look for a difference between them in terms of performance on some dependent variable that we have chosen. Alternatively, we might use a correlational method: in this case, we look for a relationship between a person's scores on one variable and their scores on another variable. Different statistical tests will be appropriate in each case, so you need to decide which kind of design you have.

Suppose we were interested in age-changes in driving ability. One way to tackle this would be to use an experimental design, in which we looked for differences between different age-groups of drivers. Another way to address the same issue would be to use a correlational technique, and look for a relationship between age and some measure of driving ability. Most studies have either an experimental or a correlational design: you are looking either for differences between groups or conditions (for example differences in driving ability between young, middle-aged and elderly drivers), or you are looking for relationships between variables (a correlation between age and driving ability).

Question 4: Independent Measures or Repeated Measures?

If each participant participates in only one condition in your experiment, so that different groups of participants do different conditions, then your study has a wholly independent measures design. If each participant takes part in all of the conditions in your study, so that they give a score for each and every one of those conditions, you have a repeated-measures design. If participants participate in some, but not all, conditions, you have a 'mixed' design (so called because it's a mixture of the other two kinds).

Note that this question only applies if your design is an experimental one: it doesn't have any relevance to correlational studies or studies involving frequency data (and hence analysed by using Chi-Squared).

Question 5: Are My Data Parametric or Non-Parametric?

As we saw in Chapters 5 and 6, one distinction which you will encounter frequently in statistics is between parametric and non-parametric tests. Hopefully, you recall that parametric tests assume that your data have certain characteristics: specifically, they assume that your data are

1. normally-distributed;
2. measurements of a continuous variable, on an interval or ratio scale of measurement;
3. the amount of variation amongst the scores in each condition or group is roughly comparable (the conditions or groups have equal variances).

Non-parametric tests make no such assumptions, but are generally less powerful than their parametric equivalents (see page 234). For the purpose of this book we call data that meet these assumptions parametric data, and data that do not non-parametric data.

8.3 Specific Sources of Confusion in Deciding Which Test to Use

There are a couple of problems which seem to crop up frequently when students first start getting to grips with deciding which test to use.

Should I use Chi-Squared or a Correlation?

Sometimes students get confused about whether they should be using the Chi-Squared Test of Association, or a correlation. Both of these tests look for a relationship between two different variables, but they do so in quite different ways. Suppose we wanted to know whether there was a relationship between age and fearfulness. Which test should we use? The answer is actually quite straightforward, once you think about how each participant is contributing to your data. Does each participant provide a pair of scores, or do they just contribute to a 'head count'? If it's the latter, and each participant merely falls into a category (e.g. 'old' or 'young', 'fearful' or 'fearless') then the Chi-Squared Test of Association is the one to use. You have frequency data (i.e. number of people in each permutation of categories), and Chi-Squared will tell you if the frequencies in the categories of one of the variables (e.g. age) are non-randomly related to the frequencies of the categories of the other variable (e.g. fearfulness).

If, on the other hand, each participant provides a pair of scores (in this case, a score for their age, and another score for their level of fearfulness), and you want to know if there is a relationship between the scores, then perform a correlation.

Should I Use a Correlation or a *t*-Test?

If you have pairs of scores from each of a number of participants, how do you decide whether to use a correlation test or a repeated-measures *t*-test? After all, you have pairs of scores in both cases! (In fact, if you use SPSS to perform a repeated-measures *t*-test, it will also give you the results of a correlation test on the same data, just to confuse you). The answer is to think of what the data represent, and precisely what it is that you are trying to find out. You use a correlation if you want to find out if there is a relationship between two sets of scores, and a *t*-test if you want to see if there is a difference between them.

Suppose we take a group of lecturers, and measure their level of anxiety under two conditions: while they are with a small seminar group, and while they lecture to a large audience. Each lecturer is giving us two scores, so should we run a correlation or a repeated-measures *t*-test?

A correlation test would tell you whether there is a systematic relationship between the level of anxiety in small-group situations and the level of anxiety in large-group situations: as one increases, does the other increase (or decrease) too? A significant positive correlation would tell us that lecturers who are highly anxious in seminars are also highly anxious in lectures (and that lecturers who are not anxious in seminars are also not anxious in lectures). In most cases, in a correlational study, neither variable is being manipulated by the experimenter: we merely record what is given. In this example, each lecturer would come along with their own two levels of anxiety, and we would record them: we wouldn't be able to say to them 'hello, you're going to be extremely anxious in seminars today, but not so bothered about lectures!'

In the case of a repeated-measures *t*-test, the pairs of scores per participant correspond to measurements of the same dependent variable measured under different conditions. You look for differences between the two measurements, that have been produced by your experimental manipulations. So, in this case, we might have pairs of scores from each lecturer, but these would have been produced because we have manipulated the conditions. For each lecturer, we would decide whether they were going to give a lecture or a seminar – this decision would represent our way of manipulating their anxiety level. The *t*-test would tell us if putting lecturers into different situations (seminars or lectures) produced changes in their anxiety levels.

8.4   Examples of Using These Questions to Arrive at the Correct Test

Answering these five questions correctly should enable you to cope with the two situations described at the beginning of this chapter. You should be able to decide correctly which statistical test should be used in any particular set of circumstances. So, if you are faced with a description of a study (either in a journal article or as part of a statistics test) you should be able to work out which test is most appropriate. If you are designing a study, you can use these questions to help you decide what kind of data you should be aiming to obtain, and hence what kind of statistics test you will be able to use to analyse those data once you've got them.

Here are a few fictitious studies, with demonstrations of how answering the five questions above enables you to arrive at the most appropriate test for those circumstances.

Example 1: The Effectiveness of 'Flooding' as a Treatment for Different Phobias

Ooerr! Hope I never get phobic about cats...

A psychologist wanted to know whether the effectiveness of 'flooding' as a treatment of for phobias varied according to the particular phobia concerned. (The 'flooding' technique consists of taking the phobic and whatever it is that they are phobic about, throwing them into a room together, locking the door and waiting for the screams to subside. In other words, you confront them with their phobia in a big way!) Four groups of phobics (snake-phobics, spider-phobics, agoraphobics and claustro-phobics) were given this treatment. (For simplicity's sake, we'll assume that each person has only one of these particular phobias). Each participant provided a rating for their perceived level of improvement, on a scale from '1' (phobia much worse) through '4' (no change) to '7' (phobia much improved).

Question 1: What kind of data do I have?

The dependent variable is perceived improvement. The data consist of each phobic providing a rating of how much they feel they have improved. Ratings are generally ordinal-scale data (although you will see instances in the psychological literature of researchers trying to use tests on these data which, strictly speaking, should be reserved for interval or ratio data, at this stage you should play by the rules and be very principled about which test you pick!). We can be reasonably confident that a score of 6 represents more improvement than a score of 5, and that a score of 7 probably represents more improvement than a score of 6; however, we can't know by how much someone scoring 7 is improved compared to someone scoring a 6 or a 5. A score of 6 might represent an enormous improvement over a score of 5, whereas a score of 7 might represent only a minor gain over a score of 6 – or vice versa. So, we'll treat this as ordinal data.

Question 2: How many independent variables do I have?

There is one independent variable, type of phobia. It has four levels: snake-phobic, spider-phobic, agoraphobic or claustrophobic. This is one of those independent variables like gender – one in which the experimenter is not free to manipulate the independent variable completely, but is able to pick certain levels of it (i.e. the experimenter can't randomly assign people to the different phobia categories because participants come ready-made with their particular type of phobia; but the experimenter can decide which levels of the independent variable to use in the study, for example choosing to examine snake-phobics rather than needle-phobics, etc.).

Question 3: What kind of design do I have (experimental or correlational)?

This is an experimental design. We are giving all of our phobics the same treatment (flooding) and then looking for differences in perceived improvement between the four different types of phobic.

Question 4: Does my study use a repeated-measures or independent-measures design?

This is a wholly independent-measures design. Each phobic can only be in one group, and gives just one score – their rating of perceived improvement.

Question 5: Are my data parametric or non-parametric?

Are the data that would be obtained in this study likely to satisfy the requirements for a parametric test? Consider each of the three requirements for a parametric test. First, are the data normally distributed? To some extent, we would have to see the actual data before making this decision. What we would be looking for is a roughly bell-shaped frequency distribution of scores in each group, around the mean of that group. Do the data show homogeneity of variance? Again, this is normally something you can only be certain about once you have collected the data. We would be looking for spreads of scores in each group that weren't wildly dissimilar from each other. Are the data measurements on an interval or ratio scale? We have already discussed this, in answering Question 1. The answer is 'no', they are ordinal-level measurements. Failure on any one of these three questions means that the data do not win the prize of having a parametric test done on them: we have to find a suitable non-parametric test instead. That will teach them to be failures…

Using the flow-chart in Box 8.2, together with our answers to the five questions, we can now decide what test we should conduct on our data.

Starting at the top, we know that our data consist of scores; so that rules out Chi-Squared as an option. We have an experimental design, so that rules out using correlations. We have one independent variable, and we have an independent-measures design. There are three or more groups. We have now narrowed our choice of test down to either a one-way independent-measures ANOVA, or its non-parametric equivalent, the Kruskal-Wallis test. Since our data do not satisfy the requirements for a parametric test, we should use the Kruskal-Wallis test on our data.

Example 2: The Relationship Between Optimism and Watching 'Star Trek'

Are people who watch 'Star Trek' more optimistic about the future of humanity than people who don't? 500 people will be interviewed, and asked to provide (a) an estimate of how many 'Star Trek' episodes they have watched, and (b) asked to provide a numerical estimate of how long the human race will survive.

Are Trekkies optimistic about humanity? Fascinating, captain!

Question 1: What kind of data will I collect?

There are two measures here. Participants' estimates of how many 'Star Trek' episodes they have watched is a measurement on a ratio scale: it is quite possible to have watched no episodes of 'Star Trek' at all, so that there is a true zero on the scale; and someone who has watched ten episodes has watched half as many as someone who has watched twenty, and twice as many as someone who has watched five. The numerical estimate of how long the human race will survive is a little less

■ Box 8.2: Which test do I use?

Use this flow-chart in conjunction with the answers to the five questions in the text, to decide which statistical test is most appropriate for your data.

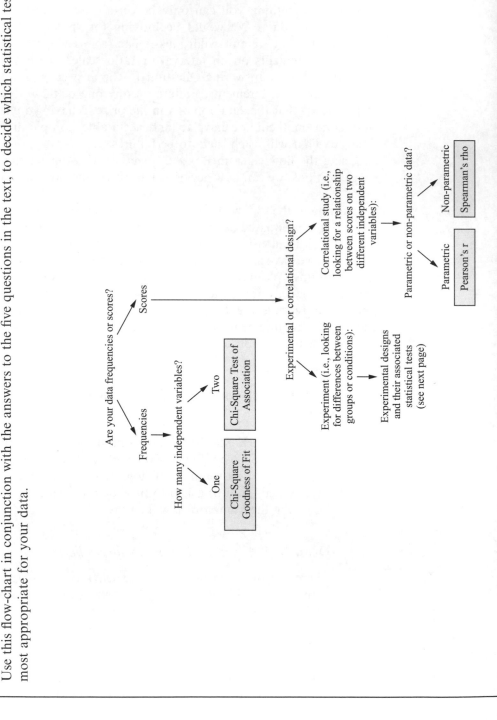

Experimental designs and their associated statistical tests (continued from Box 8.2)

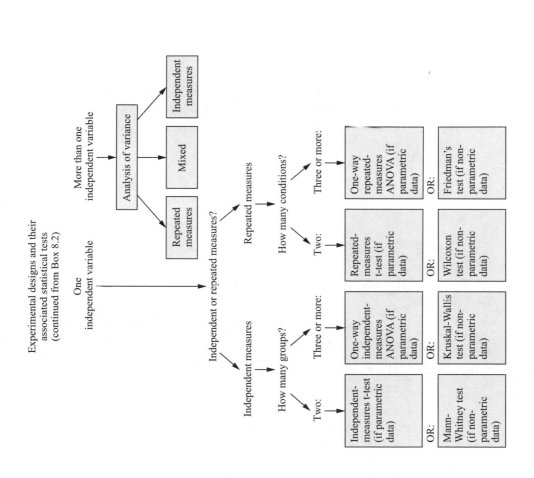

clear-cut, but can probably also be considered as ratio data, for the same reasons (intervals on the scale are equally spaced and there is a true zero point).

Question 2: How many independent variables will I use?

There are two independent variables here: number of 'Star Trek' episodes watched, and 'level of optimism about the human race'.

Question 3: What kind of design will I use (experimental or correlational)?

We are not manipulating anything in this study, merely recording data on two independent variables. We are looking for a relationship between the two independent variables, so this is a correlational design.

Question 4: Does my study use a repeated-measures or independent-measures design?

This is a correlational design, so we don't have to answer this question.

Question 5: Are my data parametric or non-parametric?

First, are the data normally-distributed? We have two independent variables and the scores on both would need to be roughly normally distributed. We would have to look at the data to be sure, but the frequency of watching 'Star Trek' is unlikely to be normally distributed. Fans tend to watch it avidly, whereas non-fans might only watch the occasional episode. Therefore the frequency distribution of scores is more likely to be bimodal than normal. It's hard to make any firm predictions about the optimism scores, but they are likely to be skewed towards the upper end of the distribution of possible scores – only a few pessimists (realists?) are likely to give very short estimates.

Secondly, are the scores measurements on an interval or ratio scale of measurement? We have already answered this question, and decided that both independent variables may be considered to be measurements on ratio scales.

Finally, is the amount of variation amongst the scores in each condition or group roughly comparable? This doesn't really apply in the case of correlational designs, so we'll ignore it.

Overall, it looks like we are safest treating these as non-parametric data, given our doubts about whether scores on the two variables are normally distributed. However, we should check the distribution of scores after the data have been collected, just to be sure.

Working through the flowchart, we make the following decisions. The data are scores, so we can forget about using Chi-Squared. We have a correlational design, so we are faced with a choice between using either a parametric correlation test (Pearson's r) or a non-parametric correlation test (Spearman's rho, ρ). Once we have collected the data and looked at the distribution, we can make a final choice of test: if the distribution is not normal, we'll use Spearman's ρ, and if it is, we'll use Pearson's r.

8.5   Summary

1. When you design a study, at the very outset think about what type of data you will collect, and what statistical tests you will use on them – don't defer thinking about these issues until after you have obtained the data!
2. Minor changes in the design of your study (and in particular, in your choice of dependent variable) can have a major effect on the conclusions that you will be able to draw from its results.
3. By answering the following five questions, you should be able to decide which statistical test is the most appropriate one to use. Question 1: what kind of data will I collect? Question 2: how many independent variables will I use? Question 3: what kind of design will I use (experimental or correlational)? Question 4: will my study use a repeated-measures or independent-measures design? Question 5: will my data be parametric or non-parametric?

8.6   Practical Tasks

Using the five questions in the text, plus the flowchart in Box 8.2, work out which statistical test you would use for each of the following studies:

1. Is there a relationship between political affiliation and attitudes to the Millennium Dome? A psychologist asked 100 supporters of each of the main political parties whether they approved or disapproved of the project.
2. Does exposure to mis-spelt words affect spelling ability? A psychologist takes two groups of students. One group is exposed to a list of mis-spelt words, while the other group is exposed to the

same words, but correctly spelt. All participants' ability to spell these words was then tested a week later. The measure was the number of words correctly spelt out of 40.

3. Do rats make better pets than hamsters? Twenty individuals who had owned both as pets, were asked to provide ratings of hamsters and rats for suitability as pets.

4. Is there a relationship between belief in flying saucers and watching the 'X-Files'? A group of 200 people were interviewed about their belief in flying saucers. Seventy said they believed in flying saucers, while the rest said they didn't. Each was also asked whether they were a regular viewer of the 'X-Files'.

5. Does shift-work affect cognitive performance? The performance of two groups of workers on a mental arithmetic test was compared: one group did permanent night shifts, and the other group did permanent day shifts.

6. Do working mothers differ from non-working mothers in terms of the quality of their interactions with their children? Fifty of each type of mother were video-filmed playing with their child for 30 minutes: one measure taken was the number of positive actions initiated by the mother rather than by the child. The variances were rather different between the two groups.

7. Are men's pain thresholds affected by what they see on TV? Fifty men's pain thresholds are measured three times – once after having watched a video of Clint Eastwood, and again after watching videos of Noddy and Mr. Bean.

8. Does drinking 'Diet Coke' affect window-cleaners' attractiveness? Each of several women in an office-block is asked to assess the attractiveness of their window-cleaner on two separate occasions: on one occasion, he drinks 'Diet Coke', while on the other he does not.

9. Is there a relationship between the amount of personal possessions one has, and happiness? Three hundred people are interviewed, and asked to provide estimates of how many possessions they have (where 'possession' is defined as a single article costing over £100) and how happy they are (on a seven-point scale).

10. Do different types of road-sign affect speeding behaviour differently? A psychologist set up four different road signs: 'Slow', '30 MPH', 'Reduce Speed NOW' and 'Police Speed Check'. He then measured the speed of each of the first 40 motorists encountering each sign.

Answers:

1. Is there a relationship between political affiliation and attitudes to the Millennium Dome? The appropriate test is the Chi-Squared Goodness of Fit. We have frequency data rather than a score per participant: all we know is how many people approve or disapprove of the Dome. This narrows down our choice of test to Chi-Squared. We have only one independent variable (political party), so it must be the Goodness of Fit version of Chi-Squared.

2. Does exposure to mis-spelt words affect spelling ability? The number of words spelt correctly is a ratio measure (you could have a score of zero if you were an atrocious speller!) Each participant gives us a single score. We have one independent variable, with two levels (exposure or non-exposure to mis-spellings). It's an experimental design (we randomly allocate people to one condition or the other, and look for differences between the two groups as a consequence of our manipulation of the independent variable). It's an independent-measures design, since each participant takes part in only one condition in the experiment. The appropriate test is therefore the independent-measures *t*-test.

3. Do rats make better pets than hamsters? Our data consist of attitude ratings. We have one independent variable, with two levels (type of animal: hamster or rat). It's an experiment, given that we are looking for differences between ratings for rats and hamsters. It's a repeated-measures design, since each participant is providing two scores, a rating for their pet rat and a rating for their hamster. The data are most likely to require a non-parametric test, firstly because ratings are measurements on an ordinal scale, and secondly because the ratings are likely to be skewed and hence not normally distributed (most people like their pets!) The appropriate test here is the Wilcoxon test.

4. Is there a relationship between belief in flying saucers and watching the 'X-Files'? Don't let the word 'relationship' fool you into thinking a correlation should be used here! We have frequency data (the number of people who do or do not believe in flying saucers, and the number who do or do not watch the 'X-Files'). Thus we're pretty well stuck with using Chi-Squared. We have two independent variables (belief in flying saucers; and 'X-Files' watching habits), so it must be the two-independent-variable version of Chi-Squared, the Chi-Squared Test of Association.

5. Does shift-work affect cognitive performance? Performance on the mental arithmetic test is almost certainly going to be measured in terms of the number of questions correctly answered, which is a ratio measure. Each worker will give us a single score. We have one independent variable, with two levels (time of shift: night or day). It's an experimental design. It's an independent-measures design, since each participant takes part in only one condition in the experiment. We would have to check the data after we collected them to check that they satisfied the other requirements for a parametric test, i.e. homogeneity of variance and normality of distribution. If they did, we would use the independent-measures *t*-test. (If they didn't, then we'd fall back on its non-parametric counterpart, the Mann-Whitney test.)

6. Do working mothers differ from non-working mothers in terms of the quality of their interactions with their children? The number of positive actions initiated by the mother is a ratio measure. Each mother gives us a single score. There is one independent variable (mother's status: working or non-working). It's an experimental design, because we are looking for differences between the two groups of mothers. It's an independent-measures design, since each mother is either working or non-working. So why not use an independent-measures *t*-test? Well, it says in the question that 'the variances were rather different between the two groups'. This inhomogeneity of variance violates one of the requirements for using parametric tests such as the *t*-test, and means that we therefore have to use the *t*-test's non-parametric brother, the Mann-Whitney test.

7. Are men's pain thresholds affected by what they see on TV? The answer to this question depends on how pain thresholds were measured. We could do this in all sorts of ways (some of which are best left to the imagination!). Let's suppose we measured the amount of time that each participant could keep their hand in freezing cold water (something which is painful but unlikely to cause significant tissue damage). This would be a ratio measure. We have one independent variable: type of video watched, with three levels (Noddy, Clint or Mr. Bean). It's an experimental design, since we are looking for differences between these three conditions. It's a repeated-measures design, since each participant is watching three videos and hence takes part in all conditions of the experiment. Assuming the data turn out to be normally-distributed and that the variance is similar in all three conditions, then the appropriate test is a repeated-measures Analysis of Variance. If these requirements weren't

met, or if the measurements had been participants' pain ratings (and hence measured on an ordinal scale), we would have used the non-parametric equivalent of the repeated-measures ANOVA, the Friedman's test.

8. Does drinking 'Diet Coke' affect window-cleaners' attractiveness? The appropriate test here is the Wilcoxon test. We have measurements on an ordinal scale (ratings of attractiveness). There is one independent variable, 'type of drink consumed' (with two levels: Diet Coke or water). This is an experimental design, since we are looking for differences between conditions, and we have repeated measures (since each woman is asked to give a rating for both of the conditions of the study). Since we have ordinal data, we should be looking for a non-parametric test: Wilcoxon is therefore the test to choose.

9. Is there a relationship between the amount of personal possessions one has, and happiness? 300 people are interviewed, and asked to provide estimates of how many possessions they have (where 'possession' is defined as a single article costing over £100) and how happy they are (on a seven-point scale). 'Number of possessions' is a measurement on a ratio scale, but 'ratings of happiness' is an ordinal-scale measurement. We have a correlational design, since we are looking for a relationship between possessions and happiness. This comes down to deciding whether we should use a parametric or a non-parametric correlation test. We have already noted that one of the variables (happiness) is measured on an ordinal scale: hence the data do not satisfy the requirements for Pearson's *r*, and we should use Spearman's rho.

10. Do different types of road-sign affect speeding behaviour differently? Our dependent variable here is 'speed', which is a ratio measure. We have one independent variable: type of road sign (with four levels, corresponding to the four different types of sign). Different groups of motorists respond to each sign, so it's an independent-measures design. There are no a priori grounds for thinking that the data won't satisfy the requirements for a parametric test (although this is something to be checked after the data have been collected). The appropriate test is therefore a one-way independent-measures Analysis of Variance.

A Further Practical Test

Suppose we want to find out if listening to Bedraggled's singing shrinks your brain. Think about how you could turn this idea into a workable study. Design a study that would give results that could be analysed using (a) a correlation; (b) Chi-Squared; and (c) a parametric statistical test. Think about the advantages and disadvantages in each case.

Answer:

There is no one perfect answer to this question: however, here are some things that you might have considered when designing your studies.

(a) A study designed with a view to using a correlation on the results:

We could get a large group of pop music fans, and get two measures from each one: firstly, an estimate of how frequently they listen to Bedraggled's singing, and secondly, a measure of their brain size (perhaps by taking an MRI scan of their heads). Both of these measures are ratio data; assuming that the data satisfy the other requirements for a parametric test, (something we could check once we have obtained the data) we could perform a Pearson's r on the results. A significant positive correlation would tell us that brain shrinkage was associated with listening to Bedraggled – the more you listened, the more your brain shrank.

Advantages:

We can make use of naturally-occurring variations in people's behaviour: no-one is forcing them to do something unnatural, like listening to Bedraggled if they don't want to.

Disadvantages:

This has the usual disadvantage of a correlational study: it tells us nothing about causality. In theory, it is just as likely that brain shrinkage causes a person to listen to Bedraggled, as it is that listening to Bedraggled causes brain shrinkage. (Or there might be a third variable that gives rise to variations in the other two: for example, listening to Strides might cause brain damage and a desire to listen to Bedraggled.)

(b) A study designed with a view to using Chi-Squared on the results:

We could take a large group of people and divide them into four categories, based on the permutations of our two independent variables (Bedraggled-listening and brain size): frequent listeners to Bedraggled who had experienced brain shrinkage; frequent listeners to Bedraggled who had not experienced brain shrinkage; infrequent listeners who had shrunken brains; and infrequent listeners whose brains remained unshrunken. To do this, we would have to devise some criteria as a basis for allocating people to one category or another. So, for example, we might define 'frequent listening to Bedraggled' as listening for more than seven hours a week, and 'brain shrinkage' as having a brain that was 10% smaller than the norm for that person's age. Our results would be the frequencies with which people fell into our four categories. We could perform a Chi-Squared Test of Association on the data: if Bedraggled listening was associated with brain shrinkage, there should be considerably more people in the category of 'Bedraggled fans with small brains' than in the other categories.

Advantages:

Again, it makes use of naturally-occurring variations in people's behaviour, as in the correlational study.

Disadvantages:

It doesn't give us much information. We have simply lumped people into listeners versus non-listeners, and brain-shrunk versus non-shrunk. In this particular case, our criteria for lumping are fairly arbitrary - someone else might have defined 'frequent listening' as anything over 10 minutes per week, or 'brain shrinkage' as having occurred only if the brain was 20% smaller than average. If we used different criteria, we might have obtained different results. In any case, we get only a crude idea of what the effects of listening to Bedraggled might be. The results might tell us that listening to Bedraggled for more than seven hours a week is associated with brain shrinkage, but it doesn't tell us whether the effects of Bedraggled listening are cumulative (i.e. the more you listen, the more your brain shrinks) or all-or-none; and it still tells us nothing about the causal relationship between Bedraggled-listening and brain-shrinkage.

(c) A study designed with a view to using parametric statistics on the results:

We could do an experiment on this issue. We could take some participants, and randomly allocate them to one of two conditions: half get prolonged exposure to Bedraggled's singing, and the other half are exposed to an equivalent amount and volume of harmless music (for example by Riff Clichard, whose music has been around long enough for it to be known that it poses no serious threat to health). After the exposure period is finished, we measure the brain-size of each participant. If Bedraggled's music produces brain shrinkage, then participants in the Bedraggled-exposure condition should have smaller brains than participants in the Riff Clichard condition. 'Brain shrinkage' is a ratio measure, so as long as the data turn out to satisfy the other requirements for a parametric test, we could use an independent-measures *t*-test.

Advantages:

We can directly and unequivocally determine cause and effect: we manipulate Bedraggled-listening, and examine the effects of our manipulations on brain shrinkage. If brain shrinkage has occurred, it must be due to what we did to the participants, since they were randomly allocated to the two conditions of the study.

Disadvantages:

If we really did think that listening to Bedraggled caused brain damage, this would be a highly unethical experiment! That apart, we would be getting participants to listen to Bedraggled when this was not necessarily something they would do voluntarily. Consequently if the study found evidence of brain damage as a result of listening to Bedraggled, we still would not know if shrinkage would occur in people who voluntarily exposed themselves to their music. (It might be that shrinkage has been caused by listening to Bedraggled in conjunction with the stress of not being able to turn them off!) Finally, we still know nothing about how much Bedraggled listening is required for brain shrinkage to occur. However, we could find this out by testing more experimental groups, each of which received a different duration of exposure to Bedraggled. (We would then analyse the data using a one-way independent-measures Analysis of Variance).

Hopefully you have learnt from this example, that (a) no one design is foolproof – each has its merits as well as its disadvantages; and (b) decisions made about statistics at the outset have major consequences on what you will be able to conclude from your results.

PART 3   WRITING UP YOUR RESEARCH

9 A Quick Guide to Writing a Psychology Lab-Report

The following chapters give a detailed explanation of how to write a psychology lab-report. If you are new to psychology, you might want to read this short chapter first, to give yourself an overview of what's involved.

9.1 An Overview of the Various Sections of a Report

Lab-reports are modelled on the scientific journal article. Like them, the report is divided into sections, each of which provides a specific type of information. Here, we provide a short description of what should be contained in each section, followed in each case by a brief illustration from a wholly fictitious and potentially offensive study on national stereotypes. Chapter 16 shows a complete, and fuller, sample report: you might want to have a quick look at that as well, to give yourself a feel for what a lab-report should look like, before going on to read Chapters 10–15.

   The precise length of each section will vary, depending on the nature of the study (some studies have more complicated procedures than others, for example, and so need a lengthier description in the 'Procedure' section). However a reader would expect to find all of these sections in the report, in this particular order:

- Title
- Abstract
- Introduction
- Method (sub-divided into the following sections:)
  - Design
  - Participants
  - Apparatus and Materials

- ○ Procedure
- ● Results
- ● Discussion
- ● References
- ● Appendices (not always present).

These sections answer four basic questions:

1. 'Why?' Why did I do this particular experiment? What did I expect to find out by doing it? This question is dealt with in the Introduction section.
2. 'How?' How did I actually carry it out – what procedures and apparatus did I use? This question is covered in the Method section.
3. 'What?' What did I find? What were my results? This information is provided in the Results section.
4. 'So What?' What does it all mean? How do my results relate to previous research on the same topic, and what are their theoretical implications? What are my conclusions? These issues are all dealt with in the Discussion section.

What about all the other bits – the Title, Abstract and References? These have important functions too. The Title enables the reader to get a very quick idea of what the report is about. If they are still interested, they can read the Abstract, which is a summary that provides a brief outline of the main procedures, results and findings of the study. The Reference section allows the reader to obtain further information on the topic of the report, by providing full details of any previous work that the author has referred to. (It also enables the reader to check that the author hasn't misquoted or misrepresented the work of others in the course of citing them!)

The overall length of the report will vary according to the precise nature of the study that's being described, and on whether your tutor requires you to include Appendices. As a very rough guide, a journal article which describes only a single experiment usually comes out to no more than 20 pages or so of double-spaced manuscript, including references, tables and graphs: about 5000 words in all. The Introduction and Discussion account for about half of this total length.

In the following chapters, we are going to look in detail at what should be included in each of these sections. See also the checklist in Box 9.1 at the end of this chapter.

9.2 Title

Provide a succinct title of no more than about 15 words. If it were the title of a journal article, it would be informative enough to enable the reader to identify the paper from the journal's index as something that they would be interested in reading: for example 'Sex differences in problem solving behaviour' rather than 'Sex differences' or 'An experiment on problem solving'. The following sections will describe a report that could be entitled *'The effects of nationality and age on sun-bed claiming behaviour'*: fairly self-explanatory, isn't it? Your title should be too.

9.3 Abstract

This is a brief summary (150 words maximum) of the report. (The American Psychological Association stipulate a 120-word limit, but we'll settle for 150 for now). It gives the reader a quick idea of what you did, the main results, and their theoretical implications. It's easiest to write this last, once you have written the rest of the report. Here's the abstract to go with our study of sun-bed claiming behaviour: note that it's only 119 words long, but it gives all the essentials of the study.

The effects of nationality (German, English or American) and age ('young', 20–30 years; or 'old', 60–70 years) were measured on latencies to claim sun-beds at an international resort. Ten males of each nationality (five for each age-group) were selected randomly and covertly filmed during the 30 minutes after the pool was opened in the morning. The speed with which each individual moved from the dining room to the sun-bed was recorded. Significant effects of nationality and age were found, but no interaction between them. Germans were faster than the British, who in turn were faster than the Americans. The young of all nationalities were faster than their older counterparts. It is concluded that national stereotypes have some basis in fact.

9.4 Introduction

This part of the report introduces the reader to the topic on which you are going to do your experiment, and provides a justification for *why* you did the experiment. You provide some background information about previous research in this area, and explain why your study was worth doing – how is it likely to add to our knowledge of this topic? Your experiment might aim to plug a gap in our knowledge, or clarify some issue which has arisen from previous research – perhaps previous experiments have produced inconsistent or conflicting results, or perhaps experiments have been done in two separate areas but no-one has thought of linking them together before.

Previous work is cited in a standardized way: in the text of the report, you refer to all previous work by means of the authors' surnames followed by the date of publication (e.g. 'Bonkers (1955)', 'Twitch and Cackle (1976)' etc.); at the end of the report, there is a reference section which gives the full reference for each work mentioned in the text. See Chapter 15 for full details.

The final paragraph or so of the introduction should outline your proposed experiment, and state (in an informal way) what you predict your results will be, given your knowledge of previous research in this area. Here's an abbreviated example of an introduction (in practice, you might include more information on previous studies and theories):

> In recent years, there has been considerable interest in national stereotypes and the extent to which they are valid. Ever since Biggott (1967) reported that French shoppers were significantly more likely to push into a bus queue than were Swiss shoppers, studies have been performed that appear to show that reliable cross-cultural differences exist in what is considered 'acceptable' behaviour, even within the Western 'developed' nations. For example, Raciste, Morone and Kruelle (2000) recently presented evidence that people from Alsace are significantly more likely to consider dog-beating acceptable than are people from Labrador. Wikked and Hartless (2001) found that 95% of Welsh interviewed claimed that they had watched ritual poodle-drowning; in contrast, 68% of Swedes claimed to find this practice abhorrent.
>
> One problem with all of these studies is that, with the exception of the original work by Biggott, they rely on responses to questionnaires: given that there is often some disparity between what people say they do and their actual behaviours (ThynKin, SeyYing and Doowing, 1978), the questionnaire studies may have overestimated the strength of these cultural variations.
>
> One behaviour which has attracted considerable interest is sun-bed claiming: the establishment of priority of access to a sun-bed at a resort by means of placing a towel on it. While there have been previous studies of this phenomenon, they are either so old that cultural practices might have changed in the meantime (e.g. Buonaparte and Nelson's (1805) study of sun-bed claiming beha-

viour on the Western European coast) or they have failed to use objective behavioural measurements (e.g. as in Krapp and Fewtile's (1966) study, in which individuals of two countries were asked to give ratings of the acceptability of each other's toenail-clipping behaviour). Also, previous studies have failed to take account of the age of the participants, and yet recent research has shown this to be an important variable in cross-cultural behavioural variation. For example, Kebbab, Burghur and Schnitzel (1995) have found that European young people are more pushy at supermarket checkouts than American young people, whereas the reverse is true for old people.

The present study therefore sets out to examine age and cultural differences in an overt behaviour (sun-bed claiming behaviour around a hotel pool) using a valid and objective measure of performance: the speed with which individuals moved from one clearly-defined part of the hotel (the dining room) to the sun-bed. On the basis of previous research, it was predicted that there would be national differences in this behaviour which conformed to widely held national stereotypes – namely, that German tourists will be faster to claim sun-beds than American tourists, who in turn will be faster than the English. It was also expected that there would be some form of interaction between the age and nationality of participants, although the precise nature of that interaction is difficult to predict in advance.

9.5   Method

This tells the reader what you did in your experiment, in enough detail that they could replicate the study in all its important details. It breaks down into sub-sections.

Design

This gives details of the formal design of the experiment – such as whether it was an independent- or repeated-measures design (see Chapter 3). It identifies the independent and dependent variables in the study. Remember, the independent variable is what you manipulate, in your role as experimenter, and the dependent variable is what you measure. Here's our 'design' section:

This study used a between-subjects design. There were two independent variables: nationality (with three levels: English,

German or American) and age (with two levels: 20–30 years old or 60–70 years old).

The dependent variable was 'sun-bed claiming speed', defined as the time (in seconds) that it took a participant to run from the hotel dining-room to a sun-bed by the hotel swimming pool.

Participants

Give details of who took part in your experiment: provide details of their sex, age and any special characteristics of them that might be relevant to your particular experiment (e.g. handedness, bilingualism, etc.). State whether they were volunteers; whether they were paid for participating; how they were allocated to the different conditions of the study; and of course, how many there were per condition.

There were 30 participants (10 German, 10 English and 10 American), residents of the 'Hotel Ripov' during the first week of July 2000. Half of each nationality were between 20–30 years of age (*M* 26, *SD* 3.2), and the rest were 60–70 years old (*M* 64, *SD* 4.8). All were male, and free from any obvious physical or sensory impairments. Participants took part in the study unwittingly, and therefore remained completely naive about the aims and purpose of the study.

Apparatus

'Apparatus' in this context means things like stopwatches, computers, questionnaires, etc. Give important relevant details (e.g. brand-names and model numbers if the equipment is unusual), but omit trivial and unnecessary details like whether they used an HB pencil or a biro to fill in a questionnaire! Write this section in full English sentences, not as a 'shopping-list' of equipment.

Participants' running speeds were measured with a hand-held stopwatch. A video-camera was used to film the participants' behaviour: this was done so that inter-rater reliability checks could later be made on the accuracy with which running speed had been recorded, and also to provide a means of enabling the hotel staff to identify the participants and thus provide the experimenter with information about their nationality and age.

Procedure

Explain how you actually carried out the experiment in practice. Give details of exactly what was done to participants; what they had to do; the order in which tests were administered; and how long test sessions took.

> From 7.30 to 8.00 a.m. each morning, the experimenter hid in a clump of bushes in a position that enabled him to see both the hotel's swimming pool and the exit to the hotel's dining room. As a person passed through the French windows of the dining room, the stopwatch was started. It was stopped when the person either placed their towel on a sun-bed (thus establishing 'ownership') or sat or lay on the sunbed. This procedure was followed for one week. At the end of each day's covert filming, the film was shown to the hotel manager, who identified the guest and provided information about the guest's nationality and age. The first ten people of each of the predetermined permutations of nationality and age that were filmed, were chosen to be the experimental participants.

9.6   Results

This section falls into two parts, although they don't have sub-headings. First, give descriptive statistics, such as means and standard deviation for each group or condition. Follow these with inferential statistics – the results of statistical tests used to decide whether any differences between groups or conditions were 'real' as opposed to merely due to chance. (See Chapters 5, 6 and 7). For the inferential statistics, state which test you used; the value of the test statistic; the number of degrees of freedom (where appropriate); and the significance level for this. Although generally you do not need to provide a justification of *why* you picked a particular test – it is usually self-evident – there are circumstances when you do (for example, explaining why you chose a non-parametric test, or saying why you picked a particular post-hoc test). One thing you should never include is the calculations for the test.

In most cases the information can be inserted into the text like this: 'an independent-means *t*-test was performed. This showed that participants who had received 40 mg of the drug 'Pukupp' recalled significantly fewer words than those who had consumed 20 mg (t (29) = 3.65, $p < .001$)'. If you have lots of results, consider using tables or graphs to display them. However, don't duplicate information unnecessarily: if the results are shown in a table, don't also show them in a graph, or vice versa. Make sure that all tables and graphs are clearly labelled with self-explanatory titles and legends. A good rule of thumb is that the text of the results section should be intelligible to a naive reader without reference to any tables or graphs; and similarly, the tables and graphs should be understandable without reference to the text.

Don't put raw data in this section – put them in an appendix at the end of the report if your tutor says you need to provide them. Explain in words what the descriptive and inferential statistics show, but don't interpret them – that's left until the next section. (So, for example, in this section we describe the data on sun-bed claiming speed that we have recorded, and say whether there were any significant differences between the ages and nationalities. Here, you wouldn't speculate about *why* these differences had occurred, or relate these findings to previous data or theories on age and cultural differences in behaviour – all of that should be left until the Discussion).

Figure 9.1 shows the mean latency to claim a sun-bed (time from dining room to sun bed) for each permutation of nationality and age. (Note that the shorter the latency, the faster the participant). The error bars represent the 95% confidence interval for the mean. Inspection of Figure 9.1 suggests that the three nationalities differed in sun-bed claiming speed, with the Germans being fastest, the Americans slowest, and the English falling between these two extremes. There also appears to be some effect of age, with the younger participants of all nationalities being somewhat faster overall than their older counterparts.

A two-way independent-measures ANOVA (nationality: three levels, American, German and English; age: two levels, younger and older) was performed on these data. There was a significant main effect of nationality (F (2, 30) = 21.03, $p < .0001$, $r = .36$).

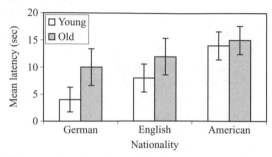

Figure 9.1   Effects of nationality and age on sun-bed claiming behaviour

Post-hoc tests revealed that, overall, the German tourists were faster to claim a sun-bed than were the English tourists, who in turn were faster than the Americans (Bonferroni tests, $p < .05$ for all tests). There was also a significant main effect of age ($F (1, 30) = 14.88$, $p < .01$, $r = .28$): regardless of nationality, younger tourists were faster to claim a sun-bed than were older tourists. From Figure 9.1, it appears that the effects of age were more marked for the Germans and English than they were for the Americans. However, the ANOVA failed to support this interpretation, revealing no significant interaction between age and nationality ($F (2, 30) = 2.34$, *ns*, $r = .04$).

9.7   Discussion

Start by briefly restating the main results, in words. Say whether or not they support your experimental hypothesis (as stated at the beginning of the Introduction). Then relate your findings to those of previous studies: do your results support previous work, refute it, or force a re-evaluation of earlier findings? If your results are at variance with previous work, why do you think this has happened? What theoretical implications does this have? Basically, you are assessing your experiment's contribution to knowledge in this area of psychology. What faults or limitations did your study have? Do these seriously affect confidence in your findings? How might they be remedied in future work? Suggest possible worthwhile future experiments in this area. Finish by summarizing the main conclusions that can be drawn from your study.

> Clear effects of nationality and age on sun-bed claiming behaviour were found in this study: German tourists were faster than English tourists to claim a sun-bed, and the English were in turn faster than the Americans. For all nationalities, younger tourists were faster to claim a sun-bed than were older tourists.
>
> These results are in line with previous research showing that there is some validity to commonly-held national stereotypes: there appear to be real cross-cultural differences in behaviour which underlie these beliefs (Biggott, 1967; Raciste, Morone and Kruelle, 2000; Wikked and Hartless, 2001). Biggott's 'Theory of Racially Induced Patterns of Expression' (TRIPE) suggests that cultural and racial stereotypes have their origins in early socialization patterns which have become slightly different around the world due to geographical isolation. In Raciste et

al.'s 'Framework Accounting Specifically for Culturally Induced Social Traits' (FASCIST) theory, cross-cultural differences stem not from childhood experiences, but instead arise when adults of one culture interact with people of another: The stereotypical behaviours are seen as an attempt by the native population to maintain their social identity in the face of threat from a 'foreigner' or 'outsider'. There is evidence in support of both of these theories, and the present study cannot decide between them conclusively. However, it does demonstrate that, contrary to Raciste et al.'s assertions, these cross-cultural differences stem from the behaviour of the 'foreigner' rather than the perceptions of the native population in which they find themselves.

Furthermore, most of the earlier researchers based their conclusions on people's verbal reports of how they would behave in various situations: for example, even in Raciste et al.'s comparatively recent study, participants were merely asked how acceptable they would find dog-beating. How these participants' reactions to a real dog-beating would relate to their verbal claims was not investigated, and yet the relationship between overt behaviour and self-report has been shown to be an important issue (ThynKin, SeyYing and Doowing, 1978). In the present experiment, participants' overt behaviour in a naturalistic situation (sun-bed claiming around a hotel pool) was recorded, without their knowledge that their behaviour was being scrutinized. The present study therefore provides important information on how different nationalities behave in practice, and suggests – contrary to ThynKin et al.'s claims – that cross-cultural differences in overt behaviour are very real and pronounced. The results described here also suggest that these differences have persisted over a comparatively long period of time, given their consistency with the findings of Buonaparte and Nelson (1805).

However, there are several factors which need to be considered in evaluating the findings of the present research. First, although the observed differences in sun-bed claiming behaviour were statistically significant, they are small in absolute terms: all nationalities were comparatively quick to claim a sun-bed. The maximum difference in latency, between the young Germans and the old Americans was still only approximately 10 seconds; given that the swimming pool was 200 metres from the dining room, it is clear that all participants were in a hurry to claim a sun-bed. The fact that the hotel had only three sun-beds for 200 residents may have had a part to play in this: a future study should include a greater range of hotels, to determine whether the present results generalize to situations in which the resource (i.e. sun-beds) is not in such short supply.

Secondly, although participants were selected who lacked obvious physical infirmities or disorders, it became apparent during the course of the study that the nationalities were not strictly comparable in terms of physical fitness. The Germans had lithe, firm, fit bodies, in contrast to the American and English tourists, most of whom were somewhat rotund. Although it was not possible to measure fitness objectively in the present study (measurements of waist-size obtained from the video proved unreliable) it was noticeable that many of the English and American tourists waddled to their targeted sun-bed, and then collapsed upon it with a noticeable shortness of breath. Similar behaviour was rarely observed amongst the German tourists. Differences in physical fitness, as opposed to desperation to claim a sun-bed, may therefore have contributed to the observed differences in running speed. Most of the difference between the younger and older participants could be attributable to fitness, rather than due to motivational differences. A future study should take care to ensure that participants are more evenly matched in terms of physical fitness than was the case in the present work.

A third problem with this study was that most of the German tourists were on a 3-day holiday, whereas the American and English tourists were all booked into the hotel for 14 days. The Germans therefore had less time in which to sun-bathe, a factor which may have contributed to the difference between their behaviour and that of the other two nationalities. However, clearly not all differences in sun-bed claiming behaviour can be attributed to this factor, given that there was also a difference in behaviour between the American and English tourists. Future research should take greater care to ensure that the participants are better matched on any factors such as holiday stay, which might have a significant effect on their motivational level.

Finally, the present study demonstrates a behavioural basis for a national stereotype in only one domain: sun-bed claiming behaviour. It remains to be determined whether these differences hold true across other situations, or are specific to the hotel pool environment.

9.8   References

See Chapter 14 for full details; basically, here you provide, in alphabetical order and in a very standardized format, full details of every work that was cited in the body of the text. Here are the references from our fictitious study:

Biggott, R.S. (1967) National differences in queue-jumping behaviour: an observational study. *Journal of Irreproducible Results*, *17* (1), 296–305.

Buonaparte, N. and Nelson, H. (1805, March 21). An analysis of sun-bed claiming behaviour in Western Europe. *Seafaring Weekly*, *75*, 46–49.

Kebbab, D., Burghur, S. and Schnitzel, Y.P. (1995) 'Pushiness' at supermarket checkouts as a function of age and nationality. *Journal of Shopping Behaviour*, *5* (2), 36–42.

Krapp, N.A. and Fewtile, T. (1966) Cultural differences in the acceptability of toenail-clipping behaviour. *Pedicure*, *36* (1), 12–15.

Raciste, P., Morone, C. and Kruelle, W. (2000) Alsatians and Labradors have different attitudes to dog-beating. *Trivia*, *4* (3), 1215–1320.

ThynKin, P.P.O., SeyYing, M.G. and Doowing, D. (1978) An assessment of the validity of measuring cultural variations by questionnaire. In R.S. Biggott, (Ed.) *Cultural Variation* (pp. 114–190). Ohio: Worthless Books.

Wikked, H. and Hartless, P. (2001) A survey of poodle-drowning practices amongst the Welsh and Swedish. *Marie Eclair*, *101* (2), 200–203.

■ Box 9.1: Things to check that you have covered in your report

When you are writing your lab-reports, check that you have covered the following points.

General:
Write clearly and simply, but in a formal style, using the passive voice. (e.g. 'an experiment was performed' rather than 'we performed an experiment').

Title and Abstract:
1. Give your report a clear and informative title, no more than 10–15 words long.
2. The Abstract is a clear summary of the study's aims, methods, findings and conclusions, all in no more than 150 words.

Introduction:
1. Summarize RELEVANT experimental findings and theories which relate to the aims of your experiment. Use this information to provide a justification for why your experiment is worth doing.
2. Outline your proposed experiment.
3. Make specific predictions about the outcome of the experiment, on the basis of the literature you have reviewed.

Method:
1. Include sub-sections on: Design; Participants; Apparatus; Procedure.
2. Make sure there is enough RELEVANT detail for the reader to be able to repeat the experiment purely by reading your Method section.
3. In the Design section, identify the independent and dependent variables, and say whether you used independent measures, repeated measures or a mixed design.
4. Make sure you give RELEVANT background characteristics of the sample of participants, as well as saying how many took part.
5. Make sure the Apparatus and Procedure sections are written in proper English, and not like a recipe.

Results:
1. Make sure you have clearly described the results and explained whether the evidence (in general) supports the hypothesis under consideration. Describe them, but leave interpretation (in terms of relationship to theories and previous experimental work) until the Discussion section.
2. If you have a fair amount of numerical data, put it in a table or graph, whichever seems clearest.
3. Number your tables and figures so that you can refer to them in the text. Figures and tables are numbered independently of each other, so if you have, say, five graphs or diagrams and three tables, these would be numbered as Figures 1 to 5 and Tables 1 to 3. Even if you have just one table or figure, refer to it as 'Table 1' or 'Figure 1' – rather than using phrases like 'the graph shows…'
4. Make sure each table or graph is clearly labelled and has a self-explanatory title.

continues

■ **Box 9.1:** *continued*

5. Make sure tables and graphs are intelligible without reference to the text, and vice versa.
6. Where inferential statistics are used, indicate the statistic that was used (e.g. t, F, etc.). Give the value of the statistic used, the number of degrees of freedom, the level of significance reached, and whether the test was one-tailed or two-tailed (see Box 5.3).
7. Put raw data and statistical calculations in an appendix, not in the main text.
8. Remember to include means and standard deviations (or medians and ranges or semi-interquartile ranges, if these are more appropriate).

Discussion:
1. Summarize your main results.
2. Provide some interpretation of what your results mean, in theoretical terms.
3. Indicate clearly whether or not your initial hypothesis has been accepted.
4. Discuss your own data with reference to other experimental findings and theories in the area, particularly those summarized in the Introduction.
5. Identify potential problems with your study, but don't produce a litany of trivial criticisms. Make intelligent suggestions for future studies.

References:
1. Give only the surname(s) of the author(s) and the date of the relevant publication in the text, unless you are acknowledging the source of a direct quote – in which case give the number of the page on which the quote can be found.
2. In the reference section itself, at the end of the report, give the references in the correct format (see Chapter 14).
3. If a source you have used (e.g. Smith, 1991) cites an author to whom you wish to refer (e.g. Bloggs, 1950), it must appear in the text as follows: 'Bloggs (1950, cited in Smith, 1991)'. Smith (1991) should be the reference which appears in the list at the end of your report, not Bloggs (1950).

10 General Points When Writing a Report

Having to produce lab-reports is one of the big bugbears about psychology for many students, especially at the beginning of their course. This is especially true for students with non-science backgrounds. Some regard writing a lab-report as a tedious chore; they consider that it's non-creative and that the formal, jargon-laden 'scientific' style is an affront to their writing skills, honed previously on insightful criticisms of 'King Lear' and the Metaphysical Poets. Others are simply scared by the whole idea: it appears to be dry, 'scientific' and hard, when all they really wanted to do was find out what makes people tick.

10.1 The Standardized Format of the Report

Actually, writing a report is none of these things: it can be a highly creative exercise, it should be well written, and it's not really as difficult as it looks. Reports have a clearly specified format, and much of report-writing is a bit like painting by numbers – you just fill in the blanks with the required stuff. (Using words rather than blobs of paint, preferably).

A report's highly standardized format helps readers find information easily.

The standardized format of the psychology lab-report is based on the format used by academics when they publish their findings in academic journals. Journal articles are one of the main ways in which psychologists communicate their ideas and discoveries to their colleagues. (Another way is in drunken conversations at conferences, but we won't go into that). Each issue of a journal consists of a number of articles, each written by a researcher or group of researchers. A typical article consists of research findings, prefaced by a brief explanation of the background to the research and followed by a discussion of what the study's results contribute to our knowledge in that particular area of psychology. The article also provides details about the methods, procedures and apparatus that were used, so that other researchers know exactly how the results were obtained and would be able to replicate the study if they so wished.

Once you are familiar with the conventions that are used, the standardized format enables you to assimilate the information quickly and efficiently. The title of the article should give you a good idea of the specific topic of research; the article itself is preceded by a summary ('abstract') that gives you a quick overview of what was done and what was found; and reading the article itself is facilitated by its standardized presentation. The reader knows exactly where everything is likely to be within the report: if they want to check up on a matter of procedure, or remind themselves of the authors' findings or conclusions, they can go straight to the appropriate section of the report to find the relevant information.

Where to Find Guidance on the Formal Aspects of Report Writing

When in doubt about any aspect of how to write a practical report, there are two ultimate sources of authority. The first and most accessible are journal articles: just go to the library, pick up a journal and see how 'real' researchers do it. (Although you don't have to make your report as tedious as some of the ones you might find!) Don't worry too much about the technical bits, the scary statistics and so on: just aim to get a feel for the general style in which articles are written. Pretty much any journal will do, as they all use much the same format, but the 'British Journal of Psychology' or the 'Journal of Experimental Psychology' spring to mind as good role-models.

The second and definitely the most authoritative source of information are the style guides produced by the British Psychological Society (BPS) and the American Psychological Association (APA). These contain detailed information on every aspect of report writing. Most journals expect submissions to conform to these guidelines: in fact, many American journals will not even look at a manuscript unless it adheres to 'APA format'. The APA are currently up to the fifth edition of their 'Publication Manual of the American Psychological Association'. This is, believe it or not, 439 pages long, and it covers every aspect of report writing from Abbreviations to Zero (the latter is covered on pages 126 and 294: I just thought I'd mention that in case you've been losing sleep over nothing. Nothing? Zero? Oh, never mind!) While some of it verges on the pedantic, much of it is sound advice, and there are some excellent tips on how to express yourself clearly.

Obviously we can't cover everything that the APA manual says, because that would make this book twice as thick as it already is. However, in the sections that follow we will mention some of the manual's more important suggestions.

In the rest of this chapter, we will outline the various sections that should be present in a practical report; tell you what should (and shouldn't!) go in each one; and finally, give you a specimen report that you can use as a rough model for your own write-ups.

10.2   Some Important Considerations When Writing a Report

Keep the Audience in Mind

When writing the report, try to keep your audience in mind. A useful strategy is to imagine that you are talking to someone, and explaining what you did. (Ahah! Finally those voices in your head can be put to some use . . .). This 'someone' is an interested, intelligent person who knows something about psychology, but isn't familiar with the area in which you have performed your experiment.

When writing a report, you have to continually bear in mind that the reader only knows what you have told them up to that point. They shouldn't have to read later parts of the report to make sense of the earlier sections. This can become a little tricky when it comes to describing the study's methods and procedures: if they are complicated, it's sometimes hard to describe them in a way that doesn't presuppose that the reader already knows what you did before you tell them! In these cases, try giving a draft to a friend who doesn't know what the study involved, to see if they can make sense of it.

Substantiate Your Claims and Assertions

You should imagine that your hypothetical non-specialist psychologist is highly sceptical, so that everything you say needs to be supported. In the Introduction, if you make claims you should back them up with references to previous research. In the Results section, if you say there are differences between conditions in your experiment (or even if you say there are no differences!) you should support these claims by referring to the results of statistical tests that you have performed on the data. In the Discussion, you support any conclusions that you draw about what the results show, by reference to your own results and, where appropriate, to those of previous researchers (in a similar way to how you did it in the Introduction).

When supporting claims and assertions by referring to previous work, don't fall into the trap of appealing to authority: sometimes students write statements like 'but Tardive's work is rubbish, according to the esteemed and highly respected psychologist Professor Doodle'. Other people's unsubstantiated opinions are as irrelevant to science as are your own. If Doodle has presented evidence that Tardive's work is problematic, then by all means cite this in support of your argument. Mere appeals to prestige have no place in science.

Avoid emotive or potentially offensive references to other people's work. Rather than write a phrase like 'Tardive's work is rubbish' or 'Tardive is an arrant fool', it's better to say something like 'There are several problems with Tardive's work' or 'However, Tardive failed to consider the following points'.

'Cats are stupid and make lousy pets!' (Woofer 1995; Bach 2001).

Lastly, and perhaps most importantly, all mentions of other people's work should be acknowledged by suitable references. (Specific details on how to provide references are given in Chapter 15). Failure to do this is plagiarism, a serious offence. Make sure you write things in your own words, rather than copying the original authors too closely. If you find you cannot express a point in your own way, it may be because you don't fully understand it enough to be able to paraphrase it – in which case adhering too closely to the original wording will betray your lack of comprehension to any reader who is familiar with the text concerned (e.g. your tutor). Once in a while (given the sub-Shakespearian writing abilities of most academics) it may be that an author makes a point in such a neat and elegant way that you feel you can't improve upon it. If so, you can use a direct quotation from the original text, but surround it by inverted commas and give the reference (surname and date of publication) accompanied by the page numbers in the original text. Use direct quotations very sparingly, as they quickly become irritating to the reader. Good reports (and essays, for that matter) do not consist of a collection of quotations linked by a few sentences of your own.

10.3   Writing Style

Write in a Formal but Clear Style

Most journal articles are written in a 'passive' and 'impersonal' style. Instead of writing in the first person ('I attached the electrodes to our participants' earlobes and administered 240 volts'), you should write in the third person ('electrodes were attached to the participant's earlobes, and 240 volts were administered'). It's just a convention really, that makes psychological writing look impressive and 'scientific'. However, nearly everyone uses it, so you should too. (There are some exceptions. The journal 'Perception' is a notable example: it often has articles written in the first-person singular. Also this convention may die out soon, given that the Fifth Edition of APA Publication Manual now suggests using 'I' or 'we' instead of 'the experimenter(s)'.) This formal style takes a bit of getting used to (and your word-processor's grammar-checker will constantly berate you for writing sentences in the passive tense). However, it's not an excuse for producing writing that's not clear and readable.

Strive for simply-constructed, short sentences. Use short Anglo-Saxon words wherever possible, and avoid words like 'utilize' (what's wrong with 'use'?) and 'posit' (possibly the ugliest word in the English language). Write 'X depends on Y' rather than 'X is dependent on Y'. 'It is to be expected that participants will utilize the manipulandum in an endeavour to effect door opening' is better expressed as 'It is predicted that participants will open the door with the stick' – it's the same information, but presented in a much simpler and straightforward manner.

Personally, I'd suggest that you go and read some George Orwell if you want to learn how to write well. (Sadly, many students appear only to have existed on a diet of Charles Dickens, judging by the inordinate length of their sentences). Avoid jargon, redundancy (for example the 'both' is superfluous in 'they were both alike') and malapropisms – make sure words mean what you think they do. There are lots of examples of good and bad practice in the APA Publication Manual, which even a good writer like wot I is can benefit from having a look at. Another book well worth looking at is Larry Trask's (see the references at the end of this chapter), which identifies many words and phrases that you should avoid (unless you *want* to sound like a pretentious fool, of course).

Read through what you have written, and see how many superfluous phrases you can ditch without doing any violence to the meaning of the text, and to what extent you can simplify and clarify what you have written. For every 100 superfluous words you eliminate, treat yourself to an extra bar of chocolate/pint of beer/snort of cocaine (delete as appropriate) after you have submitted the report.

Avoid Biased Language in Your Writing

Bias can take many forms, and the APA encourages you to read through your report to see if you have unintentionally included any terms which are potentially offensive, patronizing or stigmatizing to the individuals being referred to. So, avoid sexist, racist and ageist terms. Rather than using 'he', use 'he or she' or 'they' to refer to 'Mankind' – whoops, sorry, 'Peoplekind'. Use 'gender' to refer to men and women as social groups, and 'sex' to refer to the biological distinction between them. Generally, refer to groups of people by the labels that they prefer. Avoid labelling groups – talk about 'gay men' or 'gay people' rather than 'the gay', and refer to 'people with disabilities' rather than 'the disabled'. The APA doesn't like 'homosexual' because of its past association with negative stereotypes: 'gay (men)' and 'lesbian' are considered preferable. (One issue you probably won't have to worry about is whether to use 'American Indian' or 'Native American'; but if you do, you might be interested to know that the latter includes Hawaiians and Samoans, so it's a bit less precise than 'American Indian').

   The APA suggests using the term 'people diagnosed with schizophrenia' rather than 'schizophrenics'. 'Depressives' are 'people who are depressed'. 'Amnesics' are 'amnesic people', and they are no longer 'amnesic patients' either. Someone is no longer a 'mentally ill person', but a 'person with a mental illness'. The 'elderly' are now 'older people' (and 'geriatric' is definitely out!) The idea in all these examples is to emphasize the fact that a person is not just their disability. Avoid terms like 'normal', as they tempt the reader to consider others as 'abnormal'.

The Use of Abbreviations

The APA suggests that you use abbreviations only if they are in common use (e.g. for example!) or if using them saves a lot of space. If you do use abbreviations, make sure they are meaningful. For example, using 'Group A' and 'Group B' to refer to groups of participants presented with words or pictures is a lot less helpful to the reader than talking about the 'Word group' and the 'Picture group'. Introduce the abbreviation the first time it is used by placing it in brackets after the term that it will replace, and thereafter use only the abbreviation. ('We measured each participant's reaction time (RT) to the stimuli'). Abbreviations in a figure must be explained in its caption or legend; abbreviations in a table must be explained in the table's title or in a note to the table. (This should be done in every one of the tables and figures, not just the first one, even if it's the same abbreviation being used each time). Don't use the abbreviations 'S' and 'E' for 'subject' and 'experimenter' (you may well see these used in journal articles dating back to the 1950s and '60s). 'For example' and 'and so forth' should be used in text that is outside of brackets (and 'e.g.' and 'etc.' in text that's inside them).

The APA Publication Manual gives a list of abbreviations: ones that you are quite likely to use include 'cm', 'lb', 'kg', 'IQ', 's' (for 'second') and 'ms' (for 'millisecond', a thousandth of a second and a commonly used unit of measurement for reaction times). Note that you use 'cm' even when you're referring to several centimetres: thus you would write 'it was 5 cm long', and not 'it was 5 cms long'. (The same goes for other abbreviations). All units should be metric.

How to Write Numbers

Now, you might think this was pretty straightforward: after all, they are arranged in a row at the top of your keyboard! However, there's more to it than that. For numbers of 10 and above, use figures rather than words. However, if a number less than 10 is part of a comparison in which there is also a bigger number, write them all as figures: for example, write '3 out of 30 participants' rather than 'three out of 30 participants'. Similarly, if numbers precede a unit of measurement, use figures rather than words – as in 'a 5-mg dose'. Also use numbers for percentages, time, dates, ages, sample sizes and the like. All numbers in the abstract of a report should be presented in figures.

Use words for numbers below 10, especially if they don't represent precise measurements: thus you would write 'only one participant died this time', 'we had to ask them three times before they agreed to enter the piranha tank', and 'they completed eight questionnaires before escaping'. Also, use words for any number that begins a sentence or a heading, as in 'Ninety-eight percent of our sample turned grey overnight', Finally, use words for common fractions such as 'fully three-quarters of participants vowed never to return to our laboratory'.

10.4   Give Yourself Enough Time

Many students don't allow themselves enough time to write a good report. Through fear or complacency, they leave writing-up until a day or so before the final deadline for submission, and then end up sprinting to the submission point with only hours or minutes to spare.

The result is a rushed lab-report that shows it. So many students lose marks unnecessarily, through simple mistakes that could easily have been corrected if only they had taken a bit more time and care over the final version of the report.

You should expect to go through several drafts of the report. Few people can write a report that's perfect first time. Even academics will do several drafts of a report before submitting it to a journal.

Whew! There are a lot of drafts in here!

These days, with word-processors, producing successive drafts is a whole lot easier than it used to be. Write a first draft, and then leave it for a couple of days so that you become a little distanced from it. This should enable you to notice mistakes that you overlooked when you were immersed in writing it. Try to look at your writing critically and dispassionately, from the viewpoint of our hypothetical 'intelligent non-specialist psychologist'. Aim to produce a second draft that is both clearer and more succinct than the first. Give this to any friend who is both obliging and a competent writer themselves, and ask them for their honest opinion. Writing good, clear reports isn't easy – it takes work, but most students can write better reports than they actually do.

Producing the first report is always a bit of a step into the unknown, especially if you have never written a report before. However, if you follow all of the advice above, you should get a reasonably good mark. It's a hackneyed phrase, but practice makes perfect, in lab-report writing as in all skills.

10.5   Summary

1. The purpose of a psychology lab-report is to communicate research findings in a clear and systematic way. Reports therefore have a standardized format that is modelled on that of the scientific journal article, and your report should follow this closely.

2. Keep in mind that, up to any given point in the report, your reader knows only what you have told them so far.

3. All claims and assertions need to be supported by references to previous work.

4. Use the formal 'passive' past tense throughout the report, but aim for writing that is as clear and as simple as possible. Avoid jargon and circumlocution.

5. Be prepared to write multiple drafts – good reports do not just happen, they take work!

10.6 Practical Tasks

Rewrite this atrociously badly-written piece of text in a clearer and simpler style, using no more than 50 words.

'Notwithstanding the egregiously fallacious conclusions drawn by the internationally-famous Professor A.R. Dogwitt of the Animal Research Laboratory at Analgland University (as published in the December 1995 edition of the esteemed journal 'The International Journal of Canid and Mustelid Behavioural Research') a propos the efficacy of the 'Snuffyaworms' dog-worming tablets purveyed by the drug company Messrs. Mouseanthill in improving the performance of our canine relatives in laboratory T-maze situations by attenuating the distractive effects of anal itching, the research of Dr. Iva Lotta Slobber and her colleagues at the Behavioural Research Institute of Wolferhampton State University does corroborate Professor Dogwitt's principal conclusion – namely that the said pills, when utilized, do indeed confer some measurable advantages in maze-learning performance in this particular species of infra-human animal. However, Dr. Slobber and her team of co-workers are somewhat more tentative in the conclusions that they draw from their research than is Professor Dogwitt, it must be said. The aforesaid Dr. Slobber, in a paper entitled 'Stop the scratching and start the learning', published in the 'Journal of Pointless Research' in November 2000, posits that canine attentional mechanisms are sorely limited in terms of the diversity of environmental stimuli that can be attended to at any given moment in time; more specifically, their principal claim – which I think is a valid one – amounts to saying that the dog has the facility for attending to only one thing at a time.'

Answer:

Dogwitt (1995) concluded that 'Snuffyaworms' dog-worming tablets improved dogs' maze-learning performance by reducing the distraction produced by anal itching. Slobber et al.'s (2000) findings were similar, though more tentative: they suggested that a dog's attention can be directed only to one thing at a time.

10.7 Further Reading

American Psychological Association (2001). *Publication manual of the American Psychological Association* (5th edition). Washington, DC: APA Books.

Degelman, D. & Harris, M. L. (2000). APA style essentials. Retrieved February 8th, 2002, from Vanguard University, Department of Psychology web site: http://www.vanguard.edu/faculty/ddegelman/index.cfm?doc_id = 796. A succinct guide to APA format, if you can't get hold of the APA Manual itself.

Trask, R. L. (2001). *Mind the Gaffe: The Penguin Guide to Common Errors in English*. London: Penguin. One man's heroic attempt to save the English language from its (mis)-users. Well worth reading.

11 Answering the Question 'Why?' The Introduction Section

The purpose of the Introduction to your lab-report is to provide a rationale or justification for your particular experiment. Why did you bother to do this study? What's the background behind it, in terms of previous research on this topic?

Introductions generally have three parts, which increase in specificity as you go through the Introduction. First, you explain to the reader what the problems and issues are in this particular area of research; this provides a general context for the study. Then you outline your own experiment, and explain how it will progress our scientific understanding in this field. Finally, you summarize the possible outcomes of your experiment, and (usually) make some specific predictions about which of these outcomes is most likely to occur and why. The first part is generally the longest, and the final part the shortest.

11.1 Providing a Rationale

Describing the background to your study will be the largest part of the Introduction. Almost all research is based on previous research findings or theoretical ideas, and you need to give the reader some idea of what the issues are in your chosen area, what's been found out already, and what remains to be discovered or clarified. Essentially, what you are trying to do in this section is to persuade the reader that there is a 'gap' in our knowledge of this particular area of psychology, and that your experiment is worth doing because it will help to fill that gap.

Does your study test a theory; replicate or extend findings; or resolve an anomaly?

Someone once said that all literature involves one of only three basic plots. In the same way, there are four basic reasons why a study is performed.

To Test a Theory

If a theory is any good, it makes specific predictions about what will happen under particular circumstances. In this way, it is potentially open to disproof. (Any theory that isn't, is not truly scientific: see Chapter 1). Consequently, sometimes an experiment may be set up to test a theory's predictions, to see how well they hold up in practice. For example, suppose Professor Tardive has a theory that schizophrenia is due to high blood pressure. A specific prediction follows from this, that blood-letting will be an effective treatment for schizophrenia. I could test this by taking, at random, two groups of people diagnosed with schizophrenia, draining blood from one group but not the other, and then measuring how schizophrenic they were afterwards.

To Replicate (i.e. Confirm) an Existing Finding

Sometimes an experiment is done to replicate previous findings, either by using the same method as the people who originally demonstrated it, or more often, by using a slightly different method (so that one can be sure that the previous results were not simply due to the particular techniques that had been used). Scientists are (or should be!) fairly sceptical individuals, who often like to confirm the existence of some psychological phenomenon by demonstrating it for themselves, in their own laboratory, rather than taking someone else's word for it.

To Extend the Findings of Previous Research

This is closely related to the previous category; when researchers attempt to replicate a finding, they often include additional manipulations so that their own research does not merely 'copy' the previous work, but adds to our knowledge of the phenomenon in question. Often one wants to see how generalizable a phenomenon is: by finding out under what conditions it does and does not occur, we may find out a lot about it. For example, suppose it has been established that blood-letting helps people diagnosed with schizophrenia. Various questions then arise. For example, does it aid men and women equally? Does it help people diagnosed with schizophrenia early in life as much as those in whom schizophrenia develops later in life? How much blood needs to be let? Is it the blood-letting itself that is important, or some other aspect of the procedure, such as the stress of undergoing blood-letting?

For most first-year psychology practical reports, providing a rationale is sometimes a little artificial: you are unlikely to be doing an experiment that hasn't been done before. However, the rationale described in this section is probably the one that applies best: you will probably have replicated some well-established psychological phenomenon, perhaps with a slightly novel twist.

To Resolve Some Anomaly that has Arisen in Previous Research on this Topic

Suppose that Dr. Bullworker has found that exercise improves mood, whereas Dr. Flabby has found the opposite. What has produced this discrepancy in their findings? Perhaps neither has considered the effects of chocolate consumption as an influence on mood: in Bullworker's study, the exercisers ate chocolate before exercising, while in Flabby's study they didn't. There is a need for another study to be performed, that systematically manipulates those factors that differed between the Bullworker and Flabby studies.

11.2 How to Describe Previous Research and its Findings

So one function of the Introduction is to explain to the reader why you are performing your experiment. To explain what the issues are, you need to provide background information about relevant previous research and theory in this particular area. You must confine discussion to material that is directly relevant to your study. So, for example, if your project was on short-term memory problems in the elderly, the relevant stuff is previous research on that topic, and not on memory in general, or the elderly in general. Try to keep the description of the background material focused. A common mistake is to be too unselective: in this case, for example, some students would ramble on about memory in general and end up with a mini-essay that could have been entitled 'everything that I could find out about memory from a basic textbook and pack into three sides of A4'.

In referring to previous research, you need to describe it at an appropriate level of detail. For most studies that you cite, you will

The Introduction is a justification for why you did your study – it's not an essay!

probably need only to give a bare outline of the procedures used and the results that were obtained. The reader usually doesn't need to know how many participants were involved, what statistical tests were performed by the previous authors, precise details of the procedures used, and so on. If they want all of that information, they'll just have to go to the original source to read it for themselves. (That's one of the reasons why you provide detailed references to any work cited).

Here are examples of the level of detail that will usually suffice:

- 'Pike, Kemp, Towell and Phillips (1997) found that moving faces can be recognized more accurately than faces seen in multiple static views that provide comparable amounts of perspective information about the face. This suggests that motion *per se* may provide important information for face recognition, perhaps by aiding in the derivation of 3D structure.'
- 'Rensink et al.'s (1997) demonstrations of 'change blindness' show that observers often fail to notice quite marked changes that are made between successive views of a scene.'

We don't need to tell the reader any details of how these results were obtained, unless those details are important to our argument. Only if we thought that these workers' testing procedures contained a serious flaw, would we consider providing a little more detail on those procedures. So, for example: 'Rhubarb's (2000) conclusion was based on data from only five participants, and subsequent studies (e.g. Custard, 2001), using larger numbers of participants, have failed to replicate his findings'. Here, the number of participants is a potentially important issue, and we would mention it; if Rhubarb had used enough participants for this not to affect his conclusions, then we wouldn't bother discussing it.

Only if a previous study is central to your own research (as, for example, when your experiment is a direct replication of a previous study, or uses a complicated procedure that was used in previous research) should you go into any great detail – and even then, you should focus on what the reader needs to know to understand what you are doing, or to get a grasp of the issues involved in this area of research. As a rough guide, if you have spent more than half a page of A4 on describing a single study, then you are probably going into too much detail.

One aid to writing the rationale for your study is to imagine that you are at a party, and that you have trapped someone in a corner of the room. This person is a psychologist, but not a specialist in the area of research within which you have performed your study. They make the fatal mistake of asking you what you are researching: you explain that you have just completed an experiment on how many words people can remember while their head is immersed in a bowl of condensed soup. The psychologist then compounds their error by saying: 'Really? How interesting. Why did you do that experiment? What does that tell us about memory?' You answer their question, by explaining what previous studies on soup immersion and memory have found, and what remains to be discovered. Unless you are seriously lacking in social skills, (in which case you're probably a psychology lecturer and this analogy won't help anyway) you would not respond to their question by telling them everything you knew about memory or psychology in general. For fear of them making a feeble excuse and leaving you alone in the corner of the room, or committing hara kiri on the carpet in front of you, you also wouldn't go into too much detail about the previous studies in the area, or ramble on for hours about the theoretical issues.

11.3   Outlining Your Own Experiment

Once you have given the reader a fair idea of what the issues are, and why you have decided it is worth doing your experiment, it is time to outline what it is you propose to do. You only need to give a fairly general outline, since all of the minutiae are going to be described in the following sections. Suppose we wanted to resolve the discrepancy between Bullworker and Flabby's studies on the effects of exercise on mood. We might have four group of participants: chocolate-guzzling exercisers, chocolate-guzzling non-exercisers, chocolate-deprived exercisers, and chocolate-deprived non-exercisers. We could measure each participant's mood after a week of whichever of these four treatments they had been assigned to. If our hypothesis is that mood is affected by the combination of chocolate and exercise, we might predict that the chocolatey exercisers should be the happiest of all, followed by the chocolatey couch potatoes and the non-chocolatey exercisers. The non-chocolatey couch potatoes should be the most miserable of all.

Something like the previous paragraph is all the level of detail that you need to write at this stage – all the particulars of how the groups will be treated and measured are deferred until later in the report. Explain briefly why you expect these particular outcomes, from a theoretical point of view. For example, here we would probably have already discussed the effects of exercise and chocolate on endorphin levels in the brain, and so this would be the motivation for our predicted outcomes.

It's a little dishonest, but sometimes outcomes are 'predicted' after the results have been analysed. With the benefit of hindsight, you can often see what you should have expected in the first place; it's then easy to rewrite the Introduction to make your 'predictions' fit the data that you actually obtained. This accounts for why the Introductions of journal articles sometimes seem amazingly prescient about what the results are likely to be – it's because they were known to the author at the time of writing the Introduction!

11.4   Providing Predictions About the Experiment's Outcome

One thing that A-Level and Access to Higher Education students often do is to make formal statements of the 'experimental' (or 'alternative') and 'null' hypotheses at the end of the Introduction section. In other words, they write something like this:

'The experimental hypothesis is that there will be a statistically significant difference between the four groups. The null hypothesis is that there will be no statistically significant difference between the four groups.'

Outline your predictions clearly, simply and informally.

Real psychologists never write this kind of stuff in their Introductions. Just outline the study's predictions in a clear but informal way, like this:

'If chocolate consumption and exercise interact in their effects on mood, then it is predicted that the four groups will differ in their moods as follows: the chocolate-consuming exercisers should produce the highest mood ratings, the non-chocolate consuming non-exercisers should give the lowest ratings, and the other two groups should produce mood ratings somewhere between these two extremes.' Don't bother stating the null hypothesis – because it's invariably that there is no statistical difference between the experimental conditions, it goes without saying and hence is completely superfluous.

Essentially, what you are trying to do at the end of the Introduction is to produce a cliff-hanger: you are leaving the reader on the edge of their chair, desperate to read on and discover what results you actually obtained. First though, you have to tell them exactly how you carried out the study.

11.5   Summary

- The Introduction's main purpose is to explain to the reader the reasons why you did your study. What has been done in this area before? Why is your study worth doing?
- Introductions normally have three main parts: a description of relevant previous research and theories; a brief outline of your experiment; and an informal summary of what you expect to find and what your findings might imply theoretically.
- Reasons for doing a study include all or some of the following: to test a theory; replicate or extend previous findings; or to try to resolve anomalous or contradictory findings from previous work.
- In referring to previous research, make sure you stick to studies which are directly relevant to your own, and avoid going into too much detail about them.
- The Introduction ends with a statement of what you expect to find: write this in everyday English, rather than the stilted formal exposition of hypotheses beloved of A-level tutors!

11.6   Practical Tasks

Suppose you wanted to write the Introduction to the following experiment. Which of the following numbered points would you include in the Introduction of a report entitled 'Realism as a Factor Affecting Observational Learning in Children'? Which would you leave out, and why?

1. Bandura, Ross and Ross (1963) showed that children imitated aggressive behaviours performed by an adult towards an inflatable doll called 'Bobo'.
2. It has been inferred from this research that children will copy cartoon characters performing aggressive acts, and that therefore cartoon violence is undesirable. However, Bandura's studies used a human actor: perhaps children may not be so susceptible to imitating cartoon characters behaving aggressively, since they know that these are not real people.

3. In the present study, the extent to which the actor looked human was varied. There were two conditions. In the 'human' condition, children saw a male actor behaving aggressively towards a Bobo doll. The 'rabbit' condition was identical, except that a man dressed in a rabbit suit performed the aggressive acts.

4. Twenty children recruited from a local primary school took part in this experiment. Permission for them to take part was obtained from their parents. The children's mean age was 5 years and 6 months. Ten were allocated randomly to the 'human' condition, and the rest were allocated to the 'rabbit' condition.

5. The principles of operant conditioning were originally worked out using mainly rats and pigeons, but they have been applied to humans as well. For example, the behaviour of gamblers has been explained as being due to them operating on a variable-ratio schedule of reinforcement.

6. Piaget (1963) claimed that children pass through several stages in their development. At around the age of six or seven (the age of the children in the present experiment) they enter the stage of 'concrete operations', when their thinking is dominated by physical appearances.

7. Even children less than a year old can imitate previously seen actions: for example they may copy an adult who pokes out their tongue (Meltzoff and Moore, 1977).

8. Psychologists have studied children's development for over a hundred years, but still have much to learn about it.

9. The experimental hypothesis is that children in the 'human' condition will be significantly more likely to imitate the aggressor against the doll than will children in the 'rabbit' condition, as measured by an independent t-test comparing the two conditions. The null hypothesis is that there will be no difference between the two conditions, in terms of their propensity to copy the aggressor's acts.

10. Developmental psychology investigates how cognitive, emotional and social behaviour develop during infancy and childhood, as a result of the interaction between genetics and experience.

Answers:

1. Include: it's a description of a study that is relevant to the topic of the current research.

2. Include: this provides a rationale for the current study. It shows that there is a problem with the conclusions that have been drawn from previous research, and hints at what kind of study needs to be done to address this problem.

3. Include: it gives a brief overview of the experiment that is the subject of this report. It is only an outline: fuller details will be given later in the report.

4. Omit: the level of detail about the participants is more appropriate to the 'Method' section than the 'Introduction'. All we need to know at this stage is that 5 year-old children took part in two conditions in the experiment.

5. Omit: the present study is on social learning, not learning in general. This study on operant conditioning appears to have no relevance to the current experiment.

6. Omit: a discussion of theories of social learning or social development might be appropriate, but there seems no good reason to discuss theories of cognitive development here.

7. Omit: this study is about imitation, but has apparently only superficial relevance to the present study, which is on much older children and involves a different kind of imitation.

8. Omit: this is such a superficial and axiomatic statement that it's just a waste of space.

9. Omit (most of it, anyway!): the first part of the first line is worth including. In this section of the report, there's no need to state which statistical test will be used; that can be left until the 'Results' section. The second sentence, about the 'null hypothesis', can be dispensed with: because it merely says the opposite of the 'experimental' hypothesis, it goes without saying.

10. Omit: you don't need to define 'Developmental psychology' for the reader – you can assume they know that much!

12 Answering the Question 'How?' The Method Section

The idea of this section is to provide the reader with a clear idea of what you did and how you did it. The standard by which this section will be judged is: would it be possible to replicate this study, in all its important aspects, solely on the basis of the information that is provided in this section? The tricky bit is to walk the tightrope between providing too much information (including irrelevant information) and too little.

This section is sub-divided into several sections. The 'Design' section provides an overview of the overall structure of your experiment; the 'Participants' section provides the necessary information about the people who took part in your experiment; the 'Apparatus' section gives details of any equipment used (including things like questionnaires and other tests); and the 'Procedure' tells the reader how the study was carried out in practice.

12.1 Design

This section provides an overview of the formal design of the study. What were the 'independent variables' in the study? (Independent variables are the factors that you, the experimenter, manipulate: see Chapter 2).

How many conditions were there? Was it a repeated-measures design (with each participant taking part in all of the conditions of the study), an independent-measures design (in which participants performed in one and only one condition), or a more complex, 'mixed design' (using a combination of repeated-measures and independent-measures variables)? (See Chapter 3). What was measured – in other words, what were the dependent variables?

The 'Design' section summarizes the formal structure of your study.

This may all seem rather arcane, so here's a concrete example that will hopefully clarify what's required. Suppose you are interested in factors affecting how well factory workers can spot black cornflakes on the cornflake production-line. You might devise an experiment in which you examine the effects of age and time of day on workers' ability to detect the dodgy cornflakes. You obtain groups of young, medium and old workers. For each of these age-groups, you have a group of morning-shift workers, and a group of evening-shift workers. You measure the number of black cornflakes that each worker detects during a four-hour shift. (You cunningly arrange it so that, unknown to the workers, the same number of black cornflakes is presented during each worker's shift).

The formal design section for this experiment would look something like this:

'There were two independent variables: age of worker (with three levels: young (21–30 years), medium (31–40 years) and old (41–50 years)) and time of shift (with two levels: morning or evening). The experiment used a wholly between-groups design, with each worker assigned to only one of the permutations of age and shift. The dependent variable was the number of black cornflakes detected within a shift (out of a maximum of 20).'

12.2 Participants

These used to be called 'subjects', but psychology is as vulnerable to political correctness as anything else! Give details of how many participants you used, and how many took part in each condition (if a between-groups design was used). Include information on demographic variables such as age and gender, and provide brief details of how you obtained the participants – for example, did they volunteer, and were they paid for taking part? Were they naive about the purpose of the experiment? Participants in psychology experiments are often 'blind' to the purposes of the study. However, you need to be careful about how you express this – reading some practical reports, with phrases such as 'blind participants were used' or 'all participants were blind', you could be forgiven for thinking that many participants in psychology experiments have profound eyesight difficulties!

Give the relevant characteristics of the poor gullible fools who took part in your study.

Sometimes, you might use a special population of participants, such as colour-blind individuals, learning-disabled people, hyperactive children or spider-phobics. If so, further relevant details should be provided about them. For example, in the case of the spider phobics, give brief details of the criteria by which they are defined as 'phobic', such as their mean scores on some recognised phobia test.

As mentioned earlier, you need to think about what information is relevant and what's not relevant. This may depend on the circumstances. Thus, if you are measuring people's ability to estimate distances, the issue of ethnic grouping is irrelevant and need not be mentioned, but details of whether the individuals concerned had normal stereoscopic vision should be given. Conversely, if you are conducting a study on attitudes to racial prejudice, ethnic grouping might be highly relevant and hence details should be provided in this section.

12.3　Apparatus

This section is reasonably straightforward. You have to provide enough details of the apparatus that was used, for someone to be able to replicate the experiment. Avoid writing 'shopping lists' of apparatus – write in full English sentences. Instead of writing 'Stopwatch. Questionnaire. Tape recorder', write 'The apparatus consisted of a stopwatch, a questionnaire, and a tape-recorder'.

In the case of questionnaires and other pencil-and-paper tests, if it's widely used (such as Eysenck's Personality Inventory and Witkin's Embedded Figures Test, tests which are in common use amongst psychologists) give its name, a reference to where a full account of it can be obtained, and some justification for why you used that particular test. Briefly provide evidence that it's a good measure. This might include reference to studies which have shown that the measure is reliable, valid and is appropriate for participants similar to the ones you are testing. (Many widely-used questionnaires and pencil and paper tests have been standardized on different sub-groups of people, so that there are sub-group norms for performance which differ according to the group under consideration).

If you are using a novel or home-brewed test (e.g. a questionnaire that you have devised yourself) then put the test or questionnaire in an appendix at the end of the report, and state in the apparatus section that it can be found there.

If the experiment involves presenting stimuli and/or recording responses on a computer, it is normally sufficient to give the generic type of computer used, plus a brief mention of what software was used. For example, 'The stimuli were presented on the screen of an Apple Macintosh Quadra, using a program written in Supercard'. If the equipment is a little more out of the ordinary, give the name of the manufacturer and of the product. For example, 'Electric shocks were administered using a 'Sizzler Mk. II' shock-generator (manufactured by Megajolt Ltd., Ohio)'.

Once again, consider the issue of relevance. If the experiment consists of completing a questionnaire, you probably need only mention the questionnaire itself: you can reasonably assume the reader realises that a pen or a pencil was required to fill in the questionnaire, and you might even be bold enough to let them assume that doing the questionnaire involved using a table, a seat and a floor. You certainly wouldn't need to mention how the room was lit, unless it was something out of the ordinary. Details of the typeface and font size in which the questionnaire was written would also be superfluous. However, if you were doing a study of eye-movements during reading, the ambient lighting and typeface might well be influential factors, so they should be clearly specified. In short, only mention things that could reasonably be expected to have a bearing on the outcome of the study.

Sometimes you may see this section divided into two, 'Apparatus' and 'Materials'. If so, 'Apparatus' is the place in which to describe things like computers and other hardware, whereas details of questionnaires, visual stimuli and the like should go in the 'Materials' section.

12.4　Procedure

This section gives details of how you carried out the experiment in practice. Suppose your experiment involves examining the effects of cerebral blood-flow on memory. Participants are given a memory test twice, once after being held upside down on a rope, and once after being allowed to stand upright. How were these two conditions administered? Were all participants exposed to them in the same order, or was order of presentation randomized? Were participants tested one at a time, or in groups? How long did they dangle upside-down on the rope? How long did they stand? How long was the interval between these two experiences? How long was the memory test, in terms of time and number of items? What instructions were given to the participants? If there were long and detailed instructions, consider putting them in an appendix and referring the reader to that. However, if the instructions were short and fairly simple, this may not be necessary: it

Give relevant details – the rope's colour appears to be irrelevant to this experiment!

may suffice to mention them briefly only in this section of the report. Here's an example from a face-recognition experiment in which measurements are taken of the speed with which participants can make judgements about whether or not a face is familiar to them.

'Participants were asked to press the letter 'S' on the keyboard if the face was familiar to them, and the letter 'L' if it was not. They were asked to respond as quickly but as accurately as possible'.

As with the 'Apparatus' section, provide details only if they are needed for replication purposes, and if they are potentially relevant to the outcome of the experiment.

12.5 Summary

The 'Method' section sub-divides into the 'Design', 'Participants', 'Apparatus' and 'Procedure' sections. Together, they give the reader enough details for them to replicate the study should they wish to do so. The 'Design' section outlines the formal structure of the study: it identifies the experiment's independent and dependent variables (i.e. the things that you, as experimenter, manipulate and measure, respectively). It also tells the reader whether you used an independent-measures, repeated-measures or 'mixed' design. The 'Participants' section gives relevant details of the people who took part in your experiment. The 'Apparatus' section provides information on what equipment you used to run your experiment. Depending on the nature of your research, 'equipment' may include questionnaires and pencil and paper tests, as well as computers and the like. Provide enough details for replication purposes, but don't include irrelevant and unimportant details. The 'Procedure' section describes how you actually carried out the study in practice: again, include only details that would be required for replication purposes.

12.6 Practical Tasks

Identify the problems with the following procedure section:

Subjects were tested one at a time. Each subject arrived at the time that their appointment had been set for, and was asked to sit down at the table and to fill in the first questionnaire, which measured their mood before the experimental manipulations were administered. The questionnaire was administered via an

EverKrash™ 1 GHz PC, with a 17 inch Trashiba™ monitor screen. This was placed by the window of the test room. The room measured approximately 10 ft by 15 ft. After they had completed the first questionnaire, which took about 10 minutes, half of the subjects listened to a tape of sad music, while the other half listened to a tape of dance music. The mood of all subjects was then re-tested with a second questionnaire, administered under the same conditions as the first. Subjects were then debriefed and thanked for their participation in the study. The results were then analysed on the same computer by the experimenter, using Excel.

Answers:

1. The writer should refer to 'participants' rather than 'subjects'.
2. It's not really necessary to know that the participants had made an appointment to take part in the experiment and had arrived on time.
3. You need to use your judgement about whether or not to give precise details of equipment used. In this particular case, we probably don't need to know the make and model of the PC and its screen because the computer is merely a vehicle for administering the questionnaire: presumably using a different computer – or even pencil and paper – would have made little difference to this particular study.
4. The computer's location in the room is irrelevant detail that can be dispensed with.
5. We do not need to know the room's dimensions in this case: and if we did, they should be presented in metric units, rather than imperial.
6. We are told how long participants took to complete the first questionnaire, but other – more important – information is missing: for how long did the participants listen to the mood-inducing music? How long afterwards did they complete the second questionnaire?
7. More details of the music should be given, such as the name of the composer and the title of the piece of music, so that the reader could use the same music in their own study if they so wished. Otherwise the study is potentially unreplicable – what constitutes 'sad' music? Does 'dance' music refer to modern popular music with no tune and an irritatingly monotonous beat or to the exquisite creations of someone like Johann Strauss?

8. We probably don't need to know that 'subjects were then debriefed and thanked for their participation in the study': this should occur as a matter of course.

9. We do not need to know the mechanics of how the experimenter analysed the results, such as which computer was used and which software.

Here's a better version of the same procedure section:

> Participants were tested one at a time. Each participant completed the first questionnaire, which was administered by computer. After they had completed the first questionnaire, which took about 10 minutes, half of the participants listened to a tape of sad music (Samuel Barber's 'Adagio') for ten minutes, while the other half listened for the same amount of time to a tape of dance music (J. Strauss' 'The Blue Danube' waltz). The mood of all participants was then re-tested with a second questionnaire, administered under the same conditions as the first.

13 Answering the Question 'What Did I Find?' The Results Section

In this section, you present the results of your study. At this point, you don't go into their theoretical implications – that will be covered in the next section of the report, the Discussion (see Chapter 14). All you do here is tell the reader what you found.

There are two basic kinds of statistics that need to be described here: descriptive statistics (such as group means) and inferential statistics (the results of statistical tests). Before giving the descriptive statistics, you may also need to provide information on any treatments that you have applied to the data.

13.1 Tidying Up Your Data

Sometimes when you run a study, the data need some kind of pre-treatment before you carry out the processes of obtaining descriptive and inferential statistics. Take the example of reaction time data: every now and again, a participant produces an abnormally long reaction time (compared to the rest of their reaction times). This is usually for uninteresting reasons: their concentration might have lapsed on that particular trial, or perhaps they hesitated because they momentarily forgot which button to press. If you retain these long reaction times in your data, they may distort your findings or add so much 'noise' to the data that any effects which are lurking in the data become impossible to detect. Therefore, it's considered OK to remove these spuriously long scores. This has to be done in a fair, principled way – you can't merely discard data that you don't like the look of, or which don't fit in with your expectations! (In the case of reaction time data, one way to do it is to remove all reaction times longer than a certain pre-specified duration; or, if each

What should I do about participants who produce poor-quality data?

participant is providing several responses, you can find the mean and standard deviation of them and then discount all scores which fall more than, say, 2 standard deviations above the mean. So that you don't systematically bias the results, you must apply the same procedure to the data from all of the groups in your study.)

Because it is easier to get long reaction times than short reaction times, reaction-time data tend to be negatively skewed, rather than normally distributed around their mean. (See Chapter 4). This poses problems for statistical analysis, so some workers apply a corrective transformation (such as taking the logarithm of the reaction time, rather than using the raw RT) to compensate for the skew and make the data look more normally distributed.

Another way in which data may be treated is that certain participants may be excluded for one reason or another: perhaps they didn't provide a complete set of data, or were unable to do the set task well enough to provide meaningful data. (I used to run face recognition experiments on Open University students. They are the most enthusiastic and obliging participants I have ever worked with. Unfortunately, they are often not much use for any experiment involving recognizing famous faces, because they don't get time to watch the telly or go to the movies! Therefore I sometimes had to exclude participants from my results because they simply didn't know the celebrities whose faces I was asking them to recognize. To have retained them would have distorted the results, because their data would have been mixed up with data from participants who did know the celebrities in question, but couldn't recognize them from the pictures that I was using in my study.)

Any treatments such as these that you have performed on your data should be described clearly in this section, as they are obviously essential for a would-be replicator to know about.

13.2   Descriptive Statistics

Descriptive statistics provide summaries of group performance (see Chapter 4). They include things like averages (means, medians and modes), measures of how scores are spread out around the average (things like ranges or standard deviations) and frequency data, if relevant. The idea is to give the reader a clear idea of what you found, by presenting a clear and succinct summary of all the data that you have collected in your experiment. Thus, in the case of the

chocolate and exercise experiment mentioned earlier, you would probably have collected mood measurements from each of the participants
in each of the experimental conditions. The reader of your report
would be spared all these gory details, however. You might provide
them merely with the mean mood rating for each condition, each
mean being accompanied by some indication of the spread of scores
around it. (The most frequently used measure of spread is the standard deviation, but the American Psychological Association now
recommend giving the standard error of the mean. These two measures of spread are covered in Chapter 4.)

Data Presentation

You are aiming to enable the reader to get an immediate idea of what
you found, so things like means need to be presented clearly. If you
have just one or two means, it may be simplest to mention them within
the text itself. If you have more than a couple, it may be clearer to
present them in a table or graph. Which should you use? There are no
hard and fast rules about this. Sometimes, means and standard deviations are best presented in a table. Other times, it might be clearer to
display them in a graph. If you have only a few means, graphs generally are clearer. If you have a lot of means, or if you want to present
additional information such as standard deviations, ranges, number
of participants per condition, etc., a table might be preferable.
Whichever you decide to use, avoid duplication of information. If
you have shown data in a table, don't present it in a graph as well
– pick one method of presentation or the other, depending on which is
clearest to the reader. (See Chapter 4 for details on how to do graphs).

Tables and 'figures' (graphs and any other pictures) are numbered
in order of presentation. Numbering is done separately for tables and
figures. Thus the first table is 'Table 1', the second is 'Table 2', and so
on. The first graph or picture is 'Figure 1', the second is 'Figure 2',
and so on, even if a table has been presented in between the two
figures. Figures and graphs are always referred to in the text by
these labels. For example, you might write 'Figure 1 shows the
mean performance in each condition'.

This may seem like labouring a pretty simple point, but many students appear to be unable to do this properly! A common mistake is
to write things like 'Graph 1', 'Picture 1' or 'the accompanying graph
shows'.

13.3   Inferential Statistics

Inferential statistics (or 'infernal statistics' as we've seen it mis-typed!) are the results of statistical tests on the data, aimed at discovering whether there are statistically significant differences between the groups or conditions in your study (see Chapters 5, 6 and 7). For

Time to consult a good statistics book (Never mind, Andy's one will have to do).

example, in the study mentioned earlier in which we measured people's memory scores once when they were upright and once when they were upside-down, we might have performed a repeated-measures *t*-test to see if there was an effect of orientation on memory scores.

The results of such tests confirm and support the impressions that you obtain by 'eyeballing' the data. As a general rule, the results of the inferential tests determine whether or not you have an 'effect', and whether or not you can treat it as 'real' as opposed to merely a chance, freaky result. Once again, it's a case of having to substantiate your claims, in this case with references to your test results (rather than to previously published work as is done in the Introduction and Discussion).

Sometimes students (and researchers too!) look at the descriptive data that they have collected, and are struck by an apparent difference between conditions. However when they perform an inferential test on the data, they obtain a non-significant result. If this is inconvenient or undesirable, they ignore the test result completely, and proceed to talk about the 'difference' between means as if the test had been significant! Ignoring the outcome of the test negates the whole point of doing it in the first place. If a statistical test shows that a 'difference' is not significant, you have to accept this, awkward though it might be.

Presentation of Inferential Statistics

As with descriptive statistics, how you present inferential statistics depends largely on how many of them you have. Statistics can be displayed in the text itself; as tables; or in figures (graphs or diagrams). The APA suggest the following rule of thumb: if you have three numbers or less, put them in a sentence; if you have from four to 20 numbers, use a table; and if you have more than 20 numbers, consider using a graph instead of a table. As with descriptive statistics, if you opt for putting statistical test results in a table, make sure that the reader knows what the tests are doing (i.e., which conditions are being compared with which). You will still need to explain in words, in the text of the Results section, what the tests are showing.

In general, the neatest way of presenting the results of a statistical test is to state a result (and its associated descriptive statistics) and then follow it with the relevant supporting inferential statistics enclosed in brackets. Here are some examples:

- 'The mean reaction time of the group that took amphetamines (977 ms) was significantly faster than that of the group that did not (1004 ms) ($t(30) = 2.66$, $p < .01$, $r = .44$, one-tailed test).'
- 'The number of participants saying that they liked chocolate were as follows: 38 young women; 15 elderly women; 10 young men; and 5 elderly men. It thus appears that there is a significant relationship between age and gender in terms of chocolate preference (χ^2 (4, $N = 68$) $= 10.85$, $p < .001$).'

In both these cases, note that we show the generally-accepted abbreviation for the test (e.g. t for t-test, χ^2 for Chi-Squared); the degrees of freedom or number of participants (depending on the test); the value of the test statistic (e.g., the obtained value of t, χ^2 or whatever); and the probability value associated with it. (Further examples of how to report inferential statistics can be found in Chapters 4, 5, 6 and 7, in the sections entitled 'Interpreting and Writing the Results' which follow each of the tests covered there).

Dogs are significantly smarter than cats ($t(92) = 2.06$, $p < .01$, $r = .21$).

There are several ways of reporting probabilities associated with test statistics. Sometimes you'll see them reported as an exact probability, for example '$p = .024$' or '$p = .036$'. In other places, you'll see them reported as the nearest landmark probability under which the obtained probability falls: thus '$p = .024$' and '$p = .036$' would both be written as '$p < .05$'. The American Psychological Association prefer yet another method; they now like the author to state, at the start of the results section, the level of probability that will be used for all tests in that section, rather than reporting probability values for each test separately. (The APA also like authors to report 'effect sizes': see Chapter 5).

Whichever method you opt for, make sure you get the 'less than' sign the right way round: '$p > .05$' means 'p greater than .05', and hence means completely the opposite to '$p < .05$'! Failure to use the correct sign tells your tutor a lot about your statistical abilities, or rather the lack of them. Various commonly-used abbreviations and symbols are shown in Box 13.1.

You don't need to put the calculations of statistical tests into your 'Results' section, just the end-results: the reader just needs to see the value of t, not the laborious computations that went into obtaining it! Neither do you need to give a reference for statistics that are in common use. Pearson's *r*, *t*-tests, ANOVA, multiple regression and the like can all be referred to by their names, without you having to provide a source. If a statistic appears in a psychology statistics textbook, it's safe to assume that it needs no further explanation in your report. You only need to provide supporting references if the statistic is an unusual one, or if it's the main topic of your report.

As a rule, you only need to justify why you used a particular test if the reasons are not immediately obvious. For example: 'Since the range of performance was markedly different for fetishists and non-fetishists, a Mann-Whitney test was used to analyse the data, rather than a *t*-test'. Here, the brief explanation justifies to the reader what might otherwise appear to be an odd choice of test. You can assume that your hypothetical audience, the non-specialist psychologist, doesn't need to be reminded of the assumptions that underlie the use of a parametric test, so avoid statements like the following:

'The data were normally distributed, showed homogeneity of variance and were measured on an interval scale, and so we decided to use a *t*-test.' All perfectly correct, perhaps, but completely unnecessary in a 'Results' section!

Finally, a couple of minor points on presentation of numbers. Use a zero before the decimal point when the number is less than 1 (e.g. write 'The mean error rate was 0.73.') but not when the number cannot be greater than 1. This applies in the case of correlation coefficients (which can only range from -1 to $+1$) and probabilities (which cannot be larger than 1). Thus you would write 'Pearson's *r* was $-.55$'. While we're on numbers, it's worth mentioning that the APA suggests that, in the interests of clarity, it's generally best to round to two significant digits, as in '$p < .01$'. There may be situations in which more decimal places are appropriate of course, in which case use them. However, most of the time, using more decimal places merely adds spurious precision while reducing clarity. (This applies with equal force to descriptive statistics, of course).

13.4   Make the Reader's Task Easy

Always explain to the reader, in words, what the results show. Never just dump down descriptive or inferential statistics and expect the reader to work out for themselves what it all means. A good rule of thumb is that the text of the results section should remain comprehensible even if the tables and graphs were missing, and vice versa. Tables and graphs should be self-explanatory: the title, labels and legend should be clear, and should provide enough information for the reader to be able to figure out what is being displayed. A common mistake nowadays is for students to 'cut and paste' tables and graphs into their report from statistical packages such as SPSS or Excel, without replacing the arcane labels that are often supplied by these programs. Labels like 'var000001' or 'condition X' will probably mean nothing to the reader, and must be replaced by more meaningful labels.

Andy likes to end his 'Results' section with a summary of the key results: this is especially worthwhile if you have described a lot of complex analyses and findings, so that the reader might well have lost sight of the wood for the trees.

13.5 Be Selective in Reporting Your Results!

In Results sections, less is often more: just because you can produce the mean, median and mode on a group's scores, it doesn't mean that you have to present them all to the reader. Pick whichever average is the most appropriate, and show only that one (plus its associated measure of spread, namely the range or semi-interquartile range if you show the median; or the standard deviation or standard error if you use the mean).

Similar considerations apply to inferential statistics. Just because you have worked out how to get a statistics package to produce a zillion different tests on the same data, it doesn't mean that you should show them all. Pick the most appropriate statistical test, and show the results of that. As with the Introduction, the basic idea is to show the reader enough statistical information to give them a clear idea of what you have discovered – anything extra detracts from your 'message' and makes it hard to see the wood for the trees. Some students seem to think that the more statistics they can squeeze into their 'Results' section, the better the mark they will receive. However, often it's the opposite – all they have done is demonstrate their unintelligent and unselective use of statistics software.

13.6 Summary

- This section tells the reader what you found, but leaves the interpretation of your results for the next section (the Discussion).
- You may need to 'tidy' your data before analysing them, but this has to be done in an honest way – you shouldn't discard

participants' data just because they didn't fit in with what you expected to find!

- The 'Results' section will normally consist of descriptive statistics and inferential statistics.

- Descriptive statistics may be presented within the text of the 'Results' section, in a table, or in a graph. If you use tables or graphs, they should be labelled clearly enough for them to be understandable without reference to the text of the report.

- Inferential statistics are usually (but not invariably) presented within the text of the 'Results' section. They should be presented in a standard way, and accompanied by a brief explanation of what they show.

- Statistical calculations (whether by hand or computer) and raw data should not appear in the 'Results' section: if they must be included, put them in an Appendix.

■ Box 13.1: Some commonly used statistical symbols and abbreviations:

ANCOVA	Analysis of Covariance	ANOVA	Analysis of Variance
df	degrees of feedom	*F*	*F*-ratio (ANOVA test statistic)
H	Kruskal-Wallis test statistic	*HSD*	Tukey's Honestly Significant Difference test
LSD	Fisher's Least Significant Difference test	*M*	Mean
MANOVA	Multivariate Analysis of Variance	*Mdn*	Median
MS	Mean Square	*MSE*	Mean Square Error
N	Total number in a sample	*ns*	Non-significant
p	Probability	*N*	Numbers of members in an entire sample
n	Number of members in a subset taken from an entire sample	*r*	Pearson's correlation coefficient
r^2	Coefficient of Determination (Pearson's correlation squared)	r_s	Spearman's correlation ('rho')
R	Multiple correlation	*SD*	Sample standard deviation
σ	('Sigma') Population standard deviation	*SE* or *SEM*	Standard error (of measurement)
SS	Sum of Squares	*T*	Wilcoxon's test statistic
U	Mann-Whitney test statistic	α	Alpha: probability of a Type 1 error
β	Beta: probability of a Type 2 error	χ^2	Chi-Squared test statistic
$<$	less than	$>$	greater than

14 Answering the Question 'So What?' The Discussion Section

In the Results section, you told the reader what you found. Now it's time to tell them what it all means, in relation to your hypotheses as outlined in the Introduction, and in relation to relevant psychological theory and previous research. As with the Introduction, the Discussion tends to fall into several sub-sections. However, again as with the Introduction, don't use section headings: the discussion's 'flow' from each of these issues to the next should be obvious enough, without any need for headings.

14.1 Summarize Your Findings

Start the Discussion by briefly summarizing the principal results of your study. Assume your reader has the attention span of a goldfish, and has either completely forgotten what you said in the 'Results' section or got so thoroughly confused by it that they need a brief overview of your main findings before they continue reading. Make sure you summarize the results without any statistics or excessive detail – after all, if the reader wanted all that, they would merely re-read the 'Results' section that they have just finished!

14.2 Relate Your Findings to Previous Research

Explain how your results fit in with previous research in this area (generally, all that stuff you mentioned in the Introduction: the same considerations about relevance apply here too). How are your results explained by psychological theories on the phenomenon in question? Do they pose problems for current theoretical accounts, or are they consistent with them? Do they support one theory rather than another? Are they consistent with previous research findings in this area, do they contradict them, or do they qualify them? For most reports, this will be the longest part of the Discussion.

In most cases, the level of detail in which previous research is described should be similar to that used in the Introduction. There may be cases where you need to provide a little more specific information about a particular study however. Suppose, for example, that your study has produced findings which are at odds with those of previous research: in this case, you might want to argue that the discrepancies have arisen from procedural differences between your study and the previous ones, in which case you might need to elaborate on the details of those procedures.

Personally, I find writing this section is the most interesting part of the whole report. Sometimes your results fit in with previous findings fairly straightforwardly; sometimes they seem at odds with past findings, and you have to work out a plausible explanation for why this might be so. This is an opportunity for you to demonstrate some imagination (but not too much!) and show off your flair at being able to understand the previous research and your own findings well enough to be able to fit it all together into a more or less coherent story.

To make this section more concrete, let me take you briefly though the discussion of a paper that I was working on recently (Hole, George, Eaves and Rasek, 2002). This investigated the effects on face recognition of various distortions: for example, are faces still recognizable after they have been stretched to twice their original height? Why should anyone bother to investigate this? Well, it's come to be appreciated that so-called 'configural' information (the precise spatial relationship of the eyes, nose and mouth to each other and to the rest of the face) is very important for face recognition. People can easily detect very tiny movements of facial features in pictures, especially displacements of the eyes. However, in real life, you see 'distorted' faces all the time, due to perspective changes, alterations in a person's expression, etc., and yet still manage to recognize them. What we wanted to know was how well face recognition could tolerate various kinds of distortions to the configural information in a face. Stretching a face for example, greatly disrupts the relationship of horizontal distances (such as the distance between the eyes) to the vertical distances in a face (such as the distance between the tip of the nose and mouth, for example).

I won't bore you with the details, but essentially we found that people could recognize faces virtually as easily when they had been stretched or squashed as they could if they had been left untouched, but only if the distortion was applied to the whole face (as opposed to just half of it). That was our main finding: in the Discussion of our paper, we set about trying to relate this to previous relevant work on face recognition and trying to explain the implications of our results for theories of how face recognition is carried out by the visual system.

First of all, we tried to relate our findings to those of previous studies. I have just mentioned the studies showing that we are highly sensitive to feature displacements; our findings needed to be discussed in relation to these. To our knowledge, no-one had used the particular kinds of distortions that we used (which is why we used them!). However, other manipulations have been used to investigate the limitations of the processes underlying face recognition – for example, turning a face upside down disrupts recognition considerably, so we compared the effects of our distortions to manipulations such as this. Previous work has also shown that people can recognize faces from isolated features, so we had to consider whether our participants were resorting to this strategy. For various reasons we didn't think this was a likely explanation, so we devoted some space to arguing against this interpretation of our results.

We then went on to consider several theoretical accounts of how face recognition occurs, using our findings to try to evaluate the plausibility of each one. How well could each theory account for our results? To give just one example: one kind of theory suggests that we compare the face that we are seeing now, with our memories of all of the faces that we know. If there's a match, we recognize the face that's in front of us. Hopefully you can see that a straightforward matching strategy would fail with our distorted faces, because a distorted face will fail to match any of the faces in memory. So, our results rule out this kind of explanation of how face recognition occurs.

More sophisticated versions of this theory suggest that perhaps we can apply the inverse transformation to a distorted perceptual input – so that we can 'unstretch' a stretched face, and then compare this unstretched version to our memory of faces that we know. We considered theories of this kind, and suggested that while we couldn't rule them out altogether, they were implausible as an explanation of our results for two reasons. One argument was based on our results: one might expect such a transformation process to take some time, and we found no evidence of this in our reaction time data. The other argument was based on logic: how would the visual system know when to stop the transformation process and start trying to match the transformed face to stored memories of faces?

A final type of theory that we considered takes these kinds of issues into account, and suggests that we transform the distorted perceptual input until it matches a kind of 'prototypical' face, a 'template'. We described a couple of theories of this type, and concluded that our results did not rule out this kind of explanation. We suggested that theorists who advocate these types of theories might want to see how their computer simulations of face recognition coped with our distorted faces.

Hopefully, you can see from this example what you should be trying to achieve in the main part of the discussion. You are trying to see how your results fit in with previous work in that area, and you are trying to use your findings to clarify unresolved theoretical issues. We tried to do three things in this section of the Discussion of our paper. The first was to demonstrate a novel phenomenon: distorted faces remain highly recognizable. This is interesting, but it's just an isolated 'fact' as it stands. Therefore our second aim was to show how this fits in with what's already known in this area: other manipulations, such as inversion, have been found to disrupt recognition considerably. By discussing our findings in relation to previous work, we start to build up a bigger picture of what's going on when we look at a face: we've found a particular manipulation that doesn't have much effect on recognition, other people have found manipulations that do, and so we can use these snippets of information to start to develop an understanding of face recognition in general. Our third aim was to show how our findings could be used to assess the merits of various theories of face recognition; while one study is probably unlikely to settle an issue like this, nevertheless our results support some theories and fail to support others. (Note that, in science, we can't prove a theory, but we can provide support for it, and we can certainly disprove a theory by producing findings that it cannot explain. In this particular example, we are able to conclude fairly conclusively that face recognition cannot be based on simple measurements taken straight from a face – because if it were, recognition of distorted faces would be very difficult. We have therefore disproved any theory of face recognition that's based on simple-minded measurements of facial proportions.)

Doing a jigsaw is a good analogy for all of this. Imagine that there are hundreds of people who are all working on a jigsaw. Nobody knows what picture is depicted on the jigsaw. Each of us brings an individual piece to the jigsaw every now and again, and tries to fit it in with the other pieces that are lying around. As we are trying to fit pieces together, we come up with theories about what the picture is of. Sometimes – but not often – a whole load of pieces fit together, and you suddenly realize that you've got a fair bit of the jigsaw done. On other occasions, you try to fit the pieces together, but they don't all fit correctly, or you see that a crucial piece is missing, or that you've forced together pieces that don't really belong together. This is essentially what you are trying to achieve in this part of the Discussion: you are trying to tell everyone (i.e., other scientists) what new parts of the jigsaw you have found; explain how you think they fit in with the other bits that are already on the table; and discuss a few of the theories about what's in the picture on the jigsaw, arguing in favour of some possible interpretations and against others.

14.3   Discuss the Limitations of Your Study

You should show that you are aware of the limitations of your study, and the conclusions that can be drawn from it. These may include possible methodological problems: maybe next time you'll use a lower shock voltage, so that more participants survive to contribute to the results; or perhaps the memory scores of the Attention-Deficit Hyperactivity Disorder children might have been higher had your rewards for learning a list of items not been sweets containing food-colourings. Another possibility is that there are limitations on the generalizability of the results obtained: for example, girl guides are not necessarily representative of the general population.

Don't go into an orgy of self-abuse: no study is perfect, and just because you left one of the participants with their head in the condensed soup for six seconds longer than the rest, it doesn't necessarily mean that your results are wholly invalid. Also, avoid mechanically trotting out standard problems with experiments. Some students will routinely write statements such as 'it would have been better to use more participants' or 'the experiment should be done again, using a more representative sample of the general population than undergraduates'. Don't include statements like these unthinkingly. At one level, the statement about participant numbers is so obvious that it is not worth saying, because it would be true for any research that was done. (No matter how many participants are used, it would always be better to run more, to get a more reliable sample). Perhaps what you really mean is that, with hindsight, you don't think that you ran enough participants to find any effects of your experimental manipulations. If that's the case, and it would have been better to use more participants, the obvious question is – why didn't you do that in the first place? The issue of how many participants to use should have been considered before the study was conducted anyway (see the section on statistical 'power' in Chapter 4).

The second statement, about students being unrepresentative of the world at large, is not necessarily true. It all depends on the nature of the phenomenon under investigation. If the study is influenced by factors such as educational level, IQ, conservatism, youth, etc., then it is true that using students may produce a biased picture. For example, it's probably highly likely that, overall, students' attitudes to race relations are different to those of the general population. However, if the experiment is on something which is unlikely to be affected by student characteristics, such as low-level visual perception or memory span, then students are as 'representative' of humanity as anyone else.

Essentially, this part of the Discussion is an opportunity for you to demonstrate your ability to be self-critical and sufficiently evaluative about the research that you have performed. The idea is that you should anticipate the reader's criticisms of your research and pre-empt them. 'Attack is the best form of defence', in research as it is in life. In the case of a journal article, by the time the reviewer has reached this point in the report, they have thought of various problems and unresolved issues that have been raised by the research; this section is the researcher's opportunity to try to put the reviewer's mind at rest, effectively saying 'yes, with hindsight I'm well aware that using a repeated-measures design was not the best way to tackle this problem, and that the results for group X are rather odd; however, I can still persuade you that these problems haven't totally invalidated my study, and that my results are still worth publishing'. If you are writing a lab-report, you have a comparable task – to persuade your tutor that you have a sophisticated understanding of experimental design, by showing that you are aware of the methodological and conceptual weaknesses of what you have done.

14.4   Make Suggestions for Further Research

Finish off the discussion with some suggestions about what issues remain unresolved, and where the research could go from here. You could make some brief suggestions for future studies. However, be intelligent about this, and make sure there is some rationale for these suggestions. Don't just write something like 'Future studies might look at gender differences on these measures' or 'It would be worth repeating this experiment using a group of Botswanan participants instead'. Explain briefly why this would be worth doing, and what it might show.

14.5 Draw Some Conclusions

Consider rounding off the Discussion with some final conclusions about what your study has shown. These should be at the end of the Discussion section itself, rather than in a separate section labelled 'Conclusion'. Try to avoid merely repeating what you said earlier in the Discussion. Avoid hackneyed, empty phrases like 'Clearly, much more work needs to be done in this fascinating area'. Statements like this ultimately say nothing other than that you are desperately trying to 'round off' your report. (It's self-evident that more work could be done in any area of psychology, and we can safely assume that it's fascinating to someone!)

14.6 Summary

The purpose of the Discussion is to interpret the results that you have found, in relation to previous research: how do your findings fit in with what's already known on the topic in question?

The Discussion has three main parts: a brief recapitulation of your main findings, a discussion of how these results fit in with previous research in this area; and a discussion of possible problems and limitations with your study, perhaps with intelligent suggestions for future research.

As with the Introduction, make sure that the research and theories that you describe are relevant to your own study.

15 Title, Abstract, References and Formatting

The title, abstract (summary) and references are the last bits of the report that you should write, but they are important nevertheless: the title and abstract provide the reader with their first indications of what your study was all about, and the references provide them with the opportunity to find out more by reading research that is related to yours. For an assessed report, there's also a pragmatic consideration: the title and abstract will give the marker a first impression of the likely quality of the rest of your report, and the reference section will give them an idea of how well read you are, and how thorough and careful you have been in producing the report. So, for a variety of reasons, although these may be small sections, it's important to get them right.

15.1 The Title

This should be clear and specific, but not too detailed. For example, suppose we had done an experiment in which we had investigated whether or not having breakfast affected people's ability to concentrate later in the day. A good title would be something like 'The effects of breakfast on mid-morning concentration levels'. Avoid using a title which is vague or not detailed enough, such as 'An experiment on concentration' or 'Breakfast and concentration'. Similarly, avoid producing a title which is too long and convoluted, and unnecessarily detailed, such as 'The effects of having breakfast or not having breakfast on the concentration levels of my fellow students, as measured with a selective attention task'. The American Psychological Association suggest the title should be about 10 or 12 words long.

Suppose we were interested in gender differences in the emotions that Navaho Indians display in relation to tear-jerking stimuli (such as

---

■ **Box 15.1: Examples of good and bad report titles:**

'The 'Beer-Goggles' effect'	Too vague.
'Investigation into the effects of drinking 6 pints of Guinness in a night-club in Brighton at 11.30, while listening to drum and bass played at 100 db through a good sound system, on 12 men's and 15 women's ability to accurately judge the attractiveness of members of the opposite sex'	Over-specific, over-detailed and over-long.
'The 'Beer-Goggles' effect: the effects of alcohol on ratings of the attractiveness of members of the opposite sex'	OK (but still a bit long).

Walt Disney's 'Bambi' film). The title should give a clue to the important aspects of the study. Thus 'Emotion and Indians' or 'Navaho emotional expression' would be uninformative titles: 'Gender differences in emotional expression in Navaho Indians' would be preferable, as it encapsulates, succinctly, the dimensions of interest. Anyone interested in Navahos, gender differences or emotional expression (or maybe all three!) would be able to spot at a glance that this was a study that they might well be interested in knowing about.

A good rule of thumb is to make sure that your title includes a mention of the independent variables in your study (i.e. the factors that you, as experimenter, are manipulating in the study), and the dependent variables (the things that you are measuring). (See Chapter 2 for more explanation of independent and dependent variables). Thus, in our title 'Gender differences in emotional expression in Navaho Indians', 'gender differences in Navaho Indians' is our independent variable, and 'emotional expression' is our dependent variable.

Look at your title and ask yourself: does it give the reader a good idea of what the experiment's about, while remaining fairly snappy? In the case of journals, a researcher would skim the contents page, looking for any articles that looked likely to be of interest to them: succinct but informative titles are a great aid to doing this quickly and efficiently.

15.2　The Abstract

This is the first section of the lab-report. It is placed immediately after the title, but write it last of all – it's much easier to write it once you have done the rest of the report. Aim for a 150 word summary of what you did, what you found, and what it means. (The American Psychological Association enforce a 120 word limit very strictly). You don't need to go into much detail – if the reader wanted the details, they'd go ahead and read the report itself. In the case of a journal article, the idea is to give an overview that will enable the reader to quickly decide whether or not the paper is of interest to them. Aim for one or two sentences describing each of the following: the reason for the experiment; the methods used; the main results found, and the principal conclusions to be drawn from them.

Don't include references, excessive amounts of procedural detail, or details of statistical tests. Keep it simple, clear and to the point, and make sure that it's understandable without reference to the main text.

15.3 References

In a lab-report, there are two main ways of referring to previous work. Within the text of the report itself (i.e. principally in the Introduction and Discussion), references are cited by giving the author's surname and the year of publication. At the end of the report, there is a section entitled 'References', and this gives full details of all of the references for which you gave surname and date in the text. This is the so-called 'Harvard' system of referencing. There is another method, the 'Chicago' system, that is used in 'Science' and many medical journals. Little numbers in the text refer to the full references in the Reference section at the end of the article. In the Reference section the references are listed in order of appearance in the text. Unless you are going to submit your lab-report for publication in 'Science', don't use this system.

The whole purpose of the reference section is to enable the reader to gain access to the works that you have cited throughout your report. To ensure that sufficient information is provided in a reference list for this to be possible, the American Psychological Association and the British Psychological Society have laid down very clear, specific and detailed conventions for how to produce reference lists. In what follows, we will follow the APA's guidelines on referencing.

Conventions for References Cited in the Body of the Report

Citing works by a single author

Give the author's surname and the year of publication, as in the following examples. You can write them like this:

◼ Box 15.2: Examples of good and bad abstracts:

Gender differences in essay writing were examined. Essays written by ten boys and ten girls (mean age 12 years), and ten men and ten women (mean age 20 years) were assessed by 40 naive raters on four dimensions: readability, coherence of argument, degree of balance in the argument, and degree of scholarship. Raters judged the women's essays to show significantly greater readability and coherence of argument than the men's. There were no significant differences for balance or scholarship. No gender differences of any kind were found for the children's essays. It is concluded that post-adolescent educational experiences may influence writing style in different ways for men and women.

A good abstract. In 108 words, this specifies the two independent variables (gender and age); gives brief details of what was done, and the main results; and ends with a brief conclusion.

Previous research, for example by Riterskramp et al. (1948), has suggested that there might be gender differences in some aspects of essay writing but not others, so an experiment was conducted in order to investigate this, and see whether or not there were gender differences in the ability to write essays. First, essays were obtained from ten boys and ten girls (mean age 12 years) at a local secondary school, and from ten men and ten women (mean age 20 years) who were undergraduates at the University of Nohope. These essays were rated by 40 naive participants on four dimensions: how readable the essays were, how coherent their arguments were, the extent to which the writer showed a degree of balance in the argument, and the extent to which the essay showed scholarship (in the sense of being well-researched and well-referenced). Nine-point Likert Scales were used by raters to rate each of these dimensions: in each case, these ranged from 1 = 'atrocious' to 9 = 'excellent'. The naive raters judged the women's essays to show significantly greater readability and coherence of argument than the men's (Independent t-test for readability: $t = 2.04$, with 39 degrees of freedom; $p < .05$. Independent t-test for coherence of argument: $t = 2.62$, with 39 degrees of freedom; $p < .05$).

A poor abstract: this is 390 words long (and believe me, we've seen students produce longer ones in real life!). It's fairly clearly written, but the style is too discursive – it could be much more succinct without any loss of clarity. It contains too much information about related research (summarize your *own* study, not other people's!) and goes into too much detail about the procedures used and the results that were found.

There were no significant differences for balance or
scholarship (Independent t-test for balance: $t = 0.56$,
with 39 degrees of freedom: $p > .10$. Independent t-test
for scholarship: $t = 1.03$, with 39 degrees of freedom,
$p > .10$). In the case of the children's essays, there
were no apparent gender differences of any kind
(Independent t-test for readability: $t = 0.99$, with 39
degrees of freedom; $p > .10$. Independent t-test for
coherence of argument: $t = 0.62$, with 39 degrees of
freedom; $p > .10$. Independent t-test for balance:
$t = 1.10$, with 39 degrees of freedom; $p > .10$.
Independent t-test for scholarship: $t = 1.16$, with 39
degrees of freedom; $p > .10$). It is concluded that the
kind of educational experiences that people have
during their secondary school education may influence
writing style in different ways for men and women,
thus producing the gender differences found in the
present study. This is in line with Scribble and
Submititt's (1998) theory of essay-writing behaviour,
which suggests that boys are encouraged to write in
different ways to women during the course of their
secondary education.

- 'Tardive (1995) claimed that schizophrenia was caused by evil spirits.'
- 'Studies by Legless (1987, 1994) indicate that drunk people tend to overestimate the attractiveness of members of the opposite sex.'

Or like this:

- 'It has been claimed that schizophrenia is caused by evil spirits (Tardive, 1995).'
- 'Evidence suggests that drunk people tend to overestimate the attractiveness of the opposite sex (Legless, 1987, 1994).'

Both versions use only the surname and date. The only time you include the author's initials is to differentiate between two different authors with the same surname, as in this example:

- 'J. Tardive's (1995) results are at odds with those of C. Tardive (1955).'

Citing works by multiple authors

How you refer to these depends how many authors there are. If there are only two authors, give both surnames each time the reference is cited, as in 'Tardive and Kattatonier (2000) have now abandoned exorcism as a treatment for schizophrenia' or 'Exorcism has now been abandoned as a treatment for schizophrenia (Tardive and Kattatonier, 2000)'.

If there are three, four or five authors, the first time a reference is mentioned, give the surnames of all of the authors and the date of publication. Thereafter, if there are more than two authors, use only the first author's surname, followed by 'et al.' and the date. ('et al.' is Latin for 'and all the rest of 'em'). So, the first time a study is mentioned, you might write:

'Tardive, Kattatonia, Diskenisia and Parrenoide (2000) claimed that schizophrenia could be alleviated by blood-letting.' Later on, referring to the same study, you would write 'There were a number of problems with the study by Tardive et al. (2000).'

If there are six or more authors, use the first author's name and 'et al.' from the very first mention of the reference.

Sometimes the same authors manage to churn out more than one paper or book in a year. In this case, differentiate between them by using letters after the date. Thus, you might refer to Tardive and Wibble (1981a) and Tardive and Wibble (1981b). What if two multi-author references shorten to the same form? For example, 'Tardive, Kattatonia and Diskenisia (2000)' shortens to 'Tardive et al. (2000)', but so too does 'Tardive, Diskenisia, Kattatonia and Parrenoide (2000).' In situations like this, cite the first author's surname plus as many of the subsequent authors as are needed to distinguish between the two references. So, in this example, the abbreviated versions would be 'Tardive et al. (2000)' and 'Tardive, Diskenisia et al. (2000)' respectively.

Citing works by organizations or groups

Sometimes works are produced by anonymous, faceless organizations or committees rather than individuals. If the organisation has a long and unwieldy name and a familiar or easily understandable abbreviation, mention the name in full the first time you cite the study, and use the abbreviation subsequently. For example, 'Consumption of carrots improved readers' eyesight (Centre for Research into Applied Perception [CRAP], 1995).' If the name is short or the abbreviation would not be easily understandable, use the full name each time the work is cited. (Thus, if you happen to be citing both 'Alcoholics

Anonymous' and the 'Automobile Association' in the same report, write them out in full each time).

Citing multiple references

You might want to refer to several studies all at once. The most succinct way of doing this is to put all of the references that you want to cite in brackets at the end of the statement to which they refer. Arrange them in the same order as they will appear in the reference list at the end of the report, and separate them with semi-colons. For references within parentheses you can also replace the word 'and' with the symbol '&'.

'Blood-letting and purges have been claimed to be effective treatments for schizophrenia (Dobbs, 1998; Tardive, Dobbs, Wibble & Wobble, 1995; Wibble & Wobble, 2000).'

Note that these surnames are in alphabetical order (i.e. as they will be shown in the Reference section).

If there are two works by the same author, put the references in date order. You don't need to repeat the name. Thus you would write '(Dobbs, 1998, 1999)' or '(Dobbs, 1998a, 1998b)'. The same goes if you are referring to more than one work by the same set of authors (as long as their names appear in the same order each time). Thus you would write 'Little is known about the aetiology of long-term coma (Sneezy, Bashful & Dopey, 1978, 1999, 2001)' to refer to three works by Sneezy and his chums that all had the authors' names in this order. However, suppose the names had appeared in different orders; then you would write all of the references in full and put them in alphabetical order within the brackets: '(Bashful, Sneezy & Dopey, 1999; Dopey, Sneezy & Bashful, 2001; Sneezy, Bashful & Dopey, 1978)'.

Personal communications

Occasionally you might need to refer to something that has been said to you, or written in an email or a letter to you: this is a 'personal communication'. To be honest, it's not likely to be something that crops up in your lab-report, but you'll see references made to personal communications in journal articles and books, so you may as well know how to reference them correctly. In the text, you give the author's surname, initials and as precise a date as you can: 'Graham, don't keep putting bloody dogs in our lovely book (A. Field, personal communication, September 10, 2001)'. Note that personal communications are the one type of reference that does not have a corresponding entry in the reference list at the end of the report. (This makes sense if you think about it, because the reader has no way of obtaining a copy of this type of reference – well, OK, if it was in the form of a letter, they could in theory burgle your house or office to get hold of it . . .)

Quotations

'Whoahh, mate, looking at the state of that guttering, I reckon it's gonna cost ya at least 500 quid.' Whoops, sorry, wrong type of quotation: the ones we're going to discuss here are the elegant bon mots bandied about by previous researchers that you want to cite word for word in your report. The APA suggests that short quotations (less than 40 words) should be incorporated into the text, surrounded by double inverted commas, like this: "The minute you have a couple of pints, ugly blokes transform miraculously into Brad Pitt" (Drunkwoman, 1996: p. 154).

Longer quotations should be in a separate block of text, with no quotation marks. The whole block should be indented by about half an inch from the left margin, like this:

> Quotations are no substitute for trying to put things into your own words. Don't think you can hide your own poor writing style by just cobbling together lots of extended quotations – your tutor will probably see through the ruse (Hole, 2001, p. 999).

As in these examples, give the author, year of publication and the number of the page from which the quotation came. In the references list, of course, you supply the complete reference. Quotations should be accurate: this may seem an odd thing to say, but you would be surprised how many times I've marked an essay or a report in which a quotation was very obviously reported wrongly. If you want to emphasise part of the original, use italics, but make it clear that they are your italics rather than the original writer's, like this: 'Professor Kwotashun is an *arrant knave*, [italics added] as well as a complete charlatan'. If you want to distance yourself from the original writer's grammatical or spelling errors, show the errors are theirs by using 'sic', in italics and enclosed in square brackets: 'Professor Kwotashun is an arrunt [*sic*] knave'.

There are minor changes you might need to make to a quotation, so that it fits in with your own text. Some of these don't have to be acknowledged: for example, you might want to change the first letter of the quotation from upper case to lower case, or alter the final punctuation mark in the quotation from a comma to a full stop.

Sometimes you may want to omit material from a quotation, to shorten it or because some of the material is irrelevant to your argument. If you do this, you show that you have shortened the quotation by using three full stops, in place of the missing material. For example, suppose the original quotation was 'Professor Kwotashun's hobbies include gerbil grooming, delousing his cat, and – when he can find the time in his busy daily schedule of elephant hunting – cultivating bonsai Venus Flytraps'. This might be shortened to 'Professor Kwotashun's hobbies include gerbil grooming, delousing his cat, and . . . cultivating bonsai Venus Flytraps'.

If you want to add material to a quotation (perhaps because it wouldn't make sense out of context), enclose it within square brackets like this: 'Professor Kwotashun's hobbies [following his decline into insanity] include gerbil grooming'.

What do you do if the author of the quotation has included a reference to another work, like this? 'According to Kohma (2000), the best thing that you can say about Sopperifik's new book is that it does have a nice cover' (Sparkout, 2001, p. 366). In these circumstances, retain the citation within the quotation (after all, it is part of the quotation). However, unless you cite Kohma (2000) yourself, elsewhere within your own report, you don't have to include her work in your reference list.

Conventions for the Reference Section at the End of the Report

As a basic guide, you need to provide enough information for the reader to be able to track down the references that you used in the text. This enables the reader to go off and read these references for themselves, to see if you have misquoted or misinterpreted the authors concerned. Science is all about having a healthy distrust for everyone else's research and claims. With the exception of personal communications (see preceding section), every reference cited in the text should have a corresponding full version in the reference list, and vice versa.

The APA make a useful distinction between a 'Reference List' and a 'Bibliography'. A 'Reference List' contains references to material directly used in the research and preparation of the report, that is the stuff cited in the text. A 'Bibliography' contains references to works for further information or background reading. A journal article (and your lab-report) should contain only a Reference List, and not a Bibliography.

Where full examples are given below, note that they follow APA format to the letter (and to the punctuation mark as well!) Your own references should be exactly the same. Only a selection of all the possible types of reference that you might need to supply are listed here: for a truly exhaustive account, consult the APA Publication

Manual, which contains 74 pages on the issue of referencing, and includes many examples of how your references should look.

Journal articles

Give each author's surname, followed by their initials; the year of publication; the title of the journal; the volume (including part number, where appropriate – see below); and the page numbers. The title of the journal and its volume number should be in italics.

- Tardive, A.H., Diskenesia, K., & Parranoide, W.M. (1995). Trepanning as a cure for schizophrenia. *Journal of Dubious Research, 26,* 225–226.

If there are more than six authors (!) list the first six, and then use 'et al.' to refer to the rest.

Most journals are published in parts during a calendar year, usually one part appearing every three months. In most journals, the page numbers start at 1 at the beginning of the year, and continue throughout the various parts for that year. However, some journals start each part with 1. In the case of the latter, give the part number of the journal as well as the volume number, like this:

- Tardive, A.H., Diskenesia, K., & Parranoide, W.M. (1995). Trepanning as a cure for schizophrenia. *Journal of Dubious Research, 26* (3), 225–226.

Some journals are published more frequently, either monthly or weekly ('Nature' is a good example of this). In these cases, give the month (if it's published monthly) or month and day of publication (if it's a weekly), like this:

- Obsessive, A., Compulsive, D. & Disorder, T. (2000, November 21). Yet another modification to our revised model of the causes of OCD. *Nature, 300,* 1110–1105.

Books

Give the author's surname and initials; the year of publication; the title of the book; the geographical location of the publisher; and the publisher's name. The title of the book should be written in italics.

- Tardive, A.H. (1992). *My life as a quack.* Beirut: Walford University Press.

Articles or chapters in a book

First, give the author and title of the chapter, then the details of the editor, title and publisher of the book. The title of the book (*not* the name of the chapter) should be in italics. For example:

- Tardive, A.H. (1992). How to avoid litigation from schizophrenics. In H. Hamster, (Ed.), *Dubious research and how to conduct it* (pp. 119–155). Liverpool: Brookside Associates.

(Note how, in this case, the surname and initials of the book's author are not switched round: in other words, write H. Hamster rather than Hamster, H.).

Electronic references

It is becoming increasingly commonplace for students and researchers to cite information that they have obtained via the Internet. This information comes in various types: it might be an electronic version of an article which is also published on paper, say in a journal; or it might be material which is available only on a person's web-site (perhaps because it's a lecturer's teaching notes, or some other form of material which is not otherwise published). As with more traditional references, the idea is to make it as easy as possible for the reader to track down the original source if they so wish. However, there are a few differences. First, a complication with Web-based materials is that they are rather more ephemeral than books and journals, since they are so easily changed or moved to another location. Therefore the reference should give the precise address of the material (its 'uniform resource locator' or 'URL', in the jargon) but also the date on which you retrieved the material. Second, page numbers generally don't have much meaning as far as electronic sources are concerned, so you normally won't have to provide these. Thirdly, a minor typographical error will probably make little difference to a conventional reference, but will probably make a URL unusable, so make sure your URLs are perfectly correct. Here's an example of how to cite a Web address:

- Electronic reference formats recommended by the American Psychological Association. (2000, October 12). Retrieved October 23, 2000, from http://www.apa.org/journals/webref.html

(Notice that if the reference ends with the Internet address, as it does here, you don't end it with a full stop: that's so readers don't mistakenly think the full stop is part of the net address).

If there's no date to the document, use (n.d.) in your reference to show this. Where possible, give a URL that will take the reader directly to the material that you cited, rather than to a home page.

Order of presentation of references

References should be placed in alphabetical order. If you have more than one reference from a given first author, place them in date order, earliest first, and then arrange them in this sequence: single-author first; multiple authors second. Where there are several works by a given author in collaboration with other authors, arrange these references in alphabetical order based on the surnames of the other authors.

Here's a set of references in the correct order, worth an explanation of why each one follows the one before it in the list:

> Tardive, G. (1922).
> Tardive, G. (2000). (It's the same author as the previous reference, but a later date).
> Tardive, P. (1996). (P. comes later than G. in the alphabet).
> Tardive, P., Waggle, A. and Wobble, R. (1967). (Multi-author works by an author follow that author's single-author works).
> Tardive, P. and Wibble, T. (1985). (Wibble follows Waggle in the alphabet).
> Tardive, P., Wibble, T. and Wobble, R. (1981). (This has the same alphabetical position as the previous reference, but it has more authors).
> Tardive, P., Wibble, T. and Wobble, R. (1992). (This has the same authors as the previous reference, but a later date).
> Tardive, P., Wibble, T., Wobble, R. and Waggle, A. (1991). (This has the same alphabetical position as the previous reference, but it has more authors).

Now suppose that Tardive and Wibble wrote two papers in 1985: if so, these would go in alphabetical order based on the title (ignoring 'A' or 'The'), like this:

> Tardive, P. and Wibble, T. (1985a) 'The Root causes of schizophrenia: excessive pressure in the head'.
> Tardive, P. and Wibble, T. (1985b) 'A Theory of schizophrenia and trepanning as a proposed cure'.

If there is no author (i.e. the work has been produced by an institution such as the American Psychological Association), treat the organization as the author, writing their name in full, and insert them into the appropriate alphabetically-determined position in your reading list:

American Psychological Association (2001). *Publication manual of the American Psychological Association* (5th edition). Washington, DC: APA Books.

Primary and Secondary References

Primary references are those that you have read yourself. Secondary references are references that you haven't actually seen yourself; you have only read a description of them in someone else's work. Ideally, you should aim to use primary references. This is generally preferable to obtaining information second-hand, via another author who might be providing a misleading, distorted or biased account of the original authors' results and conclusions. (We're not saying that secondary sources deliberately set out to mislead, but mistakes or misunderstandings can happen).

There are a few problems with using primary references. Firstly, the reference might be hard to read, for stylistic or technical reasons (it's generally easier to read an account of Piaget's work by someone other than Piaget, for example). Secondly, you might get bogged down in the details, in a way that you might not with someone else's potted account of that research. Thirdly, you may not be able to get hold of the original article or book – a variant of Sod's Law is that the articles that appear to be most interesting to you generally seem to be in the most obscure and inaccessible journals!

Because of these problems, you may be stuck with using secondary references, at least to some extent. There are two ways of referencing these. One is to lie, and pretend you have read the primary reference. The problem with this is that your tutor will probably know you are lying, especially if the primary reference is an obscure one. A good example of this was when one of our students referenced an unpublished conference paper – implausible to begin with, but even more implausible given that the student would have been about six years old when the conference took place!

The honest way to deal with secondary references is to acknowledge their origins. This is done as follows. Suppose we want to refer to work by Tardive (1995), which we have only read about in a later article by Gubbins (2000). In the text, we would write 'It has been claimed that schizophrenia can be cured by blood-letting (Tardive, 1995, as cited in Gubbins, 2000)'. Alternatively, we might write 'Tardive (1995, as cited in Gubbins, 2000) claimed that schizophrenia can be cured by blood-letting'. This makes it clear to the reader that Tardive's work is being talked

No time to read the original? Then rely on someone else's garbled account of it!

about, but that you are taking Gubbins' word for it. Secondary refer ences do not appear in the reference section: there, you would include a full reference for Gubbins (2000), but not for Tardive (1995).

15.4   Appendices

Students often get confused about what should be placed in an appendix, and what should go in the main text of the report. To some extent, this will depend on the personal preferences of your tutor, but as a rough guide, the following should normally be relegated to one or more appendices:

Ask yourself - do I really need an appendix?

(a) Statistical calculations and the output from computer statistical packages
If you calculated a *t*-test on your results, by hand, the working-out would all go in the appendix. The value of '*t*' that was obtained, the degrees of freedom and the probability value would go in the 'Results' section. If you used a computer to do the hard work, then the print-out from the computer program would go in an appendix, and the value of '*t*', etc., would go in the Results section.

In the 'Results' section of the report, one thing you shouldn't do is to describe results which are buried in an appendix! If a result warrants discussion, then it belongs in the 'Results' section itself.

(b) Raw data
You might be required to supply the raw data (e.g. individual participants' scores) for your study. If so, this should go in an appendix. But, as a general rule, don't include the raw data unless your tutor specifically requests you to do so.

(c) Questionnaires and other pencil-and-paper tests
If these are home-made or otherwise unusual, you could supply them in an appendix. If they are widely-used, you wouldn't bother; as discussed earlier, it would suffice to provide a reference in the 'Apparatus' section to where the test can be found.

(d) Detailed instructions to participants
Sometimes you might have provided lengthy and detailed instructions to participants. These might have been read out to the participant, or

given to them on a sheet of paper or on a computer screen. These instructions could be placed in an appendix.

(e) Stimulus materials

If you had run a verbal memory experiment, you might want to include an appendix which contained the word lists or text passages used as stimuli. Had you run a face-recognition experiment which involved deciding whether or not faces were famous, you could include a list of the celebrities whose faces were used. If your experiment involved remembering a set of abstract geometric shapes, you might include pictures of all of these in an appendix.

Finally, if you include one or more appendices, then acknowledge their existence in the body of the report. For example, in the 'Results' section, you might write 'Table 1 shows the mean score for each condition. (The raw data for these means can be found in Appendix 1)'.

15.5   Practical Tasks

Here's a list of publications I might have used in a paper. Put them into a reference list, in the correct order and in proper APA format.

Gordon Runt wrote 'My Life Amongst the Weeds'. This is a chapter in a book, published by Weekling Press, in Ohio, Baltimore, on the 21st November 2000. The book's title is 'Pushing up Daisies', and it was edited by Norma Lee Breffless. The page numbers for Runt's contribution were 356–393. He emailed me to say 'it's an awfully heavy book to carry around' (Runt, personal communication October 31st 1999).

I haven't seen Sid and Terry O'Coopatian's new book for 2001, 'Work – Why Bother?', published by Aardvark Publishing Co., Ltd., Bognor. However, I have read Napindi Evenning's summary of their ideas in her article 'The idolatry of idleness', in the December 2001 edition of the magazine 'Work-shy'. It was on pages 1–5 in volume 26.

Max Zillofashel and his colleagues Den Tistry, Tief Urtin and Saul Ted Peenat produced two works in 1996. The first was a journal article entitled 'A participant study of dental phobias', in volume 86 of 'The Journal of Irreproducible Results'. It was on pages 335–338. The second appeared in the 26th volume of 'The Journal of Oral Psychiatry', on pages 334–336. It was called 'My life without teeth: a participant study', and it appeared in June 1998. It had an additional four authors: Don Utt, Jerry Attrick, Beena Stripper and Paul Mateefout.

A seminal work on how alcohol makes everyone look more attractive was published by Vera Sloshed, Reilly Plasted and Ada Nuff in 1994: this was entitled 'The effect of alcohol on perception of objects', and it appeared in the weekly magazine 'Cirrhosis', on the 6th September. It was on pages 113–117. Sloshed and Nuff reprised this success with an article in 'Liver Damage' two years later: pages 10–22 of volume 86 of this esteemed publication were devoted to 'My life on a slave barge: the 'morning after effect' of excessive alcohol consumption'.

In December 2000, Wilma Leggfaloff edited a book called 'Recurrent Anxieties'. It was published by Nosedrip Press, in Oxford. Armin Payne wrote a chapter covering pages 25–40 in this book. Its title was 'No, no no! Not again!'

Chester Minitt had a prolific year in 1983: he wrote three works. Two of them were journal articles: 'Towards a theory of time estimation' and 'No time like the present'. These were pages 25–26 and 22–28 in the first and third parts of volume 66 of the 'Journal of Clockwatching Behaviour'. His other work that year was a book entitled 'Here today, gone tomorrow', published by Doomsday Press (Mozambique) Ltd., but that was in collaboration with Ivor Stopwatch, who was first author.

Answers:

Minitt, C. (1983a). Towards a theory of time estimation. *Journal of Clockwatching Behaviour*, *66* (1), 25–26.

Minitt, C. (1983b) No time like the present. *Journal of Clockwatching Behaviour*, *66* (3), 22–28.

Napindi Evenning, N. (2001, December). The idolatry of idleness. *Work-shy*, *26*, 1–5.

Payne, A. (2000). No, no no! Not again! In W. Leggfaloff (Ed.) *Recurrent Anxieties* (pp. 25–40). Oxford: Nosedrip.

Runt, G. (2000). My life amongst the weeds. In N.L. Breffless (Ed.) *Pushing up daisies* (pp. 356–393). Ohio: Weekling.

Sloshed, V. & Nuff, A. (1996). My life on a slave barge: the 'morning after effect' of excessive alcohol consumption. *Liver Damage*, *86*, 10–22.

Sloshed, V., Plasted, R. & Nuff, A. (1994, September 6) The effect of alcohol on perception of objects. *Cirrhosis*, 113–117.

Stopwatch, I. & Minitt, C. (1983) *Here today, gone tomorrow*. Mozambique: Doomsday.

Zillofashel, M. (1996). A participant study of dental phobias. *Journal of Irreproducible Results*, *86*, 335–338.

Zillofashel, M., Tistry, D., Urtin, T., Peenat, S.T., Utt, D., Attrick, J. et al. (1998) My life without teeth: a participant study. *Journal of Oral Psychiatry*, *26*, 334–336.

Note: Runt's personal communication does not appear in this list. Neither does Sid and Terry O'Coopatian's book, because that was a secondary reference. Therefore, I've only included the reference that I have read, that mentioned it (i.e. Evenning's article).

16 Example of an Experimental Write-Up

Here is an unpublished study carried out by Jayne Grimes and Graham Hole. It looked at the effects of age and training on children's ability to resist being influenced by an interviewer's distortions of their accounts of events. Comments on what has been written and why, are given throughout.

[A succinct but informative title, giving the reader a clear idea of the study's topic:]

'Empowering the child witness to correct interviewer's distortions of their testimony.'

16.1 Abstract

[The purpose of our study:]
An experiment based on the work of Roberts and Lamb (1998) was performed to determine whether children could be trained to correct an interviewer's distortions of their description of a staged event.

[An outline of what we did:]
Forty children, in two age groups (mean ages of 6 years 7 months, and 9 years 6 months) saw a staged event, and were then interviewed three weeks later. Before the interview, half of the children in each group were trained to correct any distortions made by the interviewer.

[A summary of what we found, and our conclusions:]
Older children recalled significantly more correct information than did younger children, and trained children corrected significantly more of the interviewer's distortions than did untrained children.

No relationship was found between the amount of correct information remembered and the number of distortions corrected by the child.

16.2   Introduction

[A description of previous research in this field, as a way of providing a rationale for our own study:]
Considerable research has surrounded the limitations of adults and children in providing eyewitness testimony, and explored the role of both social and cognitive factors influencing the quality of their recall. In particular, research has demonstrated the susceptibility of eyewitnesses to misleading post-event information. Since Loftus' early studies (e.g. Loftus, 1979) it has been known that adult witnesses' descriptions can be corrupted by false information supplied to them in the guise of questions. Witnesses may subsequently report the false information, rather than their original memories of the event.

These effects have also been demonstrated in children (e.g. reviews in Ceci & Bruck, 1993; Dent & Flin, 1992; Spencer & Flin, 1993), and it has been suggested that children are especially prone to 'interrogative suggestibility' (Gudjonsson, 1992) of this kind.

Several reasons have been advanced for why children might be more suggestible than adults. Children might have greater difficulty in distinguishing between real and imagined events (Johnson & Foley 1984; Lindsay, Johnson & Kwon, 1991) or they might be more liable than adults to conform to the perceived authority of the interviewer (e.g. Goodman, Sharma, Thomas & Considine, 1995), especially given that they may tend to assume that the adult knows the answers to the questions being asked.

There is some evidence that younger children are more susceptible than older children to misleading information and leading questions (Ceci & Bruck, 1993; Goodman & Reed, 1986; Shrimpton, Oates & Hayes, 1998). Younger children do not remember as much as older children when recalling an event during the free recall phase of an interview (Dent & Stephenson, 1979), and so might be more likely to incorporate into their accounts information derived from the interviewer's subsequent directed questioning.

Some researchers (e.g. Bjorklund, Cassel, Bjorklund, Brown, Park, Ernst & Owen, 2000; King & Yuille, 1987) have suggested that the child witness is susceptible to leading questions due to the perceived superior status of the interviewing adult. As Bjorklund et al. put it, 'Because young children view adults as omnipotent, cooperative, and truthful conversation partners, in their attempts to be socially com-

pliant, they agree with information they believe adults want to hear'
(page 422).

*[Homing in now, on studies that are more specifically relevant to the one
that we are reporting:]*
It is claimed that the child effectively conforms to the suggestions put
to them. This suggests that if the child were given practice in not
conforming to the interviewer's suggestions, and was made to feel
that they had permission to contradict the interviewer, the influence
of the interviewer's authority on the accuracy of the child's recall
might be minimised.

Goodman et al. (1995) conducted a study that investigated the
accuracy of four year olds' recall of a play event in which they had
just participated. Half of the children were interviewed by an unfamiliar interviewer, and the rest were interviewed by their own mothers.
The mothers and strangers were either biased interviewers (having
been provided by the experimenter with inaccurate information
about the play event) or unbiased interviewers (provided with no
prior information). Children gave less accurate accounts of the
event to the unfamiliar interviewers than to their mothers.

Dent (1982) compared the effectiveness of experienced and inexper-
ienced interviewers in eliciting information from children. Each interviewer questioned five children about a staged incident. Not only did
the experienced interviewers elicit more correct information from the
child but they also obtained more incorrect information from them.
Interestingly, it was the interviewers with a strong preconceived idea
about the incident who elicited the greatest amount of incorrect information. In the Goodman et al. study, the biased group of interviewers
(which contained both mothers and strangers) had been given some
information about the event the child was participating in; however,
this information was not always accurate. The results also indicated
that the children were more susceptible to the leading questions by the
strangers than they were their mothers, perhaps because of the former's greater authority.

Goodman and Rudy (1991, cited in Spencer & Flin, 1993) conducted a series of experiments that assessed how suggestible children
were when they had participated in a situation that was both stressful
and personally significant, such as receiving an inoculation or providing a blood sample. Children as young as four were able to resist the
suggestive questions from the interviewer that concerned potentially
abusive actions made by the adult conducting the medical procedure.
Even after a delay of about a year, the children were unlikely to make
false accounts of the events as a response to the suggestive questions.
These results indicate that in some circumstances, children are able to

resist being influenced by leading questions and the authority of the interviewer.

However, misleading information can come in a variety of forms. One is prior to the child providing their account of the event, for example by the use of leading questions. There is, however, another form that does not appear to have been very widely researched: the effects of interviewers' distortions of the child's account of events during paraphrasing. Distorted paraphrasing may happen unintentionally during interviews, if the interviewer holds erroneous preconceptions about the topics on which information is sought from the child; in courtroom situations, it may also happen deliberately, if the interrogator is seeking to cast doubt on the accuracy of the witness' testimony.

Roberts and Lamb (1998) reviewed transcripts of children interviewed in relation to suspected sexual abuse. While it was found that few of the interviewers used leading questions, some distorted the child's account of the events that had happened. Although this was infrequent, when it did occur the children tended not to correct the interviewer.

[Next, we provide a specific rationale for doing our study – to 'plug a gap' in our knowledge of this area, inspired by a suggestion from previous researchers in this field. We briefly outline what we are going to do, and we finish with a clear but informally-stated description of what we expect to find: effects of age and training on children's ability to contradict the interviewer's distortions of their testimony:]
Roberts and Lamb suggested that with training and practice, children might be empowered to correct interviewers. The present study is a test of this suggestion. The primary aims were to examine the effects on children's recall of misinformation introduced by the interviewer's distorted paraphrasing of their testimony, and to see whether training would empower the child to correct the interviewer's distortions.

We also investigated whether children who remembered more about an event were more confident in correcting the interviewer when they knew them to be wrong. Finally, since older children are generally found to have better memories for events, the effects of training might be expected to interact with age: without training, younger children should be more affected by interviewer's distortions than older children, and any beneficial effects of training should be most evident for the younger children.

16.3   Method

[Here, we give an overview of the study, to help the reader avoid getting bogged down in the details provided in subsequent sections:]
Children were exposed to a staged event (a male stooge performing various actions in their classroom). Each child was interviewed individually three weeks later, to determine what they could recall of the event. Before the interview, half of the children were given training in resisting any distortions introduced into their account by the interviewer; the remainder were given no such training.

16.4   Design

[Here, we specify the independent variables and their levels. We have two independent variables, each with two levels. This is a wholly independent measures design: each child takes part in only one of the four experimental conditions:]
There were four conditions, corresponding to the permutations of two independent variables: age of child ('younger', aged 6–7 years, or 'older', aged 9–10 years) and training condition (trained to correct the interviewer's distortions of their testimony, or not trained).

[We provide a brief mention of our dependent variables. We have two dependent variables in this study:]
Each child participated in only one condition, and provided two scores: one score for the number of times they corrected the interviewer, and one score for each piece of information correctly remembered.

Participants

[Our participants are a 'special' group, since they are all school children. Note, however, that we give all of the relevant information, but without getting bogged down in irrelevant detail:]
Participants were children at a local primary school. The 'younger' children used were 6–7 years old (mean age: 82.7 months; range: 78–89 months). The 'older' children were aged between 9–10 years (mean age 118.6 months, range 114–124 months). The parents provided

informed consent but the children were naïve as to the nature of the experiment.

16.5   Procedure

The Staged Event

[Sufficient details are given here of how the experiment was performed to enable the reader to replicate it in all its important details:]

Children were exposed to a staged event, which served as the basis for the subsequent test of their recall. The event took place between 9:45 am and 10:00 am on the last day before the start of the school's Christmas holiday. A confederate entered the classroom and shouted out the question 'Where's your teacher?' He then asked about the lights and proceeded to turn them off and on twice. Each classroom went very dark, due to the poor weather conditions outside. This served to gain the children's full attention. The confederate then walked around the classroom with a screwdriver, talking to himself, but loudly enough for all of the children to hear. He then bumped his leg on the table before asking the teacher for the time and finally leaving the classroom. The staged event was performed twice: once for the class of younger children, and again for the class of older children. The entire event lasted for approximately 75 seconds on both occasions.

The Interview Procedure

After the Christmas holiday period (approximately three weeks after the staged event), each class of children was randomly divided into two groups – those who were interviewed after being given training in correcting interviewer's distortions of their testimony, and those who were interviewed without having received such training. Those children who had been allocated to the training groups were given training in how to notice and correct any distortions made by the interviewer. This was conducted prior to the interview. The child was told that they and the experimenter were going to play a game in which the child had to say 'no that's not what I said' every time the interviewer did not repeat exactly what the child had just said. The child was given an example and then the opportunity to practice this during a conversation about Christmas. For example if the child had said they did not visit anyone, then the interviewer would repeat back that they had stayed in all the time.

Each child was interviewed individually by one of the experimenters (JG), in the teacher's staff room. The interview lasted for about fifteen minutes. At the start of the interview, the experimenter asked a couple of questions to ascertain whether the child knew what it meant to tell the truth and to tell a lie, and the child was asked to tell the truth. The experimenter reinstated the context of the staged event the child had witnessed, by reminding the child of where they had been sitting and what they had been doing on that day. The child was then asked questions about six different aspects of the scenario: what the confederate looked like; what he was wearing; what he was carrying; what time of the day the incident occurred; the confederate's actions; and what he said. After each of the six sections of the interview, the experimenter summed up what the child had just said, but with some distortion added to their responses. For example, if the child said the man had worn jeans, then the experimenter said the man was wearing work clothes. The experimenter made six distortions of this kind during the interview. All interviews were recorded on cassette tape, for subsequent analysis.

16.6   Results

[For clarity, the results are described separately for the two measures that were taken. It was decided that tables were preferable to graphs for showing the descriptive data in this particular case. Note that the descriptions of the study's main findings are perfectly intelligible without reference to the tables – all the essential information for the reader to understand what was found is located here, in the text. Note that every time we present the results of a statistical test, we also explain to the reader what they mean. Note too that the description of the results is confined to a description of what was found – not what it means in terms of psychological theory. The interpretation of the results in this sense will follow later, in the Discussion.]

Two measures were taken for each child:

(a) Number of items correctly recalled:
[First, we explain exactly what was scored.]
One point was given for each item correctly recalled, up to a maximum of 24 points.
[The descriptive statistics...]
Table 1 shows the mean number of items recalled correctly by children in each of the four groups.

Table 1. Memory scores as a function of age and training condition

	6–7 year olds		9–10 year olds	
	mean %	mean (*SD*)	mean %	mean (*SD*)
Training	26.7%	6.4 (1.6)	33.4%	8.0 (2.5)
No Training	26.3%	6.3 (2.5)	36.7%	8.8 (2.4)

The maximum score was 24.

[The inferential statistics . . .]
A two-way Analysis of Variance (ANOVA) with independent measures on both variables was conducted on these data. This revealed no significant main effect of training ($F(1, 36) < 1$): giving training to children to correct the interviewer's distortions of their testimony did not affect the children's ability to recall the events. There was a significant main effect of age ($F(1, 36) = 7.96$, $p < .01$, $r = .43$): older children recalled significantly more items than did younger children. There was no significant interaction between age and training ($F(1, 36) < 1$).

(b) Number of distortions corrected:
[Details of what was scored . . .]
One point was given for each distortion that was corrected, up to a maximum of 6 points. Correction of a distortion was held to have occurred if the child said 'no that's not right' or 'no', or if they repeated what they said originally. A sample of the replies was given to an independent rater who was naïve as to which condition the samples had come from. Cohen's Kappa was 85% for the memory scores and 93% for the correction scores.

[Descriptive statistics . . .]
Table 2 shows the distortion-correction scores for each group. It appears that, regardless of age, children in the training conditions corrected more distortions than children in the non-training conditions.

Table 2. Number of distortions corrected, as a function of age and training condition

	6–7 year olds		9–10 year olds	
	mean %	mean (*SD*)	mean %	mean (*SD*)
Training	58.3%	3.5 (2.0)	60.0%	3.6 (1.6)
No Training	16.7%	1.0 (0.7)	23.3%	1.4 (1.2)

The maximum score was 6.

[Inferential statistics...]
A two-way independent measures ANOVA confirmed this impression: it revealed a significant main effect of training ($F(1, 36) = 27.06$, $p < .001$, $r = .66$), and no significant effect of age, either as a main effect or in interaction with training ($F(1, 36) < 1$ in both cases). Thus, the children who had received training in correcting the interviewer corrected significantly more distortions than did the untrained children, and this was true regardless of the children's age.

(c) Relationship between memory score and the number of corrections made:
A Pearson's correlation test was performed to determine whether the number of details that a child could remember correctly, was related to the number of interviewer's distortions that they corrected. The results indicated that there was no significant correlation between these two measures (r (38) $= .10$, *ns*): children who were able to remember a larger number of the details of the staged event were no more or less likely to correct the interviewer than were children with poorer recall.

16.7 Discussion

[First, a summary of the principal results of this study:]
The main result of this study was that training a child to correct an interviewer who mis-reported their testimony significantly increased the child's tendency to correct any distortions made by the interviewer in a subsequent interview. This was true for both younger and older children, despite age-differences in the total amount of information correctly recalled (age-differences that were consistent with those found by previous researchers: review in Ceci & Bruck, 1993). There was no evidence that training affected the amount of information that was successfully recalled by the children.

[Next, we compare our findings to those of previous researchers, and try to account for any discrepancies between them:]
At first glance our results do not appear to replicate the findings of Roberts and Lamb (1998), who found that the children did not correct two thirds of the distortions made. However, the children in that study were involved in a real child protection interview and as such were only given a short time to practice correcting the interviewer's distortions of their testimony, as part of the rapport building phase of the interview. In contrast the children who participated in the present study were actively encouraged to practice correcting distortions made by the interviewer, for about 10 minutes. This implies that in order for

such training to be effective, the child should be formally trained and given time to practice correcting distortions. However, further research is required to confirm whether this is so, and to determine the precise factors which determine whether or not training is effective.

The present study is consistent with the work of Gee, Gregory and Pipe (1999), who trained children to resist misleading questioning by an interviewer about a trip to a science centre. Gee et al. also found that the children in the training condition were less likely to comply with the interviewer when the interviewer gave the child misleading information. Taken together, these studies suggest that if the child is given permission to correct an interviewer, and time to practice doing so, they will challenge the authority of the interviewer and correct them if they provide inaccurate information – excessive suggestibility need not be an inevitable problem when interviewing children.

[Now, we start to discuss problems and limitations of the present study. First, a limitation – the study doesn't pinpoint the source of the effect that was found . . .]
Although we have demonstrated that training increases children's readiness to correct their interviewers, the source of this effect remains to be determined. One possibility is that it arises primarily from differences between the trained and untrained children in terms of the rapport that developed between them and the interviewer. Rapport has been demonstrated to have a significant influence on adult suggestibility to misleading questions (Bain & Baxter, 2000), and there is reason to believe that similar effects occur in children (review in Ceci & Bruck, 1993). In the present study, children in the training stage spent more time with the interviewer and had time to build up a rapport with her. Evidence for the importance of a good rapport between interviewer and child comes from a study by Goodman, Bottoms and Schwartz-Kenney (1991), who interviewed 3–4 and 5–7 year olds about a visit to a Health Clinic for inoculation. If the children were interviewed with a cool and detached interview style, the 5–7 year olds performed better than the 3–4 year olds. However, a warm, empathic and encouraging interview style improved performance for both age-groups and eliminated age-differences in susceptibility to leading questions.

An alternative possibility is that the effects in the present study arose from the fact that the trained children had explicitly been given permission to challenge the interviewer, and had practice in refusing to conform to the interviewer's perceived intentions. The possibility that the untrained children conformed to the interviewer as an authority figure is in line with the results of Goodman et al.'s

(1995) study, which found that children were less suggestible when interviewed by their mother than when they were interviewed by a stranger. Similar conclusions come from Ceci, Ross and Toglia's (1987) study, which found that preschool children were less influenced by misleading information when it was given to them by a seven-year old child, than when it came from an adult.

[Suggestions for future research, to remedy the limitations of the present study, and extend the generality of its findings:]
In further research, it would be useful to attempt to identify the relative contributions to the trained children's behaviour of the rapport-building and training components. These two factors could be separated out by including a condition in which the interviewer builds up a rapport with the child but does not train them to correct the distortions, or vice versa. In the present study, the same experimenter conducted both the training and the interviewing phases of the study, and had therefore built up a rapport with some of the children prior to the interview phase. This may have given the children in the training conditions more confidence in correcting the interviewer when she distorted what the child had said. Future research could usefully investigate whether the effects of training found in the present study persist when the trainer and interviewer are different people.

There are several other issues which also need to be explored. For ethical reasons, the current experiment used a neutral event. It would be desirable to investigate the effects of training when the event is of more consequence to the child, such as when a child witnesses a criminal act. Child witnesses to a criminal event have been found to be less suggestible than those witnessing a neutral event (Ochsner, Zaragoza & Mitchell, 1999). On the basis of this, one would therefore predict that similar effects to those in the present study would be found – namely that children would correct the interviewer – but that this effect would be even more marked. Ideally, however, this prediction should be tested with more ecologically-valid events.

Finally, in the present study, distortions of the child's testimony occurred every time the interviewer summed up. In future research, ecological validity could be increased by ensuring that some of the testimony was repeated correctly and some parts were distorted, to see whether the child would continue to correct the interviewer. Additionally, in real life an interview would last longer than 10–15 minutes. As the interview progresses, it is possible that the child might not remember to correct the interviewer whenever they made a mistake, especially if the interviewer distorted only a few pieces of the information provided by the child. Consequently, future research should examine the present effects within the context of considerably longer interviews, to see if training continues to be as effective under these circumstances.

16.8 References for the Example

Bain, S.A. and Baxter, J.S. (2000). Interrogative suggestibility: the role of interviewer behaviour. *Legal and Criminological Psychology, 5*, 123–133.

Bjorklund, D.F., Cassel, W.S., Bjorklund, B.R., Brown, R.D., Park, C.L., Ernst, K. and Owen, F.A. (2000). Social demand characteristics in children's and adults' eyewitness memory and suggestibility: the effect of different interviewers on free recall and recognition. *Applied Cognitive Psychology, 14*, 421–433.

Ceci, S.J. and Bruck, M. (1993). Suggestibility of the child witness: a historical review and synthesis. *Psychological Bulletin, 113* (3), 403–439.

Ceci, S.J., Ross, D. and Toglia, M. (1987). Age differences in suggestibility: psychological implications. *Journal of Experimental Psychology: General, 117*, 38–49.

Dent, H. (1982). The effects of interviewing strategies on the results of interviews with child witnesses. In A. Trankell (Ed.) *Reconstructing the past: The role of the psychologist in criminal trials*. Netherlands: Kluwer.

Dent, H. and Flin, R. (Eds.) (1992). *Children as Witnesses*. Chichester: Wiley.

Dent, H. and Stephenson, G.M. (1979). An experimental study of the effectiveness of different techniques of questioning child witnesses. *British Journal of Social and Clinical Psychology, 18*, 41–51.

Gee, S., Gregory, M. and Pipe, M.E. (1999). 'What colour is your pet dinosaur?' The impact of pre-interview training and question type on children's answers. *Legal and Criminological Psychology, 4*, 111–128.

Goodman, G.S. and Reed, R.S. (1986). Age differences in eyewitness testimony. *Law and Human Behaviour, 10*, 317–332.

Goodman, G.S., Sharma, A., Thomas, S.F. and Considine, M.G. (1995). Mother knows best: effects of relationship status and interviewer bias on children's memory. *Journal of Experimental Child Psychology, 6*, 195–228.

Gudjonsson, G.H. (1992). *The psychology of interrogations, confessions and testimony*. Chichester: Wiley.

King, M.A. and Yuille, J.C. (1987). Suggestibility and the child witness. Pages 24–35 in: S.J. Ceci, M.P. Toglia and D.F. Ross (Eds.) *Children's eyewitness memory*. New York: Springer-Verlag.

Lindsay, D.S., Johnson, M.K. and Kwon, P. (1991). Developmental changes in memory source monitoring. *Journal of Experimental Child Psychology, 52,* 297–318.

Loftus, E. (1979). *Eyewitness Testimony*. Cambridge MA: Harvard University Press.

Ochsner, J. E., Zaragoza, M. S. and Mitchell, K. J. (1999). The accuracy and suggestibility of children's memory for neutral and criminal eyewitness events. *Legal and Criminological Psychology, 4,* 79–92.

Roberts, K.P. and Lamb, M.E. (1998). Children's responses when interviewers distort details during investigative interviews. *Legal and Criminological Psychology, 3,* 23–31.

Shrimpton, S., Oates, K. and Hayes, S. (1998). Children's memory of events: effects of stress, age, time delay and location of interview. *Applied Cognitive Psychology, 12,* 133–143.

Spencer, J.R. and Flin, R. (1993). *The evidence of children: the law and the psychology*, 2nd edition, London: Blackstone.

References

American Psychological Association (2001). *Publication manual of the American Psychological Association* (5th edition). Washington, DC: APA Books.

Baeyens, F., De Houwer, J., Vansteenwegen, D. & Eelen, P. (1998). Evaluative conditioning is a form of associative learning: On the artificial nature of Field and Davey's (1997) artifactual account of evaluative learning. *Learning and Motivation, 29*, 461–474.

Baeyens, F., Eelen, P. & Crombez, G. (1995). Pavlovian associations are forever: On classical conditioning and extinction. *Journal of Psychophysiology, 9*, 127–141.

Bandura, A., Ross, D. & Ross, S. A. (1963). Imitation of film-mediated aggressive models. *Journal of Abnormal and Social Psychology, 66*, 3–11.

Campbell, D. T. (1969). Reforms as experiments. *American Psychologist, 24*, 409–429.

Clark, D. M. & Wells, A. (1995). A cognitive model of social phobia. In R. Heimberg, M. Liebowitz, D. A. Hope & F. R. Schneier (Eds.) *Social phobia: diagnosis, assessment and treatment.* New York: Guilford Press.

Cohen, J. (1988). *Statistical power analysis for the behavioural sciences* (2nd edition). New York: Academic Press.

Cohen, J. (1990). Things I have learned (so far). *American Psychologist, 45* (12), 1304–1312.

Cohen, J. (1992). A power primer. *Psychological Bulletin, 112* (1), 155–159.

Cohen, J. (1994). The earth is round ($p < .05$). *American Psychologist, 49* (12), 997–1003.

Cook, T. D. & Campbell, D. T. (1979). *Quasi-Experimentation.* Chicago: Rand-McNally.

Darwin, C. R. (1859). *The origin of species.* London: John Murray.

Darwin, C. R. (1871). *The descent of man.* London: John Murray.

Davey, G. C. L. & Field, A. P. (in press). Learning and Conditioning. To appear in P. McGhee (Ed.), *Introduction to Contemporary Psychology.* MacMillan.

De Houwer, J., Thomas, S. & Baeyens, F. (in press). Associative learning of likes and dislikes: a review of 25 years of research on human evaluative conditioning. *Psychological Bulletin.*

Field, A. P. (1996). *An appropriate control condition for evaluative conditioning.* (Cognitive Science Research Paper No. 431). Brighton, UK: University of Sussex, School of Cognitive and Computing Sciences.

Field, A. P. (1997). *Re-evaluating evaluative conditioning.* Unpublished doctoral dissertation, University of Sussex, Brighton, UK.

Field, A. P. (1998a). A bluffer's guide to sphericity. *Newsletter of the Mathematical, Statistical and Computing Section of the British Psychological Society, 6* (1), 13–22 (available from the internet at http://www.cogs.susx.ac.uk/users/andyf/research/articles/sphericity.pdf).

Field, A. P. (1998b). Review of nQuery Adviser Release 2.0. *British Journal of Mathematical and Statistical Psychology, 51,* 368–369.

Field, A. P. (2000). *Discovering statistics using SPSS for Windows: advanced techniques for the beginner.* London: Sage.

Field, A. P. (2001). Meta-analysis of correlation coefficients: a Monte Carlo comparison of fixed- and random-effects methods. *Psychological Methods, 6,* 161–180.

Field, A. P., Argyris, N. G. & Knowles, K. A. (2001). Who's afraid of the big bad wolf: a prospective paradigm to test Rachman's indirect pathways in children. *Behaviour Research and Therapy, 39,* 1259–1276.

Field, A. P., Bodinetz, M. R. & Howley, C. (2001). The role of behavioural inhibition and verbal information in the development of fear beliefs during childhood. *Manuscript submitted for publication.*

Field, A. P. & Davey, G. C. L. (1997). Conceptual conditioning: Evidence for an artifactual account of evaluative learning. *Learning and Motivation, 28,* 446–464.

Field, A. P. & Davey, G. C. L. (1998). Evaluative Conditioning: Artefact or -fiction? A reply to Baeyens, De Houwer, Vansteenwegen & Eelen, 1998. *Learning and Motivation, 29,* 475–491.

Field, A. P. & Davey, G. C. L. (1999). Reevaluating evaluative conditioning: A nonassociative explanation of conditioning effects in the visual evaluative conditioning paradigm. *Journal of Experimental Psychology: Animal Behavior Processes, 25,* 211–224.

Field, A. P. & Davey, G. C. L. (2001). Conditioning models of childhood anxiety. In W. K. Silverman & P. A. Treffers (Eds.) *Anxiety Disorders in children and adolescents: research, assessment and intervention* (pp. 187–211). Cambridge: Cambridge University Press.

Field, A.P. & Lawson, J. (2002). Fear information and the development of fears during childhood: effects of implicit fear responses and behavioural avoidance. *Manuscript submitted for publication.*

Fisher, R. A. (1925/1991). *Statistical methods, experimental design, and scientific inference.* Oxford: Oxford University Press. (This reference is for the 1991 reprint.)

Freud, S. (1901). *The psychopathology of everyday life.* London: Hogarth Press.

Girden, E. R. (1992). *ANOVA: repeated measures.* Sage University paper series on quantitative applications in the social sciences, 07–084. Newbury Park, CA: Sage.

Greenhouse, S. W. & Geisser, S. (1959). On methods in the analysis of profile data. *Psychometrika, 24,* 95–112.

Haidt, J., McCauley, C. & Rozin, P. (1994). Individual differences in sensitivity to disgust: a scale sampling seven domains of disgust elicitors. *Personality and Individual Differences, 16,* 701–713.

Hole, G. J., George, P. A., Eaves, K. & Rasek, A. (2002) Effects of geometric distortions on face-recognition performance. *Perception, 31* (10), 1221–1240.

Howell, D. C. (2001). *Statistical methods for psychology* (5th edition). Belmont, CA: Duxbury.

Hsu, T.-C. & Feldt, L. S. (1969). The effect of limitations on the number of criterion score values on the significance level of the *F*-test. *American Educational Research Journal, 6,* 515–527.

Hume, D. (1739–40). *A treatise of human nature* (edited by L. A. Selby-Bigge). Oxford: Clarendon Press, 1965.

Hume, D. (1748). *An enquiry concerning human understanding.* Chicago: Open Court Publishing Co., 1927.

Huynh, H. & Feldt, L. S. (1976). Estimation of the Box correction for degrees of freedom from sample data in randomised block and split-plot designs. *Journal of Educational Statistics, 1* (1), 69–82.

King, N. J., Gullone, E. & Ollendick, T. H. (1998). Etiology of childhood phobias: current status of Rachman's three pathways theory. *Behaviour Research and Therapy, 36,* 297–309.

Kuhn, T. S. (1970). *The structure of scientific revolutions* (2nd edition). Chicago: University of Chicago Press.

Lord, F. M. (1953). On the statistical treatment of football numbers. *American Psychologist, 8,* 750–751.

Lunney, G. H. (1970). Using analysis of variance with a dichotomous dependent variable: an empirical study. *Journal of Educational Measurement, 7*, 263–269.

MacRae, A. W. (1994). *Models & methods for the behavioural sciences.* Leicester: BPS Books.

McNemar, Q. (1946). Opinion attitude methodology. *Psychological Bulletin, 43*, 289–374.

Meyer, T. J., Miller, M. L., Metzger, R. L. & Borkovec, T. D. (1990). Development and validation of the Penn State Worry Questionnaire. *Behaviour Research and Therapy, 28*, 487–495.

Mill, J. S. (1865). *A system of logic: ratiocinative and inductive.* London: Longmans, Green.

Orne, M. T. (1962). On the social psychology of the psychology experiment: with particular reference to demand characteristics and their implications. *American Psychologist, 17*, 776–783.

Orne, M. T. (1969). Demand characteristics and the concept of quasi-controls. In R. Rosenthal and R. L. Rosnow (Eds.) *Artifact in Behavioral Research.* New York: Academic Press.

Pavlov, I. P. (1927). *Conditioned reflexes.* Oxford: Oxford University Press.

Popper, K. (1957). *The poverty of historicism.* Routledge: London.

Popper, K. (1959). *The logic of scientific discovery.* New York: Basic Books.

Rachman, S. (1977). The conditioning theory of fear acquisition: a critical examination. *Behaviour Research and Therapy, 15*, 375–387.

Rosenhan, D. (1969). The conditions and consequences of evaluation apprehension. In R. Rosenthal and R. L. Rosnow (Eds.) *Artifact in Behavioral Research.* New York: Academic Press.

Siegel, S. & Castellan, N. J. (1988). *Nonparametric statistics for the behavioral sciences* (2nd edition). New York: McGraw-Hill.

"Student" (1931). The Lanarkshire Milk Experiment. *Biometrika, 23*, 398–406.

Turner, S. M., Beidel, D. C. & Dancu, C. V. (1996). *Social Phobia and Anxiety Inventory: Manual.* Toronto: Multi-health Systems Inc.

Tversky, A. & Kahneman, D. (1971). Belief in the law of small numbers. *Psychological Bulletin, 76*, 105–110.

Valentine, E. R. (1992). *Conceptual issues in psychology* (2nd edition). London: Routledge.

Wason, P. C. (1966). Reasoning. In B. M. Foss (Ed.) *New horizons in psychology* (pp. 135–151). Harmondsworth, UK: Penguin.

Watson, J. B. & Rayner, R. (1920). Conditioned emotional reactions. *Journal of Experimental Psychology, 3*, 1–14.

Watts, F. N. & Sharrock, R. (1984). Questionnaire dimensions of spider phobia. *Behaviour Research and Therapy*, *22*, 575–580.

Wright, D. B. (1998). People, materials and situations. In J. A. Nunn (Ed.), *Laboratory psychology* (pp. 97–116). Hove: Lawrence Erlbaum.

Wright, D. B. (2002). *First steps in statistics*. London: Sage.

Index